EARLY MAMLUK SYRIAN HISTORIOGRAPHY

ISLAMIC HISTORY AND CIVILIZATION

STUDIES AND TEXTS

EDITED BY

ULRICH HAARMANN

AND

WADAD KADI

VOLUME 21

EARLY MAMLUK SYRIAN HISTORIOGRAPHY

Al-Yūnīnī's Dhayl Mir'āt al-zamān

BY

LI GUO

VOLUME ONE

BRILL
LEIDEN · BOSTON · KÖLN
1998

This book is printed on acid-free paper.

Library of Congress Cataloging-in-Publication Data

Guo, Li, 1959-
Early Mamluk Syrian historiography : Al-Yūnīnī's Dhayl Mir'āt al-zamān / [by] Li Guo.
p. cm. — (Islamic history and civilization. Studies and texts, ISSN 0929-2403 ; v. 21)
Includes bibliographical references (p.) and index.
ISBN 9004110283 (Vol. 1 : alk. paper). — ISBN 9004110291 (Vol. 2 : alk. paper). — ISBN 9004108181 (set : alk. paper).
1. Yūnīnī, Mūsá ibn Muḥammad, 1242 or 3-1325 or 6. Dhayl Mir'āt al-zamān. 2. Syria–History–1260-1516–Historiography. 3. Mamelukes–Historiography. I. Yūnīnī, Mūsá ibn Muḥammad, 1242 or 3-1325 or 6. Dhayl Mir'āt al-zamān. English & Arabic. Selections. II. Title. III. Series.
DS97.4.G86 1998
909.07'07'205691–dc21 97-52620
CIP

Die Deutsche Bibliothek – CIP-Einheitsaufnahme

Guo, Li:
Early Mamluk Syrian historiography : Al-Yūnīnī's Dhayl Mir'āt al-zamān / by Li Guo. - Leiden ; Boston ; Köln : Brill
(Islamic history and civilization ; Vol. 21)
ISBN 90-04-11028-3 (Vol. 1)
ISBN 90-04-10818-1 (Set)

ISSN 0929-2403
ISBN 90 04 11028 3 (vol. 1)
ISBN 90 04 11029 1 (vol. 2)
ISBN 90 04 10818 1 (set)

PRINTED IN THE NETHERLANDS

CONTENTS

VOLUME ONE

Acknowledgments vii
Note on Transliteration ix

Introduction. The *Dhayl Mir'āt al-Zamān* in Modern Scholarship 1

1. The Author 6

2. The Text 22

3. The Sources 60

4. The *Dhayl* and Early Mamluk Syrian Historiography: The Making of a Model 81

5. Translation: The *Dhayl* and al-Jazarī's *Ḥawādith* 97

Appendix I. The Manuscripts of al-Yūnīnī's *Mukhtaṣar Mir'āt al-Zamān* 208
Appendix II. The Publication Record of Sibṭ Ibn al-Jawzī's *Mir'āt al-Zamān* 212
Appendix III. List of Rulers and Officers Mentioned in the Text Edited (with special reference to Syria) 213

Bibliography 217
Index 227

ACKNOWLEDGMENTS

I owe a profound debt of gratitude to my teachers and dissertation readers who prepared me for the task and saw me through it. My thanks first go to Professor Dimitri Gutas who patiently oversaw the research and writing of my 1994 Yale dissertation on which this book is based. Although Professor Gutas's own research interests lie elsewhere, it was his advice about the methodology of Arabic textual criticism that firmly guided this study. I was also privileged to have spent many profitable hours with Professor Franz Rosenthal during my student years in New Haven. Professor Rosenthal's kindness and insightful advice will always remain a source of inspiration for me. My wholehearted thanks also go to Professor Donald Little, for sharing with me his vast knowledge of Mamluk history and historiography and for his criticisms and corrections, and Professor Stephen Humphreys, for his many valuable comments and suggestions.

I also wish to thank the following scholars whose guidance and inspiration are as invaluable as their help on every step of my long journey. Professor Ulrich Haarmann not only helped me acquire microfilms, but also guided my research through his writings, correspondence and conversation. I am extremely grateful for Professor Gerhard Böwering with whom I took nearly half of my graduate course work and from whom I have received every kind of support and encouragement. I have no way to express my thanks to Professor Wadad Kadi who painstakingly read my revised edition of the Arabic text and whose advice was instrumental in helping me resolve many remaining problems.

Many individuals also contributed to the preparation of this study. I thank Dr. Numan Jubran, Dr. Gül Pulhan, Dr. Guiseppe Scattolin, for their help in acquiring research materials. Dr. Yūsuf Rāġib read some parts of the Arabic edition and provided helpful comments. I am also grateful for the assistance of many curators and librarians all over the world: Dr. Robert Babcock, of the Beinecke Rare Book and Manuscript Library, and Mr. Simon Samoil, of the Sterling Memorial Library, Yale University, New Haven; librarians in the British Library, the Library of the India Office, London, Bodleian Library, Oxford, Bibliothèque Nationale, Paris, and the Süleymaniye Library, Istanbul. My colleagues at the University of Chicago have provided me with much support and assistance. Professor Farouk Mustafa's and Mr. Bruce Craig's persistent encouragement and friendly pressure are greatly appreciated, indeed. Mr. Craig and Mr. John Meloy also carefully read various drafts of the manuscript and made many helpful suggestions. Professor John Woods helped me in trouble-shooting some computer hassles. Mr. Thomas Urban, of the Oriental Institute, and Mr. Mark Stein kindly assisted me in preparing the camera-ready copy of the book. To all of them, I wish to express my sincere gratitude.

Finally, I wish to extend my heartfelt thanks to my friends for their constant encouragement and unfailing support over the years: Rula Abisaab, Maureen Draicchio, Bassam Frangieh, Jane Joyce, Scott Long, Fred Murphy, Nada Saab, and Ray Smith. I must express special thanks to Jane who skillfully proofread volume one of the book.

I dedicate this book to my family in Shanghai and Sydney: Mom, Dad, Bei, Lei, little Xixi and Clinton, without your love and loyalty, I could not have done all this.

Chicago LG
October, 1997

NOTE ON TRANSLITERATION

The Library of Congress system has been used throughout this book with two exceptions: the non-pronounced *tā' marbūṭa* is omitted altogether; the *alif maqṣūra* is spelled as *ā* not *á*. Only those rare technical terms, e.g., *ustād-dār*, *iqṭā'*, *raṭl*, etc., and citations of Arabic text are italicized, while other commonly known Arabic words, e.g., 'ulamā', ḥadīth, madrasa, etc., are written in regular font. Arabic terms that are Anglicized are written without diacritical marks, e.g., Mamluk, Fatimid, Aleppo (not Ḥalab), Hama (not Ḥamā), etc. Names of Turkish and Persian origin are written as they appear in the *Cambridge History of Iran*. Others are transliterated according to the Arabic spelling in the texts cited.

INTRODUCTION

THE *DHAYL MIR'ĀT AL-ZAMĀN* IN MODERN SCHOLARSHIP

The work that has come down to us as Quṭb al-Dīn Mūsā al-Yūnīnī's (d. 726/1326) *Dhayl Mir'āt al-zamān* (hereafter *Dhayl*) is a continuation of Sibṭ Ibn al-Jawzī's (d. 654/1256) famous universal history entitled *Mir'āt al-zamān fī ta'rīkh al-a'yān* (hereafter *Mir'āt*). It covers the period from the year 654/1256 through the year 711/1311, the period of the late Ayyubids and Crusaders, the Mongols and the early Mamluks (the so-called Baḥrī Mamluks), an era full of interest for students of Islamic history. Although it is a *dhayl*, a supplement, the independence and originality of the work have been remarked upon by medieval and modern scholars alike, some of whom even went so far as to claim that the work does, in fact, outshine the principal work, viz. the *Mir'āt*, in functional significance. It contains much material, especially on Syria (*Bilād al-Shām*), not available elsewhere, based on the author's own observations or drawn from his contemporaries and predecessors whose works have been either lost or only partly preserved.[1]

Information about the existence of a manuscript entitled *Kitāb al-dhayl 'alā Mir'āt al-zamān* by one al-Yūnīnī was first made public as early as 1787 in Johannes Uri's catalogue of the Oriental manuscripts in the Bodleian Library.[2] The manuscript, numbered as "Arabic. Mohamm. 700" was mentioned by Heinrich Ferdinand Wüstenfeld in his *Die Geschichtsschreiber der Araber* (1882) and described as an integral part of the four-volume "Fortsetzung" of Sibṭ Ibn al-Jawzī's acclaimed *Mir'āt*.[3] In 1898, Carl Brockelmann added the three additional manuscripts of the *Dhayl* in the Landberg collection (Landberg Mss. 138, 139, and 340)[4] which was to be

[1] One such instance is the biography of Rāshid al-Dīn Sinān, the grand master of the Assassins; originally written by Ibn al-'Adīm in his *Bughyat al-ṭalab fī ta'rīkh Ḥalab,* it is now lost, along with other parts of the book, and is only preserved in detail in al-Yūnīnī's *Dhayl*; cf. Lewis, "Rāšid al-Dīn Sinān." Another example is al-Jazarī's *Ḥawādith al-zamān*, a major portion of which, i.e., the text that covers A.H. 699-711, has only survived in the *Dhayl*; see our discussion below, 54-59.

[2] Shelf number "Pococke 132"; see Uri, I:157.

[3] No. 340, the entry of "Sibṭ Ibn al-Ǧauzī."

[4] *GAL*, I:347.

moved to Yale in 1900.[5] In a handwritten checklist, Carlo Landberg called the work "außerordentlich wichtig" and predicted the importance of these manuscripts for future study inasmuch as they would fill the gap left by Sibṭ Ibn al-Jawzī's work. Landberg also noted that the *Dhayl* is in fact "eine Art Tagebuch";[6] however, he did not go further.

More manuscripts have been discovered since then: Giuseppe Gabrieli's catalogue (1916) of other manuscripts of the *Dhayl* in Istanbul (Aya Sofya 3146) and Cairo (v. 58, *ta'rīkh* 551)[7] was followed by that of Otto Spies (1932; Aya Sofya 3199 and Ahmet III 2907 were added to the list).[8] The supplement to *GAL* (1936) included all the above-mentioned manuscripts.[9] The same year Claude Cahen published a description of the *Dhayl* manuscripts in Istanbul (Aya Sofya 3146, 3199; Ahmet III, 2907/e, f, and i; Evkaf 2138-40).[10] In 1946, Fritz Krenkow discovered an anonymous manuscript entitled *Dhayl Mir'āt al-zamān* in the library of the India Office and attributed its authorship to al-Yūnīnī.[11] Other manuscripts (Istanbul, Feyzullah Efendi 282; Aleppo, al-Aḥmadīya 1213; Tehran, Maktabat-i Millī 1119) were reported by Ṣalāḥ al-Dīn al-Munajjid in 1956.[12]

Cahen was the first to point out that the work has survived in two major redactions.[13] In addition, he made an effort to trace al-Yūnīnī's sources and to describe the reciprocal borrowing relationship that exists between him and other contemporary historians. In a series of writings, he repeatedly stressed the originality of the work and the need for a critical edition of the entire text. Accordingly, all progress in this direction has been closely followed by him[14] as well as other scholars working in the field.[15]

---

[5] For the transfer of the Landberg collection to Yale, see Nemoy, 6.

[6] The five-volume handwritten checklist entitled "Kurzes Verzeichniss der Sammlung arabischer Handschriften des Dr. C. Grafen v. Landberg in Yale, München, 1900," which appears to have been made by Landberg with the assistance of his secretary on the eve of the delivery of the collection to Yale, is now preserved in the Beinecke Rare Book and Manuscript Library, Yale University, under "Landberg, O., v. 1-5." The Mss. 138 and 139 are listed in v. 1.

[7] Gabrieli, 1164; the date of publication is mistakenly given as 1911 in *GAL*.

[8] Spies, 69f.

[9] *GALS*, I:589; it has "Land. 140" for "Land. 340."

[10] Cahen, "Chroniques arabes," 344-45.

[11] Krenkow, 378-80. However, this item is not listed in the *Catalogue of the Arabic manuscripts in the Library of the India Office* (London, 1877-1991).

[12] *Al-Mu'arrikhūn al-Dimashqīyūn*, 40, 131, 444.

[13] "Chroniques arabes," 344-45; *Syrie*, 79-80.

[14] See Cahen's review of the Hyderabad edition, *Arabica* 4 (1957): 193-94; and "Editing Arabic Chronicles," 3-4 (especially note 13), 17f.

[15] Sauvaget, *al-Jazarī*, v; also *Introduction*, 177.

The work was published for the first time under the title *Dhail Mir'ātu'z-zamān* in Hyderabad in four volumes (the first two in 1954-55, and the second two in 1960-61). The edition appears to be based on the work of Krenkow, who had been studying and preparing such a project for nearly a decade,[16] but the extent of his responsibility for the final product remains unclear.[17] The Hyderabad edition was credited for its serviceable typography, its apparatus, tables of contents, and an index (only to the last two volumes), but criticized, by Cahen and Jean Sauvaget, as "badly" edited with regard to its handling of manuscript traditions.[18] Since Cahen's 1957 book review dealt only with the first two volumes which had been published at that time, some further discussion here would not be redundant.

In general, the Hyderabad edition lacks a comprehensive survey of the manuscripts and, as a result, often gives readers wrong information. For example, the third and fourth volumes, which cover the years A.H. 671-677 and 678-686 respectively, claim to be based on "the oldest extant mss. in the Libraries of Oxford and Istanbul,"[19] but the fact is that the Bodleian manuscript ends with the year A.H. 673; in other words, these two volumes *cannot* be based on the Bodleian manuscript,[20] but are, as a wealth of footnotes suggests, based on Krenkow's copy of an "Istanbul Ms." about which no information is given. To add to the confusion, in the third volume the folio numbers of the Bodleian manuscript (f. 187b to f. 210a) are given in the margins of the printed text for the years A.H. 671 to 673, though the manuscript is

[16] Krenkow's brief communication shows that his interest in the work started around the middle of the 1940s; see Krenkow, 378-80. Helmut Ritter mentioned that Krenkow had once asked his help in searching for and acquiring the *Dhayl* manuscripts in Istanbul; see Ritter, 672-73. 'Abbās al-'Azzāwī gave a detailed bibliography of the extant manuscripts as well as a brief survey about the work in medieval Muslim scholarship; see "Sibṭ Ibn al-Jawzī." Sauvaget also mentioned, in 1949, Krenkow's proposed project; cf. *al-Jazarī*, v, note 1.

[17] In the editors' postscript, we are told that the entire text of four volumes is based on Krenkow's handwritten copies of various manuscripts along with his apparatus and commentaries. In addition, the first two volumes were corrected and proofread by a group of Indian Muslim scholars; see *Dhayl*, 4:335.

[18] Cahen, "Editing Arabic Chronicles," 3, 17; Sauvaget, *Introduction*, 177. My collation of the first volume of the printed text with the two Aya Sofya manuscripts also reveals that there is a considerable number of typographic errors as well as the editors' "corrections," often without any editorial notes.

[19] See the cover and the title page of the third and fourth volumes of the Hyderabad edition.

[20] My collation shows that it was used only for cross reference for the three years (A.H. 671-673). This fact can be detected by a number of footnotes that read: "added according to *b*" (the abbreviation of the Bodleian manuscript); while the "Istanbul Ms." is often referred to as *al-aṣl* or "according to *a*" (an abbreviation for *al-aṣl*, the original).

by no means the basis of the text, while from the year A.H. 674 on, the folio numbers given (f. 24b to f. 209b) are those of the mysterious "Istanbul Ms." Moreover, readers are left in the dark about the whole manuscript situation and are never told that the published text in all four volumes constitutes only *the first half* of the entire work that is known to run through the year 711/1311.

The Hyderabad edition has been widely used as one of the primary sources on the history of Syria during the period of the late Ayyubids and Crusaders, the Mongols and early Mamluks. Unfortunately, for reasons unknown, the Hyderabad project has stopped,[21] despite the fact that the remaining part of the work, i.e., *the second half* of the work, which begins with the year 687/1288 and runs through the year 711/1311, is believed to be, in Cahen's assessment, "the most original and the most important,"[22] and, therefore, the one most needed.

The work has continued to receive the attention of modern students.[23] Ulrich Haarmann's and Donald Little's studies, both published in 1970, marked a significant step toward our better understanding of al-Yūnīnī and his work. Haarmann's study focused on Shams al-Dīn Muḥammad al-Jazarī (d. 739/1339), al-Yūnīnī's contemporary and Damascene colleague, and Ibn al-Dawādārī, an Egyptian historian, while Little's interest lay in drawing a broad picture of early Mamluk historiography as a whole; however, their source criticism and textual analysis stand as the most extensive critical study of al-Yūnīnī and the *Dhayl* to date.

Al-Yūnīnī and his *Dhayl* received independent treatment for the first time in a 1975 Freiburg dissertation by Antranig Melkonian.[24] Entitled *Die Jahre 1287-1291 in der Chronik al-Yūnīnīs*, it contains a critical edition of the part covering those years, along with an introduction, German translation,

---

[21] Cahen even went so far as to question whether the Hyderabad editors knew of the existence of the remaining manuscripts. My own suggestion would be that the well-known claim (e.g., al-Sakhāwī, Ḥājjī Khalīfa) that the work consists of "four *mujallad*s" may have contributed to this confusion.

[22] Cahen, "Editing Arabic Chronicles," 3.

[23] E.g., Farah, 2. However, some of the information provided by Caesar Farah (e.g., note 457) about the manuscripts and publication of the *Dhayl* is wrong ("the original four volumes apparently have not survived. . . ."); moreover, Farah was obviously not aware of the publication of the third and fourth volumes in Hyderabad.

[24] For the attention to early Mamluk historical writings in the University of Freiburg, see Humphreys, *Islamic History*, 136. Among the Freiburg dissertations not listed in Stephen Humphreys's survey, two are related to the current study: Melkonian's study of al-Yūnīnī and Numan Jubran's study of al-Jazarī (1987). I thank Numan M. Jubran of Irbid, Jordan for sending me a copy of his dissertation.

and commentary. Melkonian's work is, however, far from being satisfactory. It, too, lacks a basic survey of the extant manuscripts. As a result, the edition is based on a single manuscript (Ahmet III 2907/e), ignoring other extant codices (e.g., Ms. Landberg 139). The work as a whole is full of errors from which even the title cannot escape. One wonders why the title claims that it deals with the years 1287-1291, although the text in question starts in fact from A.H. 687 which, as correctly indicated in the translation, began on July 6, 1288.[25]

Some further work on al-Yūnīnī has been carried out since then. Shah Morad Elham has discussed Egyptian authors Baybars al-Manṣūrī's and al-Nuwayrī's textual relationships with al-Yūnīnī.[26] Meanwhile, the call for continuing the effort to edit the rest of al-Yūnīnī has constantly been raised.[27]

The above survey reveals what is required of our current study: 1) a biographical study of al-Yūnīnī: his life, career, and his milieu; 2) an up-to-date inventory of all the known manuscripts of the *Dhayl*; 3) an overall examination, including further source criticism, of the work within the context of the so-called "Syrian school" in early Mamluk historiography. It is hoped that this study will not only shed light on the life and writing of a prominent Syrian Mamluk historian, thus paving the way for a complete edition of his principal work,[28] but also will contribute to our better knowledge of early Mamluk historical writing in particular, and medieval Muslim historiography in general.

---

[25] Melkonian, 40.

[26] Elham, 52-53, 60-61.

[27] E.g., Little, "al-Ṣafadī," 192-93, in which he emphasizes that the unpublished part has "real value" for it covers "those years during which al-Yūnīnī was a contemporary observer." Robert Irwin observes that "until the publication of all the best sources," including "the rest of al-Yunini . . . any history of the period will be premature"; see Introduction to *Early Mamluk Sultanate* (no page number).

[28] The following table shows the publication history of the *Dhayl*:

A.H. 654-686	Hyderabad edition (four volumes)
A.H. 687-690	Melkonian's edition
A.H. 697-701	The present edition

CHAPTER ONE

THE AUTHOR

1. Al-Yūnīnī's Life

A ḥadīth scholar and historian of modest fame in his time, al-Yūnīnī has been mentioned in a variety of medieval Arabic biographical dictionaries.[1] Nearly all of his biographers acknowledge transmitting on the authority of al-Dhahabī (d. 748/1347), a younger contemporary of al-Yūnīnī who attended the latter's ḥadīth sessions in Damascus and Ba'labakk.[2] However, al-Dhahabī's short biographical sketch does not shed much light on his former teacher's life and career. Many details, especially those concerning his travels, social contacts and intellectual involvement in Ba'labakk, Damascus and Cairo are left untold. In this respect, we might find al-Yūnīnī's own work, the *Dhayl*, a more significant mine of information from which such data can be assembled. What interests us here is al-Yūnīnī's willingness to weave personal remarks into the texture of his narrative. He often uses the first person to state that "on such-and-such a day, month and year, I met with so-and-so in such-and-such city, and he told me the following story (or, recited to me

---

[1] Among these are: 1) mainstream biographical dictionaries: Ibn Kathīr (d. 774/1372), *Bidāya*, 14:126; al-'Asqalānī (d. 852/1448), *Durar*, 4:383; Ibn Taghrībirdī (d. 874/1469), *Dalīl*, 2:752; and 2) the Ḥanbalī biographical dictionaries: al-Yāfi'ī (d. 768/1366), *Mir'āt al-janān*, 4:276; Ibn Rajab (d. 795/1392-93), *al-Dhayl 'alā ṭabaqāt al-Ḥanābila*, 2:379-80; Ibn Mufliḥ (d. 884/1479), *al-Maqṣid*, 3:9-10. I have not yet seen al-Ṣafadī's (d. 764/1362-63) *al-Wāfī bi-al-wafayāt* (still in manuscript), 26:145 and *A'yān al-'aṣr* (Ms. Istanbul, Sülaymaniye, Atif 1809). Part 3 of the facsimile edition (Frankfurt, 1990) of the latter ends, incidentally, at our author. Part 4, which opens with the entry on him, is eagerly awaited.

Among post-medieval and recent writers, we may mention: Ibn al-'Imād, *Shadharāt*, 6:73-74; Ḥājjī Khalīfa, 1647, 1843; Ismā'īl Pāshā al-Baghdādī, *Hadīyat al-'ārifīn*, 2:479; *Īḍāḥ al-maknūn*, 2:47; Kaḥḥāla, *Mu'jam*, 13:45-46; Nadwi, *Catalogue of Bankipore*, XV: 12-13; al-Munajjid, *al-Mu'arrikhūn al-Dimashqīyūn*, 130-31, 444. None of these supplies any new information.

[2] *Al-Mu'jam al-mukhtaṣṣ*, 285-86; *Dhuyūl al-'ibar*, 4:76-77. Al-Dhahabī's statement that "he (al-Yūnīnī) used to dictate ḥadīth to us in Damascus and Ba'labakk" has been quoted in Ibn Rajab, *Dhayl*, 2:380 and in Ibn al-'Imād, *Shadharāt*, 6:74.

the following poem) on the authority of so-and-so. . . ." This pattern of information confirmation on a personal level, occasionally even laced with his own comments, can be witnessed especially in the *wafayāt* sections (obituary notices) of the *Dhayl* in which al-Yūnīnī's tireless effort to bring together all the details is clearly observed. It is on such grounds that we are able to have a better view of his life, the milieu in which he lived, the way he worked and the sources that he and his informants used.

Family and education: Ba'labakk and Damascus

Quṭb al-Dīn Abū al-Fatḥ Mūsā ibn Muḥammad al-Yūnīnī al-Ḥanbalī was born in Damascus on Ṣafar 8, A.H. 640 (August 7, 1242) into a family noted for its learning and Ḥanbalī affiliation. His *nisba* does not go back to his birth place, but to Yūnīn, a hamlet on the outskirts of Ba'labakk[3] where his family originated. His name is, therefore, given by some biographers as al-Yūnīnī al-Ba'labakkī, or al-Ba'lī. The family claimed descent from Ja'far al-Ṣādiq[4] and hence all members of the family, including our author, are mentioned in some biographical dictionaries[5] with the title, among others, of *baqīyat al-salaf* (the descendant of the Prophet Muḥammad), or al-Ḥusaynī.[6]

Al-Yūnīnī's father Taqī al-Dīn Muḥammad ibn Aḥmad (d. 658/1260)[7] was a renowned Ḥanbalī jurist who succeeded his mentor and father-in-law, the famous Ḥanbalī master 'Abd Allāh al-Yūnīnī (d. 617/1220)[8] as the head of the Ḥanbalīs of Ba'labakk—one of the most prestigious centers for Ḥanbalī learning of the age.[9] In this capacity, Muḥammad is said to have maintained

---

[3] Al-Yūnīnī mentioned that Yūnīn was only two parasangs (approximately six miles) from Ba'labakk; see *Dhayl*, 2:39.

[4] The family lineage, as it was told by the father Muḥammad to the brother 'Alī who wrote it down and showed it to our author, is said to be as follows: Muḥammad ibn Aḥmad ibn 'Abd Allāh ibn 'Īsā ibn Aḥmad ibn 'Alī ibn Muḥammad ibn Muḥammad al-Ḥarrānī ibn Aḥmad al-Ḥijāzī ibn Muḥammad ibn al-Ḥusayn ibn Isḥāq ibn Ja'far al-Ṣādiq ibn Muḥammad al-Bāqir ibn Zayn al-'Ābidīn 'Alī ibn al-Ḥusayn ibn 'Alī ibn Abī Ṭālib; see *Dhayl*, 2:57.

[5] E.g., Ibn Kathīr, *Bidāya*, 14:126.

[6] E.g., Ms. Bodleian Marsh 658, f. 4a.

[7] For his biography, see *Dhayl*, 1:429-30 (abridged) and 2:38-72 (detailed); also see al-Dhahabī, *Tadhkirat al-ḥuffāẓ*, 4:223-24; *al-'Ibar*, 5:248; al-Ṣafadī, *al-Wāfī*, 2:121; Ibn Kathīr, *Bidāya*, 13:227; Ibn Rajab, *Dhayl*, 2:269-73; Ibn al-'Imād, *Shadharāt*, 5:294; Ibn Mufliḥ, *al-Maqṣid*, 2:356-57; al-'Ulaymī, *al-Manhaj*, 1:388.

[8] For 'Abd Allāh al-Yūnīnī, see *Dhayl*, passim; also Laoust, "Le hanbalisme," 48-50. According to our author, his father Muḥammad's first wife was 'Abd Allāh's daughter; see *Dhayl*, 2:44.

[9] Cf. Laoust, "Le hanbalisme," 48ff.

close ties with the Ayyubids for more than 40 years. He was highly respected by the Ayyubid rulers, among whom were al-Malik al-Ashraf (d. 635/1237), his brother al-Malik al-Kāmil (d. 635/1237), and another brother, al-Malik al-Ṣāliḥ (d. 648/1250), all of whom regarded him as the one they could turn to for consultation on religious affairs.[10] Al-Yūnīnī's half brother Sharaf al-Dīn 'Alī (d. 701/1301),[11] a ḥadīth scholar, was well-known for his editing of the vulgate of al-Bukhārī's *Ṣaḥīḥ*, the version that is now in common use.[12] Among his students were the above-mentioned al-Dhahabī[13] and 'Alam al-Dīn al-Birzālī (d. 739/1339) who happened to be, as will be discussed below, one of the key figures in al-Yūnīnī's enterprise.[14]

[10] The father's connections with the Ayyubid rulers are well documented in the *Dhayl* (2:40-46), which constitutes the primary source of all later accounts on this matter. Al-Yūnīnī boasts that whenever these Ayyubid princes came to Damascus, they would send for his father for advice on religious affairs and learning. An anecdote has it that when the Prophet's sandal was discovered and presented to al-Malik al-Ashraf who was then in Damascus, al-Yūnīnī's father was invited to come and observe the holy relic. He told al-Ashraf that his mother, al-Yūnīnī's grandmother, also wished to pay her respects to the holy relic. Al-Ashraf, in his turn, thus ordered to have it sent to Ba'labakk, fulfilling the old lady's noble wish (*Dhayl*, 2:45-46; the account on al-Ashraf's obtaining the Prophet's sandal is found in *Mir'āt*, Jewett edition, 471-72). Another oft-quoted anecdote is as follows: al-Yūnīnī's father was once teaching ḥadīths to al-Malik al-Ashraf at the Damascus Citadel. Al-Malik al-Ashraf insisted on offering the turban he was wearing at the time so al-Yūnīnī's father would use it as sandals after having performed the ritual ablution. Al-Malik is said to have sworn that the turban was "pure and clean" (*Dhayl*, 2:41). This story is said to have been narrated by al-Yūnīnī's brother 'Alī to al-Dhahabī but the latter had remained skeptical about its veracity (in al-Dhahabī's own words: *wa-al-shakk minnī*); see Ibn Rajab, *Dhayl*, 2:270-71. However, al-Dhahabī agrees that the father was indeed highly regarded by the Ayyubids; see, *Tadhkirat al-ḥuffāẓ*, 4:224. For modern scholars' views, cf. Laoust, "Le hanbalisme," 48-50.

[11] For his biography, see al-Birzālī, *al-Muqtafā* (Ms. Istanbul, Ahmet III 2951), 2:55; al-Dhahabī, *Tadhkirat al-ḥuffāẓ*, 4:282; *al-Mu'jam*, 168-69; *Dhuyūl al-'ibar*, 4:4; al-Ṣafadī, *Dalīl*, 1:476; Ibn Rajab, *Dhayl*, 2:345-46; al-'Ulaymī, *al-Manhaj*, 1:410; Ibn Mufliḥ, *al-Maqṣid*, 2:259-61; Ibn al-'Imād, *Shadharāt*, 6:3. For modern studies, see *GALS*, I:261.

[12] Rosenthal, *Technique*, 24; *SEI*, 65; *GALS*, I:261. Also al-'Asqalānī, *Durar*, 3:172; al-Dhahabī, *al-Mu'jam*, 169, note 1.

[13] Al-Dhahabī states that he used to study ḥadīth with 'Alī at Ba'labakk and Damascus (*al-Mu'jam*, 169) and once had attended the latter's sessions for 70 consecutive days (*Tadhkirat al-ḥuffāẓ*, 4:282). Al-Dhahabī is also the editor of 'Alī's *'Awālī* (Ibn Mufliḥ, *al-Maqṣid*, 2:261).

[14] Al-Birzālī says that he used to be with him (*lazimtuhu*) for a long period studying ḥadīth and that he went to Ba'labakk four times in order to study with him the *Musnad* of al-Shāfi'ī; see al-Birzālī, *al-Muqtafā* (quoted in Ibn Mufliḥ, *al-Maqṣid*, 2:260-61, note 1).

Al-Yūnīnī was the only son of Zayn al-'Arab bint Naṣr Allāh (d. 693/1294), who herself came from a distinguished family of scholars[15] and is said to have been the favorite among her husband's six wives.[16] He grew up under his parents' close watch and had the unique opportunity of being exposed to the best teachers and learning of his time. In his youth, he was taught by his father who often introduced him to his fellow learned men in Ba'labakk and Damascus.[17] In the *Dhayl*, al-Yūnīnī recalls that when he was a teenager, he often accompanied his father to visit one Shaykh 'Īsā ibn Aḥmad, a revered Ḥanbalī and ṣūfī,[18] in the latter's zāwiya at Yūnīn. At the beginning of Shawwāl, A.H. 654 (November, 1256), he was sent by his father to visit the shaykh who was severely ill. On his deathbed, the shaykh recited disjointedly some fragments of ḥadīths and poems, and the zealous young al-Yūnīnī implored him to complete his recitation.[19] When his father died, al-Yūnīnī's education was guided by his older brother 'Alī. The brother not only shared his knowledge with the young al-Yūnīnī by showing him his notebooks and other manuscripts,[20] but also took him to Egypt to meet with people there.

Al-Yūnīnī's early education appears to be ḥadīth-oriented. His teachers were all prominent ḥadīth scholars. Among these, Aḥmad ibn 'Abd al-Dā'im al-Ḥanbalī (d. 668/1270) of Damascus is the one most often mentioned.[21] As al-Yūnīnī reflects, he studied with him the entire *Ṣaḥīḥ* of Muslim. Other teachers include 'Abd al-'Azīz, known as Shaykh al-Shuyūkh (d. 662/1263), of Hama,[22] Abū Bakr ibn Makārim,[23] Rashīd al-Dīn al-'Aṭṭār (d. 662/1263),[24] Ibn Ṣārim, al-Sāwī,[25] and Ibn Rawwāj,[26] all of Egypt.

---

[15] Her grandfather al-Ḥasan ibn Yaḥyā Sanī al-Dawla was a revered religious figure; her uncle Shams al-Dīn Aḥmad ibn Yaḥyā (d. 635/1237) was the chief judge (perhaps at Damascus); and her brother, al-Yūnīnī's uncle Tāj al-Dīn Ya'qūb, was a prominent scholar as well; see *Dhayl*, 2:47, 49, 71.

[16] *Dhayl*, 2:71-72.

[17] *Dhayl*, 2:49; also Ibn Kathīr, *Bidāya*, 14:126.

[18] His obituary is found in *Dhayl*, 1:24-33.

[19] *Dhayl*, 1:26-27.

[20] For instance, al-Yūnīnī reported that the death date of his teacher Ibn 'Abd al-Dā'im was Rajab 7, A.H. 668, however, "I saw my brother 'Alī's notebook stating that he died on Rajab 9, Monday. Only God knows"; *Dhayl*, 2:437.

[21] For his biography, see *Dhayl*, 2:436-37; Ibn Rajab, *Dhayl*, 2:278-80; al-Birzālī, *Mashyakhat Ibn Jamā'a*, 145-50. He was also a famous copyist; see Morray, 30-32, 160, 165, 168.

[22] Ibn Mufliḥ, *al-Maqṣid*, 3:9. His name was 'Abd al-'Azīz ibn Muḥammad ibn 'Abd al-Muḥsin, a poet and jurist. He was also the ḥadīth teacher of al-Yūnīnī's brother. For his biography, see al-Birzālī, *Mashyakhat Ibn Jamā'a*, 343-51; al-Kutubī, *Fawāt al-wafayāt*, 1:598-607; Ibn Taghrībirdī, *Nujūm*, 7:214-15.

[23] Unidentified.

Along with training in ḥadīth, al-Yūnīnī seems to have developed from his early days an interest in observing the events occurring around him and writing them down in his notebooks.[27] For instance, we are told that when the siege of the Ba'labakk Citadel in 658/1260 took place, he was then on the scene and saw the Mongol general Kitbughā Nūwīn[28] and his young son. A vivid description of the event, including Kitbughā's eccentric and savage behavior in the town was recorded and later presented in his chronicles.[29] At the time, he also saw Bohemond VI,[30] then the count (*mutamallik*) of Tripoli, coming down with his troops to the rescue. This encounter was recorded and later added to Bohemond's obituary in the *Dhayl* as well.[31]

Travels to Egypt and Mecca and gathering information for future writing

In 659/1261, al-Yūnīnī, accompanied by his brother 'Alī, made his first journey to Egypt. On the way, they arrived in Jerusalem in Ramaḍān and were received by 'Umar ibn Mūsā, then the qāḍī of Gaza,[32] and al-Musallim ibn Muḥammad al-Dimashqī, a ḥadīth scholar and then the magistrate (*nāẓir*) of Gaza.[33] Al-Yūnīnī later recalled that he and his brother, who were not keeping the fast at the time because of the circumstances of traveling, were impressed by the lavish dishes provided to them by the hosts.[34] The trip to

[24] For his obituary see *Dhayl*, 2:314-15. He was also the ḥadīth teacher of al-Yūnīnī's brother 'Alī; al-'Asqalānī, *Durar*, 3:172.

[25] Al-'Asqalānī, *Durar*, 4:382. The two are unidentified.

[26] Al-Dhahabī states that al-Yūnīnī received an *ijāza* from Ibn Rawwāj; see *Dhuyūl al-'ibar*, 4:77. Ibn Rawwāj was also his brother 'Alī's ḥadīth teacher; see al-Dhahabī, *al-Mu'jam*, 169; Ibn Rajab, *Dhayl*, 2:345.

[27] The remark that he had some sort of "*muswadda*" at hand as he was working on his manuscript is mentioned frequently in the *Dhayl*, e.g., 2:114-15.

[28] Nūwīn: an Amīr of Ten Thousand. He was Hülegü's deputy to Syria; cf. Ibn Kathīr, *Bidāya*, 13:226-27.

[29] Kitbughā is said to have urinated in public in Ba'labakk, among other things (*Dhayl*, 2:34, 36). Al-Yūnīnī's own account was widely quoted in later sources, e.g., Ibn Kathīr, *Bidāya*, 13:227.

[30] Bohemond VI, prince of Antioch and count of Tripoli (d. 1275); cf. Irwin, "The Mamluk Conquest of the County of Tripoli," 246; also Amitai-Preiss, *Mongols and Mamluks*, 265 (Index).

[31] The obituary of Bohemond VI is to be found in *Dhayl*, 3:92-94. The event was recorded by al-Yūnīnī and later presented in the *Dhayl*, 2:36, in the chapter for the year 658/1259-60.

[32] His obituary is found in *Dhayl*, 4:57-59.

[33] For his obituary, see *Dhayl*, 4:125-28. It is not out of place to note here that he transmitted the *Ta'rīkh Baghdād* on the authority of Tāj al-Dīn al-Kindī (*Dhayl*, 4:126).

[34] *Dhayl*, 4:57-59, 125-28.

Egypt was significant for al-Yūnīnī both as a young ḥadīth scholar and as a historian. It was in Cairo that he visited Yaḥyā ibn 'Alī al-'Aṭṭār, an authority on ḥadīth and a leading Mālikī scholar. In the latter's home, al-Yūnīnī was given a book of ḥadīth transmitted on al-'Aṭṭār's authority and was granted the *ijāza*, permission to transmit the materials contained in it.[35] It was in Cairo also that al-Yūnīnī's long-cherished wish to meet with 'Abd al-'Azīz ibn 'Abd al-Salām, a Shāfi'ī jurist and ḥadīth authority,[36] came true.[37] Besides pursuing ḥadīths, al-Yūnīnī also kept his eyes on other things. We are told that he encountered one Ḥasan Ibn Shāwir, a poet, and that the latter recited his own poems to the young Syrian visitor.[38] Al-Yūnīnī's keen observation and sharp memory are clearly demonstrated when, later in the *Dhayl*, he mentioned that in Cairo he also saw Kitbughā's son whom he had seen once in Ba'labakk during the siege of its citadel. Our young chronicler-to-be even noticed that the man was "wearing the clothes of Turks" at the time.[39]

Al-Yūnīnī's lifelong interest in observing and recording seemed to continue. He appeared to be very eager to gain information through any means possible. We are told by him that in 669/1270, shortly after al-Malik al-Ẓāhir's successful siege and conquest of Ḥiṣn al-Akrād (Crac des Chevaliers),[40] Khaḍir ibn Abī Bakr (d. 676/1277),[41] al-Malik al-Ẓāhir's principal advisor (*shaykh al-sulṭān*) and fortune-teller during the battle, happened to pass by Ba'labakk. The city's rulers and its elite, including al-Yūnīnī, gathered to receive the triumphant hero. Al-Yūnīnī later reports that he "overheard" one shaykh's inquiry about the siege and Khaḍir's detailed answer.[42]

The next significant journey of al-Yūnīnī was his pilgrimage to Mecca in 673/1275 with a group of Damascene learned men.[43] In Mecca, al-Yūnīnī met with Bahā' al-Dīn al-Fā'izī,[44] who had close ties to the Mamluk court through marriage and knew many inside stories, and accompanied him to

---

[35] *Dhayl*, 2:314-15.

[36] His obituary is found in *Dhayl*, 2:172-76.

[37] *Dhayl*, 3:137.

[38] *Dhayl*, M:6-14.

[39] *Dhayl*, 2:36.

[40] For the siege of Ḥiṣn al-Akrād, see *Dhayl*, 2:444-45. It lasted from Jumādā II to Rajab, A.H. 669.

[41] For this famous shaykh who played a vital role in Baybars's policy making, see Pouzet, "Ḫaḍir ibn Abī Bakr al-Mihrānī," 173-83; Peter Thorau devoted a whole chapter to this shaykh; see *Baybars*, 225-29; his biography is also found in *Dhayl*, 3:264-68; Ibn Taghrībirdī, *Nujūm*, 7:276-77.

[42] *Dhayl*, 3:266.

[43] *Dhayl*, 3:137, 187-89, 386-400; M:34f, 59-60; Ms. Landberg 139, f. 2a.

[44] His obituary is found in *Dhayl*, Ms. Landberg 139, f. 2a.

Medina.[45] However, what seems to have excited al-Yūnīnī the most at Mecca was his meeting with ʿUthmān ibn ʿAbd Allāh al-Āmidī, a ṣūfī-Ḥanbalī who had lived at Mecca for 50 years by the time al-Yūnīnī met with him.[46] On his return from Mecca to Damascus, al-Yūnīnī and his fellow pilgrims stopped by Kerak on the first of Ṣafar, A.H. 674 (July 27, 1275).[47]

Al-Yūnīnī must have married very early. Following his father's court connections, he was also allied with the Mamluk military rulers through his own children's marriages. His daughter was married to ʿIzz al-Dīn Aybak al-Iskandarī al-Ṣāliḥī, a powerful Mamluk amīr and the commander of the Baʿlabakk Citadel at the time of the wedding. During his absence on pilgrimage in 673/1275, his daughter, together with his mother, joined her husband, then the commander-in-chief of al-Raḥba Citadel.[48] Upon his return from the pilgrimage, al-Yūnīnī went to al-Raḥba in Rajab, A.H. 674 (December, 1275) for a family reunion and stayed there until his son-in-law's sudden death in Ramaḍān. Al-Yūnīnī then arranged for the funeral of his son-in-law who was 30 years his senior.[49] After the funeral, al-Yūnīnī accompanied his family and the late amīr's son and bodyguards back to Damascus.[50]

Al-Yūnīnī made his second journey to Egypt in 675/1276 and appears to have stayed there at least until 676/1277. In Cairo, he met with some of his old acquaintances such as Bahāʾ al-Dīn al-Fāʾizī,[51] and made new friends like Muḥammad ibn Aḥmad Ibn Manẓūr, a ṣūfī,[52] among others. Al-Yūnīnī's collecting of materials continued during this period: in Rabīʿ II, A.H. 680 (July, 1281), he heard one shaykh ʿImrān's anecdotes about the renowned ʿĪsā ibn Aḥmad al-Yūnīnī.[53] In the same year, in Rajab, he made his way to Hims to join (or to observe?) the battle led by al-Malik al-Manṣūr Qalāwūn against the Mongols. His companion was Muḥammad ibn Aḥmad, a learned man highly regarded by our author, who was later killed on the battlefield. Al-Yūnīnī witnessed the battle and his friend's martyrdom.[54] In 685/1286, in Damascus, he obtained information about the prices, heavy taxes and chaotic

[45] His son married the daughter of Sharaf al-Dīn Hibat Allāh al-Fāʾizī, a protégé of the vizier of al-Malik al-Manṣūr (ruled 655/1257-657/1259); *Dhayl*, 1:81-83.

[46] He died at Mecca in 674/1275, shortly after al-Yūnīnī's visit; see *Dhayl*, 3:137.

[47] *Dhayl*, 3:125-31.

[48] *Dhayl*, 3:133.

[49] He died, as al-Yūnīnī informs us, in his '60s (*Dhayl*, 3:133). Al-Yūnīnī, the father-in-law, was then 33 years old.

[50] *Dhayl*, 3:133. His stay in al-Raḥba at the time is also mentioned in 3:194.

[51] *Dhayl*, 1:82.

[52] His obituary is found in *Dhayl*, 3:280-81.

[53] *Dhayl*, 1:30.

[54] *Dhayl*, 4:121-22.

situation in Aleppo under Mongol occupation back in 659/1261 from one Taqī al-Dīn Abū Bakr al-Ṣarṣarī, a merchant who had lived there during that time.[55] In early Rabī' I, A.H. 688 (March, 1289), probably en route to Egypt, he happened to be in Tripoli and witnessed the battle between the Crusaders and Muslims. The event, from the time when the Muslims launched the attack by firing ballistae on the fortress until their triumphant conquest, was reported on his own account and that of others.[56]

Besides research and writing, al-Yūnīnī seemed quite active in day-to-day affairs in learned circles in Ba'labakk and Damascus. In 687/1288, he attended the funeral honoring Ibrāhīm ibn 'Abd al-'Azīz, a Mālikī teacher and ṣūfī. Al-Yūnīnī, we are told, even undertook the task of burial.[57]

Al-Yūnīnī's third journey to Egypt in the year 688/1289 was highlighted by his visit, in Dhū al-Qa'da, at Alexandria, to the tomb of Abū al-Qāsim Ibn Manṣūr, a Mālikī teacher renowned for his saintliness and piety.[58] In Cairo, he met with his old friend and informant Bahā' al-Dīn al-Fā'izī[59] and encountered one Muḥammad ibn 'Abd al-Razzāq, a Ḥanbalī teacher and poet. He reports that during his time in Cairo, he also saw on several occasions al-Malik al-Mu'izz's son[60] "in the clothing of the Ḥarīrī ṣūfī order (*al-fuqarā' al-Ḥarīrīya*)."[61]

After this, al-Yūnīnī appeared to begin spending more time at home, doing research and working on his manuscript. In Muḥarram, A.H. 691 (January, 1292), he was in the Ba'labakk Citadel interviewing one amīr Asad al-Dīn Ibn al-Ṣu'lūk on al-Malik al-Manṣūr Maḥmūd's biography.[62] The same year, at Ba'labakk, he heard 'Alā' al-Dīn 'Alī recounting some events that had occurred in 658/1259-60.[63] The next year (i.e., 692/1293) he was in Damascus collecting stories on the events of 658/1259-60 from Amīr 'Izz al-Dīn Muḥammad Ibn Abī al-Hayjā', one of his most frequently quoted infor-

---

[55] *Dhayl*, 1:437.

[56] *Dhayl*, M:16-31. This is one of the few instances that al-Jazarī claimed to have quoted from al-Yūnīnī's account; also cf. Haarmann, *Quellenstudien*, 94.

[57] *Dhayl*, M:3.

[58] *Dhayl*, 2:316.

[59] *Dhayl*, 1:82.

[60] Al-Mu'izz Aybak al-Turkumānī, the first Mamluk sultan, ruled 648/1250-655/1257. His son 'Alī (whose regnal name was al-Malik al-Manṣūr) ruled in 655/1257-657/1259. Here al-Yūnīnī perhaps is talking about this deposed ruler. Al-Yūnīnī's eyewitness account of 'Alī's situation was quoted by Ibn Taghrībirdī, *Nujūm*, 7:14.

[61] *Dhayl*, 1:60.

[62] *Dhayl*, M:43-46.

[63] *Dhayl*, 1:381; 2:30.

mants.[64] On Dhū al-Qa'da 22, he received in his home at Yūnīn one Amīr Ibn Yaḥyā and listened to him relating some anecdotes about the above mentioned 'Īsā al-Yūnīnī.[65] He was perhaps at Damascus in Muḥarram, A.H. 698 (October, 1298), watching the building of a royal pavilion on the Akhḍar Square. Our always curious chronicler talked to the officer in charge about the cost of the project.[66] In the same year (i.e., 698/1298), in Rabī' II, al-Yūnīnī was able to watch a comet from the Grand Mosque in Damascus and recorded his observations in detail.[67] It is noteworthy that, despite the extensive record of al-Yūnīnī's social contacts in Damascus, we have no textual evidence that he ever met with al-Jazarī, one of the most important figures for his career.

Later days: the Ḥanbalī Grand Master of Ba'labakk

A turning point in al-Yūnīnī's life came in the year 701/1301 when he succeeded his brother 'Alī, who had died in an accident earlier that year,[68] as the Ḥanbalī Grand Master (*shaykh*) of Ba'labakk.[69] The post may have had a certain impact on his life and career for after that we hardly hear anything about his long-distance travels. Though as the shaykh of Ba'labakk he may have been required to stay home for most of the time, he seems to have kept active in Damascus, enjoying high prestige in learned circles. We are told that in 711/1311, when two chief qāḍīs, Najm al-Dīn Ibn Ṣaṣrā and 'Izz al-Dīn Ibn al-Qalānisī, were at odds, it was al-Yūnīnī who mediated between the two and settled the disputes.[70]

Al-Yūnīnī was remembered also for his ḥadīth teaching. Al-Dhahabī, as mentioned above, reported that he himself had attended al-Yūnīnī's ḥadīth sessions in Ba'labakk and Damascus.[71] Ibn Ḥabīb, the author of the *Durrat al-aslāk*, the primary source of Ibn Rajab's *Ṭabaqāt al-Ḥanābila*, related that his father used to study ḥadīth with al-Yūnīnī as well.[72]

---

[64] *Dhayl*, 2:33; also cf. below, 73-74.

[65] *Dhayl*, 1:31-32.

[66] *Dhayl*, the present edition, 50.

[67] *Dhayl*, the present edition, 66.

[68] The incident has been extensively quoted by many biographers, on the authority of al-Birzālī whose version is virtually identical with that of al-Yūnīnī; see *Dhayl*, the present edition, 260; compare al-Birzālī's version, quoted in Ibn Mufliḥ, *al-Maqṣid*, 2:260, note 1.

[69] Al-'Asqalānī, *Durar*, 4:382.

[70] *Dhayl*, Ms. Ahmet III 2907/e. 4, ff. 218b-219a.

[71] *Al-Mu'jam*, 285-86; another similar statement is quoted in Ibn Mufliḥ, *al-Maqṣid*, 2:9; also al-Yāfi'ī, *Mir'āt al-janān*, 4:276.

[72] Quoted by Ibn Rajab, *Dhayl*, 3:10, note 10.

Little is known about al-Yūnīnī's later days. According to al-Dhahabī, who might have had personal contact with his former teacher at the time, al-Yūnīnī lived a secluded life in his old age, devoting himself to piety and worship[73] and earning the reputation of being an ascetic (*al-zāhid*).[74] This may be attributed to the influence of mysticism under which his father, as well as other great Ḥanbalī masters in Ba'labakk, had also come.[75]

In addition to having the customary virtues of Muslim learned men and being "noble-minded, eloquent, knowledgeable, sincere, well-versed in several branches of learning,"[76] the aged al-Yūnīnī is described by al-Dhahabī as "simply dressed, with beautiful gray hair, full of dignity and awe-inspiring," and by Ibn Kathīr as "devoting himself to Qur'ānic recitation, well-mannered, and having simple tastes in food and clothing" in daily life.[77] According to al-Dhahabī, al-Yūnīnī was highly respected in his community in his later days,[78] attaining, probably, the status of a saintly figure. Given his lifelong zeal for piety, mysticism and asceticism, this kind of description seems quite fitting. Al-Yūnīnī died on the night of Shawwāl 13, A.H. 726 (September 12, 1326) in Ba'labakk[79] and was buried at Bāb Saṭḥā, next to his brother 'Alī's tomb.[80] The family tradition of learning passed on to the next generation: al-Yūnīnī's son Muḥammad, who had studied with his cousins, his un-

---

[73] Quoted in Ibn Rajab, *Dhayl*, 2:380; Ibn al-'Imād, *Shadharāt*, 6:74; Ibn Mufliḥ, *al-Maqṣid*, 3:10. Perhaps his ḥadīth teaching had ceased as well.

[74] Ms. Bodleian Marsh 658, f. 4a.

[75] All his biographies indicate that Muḥammad, al-Yūnīnī's father, was invested with the ṣūfī mantle (*al-khirqa*) by shaykh 'Abd Allāh al-Baṭā'iḥī (*Dhayl*, 2:39) who was the famous Ḥanbalī ṣūfī 'Abd al-Qādir al-Jīlānī's disciple (Ibn Mufliḥ, *al-Maqṣid*, 2:357). Al-Yūnīnī later devoted a hagiographic work to this al-Jīlānī; cf. below, 19, note 96. According to Abū Shāma, quoted by Ibn Kathīr (*Bidāya*, 13:229), Muḥammad, following his master 'Abd Allāh, used to wear a ṣūfī's hat whenever he went out. He is said to have invested the ṣūfī mantle to al-Malik al-Ashraf at Damascus as well; see *Dhayl*, 2:41. For discussion of the relations between ṣūfīs and Ḥanbalīs in general, cf. Laoust, "Le hanbalisme," 1-71; especially 66-68 (on the inclination toward mysticism of Ḥanbalī scholars in Damascus and Ba'labakk). I have been unable to consult Makdisi's "The Hanbali School and Sufism," *Boletín de la Asociación Española de Orientalistas* 15 (1979): 115-26.

[76] Quoted by nearly all biographers on the authority of al-Dhahabī. Ibn Ḥajar al-'Asqalānī also mentioned that al-Yūnīnī, besides being *muḥaddith* and *mu'arrikh*, was also a *faqīh*, an expert on *al-shurūṭ*; *Durar*, 4:383.

[77] Ibn Kathīr, *Bidāya*, 14:126.

[78] Quoted by Ibn Rajab, *Dhayl*, 2:380.

[79] Al-Dhahabī, *Dhuyūl al-'ibar*, 4:77; Ibn Mufliḥ, *al-Maqṣid*, 3:10.

[80] Ibn Kathīr, *Bidāya*, 14:126; Ibn al-'Imād, *Shadharāt*, 6:74.

cle 'Alī's children,[81] eventually became a Ḥanbalī ḥadīth scholar, though perhaps not as prominent as his father.[82]

2. The Penning of the *Mukhtaṣar Mir'āt al-Zamān* and the *Dhayl*

We do not know for sure when al-Yūnīnī began to write. In the preface to the *Dhayl*,[83] we are told that he had first worked on the *Mukhtaṣar Mir'āt al-zamān*, an abridged version of Sibṭ Ibn al-Jawzī's *Mir'āt* and then thought to write a continuation of it.[84] At any rate, the process of abridging the *Mir'āt* and collecting materials, interviewing people and putting things down for his own chronicles, which he would later entitle *Dhayl Mir'āt al-zamān*, had obviously been taking place during the last two decades of the 7th/14th century. It seems certain that at least by the end of 690/1291, some parts of the *Dhayl* were completed. In one obituary notice, al-Yūnīnī confirms that when he "finished these lines, it was the year A.H. 690."[85] The date of completing the *Mukhtaṣar* therefore must be even earlier.

Al-Yūnīnī's self-described "obsession" with Sibṭ Ibn al-Jawzī's universal history was crystallized in his introduction to the *Dhayl:*

> [Among the historical works at my disposal] I saw it (i.e., the *Mir'āt*) to be the most comprehensive in its plan, the most reliable in its sources, the best in its presentation and the most accurate in its narratives as if its stories were eye-witnessed. Therefore, I began abridging the work in the present compendious form and then writing a continuation of it . . . [In doing so,] I [first] read the entire work thoroughly (*anhaytuhu muṭāla'atan*) and then I abridged it through continuous reference to it (*ḥarrartuhu ikhtiṣāran wa-murāja'atan*). . . .[86]

The passage is of special interest insofar as it sheds light not only on al-Yūnīnī's motivation but also on his methodology and scholarship: cautious

[81] According to Ibn Mufliḥ, based on the account of Aydughdī's *Mu'jam*, he studied ḥadīth with Muḥammad, Amat al-'Azīz, Fāṭima, and Zaynab, his uncle 'Alī's children, but his father is not mentioned as his instructor; see *al-Maqṣid*, 3:522. Another son of 'Alī, 'Abd al-Qādir is better known than all the others among the younger generation of the family; see Vajda, "'Abd al-Qādir al-Yūnīnī," 223-46.

[82] For his biography, see al-'Asqalānī, *Durar*, 5:38; Ibn al-'Imād, *Shadharāt*, 6:206-7; Ibn Mufliḥ, *al-Maqṣid*, 3:521-22.

[83] He called it "*khuṭbat al-mudhayyil*"; see *Dhayl*, 1:42.

[84] *Dhayl*, 1:2, 41-42.

[85] *Dhayl*, 2:24.

[86] *Dhayl*, 1:2; also the preface of Ms. Bankipore 967, a *Mukhtaṣar Mir'āt al-zamān*.

and meticulous, but lacking the critical spirit that the younger generation of his fellow Mamluk historians, like al-Dhahabī and al-Ṣafadī (d. 764/1363), possessed.

Regarding the *Mir'āt*, al-Yūnīnī's enthusiasm was shared by some of his colleagues,[87] but surely not all of them. Though considered by scholars, medieval and modern alike, as the basic source of all later Syrian historical writings as well as of various other historical works,[88] Sibṭ Ibn al-Jawzī's famous universal history was subject to criticism even in his own time. Many medieval Muslim scholars, while praising the work for its informative chronicles, complained about its improbable ḥadīths as well as its untrustworthy accounts relating to the Prophet and early Islamic history.[89] Among his critics, al-Dhahabī and al-Ṣafadī seemed to be the most severe, though in their own writings, they benefited from the materials provided by the *Mir'āt*.[90] Modern students of Sibṭ Ibn al-Jawzī find the work a mine of information, especially for the history of the Muslim lands during the Crusades, but are frustrated by its poor planning, confusing presentation and less-than-perfect writing.[91] In this connection, it is commonly held among modern scholars that al-Yūnīnī's *Mukhtaṣar* represents a much better version than any other textual traditions of the work. According to Cahen, the *Mir'āt* survives only in two versions. One is a whole group of manuscripts which reproduce the author's original incomplete draft that was never finally edited due to his death. Another is al-Yūnīnī's *Mukhtaṣar* version. The textual witnesses demonstrate that al-Yūnīnī on the one hand "inserted a number of additions" to

---

[87] For instance, al-Jazarī's acclaimed chronicle *Ḥawādith al-zamān* was also meant originally to be a continuation to Sibṭ Ibn al-Jawzī's work; cf. al-Zayyāt, "Ta'rīkh Dimashq fī Dhayl Shams al-Dīn Ibrāhīm al-Jazarī 'alā Mir'āt al-zamān," cited in Haarmann, "L'édition," 198, note 1.

[88] Cf. "Ibn al-Djawzī," *EI*², by Cl. Cahen.

[89] For medieval scholars' critiques, a note attached to Ms. Bodleian, Marsh 658 (a *Mukhtaṣar Mir'āt*) states that "most scholars in Sibṭ Ibn al-Jawzī's time held favorable views on his history sections, but blamed his ḥadīth sections as weak and unreliable, containing many inaccurate stories as well as false narratives." Sibṭ Ibn al-Jawzī was also blamed for showing sympathy towards the Rāfidites and Shī'īs; see Ms. Marsh 658, f. 4a.

[90] Al-Dhahabī's criticism is found in his *Mīzān al-i'tidāl*, quoted in Ms. Bodleian, Marsh 658, f. 4a. For al-Ṣafadī's criticism see 'Abbās al-'Azzāwī, "Sibṭ Ibn al-Jawzī," 377. This is quite a controversial issue. Some later authors, such as Ibn Taghrībirdī (*Nujūm*, 7:39) and al-Sakhāwī (*I'lān*, 146), were in favor of Sibṭ Ibn al-Jawzī. Others complained that al-Dhahabī and al-Ṣafadī's bitter attacks were "out of jealousy"; cf. 'Abbās al-'Azzāwī, "Sibṭ Ibn al-Jawzī."

[91] Cf. Jewett's introduction to his edition of the 8th volume of the *Mir'āt*; Chase, IX, XV, XIX; Cahen, "Ibn al-Djawzī"; Humphreys, *Ayyubids*, 395-98.

the original and on the other "cut off some lengthy passages" of less importance and thus made the edition complete and balanced.[92]

It should be noted here that the importance of Sibṭ Ibn al-Jawzī's work lies not only in its content, but also in its form. As will be discussed below, it is the *Mir'āt* that set the stage for a long tradition of historical writing in Syria, a model that was to be followed and nourished by al-Yūnīnī and his fellow Damascene historians, and handed down through them to the younger generation represented by al-Dhahabī, under whose stewardship medieval Muslim historiography reached its maturity. Al-Yūnīnī's own contribution to this whole enterprise is that he, in his *Mukhtaṣar* version, developed the framework invented by Sibṭ Ibn al-Jawzī, and later perfected this form in its continuation, i.e., the *Dhayl*.

Al-Yūnīnī acquired fame and, one may say, built his career around the *Mir'āt*: the *Mukhtaṣar* was widely read in many copies at the time;[93] and at least by 709/1309, the first volume of the *Dhayl* was already circulated, perhaps commercially, in Damascus, in a recension deriving from fellow historian 'Alam al-Dīn al-Birzālī's dictation.[94]

One issue that needs clarification here is the peculiar title of *Ta'rīkh al-Yūnīnī* by which al-Yūnīnī's chronicles were well known to many medieval authors. Al-Jazarī, for example, mentions one *Ta'rīkh al-Yūnīnī* as the source of his *Ḥawādith al-zamān*, particularly of the accounts about Ba'labakk, al-Yūnīnī's hometown.[95] Haarmann, citing Ibn al-Dawādārī's reference to al-Yūnīnī's chronicle as *Ta'rīkh Baghdād*, has suggested that at least one early version of al-Yūnīnī's *Dhayl* was perhaps so named. Unfortunately, we do

---

[92] Cahen, "Ibn al-Djawzī"; *Syrie*, 65, note 5. The voluminous *Mir'āt*, beginning with the Creation and continuing up to the author's death (654/1256), is said to have been, as Ibn Khallikān saw it in Sibṭ Ibn al-Jawzī's autograph, in 40 *mujallad*s (*Wafayāt al-a'yān*, 3:142). Al-Yūnīnī reported that he had seen the work in "37 *mujallad*s" instead (*Dhayl*, 1:41). According to al-Sakhāwī (*I'lān*, 146; and Rosenthal's translation, *Historiography*, 490-91), al-Yūnīnī abridged the work to "about half its original size (*fī naḥw niṣfihi*)," that is, to some 20 volumes. One is also interested to see how al-Yūnīnī handled Sibṭ Ibn al-Jawzī's ḥadīth sections which had been the target of critics. According to Chase, as far as the chronicles are concerned, the omissions made by al-Yūnīnī are very few; in other words, most of the omissions in the *mukhtaṣar* version must have had to do with the ḥadīths; cf. Chase, XIXff. For the manuscripts of the *Mukhtaṣar Mir'āt* and the publication record of the *Mir'āt*, see Appendix I and II. Based on our discussion above, I would suggest that any future editions of the work should consult al-Yūnīnī's epitome (*Mukhtaṣar*) as the primary textual basis.

[93] Cf. Appendix I; at least around 712/1312, copies of the *Mukhtaṣar* were made available by professional scribes.

[94] *Dhayl*, 3:110.

[95] Haarmann, *Quellenstudien*, 94-95.

not have any evidence to prove the existence of this *Ta'rīkh Baghdād*. Even if there were such a work, it seems to have hardly anything to do with the *Dhayl*, which is evidently a chronicle about Syria and Egypt, much less about other regions; it is a work that is virtually silent on Baghdad. On the other hand, given that al-Yūnīnī's early version of the chronicle was, as will be discussed below, very much focused on the affairs and people associated with Ba'labakk, the possibility of an early title like *Ta'rīkh Ba'labakk*, perhaps being confused with *Ta'rīkh Baghdād*, appears to be plausible. But again, we do not have any manuscripts to support such a hypothesis. Another explanation may lie in a hagiographic work entitled *al-Sharaf al-bāhir fī manāqib al-shaykh 'Abd al-Qādir al-Kīlānī*,[96] a monograph attributed to al-Yūnīnī about the life and sainthood of al-Kīlānī (also known as al-Jīlī, or al-Jīlānī; d. 561/1166), a revered Ḥanbalī master and ṣūfī whose activities were centered in Baghdad. The work, which is the only title ascribed to al-Yūnīnī besides the *Mukhtaṣar* and the *Dhayl*, appears to be lost today. According to Ḥājjī Khalīfa, al-Yūnīnī states that during his editing of the *Mukhtaṣar*, he came to realize that Sibṭ Ibn al-Jawzī's biography of al-Jīlānī was too scant and thus decided to devote a separate *manāqib*-type monograph to him in which he not only quoted from Sibṭ Ibn al-Jawzī, whose grandfather Ibn al-Jawzī was a leading Ḥanbalī in Baghdad, but also used many other sources.[97] By any account, even if al-Yūnīnī's original, or later, plan was to expand this *manāqib* to a larger biographical dictionary of the Ḥanbalīs in Baghdad under the title of *Ta'rīkh Baghdād*,[98] it still would be, if Ḥājjī Khalīfa's quotation of al-Yūnīnī is to be trusted, no more than a by-product of the *Mukhtaṣar*, which, at best, could not exceed the decline of Ḥanbalism in Baghdad after the Mongol invasion in 1258. In other words, this "*Ta'rīkh Baghdād*" would have nothing to do with the *Dhayl*, al-Yūnīnī's own "chronicle" *per se*.

Going back to the *Ta'rīkh al-Yūnīnī*, it is also very intriguing to note that in a marginal note to Ms. Istanbul Köprülü 1147, an abridged version of al-Jazarī's chronicle,[99] the editor al-Dhahabī claims that al-Jazarī's chronicle was "a continuation (*al-tatimma*) to [Abū Shāma's] *al-Mudhayyal 'alā al-*

---

[96] Also known as *Manāqib al-shaykh 'Abd al-Qādir al-Kīlānī*; see al-Baghdādī, *Hadīyat al-'ārifīn*, 2:479.

[97] Ḥājjī Khalīfa, 1843-44.

[98] For the close association between *ta'rīkh* and *ṭabaqāt* (or *rijāl*, *tarājim*, *wafayāt*, etc.) in medieval Islam, see al-Qāḍī, "Biographical Dictionaries," 115-16, note 3.

[99] The manuscript is said to have been published under the title of *al-Mukhtār min Ta'rīkh Ibn* [sic] *al-Jazarī al-musammā Ḥawādith al-zamān* (ed. al-Munshadāwī, Beirut, 1988). The information of its publication was given to me by Ulrich Haarmann through private correspondence, but I have been unable to locate the book.

Rawdatayn as well as a continuation to our shaykh Quṭb al-Dīn [al-Yūnīnī]'s *Ta'rīkh* which I (i.e., al-Dhahabī) have edited" (*naqqaḥtu*).[100] This short note, perhaps al-Dhahabī's autograph, raises several interesting points: 1) if al-Jazarī's chronicle, whose fragments are known to have covered from 608/1211 to 739/1338,[101] was meant to be a continuation of al-Yūnīnī's "chronicle," this chronicle in question, again, cannot be the *Dhayl*, which begins with the year 654/1256; in other words, the "*Ta'rīkh*" here is certainly referring to the *Mukhtaṣar*; 2) al-Dhahabī was evidently one of the later editors of al-Yūnīnī's manuscripts, and this is important for our examination of the transmission of the *Dhayl* that is to follow; and 3) al-Dhahabī's editorial statement quoted above was surely made when al-Jazarī was still alive, i.e., prior to 739/1338, for he mentioned the latter's name with the phrase "May Allāh spare his life (*abqāhu Allāh*)." In other words, as early as the '40s of the 8th/14th century, both al-Yūnīnī's and al-Jazarī's chronicles had already been circulated not only in their original form, but also in versions edited by others, among them al-Dhahabī.

The title *Ta'rīkh al-Yūnīnī* as referring to his *Mukhtaṣar Mir'āt*, rather than his own chronicle, i.e., the *Dhayl*, seems to have been observed by other later scribes or book collectors as well. On the title page of Ms. Landberg 139, for instance, a marginal note, apparently by a later hand, reads: "this is the 11th [sic] volume of *al-Ta'rīkh ma'a al-Dhayl*," that is, the *Mukhtaṣar* and *Dhayl* collection.

It is thus safe to conclude that, first, the title *Ta'rīkh al-Yūnīnī* is a loose reference indicating either the *Mukhtaṣar* or the *Dhayl*, both attributed to al-Yūnīnī. However, it is used most often to name the former. Second, the title *Dhayl Mir'āt al-zamān* as we know it now was perhaps not the original one in the earliest stage of the composition of the text of al-Yūnīnī's chronicles; it could have been used later, but not later than A.H. 709, when Ms. Bodleian, the earliest codex that bears this title, was copied. We also have good reason to speculate that the finalizing, or the revising, of the *Dhayl* was not too far away from this date, for it is suggested by some medieval sources that, for unknown reasons, the idea of writing chronicles seems to have been abandoned by al-Yūnīnī at some point later in his life, inasmuch as it is most likely that the *Dhayl*, which runs through the year 711/1312, was never designed to go further. In the colophon of Ms. Landberg 136 (entitled *Mukhtaṣar Mir'āt al-zamān*, dated 794/1391-92, i.e., half a century after al-

[100] Ms. Köprülü 1147, f. 1b.

[101] Haarmann, *Quellenstudien*, 27-58; "L'édition," 200-2.

Yūnīnī's death), the scribe stated that he had seen a copy of the "lengthy *Dhayl* running through the year A.H. 711" and "it was a very good continuation which follows the model of the original [*Mir'āt*] and contains a wealth of information" (*wa-qad waqaftu 'alayhi* [i.e., the *Dhayl*] *wa-qad zāda 'alā sanat iḥdā 'ashara wa-sab'imi'a wa-hwa dhayl jayyid naḥw al-aṣl wa-ḥadhwuhu wa-fīhi fawā'id kathīra).*[102] Later authors, starting from Ḥājjī Khalīfa and followed by others, all seemed to subscribe to this claim, pointing out that the four-part (*juz'*) work ends in the year A.H. 711.[103]

[102] Ms. Landberg 136, ff. 264b-265a.
[103] Ḥājjī Khalīfa, 1843-44.

CHAPTER TWO

THE TEXT

1. The Manuscripts

Various parts of the voluminous *Dhayl* are known to be extant in 23 manuscripts, some of which can be grouped in sets. They may be listed in the following roughly chronological order:

1. Ms. Oxford, Bodleian Pococke 132 (Uri 700): The manuscript, which is preserved in the Bodleian Library, Oxford,[1] is incomplete (a few folios at the beginning are missing) and includes 206 folios. It is entitled *Kitāb al-dhayl 'alā Mir'āt al-zamān*. The colophon states that it constitutes the first volume (*mujallad*) of al-Yūnīnī's chronicle and was copied by Muḥammad ibn Muḥammad 'Alī al-Ṣayrafī al-Anṣārī (d. 722/1322)[2] in A.H. 709 at Damascus under the dictation of al-Birzālī (*quri'a hādhā al-mujallad min al-Birzālī*). The manuscript begins with the event of 'Ayn Jālūt, in A.H. 658 and ends with the obituary notices of A.H. 673. Ms. Bodleian is the oldest extant manuscript of the *Dhayl* and was used as the basis of the Hyderabad edition (v. 2 and partially v. 3).

2-5. "The Khālid Set." This is the earliest manuscript set that contains the entire earlier part of the *Dhayl*, covering the years A.H. 654-690. All five volumes, of which four are extant, were copied by one unidentified Khālid ibn Yūsuf ibn Nūḥ and are preserved now in the Topkapı Sarayı Library, Istanbul, under Ahmet III 2907/f. 2, 3, 4, 5 (Karatay 5805-8).[3] The Khālid Set includes the following manuscripts:

2. *Ms. Ahmet III 2907/f. 2*: Entitled *al-Dhayl 'alā Mir'āt al-zamān*, the manuscript covers the years A.H. 658-663. According to Fehmi Edhem

[1] Uri, 1:157.

[2] His biography is found in al-'Asqalānī, *Durar*, 4:319. A contemporary of al-Yūnīnī, he was known also as the copyist of al-Dhahabī's works.

[3] Karatay, 360-61.

Karatay, it is the second volume of the *Dhayl* and includes 198 folios. The colophon states it was copied in 722/1322.[4]

3. Ms. Ahmet III 2907/f. 3: The manuscript has 196 folios and constitutes the third volume of the *Dhayl*, covering A.H. 664-674. The manuscript was copied by the same hand as Ms. Ahmet III 2907/f. 2 and can therefore be dated from around 722/1322.

4. Ms. Ahmet III 2907/f. 4: This is an incomplete codex and contains 191 folios.[5] The fourth volume begins with A.H. 675. Written by the same hand of Khālid ibn Yūsuf, it is dated from 722/1322.

5. Ms. Ahmet III 2907/f. 5: The manuscript, which constitutes the fifth volume, has 229 folios[6] and covers A.H. 680-690. Written in the same hand of Khālid ibn Yūsuf, it can be reasonably dated from around 722/1322.

6. Ms. Istanbul, Aya Sofya 3146: The manuscript is now housed in the Süleymaniye Library, Istanbul.[7] It includes 298 folios. Entitled *Dhayl Kitāb mir'āt al-zamān fī ta'rīkh al-a'yān*, the anonymous manuscript begins with the author's "preface" and covers A.H. 654-662. The manuscript is used as the basis of the Hyderabad edition (v. 1) and is of special importance for it stands as a representative witness to a version that is drastically different from the one represented by Ms. Bodleian. Copied around the 9th/15th century.

7. Ms. Istanbul, Aya Sofya 3199: The manuscript is at present preserved in the Süleymaniye Library.[8] It suffers from the misplacement of a number of folios as well as missing a block of text (from the middle of A.H. 655 to the beginning of A.H. 657). Claimed to be the first volume of *al-Dhayl 'alā Mir'āt al-zamān*, it covers A.H. 654-668. Like Ms. Aya Sofya 3146, it begins with the author's "preface." Copied around the 9th/15th century.

8-10. "The Nastarāwī Set." The fragmentary parts preserved today in several libraries (The Dār al-Kutub of Cairo and the Beinecke Library of Yale) form a *Mukhtaṣar* and *Dhayl* combination of which four volumes (13, 15, 17, and 18) have survived. The set was copied by one Muḥammad ibn

---

[4] Fu'ād Sayyid, 2:2, 141, states that the Ahmet 2907/f set was written during "the 9th century of the Hijra," which is obviously incorrect.

[5] Not listed in Fu'ād Sayyid.

[6] Fu'ād Sayyid has "227 ff."

[7] *Defter*, 189; Cahen, "Chroniques arabes," 344; Spies, 69; Gabrieli, 1164.

[8] *Defter*, 192; Cahen, "Chroniques arabes," 345; Spies, 69-70.

Muḥammad Maḥlūsī al-Nastarāwī, of al-Nastarāwa, Egypt,[9] during the '70s of the 9th/15th century. The Nastarāwī Set includes the following manuscripts:

8. Ms. Cairo, Dār al-Kutub, ta'rīkh 1516, v. 15: The manuscript, which was originally housed in the Khedivial Library under *Ta'rīkh* 551, is now preserved in the Dār al-Kutub, Cairo.[10] The manuscript is incomplete and has only 125 folios. Entitled *Dhayl Mir'āt al-zamān fī ta'rīkh al-a'yān*, it begins with the obituary notices of A.H. 655 and runs through A.H. 657. According to the colophon, the copying of the manuscript was completed in A.H. 870 by one unidentified Muḥammad ibn Muḥammad ibn Muḥammad al-Qurashī al-Nastarāwī. It is noteworthy here that the manuscript claims to be the 15th volume (*juz'*) of a *Mir'āt* (in *mukhtaṣar* form) and *Dhayl* collection whose other volumes have survived in Ms. Yale, Landberg 137 (v. 13, the *Mukhtaṣar*), Ms. Cairo 1516/17 (v. 17) and Ms. Yale, Landberg 139 (v. 18).

9. Ms. Dār al-Kutub, ta'rīkh 1516, v. 17: The manuscript is a complete codex and has 277 folios. It claims to be the 17th volume of the *Mir'āt* and *Dhayl* collection by an anonymous author[11] and begins with an obituary notice in A.H. 671 and ends at A.H. 686. The manuscript was copied by the same hand as v. 15, namely, Muḥammad al-Nastarāwī, and can thus be dated roughly from the same era (around 870/1465). A collation reveals that, as far as the years in question (i.e., until A.H. 673, where Ms. Bodleian ends), are concerned, the manuscript is identical with Ms. Bodleian in that it shares many peculiarities (even errors) with the latter. Several copies of the manuscript (e.g., Ms. Yale, Landberg 340 and, perhaps, "Ms. Istanbul"[12]) have survived as well.

10. Ms. Yale, Landberg 139 (Nemoy 1287): The manuscript is at present preserved in the Beinecke Rare Book and Manuscript Library of Yale University, New Haven.[13] It is a complete codex, with title page and colophon, and counts 277 folios. Covering A.H. 687-701, the manuscript stands as the

---

[9] An ancient town in today's al-Gharbīya Province, it was the capital of the Wilāyat al-Nastarāwīya which is no longer in existence; cf. Yāqūt, *Mu'jam al-buldān*, 4:780; *QI*, 11:56.

[10] *Fihrist* (Cairo, A.H. 1306-1309), 5:57-58; also *GAL*, I:347; Gabrieli, 1164.

[11] Ms. Yale, Landberg 340, which is a copy of this codex, has *wa-lam yu'lam mu'allifuhu* on the title page.

[12] I.e., the unidentified manuscript used by Krenkow in preparing the Hyderabad edition; see item 18 below.

[13] Nemoy, 137.

18th volume of the *Mir'āt* and *Dhayl* collection.[14] The colophon states that it was copied by the same Muḥammad ibn Muḥammad al-Nastarāwī. A detailed description of this codex, on which the present edition is based, is to be found in "Description of the Manuscripts and the Edition," volume two of the present study.

11-13. "The Evkaf Set."[15] The three extant volumes (15, 16, 17) housed in the Evkaf Library of the Türk ve Islam Eserleri Müzesi, Istanbul, apparently belong to a *Mukhtaṣar* and *Dhayl* collection and are wrongly attributed to Sibṭ Ibn al-Jawzī under the title *Mir'āt al-zamān*. No date is given as to when the set was copied. Judging from its paleographical features, it was likely copied during the 9th/15th century.[16] This set includes:

11. Ms. Evkaf 2138: The manuscript has 298 folios and is the 15th volume of the work. A note on the title page states that the manuscript was collated by one unidentified Muḥammad al-Ḥanafī. It covers the years from A.H. 620 (the *Mukhtaṣar Mir'āt*) to A.H. 659 (the *Dhayl* begins A.H. 654).

12. Ms. Evkaf 2139: The manuscript has 275 folios and constitutes the 16th volume of the work, covering A.H. 660-676.

13. Ms. Evkaf 2140: This manuscript, which has 239 folios and constitutes the 17th volume of the work, covers the years A.H. 677-691. This volume is particularly interesting in that it, as will be discussed below, represents a probable composite text wherein the two recensions (Version I and Version II) were put together (see the diagram below).

14-16. "The Buhūtī Set." Written by Muḥammad ibn Muḥammad al-Buhūtī, of al-Buhūt, Egypt,[17] in the 10th/16th century, this set, now housed in the Topkapı Sarayı Library, Istanbul, under Ahmet III 2907/e. 2, 3, 4 (Karatay 5802-4),[18] was originally a four-volume collection of the *Dhayl*, the last three of which have survived, and they are:

---

[14] However, a marginal note, perhaps by a later owner's hand, reads "this is the 11th *juz'* of the *ta'rīkh* (i.e., the *Mukhtaṣar Mir'āt*) with its *Dhayl*"; also cf. above, 20.

[15] I thank Gül Pulhan for helping me obtain the microfilms of the three Evkaf manuscripts.

[16] Cf. Cahen, "Chroniques arabes," 345.

[17] Also as Bahūt (*GAL*, II:424; *GALS*, II:447, and "al-Bahūt," *EI²*, by H. Laoust), in today's al-Gharbīya Province. It is worth noting that a great number of Ḥanbalīs came from al-Gharbīya during the Mamluk period. The fact that the two major sets (i.e., the Nastarāwī Set and the Buhūtī Set) of the *Dhayl* by al-Yūnīnī, himself a prominent Ḥanbalī, were copied in al-Gharbīya may not be merely coincidental.

[18] Karatay, 360.

14. Ms. Ahmet III 2907/e. 2: This is a complete codex, with title page and colophon, and includes 292 folios. Entitled *al-Dhayl 'alā Mir'āt al-zamān*, it constitutes the second volume of the *Dhayl*, starting with an obituary in A.H. 670 and running down to A.H. 689. A table of contents (*fihrist*) of the events of the years A.H. 671-679 is found in the first seven folios as well. The colophon states that it was copied in A.H. 988.[19] It was written by the same hand as Ms. 2907/e. 3, namely, by Muḥammad ibn Muḥammad al-Buhūtī.

15. Ms. Ahmet III 2907/e. 3: The third volume is a complete codex, with title page and colophon, and counts 240 folios, covering A.H. 690-701. The colophon confirms that it was copied by Muḥammad ibn Muḥammad al-Buhūtī and can thereby be dated from around 988/1580. A detailed description of this manuscript, on which the present edition is based, is to be found in "Description of the Manuscripts and the Edition," volume two of the present study.

16. Ms. Ahmet III 2907/e. 4: The manuscript, being the fourth and the last volume, is a complete codex, with title page and colophon, and has 234 folios. Though no information about its date and scribe is given in the colophon, it was evidently written by the same hand as 2907 /e. 2, 3, namely, by Muḥammad al-Buhūtī. The manuscript contains a number of blanks (occurring in ff. 25-28, 38a, 40b-41b, 44a, b, 46a, 47a, 49b, 89b, 90a, 92b, 93a, b, 94b-96b, 112a, b, and 113a) which were obviously reserved for original lacunae in the archetype from which it was copied. A few folios (ff. 59, 64, 69, 74, 79, 84, 179, and 184) seem to have been immersed in water but still remain legible. The special value of this manuscript lies in that it is the only extant manuscript that covers A.H. 702-711, that is, the last portion of the entire text.

17. Ms. Istanbul, Ahmet III 2907/i. 3: The third volume from a set the rest of which is lost today. It is housed, together with other Ahmet III 2907 manuscripts, in the Topkapı Sarayı Library, Istanbul.[20] The manuscript contains 287 folios, covering A.H. 676 (the end) to A.H. 688. This codex is noteworthy in that it represents a much abridged version of the *Dhayl* as opposed to the two other major redactions of the text.[21]

---

[19] Fu'ād Sayyid, 2:2, 141, states that the Ahmet III 2907/e set was made during "the 9th century of the Hijra," which is inaccurate.

[20] Karatay, 362.

[21] Cahen, "Chroniques arabes," 345.

18. "Ms. Istanbul": Neither the catalogue reference to the manuscript nor its whereabouts can be traced. According to information given by the Hyderabad edition (v. 3 and v. 4), this is the original of Krenkow's handwritten copy of one "Istanbul manuscript" upon which the Hyderabad edition (v. 3 and v. 4) is based. It is constantly referred to as *al-aṣl* (the original) in the printed text. On the basis of the information that can be gleaned from the printed text, the manuscript has 290 folios and covers the years A.H. 671-686. The colophon is said to indicate that it constitutes the 17th volume of the *Mir'āt al-zamān* [sic] and that it was copied in 1115/1703. A close reading reveals that the text is almost identical with that of Ms. Cairo 1516/17, a fact that strongly suggests that this "Ms. Istanbul" might well be a direct copy of Ms. Cairo 1516/ 17.

19. Ms. Yale, Landberg 138: The manuscript, which is now preserved at the Beinecke Library under Landberg 138 (Nemoy 1289),[22] is a collective codex, containing both *Mukhtaṣar* (ff. 1a-110b) and *Dhayl* (ff. 111a-219b). The *dhayl* part, whose colophon states that it is the 15th volume (*juz'*) of the *Mukhtaṣar* and *Dhayl* collection, covers A.H. 654-656. The date of the manuscript is uncertain but is presumably later than that of Mss. Aya Sofya 3146 and 3199, for my collation reveals that wherever a lacuna occurs in Mss. Aya Sofya 3146 or 3199, the Yale manuscript in its turn jumps to the next word without leaving a blank space; moreover, whenever both Mss. Aya Sofya 3146 and 3199 do not contain diacritical points on letters, it, too, leaves the word un-dotted. It seems plausible that, so far as the *dhayl* part is concerned, the manuscript was copied from a codex that represents the same parent manuscript from which Mss. Aya Sofya 3146 and 3199 were derived. Nevertheless, the manuscript is noteworthy for it contains three more obituary notices of A.H. 656 (f. 219 a, b; that of Yūsuf al-Kurdī, Abū 'Abd Allāh al-Ḥasan, and Abū al-Qāsim Ibn al-Layth) which are not found either in Ms. Aya Sofya 3146 nor in Ms. Aya Sofya 3199 (from which the entire year A.H. 656 is missing).

20. Ms. Aleppo, al-Aḥmadīya 1213: This is a less studied codex. According to the scattered information we have, it has approximately 200 folios, and covers A.H. 658-673.[23] The date of the manuscript is uncertain; its 11th/17th century calligraphic style might place it around that era. Judging from the fact that it covers exactly the same years as Ms. Bodleian does, this codex might well be a copy of the latter.

---

[22] Nemoy, 137-38.

[23] Al-Munajjid, *Mu'jam al-mu'arrikhīn*, 131; also Fu'ād Sayyid, 2:2, 71.

21. Ms. Yale, Landberg 340 (Nemoy 1286):[24] The colophon states that this copy of the Cairo manuscript (then in the Khedivial Library) was made in 1309/1892 by one Aḥmad 'Abd al-Wahhāb and was collated "carefully" with the original by one Muḥammad Muḥammad al-Khawājah. This relatively modern manuscript is not without interest in that it contains a good number of marginalia and notes by the scribes. A block of text (the end of A.H. 677, all of A.H. 688 and the beginning of A.H. 679) is missing between f. 140 and f. 141.

Besides the manuscripts mentioned above, two other codices have been mentioned by Ṣalāḥ al-Dīn al-Munajjid, but he gives no other information; they are:

22. Ms. Istanbul, Feyzullah Efendi 282.[25]

23. Ms. Tehran, Maktabat-i Milli 1119.[26]

2. The Formation and Transmission of the *Dhayl*

The two major recensions

Previous studies have suggested that the manuscripts of the *Dhayl* derive mainly from two drastically divergent recensions: one represented by Ms. Bodleian Pococke 132 and the other by Ms. Aya Sofya 3146.[27] A collation reveals that, as far as the years in question (that is, from A.H. 658 to A.H. 673) are concerned, Mss. Cairo 1516/17, Ahmet 2907/e. 2, and "Ms. Istanbul," and perhaps Ms. al-Aḥmadīya 1213, are essentially identical—even sharing the same errors—with Ms. Bodleian, the oldest and the most authentic manuscript of this recension. As for the rest of the text not covered by Ms. Bodleian (which ends at A.H. 673), the intrinsic similarities in structure

---

[24] Nemoy, 137.

[25] *Mu'jam al-mu'arrikhīn*, 131. The Feyzullah collection is now housed in the National Library (Millat-i Kütüphane). The old catalogue (Istanbul, 1310/1892) is useless and the recent one made by Ḥamīd Majīd Haddū, published in *al-Mawrid* (Baghdad), 7/2 (1978): 311-64, 8/1 (1979): 305-48, is not yet at my disposal; for Haddū's catalogue, see 'Awwād, *Fahāris*, 1:320.

[26] *Mu'jam al-mu'arrikhīn*, 444.

[27] Cf. Cahen, *Syrie*, 79-80; "Chroniques arabes," 344-45; "al-Yūnīnī," 193-94. Cahen was of the opinion that the Ahmet III 2907/e and 2907/f sets, the Evkaf set, and Ms. Aya Sofya 3199 all belong to the Ms. Bodleian family, which is apparently not very accurate.

and content as well as philological features indicate that these manuscripts are derived from the same manuscript family headed by Ms. Bodleian.

The earliest copy of the other major recension is Ms. Aya Sofya 3146 which shares similarities with, contrary to Cahen's assessment, Ms. Aya Sofya 3199, and Ms. Landberg 138.

A third, and minor, recension is represented by Ms. Ahmet III 2907/i. It is believed to be a short version of the text.

The relationship of the manuscripts that cover later years—that is, the *second part* of the text: A.H. 690-711; e.g., Mss. Ahmet III 2907/e. 3, 4 and Ms. Landberg 139—to the two major recensions remains unclear, for the former have attested to the existence of some new elements, the similarities of which are not found in the representatives of either earlier version.

The complexity of the situation lies in the fact that here we are not dealing with manuscripts of one single complete monograph but a host of manuscripts that represent various volumes of a lengthy text compiled and revised over a long period. Therefore, our scrutiny of the divergent textual traditions of the *Dhayl* should focus on an examination of the formation of the text from a historical perspective.

In the following, let us first note the textual dissimilarities between the two major recensions and then discuss what they can tell us about the history of the formation of the text. To facilitate the discussion, the version represented by Ms. Bodleian will be referred to as Version I and the one by Ms. Aya Sofya 3146 as Version II.

A collation reveals that the two versions demonstrate significant divergences with regard to their inner structure, contents, sources, and some philological features:

1. Structure. Following a tradition set forth by Sibṭ Ibn al-Jawzī, both versions follow the same annalistic norm in which each year is equally divided into a *ḥawādith* section (the chronicle proper) and a *wafayāt* section (the obituaries). However, in Version I, obituary entries are arranged *alphabetically*, i.e., after persons' names, exactly along the lines drawn in Sibṭ Ibn al-Jawzī's *Mir'āt*; but in Version II, they follow a *chronological order*, i.e., according to the death dates of the persons. In addition, this chronological order appears to be a loose one: only those who died in Damascus are put in a strict chronological order but all others are listed not according to the actual date of their death but the date the news of their death was received at Damascus or the date their funeral took place in the city. Additional entries, usually about those who died in remote regions such as Tunisia or those whose death dates were uncertain, are grouped at random at the end of each *wafayāt* section. This new Damascus-centered chronological order has enhanced the work's overall focus as a Damascus chronicle rather than the earlier version that is of a much more local nature, that is, of Ba'labakk. It is not out of place here to recall that this same arrangement is also found in the chronicle *Ḥawādith al-zamān* by al-Yūnīnī's fellow Damascene historian Shams al-Dīn Muḥammad al-Jazarī.

2. Content. The two versions differ largely in terms of their content. By and large, Version I contains more stories and vivid details, especially accounts of events and people associated with Ba'labakk. For example, the events of A.H. 661 occupy 43 pages of printed text[28] in Version I but only 20 pages[29] in Version II. It is to be noted that many details concerning Egyptian affairs[30] are omitted in the latter while new information on Syria, and especially on Damascus, is added.[31] In other words, the author intentionally focused his main narrative line on Damascus and Syria in Version II and his manner of presentation tended to be more succinct and precise. This tendency is similarly seen in the *wafayāt* sections as well. For instance, the *wafayāt* section of A.H. 658 is made up of 26 entries in Version I[32] but only 20 in Version II;[33] and 18[34] vs. 10[35] for A.H. 659. Some Egyptian figures have been eliminated. In those entries that remain, lengthy stories have been reduced sharply. A case in point is al-Yūnīnī's own father's obituary: full of anecdotes of a Ba'labakki flavor, it occupied some 33 pages of text in Version I,[36] but was reduced, surprisingly, to merely a few lines in Version II.[37] This could hardly be due to the author's modesty.

It is extremely interesting to note that despite the overall tendency in Version II toward condensation, the number of poems it contains has, in contrast, actually increased. Let us cite statistics again: for A.H. 658, Version I has 36 poems while Version II has 61; for A.H. 659, there are 16 (Version I)

---

[28] *Dhayl*, 2:186-229.

[29] *Dhayl*, 1:530-50. Parallel texts of the two versions that cover the years A.H. 658-662 are presented respectively in v. 1 and v. 2 of the Hyderabad edition.

[30] E.g., the accounts on the caliph al-Ḥākim bi-amr-Allāh's investiture (*mubāya'a*) in Cairo: six pages in Version I (*Dhayl*, 2:186-91) but only 12 lines in Version II (*Dhayl*, 1:530).

[31] E.g., names of the viceroy (*nā'ib*) and the chief judge of Damascus are added to the list of rulers of A.H. 661, Version II (*Dhayl*, 1:530); compare Version I (*Dhayl*, 2:186).

[32] *Dhayl*, 2:7-87.

[33] *Dhayl*, 1:378-434.

[34] *Dhayl*, 2:126-50.

[35] *Dhayl*, 1:461-83.

[36] *Dhayl*, 2:38-72.

[37] *Dhayl*, 1:429-30.

vs. 33 (Version II); and for A.H. 600, 22 (Version I) vs. 38 (Version II).[38] In other words, the number of poems in Version II is almost double that of Version I. It is also very telling that only a few of these poems, which occur in the parallel texts from the two versions, actually appear in both. That is to say, the majority of poems in Version II are evidently taken from other sources than Version I.

In short, Version I constitutes an earlier form of the work, perhaps a *muswadda*, a draft,[39] wherein much raw material is presented, while Version II shows more of an effort in editing: with the author's "preface," the selective contents, the narrative focus on Damascus, and the much terser wording; on the other hand, there is an obvious effort to introduce more poems as well as other *adab* material into the chronicle framework.

3. Sources. It is curious to note that certain sources utilized in Version I are no longer used in Version II. For example, at the end of the *ḥawādith* section of A.H. 659 (Version I), the author points out that:

> This is a summary of what has come to my attention and what has been recorded in my drafts (*muswaddāt*) regarding the events of this year. Qāḍī Jamāl al-Dīn Muḥammad Ibn Wāṣil,[40] however, has quite different stories in some of the narratives mentioned above and they are perhaps more complete than mine. So I quote his narratives as follows. . . .[41]

Ibn Wāṣil's stories are omitted in Version II, while al-Jazarī's narratives, among others, are added.

Except for one instance,[42] al-Jazarī was virtually unheard of as a source in Version I. His chronicle is first mentioned as *Ta'rīkh Ibn al-Jazarī* in Version II in the year A.H. 658.[43] Many of al-Yūnīnī's quotations from al-Jazarī are about Damascus, of which the latter was a native.[44] The particular problem here, as in other medieval Arabic writings, is to determine where in the text

[38] The only exception is A.H. 661 where only four poems are recorded in Version II while Version I contains some 22 poems.

[39] For the existence of a *muswadda*, see *Dhayl*, 2:114-15; also the quotation below.

[40] He died in 697/1298; for his biography, see "Ibn Wāṣil," *EI²*, by G. el-D. el-Shayyal.

[41] *Dhayl*, 2:114.

[42] Al-Jazarī is named as the source of a poem in the chapter covering A.H. 687; see *Dhayl*, M:4.

[43] *Dhayl*, 1:363.

[44] *Dhayl*, 1:363ff, 368-80, 389-92.

the direct quotation ends.[45] For example, in the printed text, from 1:368 on (the beginning part of Version II), al-Yūnīnī mentions that he used al-Jazarī's chronicle as the source for al-Malik al-Muẓaffar Quṭuz. As the quotation goes on (*Dhayl*, 1:369), al-Jazarī's name is mentioned once again (*ḥakā al-madhkūr ayḍan* . . .). Until the end of this year, namely A.H. 658, there is no indication of the end of al-Jazarī's quotation, which leads to the assumption that the 20 pages that follow contain al-Jazarī's account as well. However, from Ibn Taghrībirdī[46] we learn that some reports within this block of text are originally al-Yūnīnī's own stories, not al-Jazarī's.[47] Though we are now able to prove that some of these reports are indeed al-Yūnīnī's original accounts through tracking down al-Yūnīnī's direct informants, e.g., one Amīr Ibn Abī al-Hayjā',[48] many other paragraphs still remain uncertain. This instance illustrates the inconsistency in al-Yūnīnī's handling of his sources. At any rate, however, al-Jazarī's role as a primary source for al-Yūnīnī, but only in Version II, is very visible.

4. *Format and Wording*. Various philological aspects also make the two versions distinguishable. It is hard to say whether these linguistic features reveal any kind of individual style. As will be discussed below, "individuality" was hardly the case in Syrian historical writing at the time. Still, it is evident that certain relatively stable patterns, each consistently maintained for considerable lengths, can be pointed out to indicate that some remarkable changes had taken place in the process of revision or re-editing of the work, and these include:

a. The change in headings: in Version I, the *ḥawādith* section is always introduced by the heading *mutajaddidāt al-aḥwāl fī hādhihi al-sana* (this year's update); most of the events, big and small, are highlighted by the headline *dhikr* . . . (a report on so-and-so). Such a heading, nevertheless, is not found in Version II at all; and headlines are scarcely used either. Each paragraph that covers one single "event" usually begins directly with the standard phrase *wa-fīhi* . . . (and in this year).[49]

---

[45] For a general discussion of the problem of quotation in medieval Arabic writing, cf. Hitti, 17, 19.

[46] *Nujūm*, 7:86ff.

[47] Krenkow, perhaps for this reason, thought to insert the phrase *qāla Quṭb al-Dīn al-Yūnīnī* (1:380, 381, 389, 430) into the edited text in order to draw the distinction.

[48] For this amīr and his relation to al-Yūnīnī, see below, 73-74. He is named as source in *Dhayl*, 1:383, 502.

[49] For the phrase *wa-fīhi* used as the typical heading in the Arabic annalistic form, cf. Rosenthal, *Historiography*, 71.

b. The change in tone: the frequent use of the first person ("I" or "my") in Version I has been reduced to a minimum in Version II, where the author frequently begins to be introduced in the third person as Quṭb al-Dīn, or *al-mu'allif* (the author). Though it was not an uncommon practice in medieval Arabic writings to refer to the author and his work by phrases like *qāla fulān* . . . (so-and-so [the author] said) or *qāla fulān fī* . . . (so-and-so [the author] said in such-and-such [work]), what we find in al-Yūnīnī's case is an apparent inconsistency in the use of such formulas. Here the tone sounds more like someone quoting al-Yūnīnī's *Ta'rīkh*, namely the *Dhayl*, than al-Yūnīnī telling his stories. It strikes the reader that even in presenting his father's obituary, the author remains totally silent on the deceased's relationship to him.[50] In other words, the narrator's neutral tone prevails in Version II, while the personal imprint, which we encounter more often in Version I, is not apparent anymore. This curious shift of tone may well indicate al-Yūnīnī's effort to bring his text into accordance with a common model or a kind of "mainstream" formulation, as will be discussed in chapter 4 of the present study, among the Syrian historians at the time, but it may also raise the question of the real authorship of certain parts of the text, a question we will try to answer in the following chapter.

All the intrinsic features found in the representative manuscripts of Version I are continued right up to A.H. 677, where the heading *mutajaddidāt al-aḥwāl* begins to disappear altogether. The basic inner structure, including the alphabetically arranged *wafayāt* sections, remains the same through the end of these manuscripts; and among these the most complete one (Ms. Ahmet 2907/e. 2) reaches as far as the year A.H. 689.

Features of Version II have yielded some interesting observations. It is noteworthy that, though variant readings are found here and there, the beginning part of Version II (A.H. 654-657) evidently shows some features similar to that of Version I, among which are the alphabetically-arranged obituaries and the intensive use of the first person. That is to say, all fundamental changes characterizing Version II do not begin to appear until A.H. 658 onward, where al-Jazarī's accounts begin to be quoted as the primary source and his format as the model.

Version II also exhibits the struggle to add novel features to an old framework. For instance, in the chapters on A.H. 658 and A.H. 659, the author appears to have tried to group obituaries according to the status of the de-

[50] Compare the obituary of his father in Version I (*Dhayl*, 2:38-72) where the word *wālidī* (my father) is pervasive. The same treatment is found in his brother's obituary (A.H. 701); cf. *Dhayl*, the present edition, 260-61.

ceased persons in that all the Mamluk sultans and amīrs are put together, and this is to be followed by the next category, the non-Mamluks, i.e., religious figures, bureaucratic clerks, and so forth. But such a plan seems to have been abandoned soon. Another example is the inner structure of the obituary. In Version I, the typical pattern of an obituary is as follows: name / place of death / *manāqib* (virtuous character traits) / quotations from literary works (mainly poetry) / dates of birth and death[51] / funeral, and so forth. The verb *tuwuffiya* (he died) only appears once at the beginning of the first entry of each year's *wafayāt* section and all the following entries thus start with the names immediately without repeating the verb. This pattern remains the same in Version II as well, albeit the way of arranging the entries has changed. In addition, all the evidence, internal and external, and all the signs of continuity and discontinuity point to the fact that Version II is significantly influenced by al-Jazarī's *Ḥawādith al-zamān*. However, it still reflects, in many ways, al-Yūnīnī's own labor.

With regard to the rest of the manuscripts, namely Ms. Landberg 139, Mss. Ahmet III 2907/e. 3, 4, whose manuscript family affiliations remain uncertain since the archetypes of the two versions do not contain this part of the text (after A.H. 690), a close reading reveals that features of Version I (the use of the first person, the way of arranging obituaries, etc.) remain right up to A.H. 690 where some new elements begin to emerge. These new elements include:

a) A heading of *dhikr ḥawādith* for the *ḥawādith* section is used throughout the text.

b) A new pattern of obituary style is applied to A.H. 691-695: it begins with the date of the deceased's death, and continues as follows: date and place of death / name / *manāqib* / quotations from literary works, and so forth. Moreover, the chronological order of obituaries is rather loose. For example, the *wafayāt* section of A.H. 692 begins with Muḥarram (the first month in the Islamic calendar), reaching the month Dhū al-Qa'da (the second to last), and then begins again with the month Muḥarram and goes on to the end of the year.[52]

c) A heading of *dhikr man daraja fī hādhihi al-sana* (obituaries of those who passed away in this year) for the *wafayāt* section is used from A.H. 695 onward. It is also noted that the pattern of the obituary has been established

[51] Sometimes dates of birth and death are put in the middle of the obituary.

[52] My speculation would be that while compiling the *wafayāt* sections, the author quoted from several notebooks and each of these followed a roughly chronological order.

as: name / place of death / date of death and birth / *manāqib* / quotations, and so forth. The phrase *wa-fīhi tuwuffiya* (and died in this year . . .) is repeated at the head of every single entry. The overall structure of the *wafayāt* section seems to have improved as well, in that a strict chronological order is observed. By and large, this overall structure remains the same in Ms. Ahmet III 2907/e. 4 through the end of the text.

To sum up, the evidence afforded by all the available textual evidence of the *Dhayl* shows that the formation of the entire text had gone through at least three major phases:

1) Al-Yūnīnī first wrote a draft the oldest copy of which (Ms. Bodleian) serves as the archetype of this ancient version. This version runs from A.H. 654 through A.H. 690. It is very much in line with the plan in Sibṭ Ibn al-Jawzī's *Mir'āt* and has proved to be genuinely al-Yūnīnī's original writing (Version I). This version, having inherited the internal shortcomings of Sibṭ Ibn al-Jawzī's, is uneven in its coverage and is poorly organized. For instance, it is long on Ba'labakk, the author's home town, and relatively short on other parts of Syria.

2) A limited portion (A.H. 654-668) of a revised version (Version II) is extant in a group of manuscripts the chief of which is Ms. Aya Sofya 3146. It appears to have been derived from a "work-in-progress" draft in which profound changes in structure, content, sources as well as wording are found. But on the other hand, some old patterns still persist. It is noted that some portions of this version (e.g., from A.H. 658 on) quote from al-Jazarī frequently. This version also shows a tendency to concentrate on Syrian, particularly Damascene, affairs and, in general, to cut the text short. But at the same time, it has the tendency to elaborate and enrich the biographical material by introducing even more *adab* products by local 'ulamā', such as poetry, anecdotes, witty sayings, and so forth. In this regard, we do not know whether the author had in his mind a plan of penning a *mubyaḍḍa* (final version), or a *mukhtaṣar* (epitome) of the work while he was working on the revision. The only thing we know for sure is that nearly all the extant copies bear the title of *Dhayl Mir'āt al-zamān*.

3) The remaining part of the text (A.H. 690-711) continues to show the same basic characteristics in the revised draft (Version II), and becomes increasingly similar to al-Jazarī's *Ḥawādith*. As will be argued in detail below, at least until A.H. 698, the last year for which al-Jazarī's version is available

for a comparison,[53] the *Dhayl* ascribed to al-Yūnīnī and the *Ḥawādith* of al-Jazarī essentially represent a common text, with occasional omissions here and additions there, a text tradition that I would call the "Jazarī-Yūnīnī tradition."

Later history of the manuscripts

The text of the *Dhayl* has a rich and continuous record of both direct and indirect transmission, i.e., in the various manuscripts of the *Dhayl* and its frequent quotation in the works of later historians (e.g., al-Dhahabī, Ibn Kathīr, Ibn Taghrībirdī, al-Maqrīzī). Here we are mainly concerned about the direct transmission. Based on the above overview, an approximate stemma of the manuscripts of the *Dhayl* may be established, as depicted in the diagram below.

Of the extant 23 manuscripts of the *Dhayl*, at least five were made during al-Yūnīnī's lifetime. The oldest manuscript, Ms. Bodleian (copied in A.H. 709) might well be an archetype that was extremely close to the original of al-Yūnīnī's first draft (Version I). The second oldest codex, the so-called "Khālid Set," of four volumes (copied in A.H. 722), is the oldest copy of a multi-volume collection made during al-Yūnīnī's lifetime. This set ends at A.H. 690, which is, as discussed above, a sort of watershed in the formation of the entire text. Though there is no enough evidence for any further speculations, it might at least be suggested that this codex was perhaps very close to the line of Ms. Bodleian and that the year A.H. 690 was indeed some sort of limit in the author's original division of the text.

A revised draft (Version II) is represented by another group of later manuscripts, namely, Ms. Aya Sofya 3146, Ms. Aya Sofya 3199 and Ms. Landberg 138. Due to the scantiness of the copies of this version, I am unable to determine when exactly this revised draft was made or how far it went. However, in light of the above discussion it might be safe to say that this version did play a significant part in determining, or at least characterizing, the overall format of the rest of the text. Accordingly, it might have had a certain impact on its transmission as well. The original of this revised version must have been made at some point between 709/1309-10 (when Version I was already being circulated in Damascus) and 726/1326 (when the author died),

[53] Ms. Paris arabe 6739, the major testimony to al-Jazarī's version, ends abruptly with the beginning of the year A.H. 699.

and, as has previously been suggested, perhaps sometime around 711/1311, when he finally abandoned the writing project.

Next we see a gap of more than one and a half centuries until the copying of the Nastarāwī Set (copied in 870/1471) in which various parts of both *Mukhtaṣar* and *Dhayl* were brought together. The Evkaf Set (perhaps copied in this same century) should probably also be thought of as belonging to this composite set which represents a line of descent in which a final version, or a synthesis, of the "Jazarī-Yūnīnī tradition," has been preserved. But we do not know whether this version, or synthesis, was made by al-Yūnīnī himself or by some later scribe.

Another major group of manuscripts, the Buhūtī Set, was copied 100 years later. This set is the most complete for it contains the unique part of the text that runs through A.H. 711. However, the last "volume" of this set is, as will be discussed in detail below, evidently copied from a defective parent codex with a considerable number of lacunae as well as other severe textual errors.

To be sure, some gaps are to be noted in this picture. Questions of the existence of a "final version" are left unresolved: the composite version in which the entire text of the Jazarī-Yūnīnī tradition was brought together, the nature of the version of the *Dhayl* that was seen by some scribe (in 794/1391)[54] as having reached the year A.H. 711, the authenticity of the two major versions and their archetypes, the relation of these two versions to the third abridged version, and the authorship of the second part of the text (i.e., that which covers A.H. 690-711), etc. However, some speculations based on a close reading of the text are possible.

First, as mentioned above, all manuscripts that cover the years prior to A.H. 690, namely, Mss. Cairo 1516/15, 17, Ms. Landberg 139, Mss. Ahmet 2907/e. 2, 3, Mss. Evkaf 2138-40, and Ms. "Istanbul," show essential similarities in wording and even share errors with each other. They are thus close enough to permit the hypothesis that a codex was made around the first decade of the 8th/14th century, say, around or shortly after Ms. Bodleian. In this codex, a good portion (A.H. 654-677), which is evidently identical to the ancient archetype (Ms. Bodleian), co-existed along with another portion of slightly revised text (A.H. 678-690). In other words, al-Yūnīnī probably made a codex which runs through A.H. 690, and this codex, now missing, was the archetype (or exemplar) of the Khālid Set.

---

[54] Cf. above, 21.

Second, as regards the second part of the text, namely, that which covers the years from A.H. 690 onward, a considerable number of minor dissimilarities can be observed in Ms. Landberg 139 and Ms. Ahmet 2907/e. 3, the two manuscripts that are made the basis of the present edition, which covers A.H. 697-701. Some of these dissimilarities, especially those found in the verses cited, are very suggestive. As such, though the two manuscripts essentially represent a common text, they appear likely to have been derived from two sub-recensions. In this connection, it is noteworthy that Ms. Ahmet 2907/e. 3 is even closer to al-Jazarī's version in wording, particularly in poetical and other literary quotations,[55] than to another al-Yūnīnī manuscript, i.e., Ms. Landberg 139. It appears plausible that, at some point during the process of copying, al-Jazarī's work[56] was intensively cross-checked by the unknown scribes of the exemplar from which the Buhūtī Set, namely, Mss. Ahmet 2907/e, was copied. One may speculate that this exemplar was thought by later scribes to be the original of the *entire* work of al-Yūnīnī's *Dhayl*. It follows that the existence of this exemplar could not be too late, say, no later than the year 794/1391, when the entire work of *Dhayl* running through A.H. 711 was seen by one copyist of al-Yūnīnī's work.[57]

Third, the exemplar of this composite version was perhaps further contaminated; not only are al-Yūnīnī's and al-Jazarī's texts merged without the scribes' noticing,[58] but there are also cases in which the stories are known to have come from other sources. The famous "Damascus diary," for example, which describes the destruction of Damascus by the Mongols in 699/1299-700/1301 is ascribed to al-Dhahabī as well.[59] There are also a few instances that suggest some sort of misplacement. The *wafayāt* section for the year A.H. 700, for example, ends with a fragment of a certain shaykh's biography which is obviously out of context.[60]

Finally, a few words concerning the transmission of such a multi-volume enterprise are pertinent. It is noted that the extant manuscripts constitute sev-

---

[55] Examples will be discussed in the next segment of this chapter. It seems that although itself a bad manuscript (cf. "Description of the Manuscripts and the Edition," volume two of the present study), Ms. Ahmet 2907/e. 3 might have been copied from a better parent codex than that of Ms. Landberg 139.

[56] Since only one manuscript (Ms. Paris) of the relevant part from al-Jazarī's *Ḥawādith* has survived, we are not in a position to pursue this matter further.

[57] Cf. above, 21.

[58] E.g., al-Jazarī's collection of *faḍā'il* literature (including several *maqāmāt* and descriptions of Egypt) was wrongly inserted into the narrative of the events of the year A.H. 701; for details, see below, 55-56.

[59] For details see below, 54-55, especially note 78.

[60] See *Dhayl*, the present edition, 239, lines 9-16.

eral sets, each of which was copied by the same scribe and divided into four or five volumes (*mujallad* or *juz'*) depending on the way the quires (*kurrāsa*) were cut and bound. So far we have:

- *Dhayl* proper: the Khālid Set, the Buhūtī Set.
- *Mukhtaṣar* and *Dhayl* combination: the Nastarāwī Set, Ms. Landberg 138, the Evkaf Set.

Putting the *Mukhtaṣar* and *Dhayl* together seems to have been popular later. At least three such combination sets have survived, though partially, in manuscript. It is interesting to note here that the *Dhayl* part of all the combination sets begins exactly with the 15th volume. That is to say, in these *Muktaṣar* and *Dhayl* combination sets, the *Mukhtaṣar* takes up 14 volumes,[61] while the *Dhayl* part has approximately four or five volumes.

[61] The normal size of the *Mukhtaṣar* is usually 20 volumes; cf. Appendix I.

The Relationship of the Extant Manuscripts of the *Dhayl*

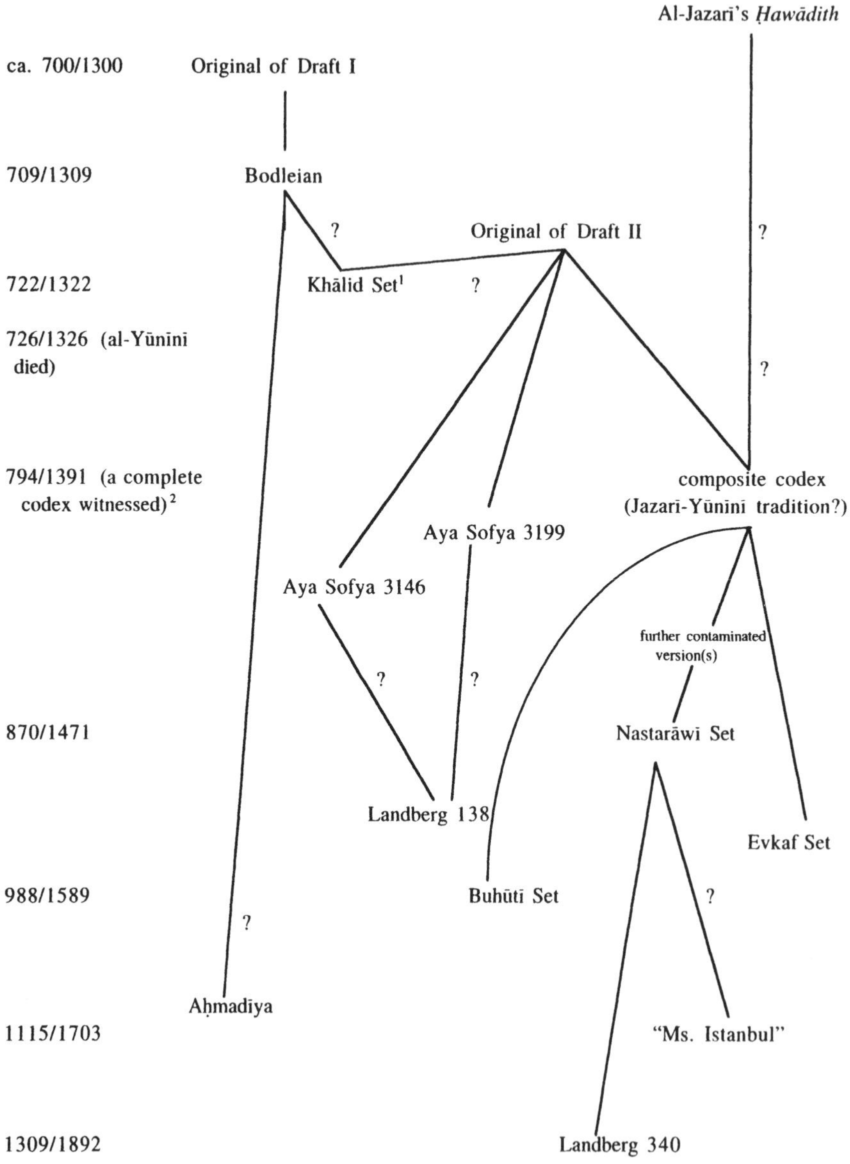

---

[1] See above 36.
[2] See above 21.

3. The Jazarī-Yūnīnī Tradition

The similarity between al-Yūnīnī's and al-Jazarī's texts has long been noticed by modern scholars, and a wide range of opinion exists among them. As Stephen Humphreys puts it: "[The writings of] al-Jazarī, al-Birzālī, and al-Yūnīnī . . . are closely linked to one another," but "in ways that are still not wholly clear."[62] Cahen's, Haarmann's, and Melkonian's studies demonstrate that the mutual borrowing between the two, often without acknowledgment, did take place in certain portions (covering the years prior to A.H. 690) of their works.[63] Little, however, challenged this notion by showing that at least for the years he examined (A.H. 694, 699, and 705), the borrowing actually took a one-way direction, i.e., al-Yūnīnī copied al-Jazarī, not *vice versa*.[64] Haarmann's and Melkonian's explanation of this puzzle is that al-Yūnīnī first wrote a *muswadda*, a draft, which was later utilized by al-Jazarī in preparing his chronicle, and then al-Yūnīnī took back his own accounts along with those of al-Jazarī when he was working on his second draft of the *Dhayl*. However, some questions remain unanswered: What exactly happened during the process? How could al-Yūnīnī knowingly copy from al-Jazarī nearly verbatim without any acknowledgment? Was this kind of "borrowing" a common practice in Damascus at that time among the ḥadīth transmission-oriented chroniclers? If yes, what were the rules of such a practice? If no, who was responsible for this confusion? Or, who was the real author of this valuable portion of the text? Here we are faced with two technical problems that can be characterized as common in Mamluk historiography: 1) both authors are inconsistent in naming each other as sources; and 2) even when they do so, they usually fail to indicate the end of a quotation. The consequence of such a practice is made worse where references of provenance such as *qultu* (I say, or, I think) or *ra'aytu* (I saw) or *sami'tu* (I heard) are exactly the same in both al-Yūnīnī's and al-Jazarī's texts, thereby losing their functional meaning.

All previous studies have touched upon selected parts of this problematic portion of the text and the conclusions they have reached are, by and large, accurate. We thus have some well observed trees, but not a view of the for-

---

[62] *Islamic History*, 240.

[63] Cahen, *Syrie*, 79-80; "Editing Arabic Chronicles," 3-4, 17f; Haarmann, *Quellenstudien*, 94-95; Melkonian, 21-37.

[64] *Introduction*, passim, especially 57-61.

est. For one thing, Cahen's, Haarmann's, and Melkonian's observations of the existence of the "reciprocal borrowing relationship" between the two are well documented. Equally supported by textual evidence, however, is Little's "one way" copying theory. The only difference here is that Cahen's, Haarmann's, and Melkonian's examinations were confined to the text that covers the years prior to A.H. 690, while Little's analysis focused on the years after A.H. 690. It is obvious that in order to get rid of this chicken-egg situation, we need, first, to carefully examine *all* the available textual evidence, in other words, to get a "big picture."

A collation of al-Yūnīnī's and al-Jazarī's texts (A.H. 691-699)

The following is the result of a textual collation between al-Yūnīnī's *Dhayl* and al-Jazarī's *Ḥawādith al-zamān*. The years A.H. 691-699 are singled out here for several reasons: 1) al-Jazarī's version only survives in Ms. Paris arabe 6739, which ends at the beginning of A.H. 699;[65] 2) previous studies by Cahen, Haarmann, Melkonian, and the present survey have convincingly shown that until A.H. 690, the two texts are clearly independent of each other and contain their exclusive stories supported by their own sources; in other words, the fundamental similarity between the two texts does not begin to emerge until A.H. 691.

Al-Yūnīnī's version is here represented by Ms. Landberg 139, and the folio numbering (a, b) will be followed. Al-Jazarī's version is represented by Ms. Paris arabe 6739 (covering the years A.H. 689-698), and the page numbering on the top center margin of the Ms. (instead of the folio numbering) will be followed.[66] From the year 697/1297 on, we deal with the portion that is covered in the present edition. Page numbers in this edition will be given. One of the goals of this edition, which presents the two texts side by side, is to give those readers who have no access to the manuscripts a chance to see

[65] For the manuscript survey of al-Jazarī's chronicle, see Haarmann, *Quellenstudien*, 27-50; "L'édition," 200-3. An edition based on Ms. Paris and Ms. Gotha 1560 (covering, incompletely, A.H. 690-695) is found in Jubran, 1-80 (Arabic text). Al-Dhahabī's *Mukhtār* version, which covers A.H. 593-699, is far too brief for the present purpose (e.g., the year of A.H. 697 occupies less than two folios [ff. 140a-141b] in the extant manuscript, Ms. Köprülü 1147).

[66] The page numbering sometimes contains errors. I will confine myself to the given numbers as they appear in the manuscript, regardless of whether they are wrong or not. Thus, all the numbers with folio indications (a, b) are from al-Yūnīnī's text and all the others are from al-Jazarī's version.

how the two texts, neither of which was published before, are closely linked and how a possibly better version of this common textual tradition could eventually be made on the basis of all variations seen in these two versions attributed to two different authors.

A.H. 691

Ḥawādith: Al-Jazarī's name is not mentioned as the source for this part of the text; however, his authorship can be attested by historical evidence, namely, his direct source Amīr Sayf al-Dīn Ibn al-Miḥaffadār,[67] who is referred to by the phrase *ḥakā lī* (119), while al-Yūnīnī has *ḥakā* (55a).

Wafayāt: 1) Al-Jazarī is clearly named, on several occasions, as the source for this section. There is a very interesting case in which al-Yūnīnī's version has preserved a passage attributed to al-Jazarī but which is missing from Ms. Paris, the sole witness to al-Jazarī's text. In 65a, al-Yūnīnī's text reads *qāla Ibn al-Jazarī ittafaqa annanī kuntu yawman bi-qal'at Dimashq 'inda al-amīr Sayf al-Dīn Ibn al-Miḥaffadār* . . . (it so happened that one day I was in the Damascus Citadel with Amīr Sayf al-Dīn Ibn al-Miḥaffadār . . .) on whose authority an anecdote about the deceased person (*ṣāḥib al-tarjama*) Fatḥ Allāh Muḥammad ibn 'Abd Allāh was narrated. Here a block of text that has been contained within al-Yūnīnī's quotation from al-Jazarī has not survived in Ms. Paris; that is to say, sometimes we rely on al-Yūnīnī to reconstruct al-Jazarī's text.

2) Other observations drawn from this section reveal al-Yūnīnī's inconsistency in naming al-Jazarī as his source. In 66b (= al-Jazarī, 154), al-Jazarī as the source for the deceased person's poems is indicated by the phrase *qāla* . . . *al-Jazarī* while elsewhere he is not; e.g., in 70a, 70b whenever al-Jazarī stated *anshadanī* and *ḥakā lī*, al-Yūnīnī would claim the same. In the last two instances, al-Yūnīnī's text also contains serious scribal errors: al-Jazarī's original text (163) reads *anshadanī lil-shaykh . . . al-Sakhāwī* (he [the *ṣāḥib al-tarjama* 'Imād al-Dīn Yūnus al-Dimashqī] recited to me a poem attributed to al-Sakhāwī) is found in al-Yūnīnī's version as *anshadanī al-shaykh . . . al-Sakhāwī* (70a), thus this al-Sakhāwī would be mistaken as al-Yūnīnī's direct source and the poem as attributed to an unknown person. Moreover, the same misidentification is repeated in 70b where al-Yūnīnī has *anshadanī 'Alam al-Dīn al-madhkūr* (i.e., al-Sakhāwī) while the original version of al-Jazarī gives the reference to *'Imād al-Dīn al-madhkūr* (164,

[67] This is attested in 65a; see the discussion below, A.H. 691 *wafayāt*, 1).

namely, Yūnus al-Dimashqī). Such inconsistency by al-Yūnīnī has caused confusion.

3) Some 17 obituaries are omitted in al-Yūnīnī's version and we do not know what the criterion for the omission was.

4) Some obituaries have been abbreviated in al-Yūnīnī's version; e.g., quotations from Zayn al-Dīn 'Umar Ibn Makkī al-Shāfi'ī's works (137-40) are omitted in al-Yūnīnī's version.

A.H. 692

Ḥawādith: Although al-Jazarī is not cited as the source of this section, a strong case can be made here through the historical evidence: al-Jazarī's authorship is firmly established through the narrative concerning a merchant and traveler 'Abd Allāh ibn Muḥammad al-Sinjārī's coming from Constantinople to Damascus in this year. This person is referred to as "my father's old acquaintance" (*kāna baynahu wa-bayna wālidī ma'rifa qadīma*) and "my father thus asked [him] about" (*fa-sa'ala al-wālid 'an*) the situation in Constantinople; and at the time, "I said to him: Uncle, please describe the city [of Constantinople] to me" (*qultu 'ammī ṣif lī ṣifatahā*, . . . 75a-76b). "My father" here without doubt refers to al-Jazarī's father, for al-Yūnīnī's father had died in 658/ 1260. And it follows that "I" in the context could be none but al-Jazarī. This whole *ḥawādith* section was most likely quoted by al-Yūnīnī from al-Jazarī without acknowledging the latter as the source. Even the indication of other direct personal contact by al-Jazarī, such as *ḥakā lī*, is quoted verbatim by al-Yūnīnī (76b = 181).

Wafayāt: 1) Al-Jazarī's name is not mentioned in this section; in the light of the analysis of historical evidence, it may be safe to say that al-Jazarī's accounts continue to be quoted nearly verbatim by al-Yūnīnī. Besides, it is significant that al-Birzālī is mentioned as the direct oral source to "me," in that we are told that al-Birzālī recited Kamāl al-Dīn 'Alī ibn Muḥammad al-Dimashqī's poems to "me" in Ṣafar, A.H. 705 (185), and the same wording, including the phrase of *anshadanī*, is found quoted by al-Yūnīnī (78a). Though we know for sure that both al-Yūnīnī and al-Jazarī were acquaintances of al-Birzālī, based on our overall survey, there is good reason to believe that it was al-Jazarī, not al-Yūnīnī, that received the related information from al-Birzālī; in other words, al-Yūnīnī recorded al-Birzālī's accounts through al-Jazarī's version. Further discussion of al-Birzālī's relation with the two is presented in our source criticism below.[68]

---

[68] Cf. chapter 3 below, 75-80.

2) Ten obituaries are omitted by al-Yūnīnī.

3) More ḥadīth citations on the authority of Taqī al-Dīn Ibrāhīm ibn 'Alī al-Wāsiṭī al-Ḥanbalī are preserved in al-Yūnīnī's version (81a-84b) than in Ms. Paris.

A.H. 693

Ḥawādith: 1) Al-Jazarī's name is not mentioned in this section of the text, but his authorship is, again, strongly suggested by certain historical evidence: e.g., the original wording *wa-ḥakā lī al-amīr Sayf al-Dīn Ibn al-Miḥaffadār . . . al-madhkūr kayfiyat qatl al-sulṭān sanadhkuruhu fī wafātihi* (Amīr Sayf al-Dīn Ibn al-Miḥaffadār also told me about how the sultan [al-Malik al-Ashraf] was murdered and we will go into details in his obituary later) has been changed to a brief *wa-sanadhkuru kayfiyat qatl al-sulṭān* (we will go into details about how the sultan was murdered) in al-Yūnīnī's version (93b); the reference to Amīr Ibn al-Miḥaffadār, who was certainly al-Jazarī's direct informant, is passed by in silence.

2) Three events are omitted from al-Yūnīnī's version and those include al-Malik al-Sa'd Shams al-Dīn Dāwūd Īlghāzī's succeeding his father as the ruler of Mārdīn (243), Hülegü's grandson Baidu's ascending the throne (243), and an anecdote about the mayor of Damascus's ordering that all dogs should be expelled from the city, perhaps out of concern for public health (244-45).

Wafayāt: 1) Al-Jazarī is mentioned by al-Yūnīnī once as source for the following purpose: the reference "my father" (i.e., al-Jazarī's father) may be thought confusing and thus al-Jazarī's name is needed; the text (105a) has *qāla . . . al-Jazarī ḥakā lī wālidī* (al-Jazarī said: my father told me that) to add to al-Jazarī's original *ḥakā lī wālidī* (256). The lengthy verbatim copying must have continued all the way through to the end of this *wafayāt* section, and therefore the phrase "my brother Abū al-'Abbās Aḥmad" (109a = 267) should be understood as referring to al-Jazarī's brother, not al-Yūnīnī's. We also see al-Jazarī's statements of *anshadanī* copied exactly the same by al-Yūnīnī; such statements usually contain very important historical background information; e.g., 110b: al-Yūnīnī's text says that Sibṭ Ibn 'Abd al-Ẓāhir "recited to me at Cairo in the year A.H. 712" some poems attributed to Fakhr al-Dīn Ibrāhīm Ibn Luqmān al-Shaybānī al-Miṣrī. The same phrase in al-Jazarī's text (271) convinces us that the person in Cairo in 712/1312 was not al-Yūnīnī, but al-Jazarī. Another telling example is found in 110b: the text reads *anshadanī al-shaykh Shams al-Dīn . . . Muḥammad li-nafsihi*; by comparing it to al-Jazarī's version, we realize that the entire passage was in fact handed down through al-Birzālī to al-Jazarī (*anshadanī shaykhunā . . .*

al-Birzālī qāla anshadanī al-imām Shams al-Dīn . . . Muḥammad li-nafsihi). That is to say, this Shams al-Dīn recited his own poems neither to al-Yūnīnī nor to al-Jazarī, but rather to al-Birzālī. Those historical details are crucial for our source criticism of a text wherein three authors are involved. A quick note here: it was al-Jazarī that was active in Cairo during the year 712/1312 and al-Birzālī was al-Jazarī's direct informant.

2) Eighteen obituaries are omitted by al-Yūnīnī. The obituary of Shams al-Dīn Ḥusayn ibn Dāwūd al-Shahrazūrī al-Kātib is moved (295) forward to follow Fakhr al-Dīn Muḥammad ibn Muḥammad ibn al-Tibnī (269 = 109b). The reason of this re-arrangement is not clear.

3) Some details are left out of al-Yūnīnī's version; e.g., an anecdote about Shams al-Dīn Muḥammad ibn 'Uthmān al-Tanūkhī (251) is not found in his obituary in the *Dhayl*.

A.H. 694

Ḥawādith: 1) This year's *ḥawādith* and *wafayāt* sections have been examined by Little who points out that:

> Al-Yūnīnī's annal for 694/1294-95 . . . is almost exactly the same as al-Ǧazarī's for this year. Al-Yūnīnī did delete notices of a few appointments and some obituaries; otherwise, he copied al-Ǧazarī's text closely, changing a few phrases here, omitting a word or two there, in the manner of a bored copyist.[69]

The only obvious such change occurs in 119b when the phrase *jā'a khabar anna Baydū* (it was reported that Baidu . . .) replaced al-Jazarī's *balaghanā anna Baydū* (we were told that Baidu, . . . 306). Al-Jazarī's name was mentioned in 117b as the source of Hülegü's conquest of Aleppo (299-300).

2) The text for this year is of special interest for it reveals that al-Jazarī's source of Ghazān's conversion was al-Birzālī who, in his turn, obtained the information from Ṣadr al-Dīn Ibrāhīm ibn Muḥammad Ibn Ḥamawayh al-Juwaynī and Zayn al-Dīn 'Abd al-Raḥmān, the brother of Ibn Taymīya. The historical value of such accounts is highlighted by the fact that Ibn Taymīya was personally involved in the contact with the Mongols (306-310 = 120a-121b).

Wafayāt: 1) We continue to witness al-Yūnīnī's editing effort in this portion of the text; on one occasion, al-Jazarī is mentioned by name as the

[69] *Introduction*, 57.

source for the events in Yemen, the details of which were told to him in A.H. 701 at Cairo by a visiting Yemeni (314 = 122b); and on another occasion, a paragraph dealing with Sharaf al-Dīn Aḥmad ibn Aḥmad al-Maqdisī al-Shāfi'ī's biography and poetry (on al-Birzālī's authority, 319f) is omitted in al-Yūnīnī's version.

2) Six obituaries were deleted by al-Yūnīnī.

3) What Little did not mention and proves to be a new phenomenon occurring in the text for the first time is that six obituaries, which were not found in Ms. Paris, were added to al-Yūnīnī's version. Judging from the fact that the first person in this list died in the village of Yūnīn, we might speculate that some of these obituaries were based on al-Yūnīnī's own accounts.

A.H. 695

Ḥawādith: Al-Jazarī proves to be the source for this year's events (132b). On the other hand, the text has undergone slight changes in wording and paragraphing:

1) Two events are found recorded in al-Yūnīnī's version while shifted to the *wafayāt* section in Ms. Paris, and they are: a thunderstorm that hit the Dome of Bi'r Zamzam, and Taqī al-Dīn Sulaymān Ibn Ḥamza's inaugural lecture at the Ashrafīya Dār al-Ḥadīth (131b = 387); one event is missing from al-Jazarī's text: Jamāl al-Dīn Sulaymān ibn 'Umar al-Adhru' al-Shāfi'ī's appointment to the office of qāḍī in Damascus (131b).

2) Some events, such as Jamāl al-Dīn Ibn al-Qalānisī's teaching in a Damascus suburb (352-53), and Zayn al-Dīn 'Abd Allāh's appointment to the office of qāḍī in Damascus (353), are omitted in al-Yūnīnī's version.

3) There is evidence of slight adjustment in wording, such as the more accurate phrase *ḥakā* (130a) replacing al-Jazarī's *ḥakā lī* (335), *wa-mimmā akhbara bihi* (among what has been reported is, . . . 130b) replacing al-Jazarī's *wa-akhbaranī* (I was told that, . . . 335; the source of Egyptian events in both cases being al-Birzālī); al-Jazarī's name was mentioned once again (132b) as the source for Egyptian events (340); some times we see the verb *waliya* (136b) substituted for al-Jazarī's *tawallā* (349), *dakhala* (136b) substituting *waṣala* (350), etc.; the details of this year's pilgrimage (137b = 352-53) were deleted in al-Yūnīnī's version as well.

Wafayāt: This year's *wafayāt* section also sees an intensive editing effort by al-Yūnīnī:

1) A total of 23 obituaries were added to al-Yūnīnī's version, meanwhile one or two were omitted.[70]

2) More poems on the authority of Amīr 'Alam al-Dīn al-Duwaydārī are found in al-Yūnīnī's version (138b).

3) Al-Yūnīnī's editing can also be seen in 138b: the phrase *ṣulliya . . . 'alā* (a prayer was held . . .) replaced al-Jazarī's *ṣallaynā 'alā* (we prayed to honor, . . . 354), and the phrase *ḥakā* (142a) replaced al-Jazarī's *ḥakā lī* (369). However, just as in the previous sections, this editing policy lacks consistency; the phrases *balaghanā* (354 = 138b), *ḥakā lī* (355 = 139a, the source being Amīr Ibn al-Miḥaffadār), *anshadanī* (358-60 = 140a-b; 378-81 = 144a), *anshadanā* (386-87 = 151b-152a, the source being al-Dimyāṭī)[71] and even *qultu* (386 = 152a) are simply repeated without referring to al-Jazarī's authority. The most interesting occurrence in this connection is in 145a where the phrase *anshadanī . . . Abū Ḥayyān* (Abū Ḥayyān recited a poem to me . . .) is copied by al-Yūnīnī from al-Jazarī verbatim with the date (Dhū al-Ḥijja, A.H. 712) and place (Cairo); the information of the date and place is lost in Ms. Paris itself (see 378). This further confirms our hypothesis that 1) al-Jazari was the one who was active in Cairo during A.H. 712-713 and 2) al-Yūnīnī's version was perhaps derived from a different archetype of al-Jazarī's text than Ms. Paris.

A.H. 696

Ḥawādith: The *ḥawādith* section of this year in al-Yūnīnī's text is nearly identical with that of al-Jazarī's with slight changes in wording, such as the use of the verb *musika* (158b) instead of al-Jazarī's *umsika* (405), *tawallā bilād al-Yaman al-sulṭān* (159b) instead of al-Jazarī's *tawallā al-salṭana bi-bilād al-Yaman al-sulṭān . . .* (408), etc.

Wafayāt: The remainder of this year's *wafayāt* section is missing from Ms. Landberg 139 after folio 170, and thus I will use Ms. Ahmet III 2907/e. 3 to complete the collation.

1) Al-Jazarī is acknowledged as the source for this year's *wafayāt* section (163b-169a), and the phrase *ḥakā lī* by al-Jazarī (450, 451) has been changed

---

[70] There is also a misplacement of folios in Ms. Paris inasmuch as the current order of folios appears to be: 180, 185, 186, 181-184 (357-364). Since the foliation on the leaves is correct, this misplacement must have occurred later during the binding and preservation process.

[71] For al-Dimyāṭī's relation to al-Jazarī as the latter's direct informant, see chapter 3 below, 74.

to *ḥukiya* (it was said that, . . . 111a, b); however, there are inconsistencies: in the obituary notice on Najm al-Dīn al-Ḥasan, phrases like *ra'aytu bi-khaṭṭihi* (I saw his autograph) by al-Jazarī were cited verbatim in al-Yūnīnī's version (112b, 114b, 119b).

2) A prayer at Damascus honoring (*ṣallū 'alā ghā'ib*) one Abū Muḥammad Ibn Abī Ḥamza, who died in A.H. 695 and whose obituary (367-68) was omitted in the previous year's *wafayāt* section of al-Yūnīnī's version, is mentioned in this year's (160b).

3) Ten obituaries are added to al-Yūnīnī's version.

4) The order of some obituaries has been changed; e.g., the obituaries of Shams al-Dīn Muḥammad Ibn Ḥāzim al-Maqdisī (445) and Ḍiyā' al-Dīn Dāniyāl ibn Mankalī (Mengli?) al-Turkumānī al-Karakī (445) which follow the obituary of Amīr 'Izz al-Dīn Azdamur in al-Jazarī's version have been moved in al-Yūnīnī's version to follow the obituary of Najm al-Dīn al-Ḥasan ibn Sirḥān al-Dimashqī (122a).

A.H. 697

Ḥawādith: Now we come to the portion for which I have prepared an edition. Following the previous year, the text for this year is evidently identical to that of al-Jazarī; however, countless slight variations in wording and paragraphing are clearly observed in the two texts, the most remarkable among them being the following:

1) The place names indicating the territories of the Mamluk sultanate are added in al-Yūnīnī's text (1).

2) More details are added in al-Yūnīnī's text; e.g., a clearer definition of the limits of the office of Jalāl al-Dīn, the son of the Ḥanafī chief judge Ḥusām al-Dīn (2), and background information about Amīr 'Izz al-Dīn Aybak (9).

3) The most spectacular is a consistent effort to change certain office titles; e.g., *mushidd* instead of al-Jazarī's *shādd*, *mutawallī barr* instead of *wālī barr*, *mutawallī al-ḥarb bi-Dimashq* instead of *wālī Dimashq* (2), etc.

4) Al-Yūnīnī's editing is also seen in the cases where the phrase *ḥakā lī* (I [i.e., al-Jazarī] was told that . . .) has been changed to *mimmā ḥukiya* (it was told that, . . . 3, 11).

5) Another spectacular phenomenon is the variant readings of the poems cited; many of these variations must have been made for a purpose and are not likely scribal errors (e.g., 4). More will be said in the following *wafayāt* section on this matter.

6) Al-Yūnīnī's tendency to alter the verbs in the topic sentence of each paragraph is also clearly seen; e.g., *tajaddada* instead of al-Jazarī's *uḥditha*

(5), *'aṭṭalahu* instead of *mana'ahu* (6), *'ātabahu* instead of *naharahu* (7), etc.

7) Some paragraphs were shifted; e.g., the events of al-Malik al-Nāṣir's exile to Kerak and this year's *Rawk* (land re-distribution) were moved forward (10-12),[72] two paragraphs (on this year's Nile flooding and Shalḥūnah's appointment) were also put later (12),[73] while some paragraphs were omitted; e.g., Amīr Sayf al-Dīn Jāghān's revenge in Damascus (5), the viceroy's investigation of the administration of the Grand Mosque of Damascus,[74] the Friday prayer began to be held in the Mu'aẓẓamīya Madrasa (12), and the ceremony of opening the Cairo Canal (*kasr al-khalīj*, 12).

8) There is also a tendency to verify some facts; e.g., the date of Fakhr al-Dīn Ibn al-Khalīlī's re-appointment to the vizier's office (5).

9) A close look at all the slight variations in a paragraph about the shortage of ice in Damascus (9-10) reveals that al-Yūnīnī's much briefer version does not make as much sense as al-Jazarī's does (e.g., Why should the price go up? Why should ice and beer be put on the roof?).

10) The variations in an important paragraph (on the *Rawk*, 11-12) also cast some light on al-Yūnīnī's opinion; e.g., his bitter comment that "such an action was extremely harmful" is not found in al-Jazarī's version.

Wafayāt: Like the previous years, the *wafayāt* section of this year contains omissions and additions made by al-Yūnīnī:

1) Nine obituaries are omitted while one is added.

2) Some details were either added by al-Yūnīnī; e.g., on Sharaf al-Dīn 'Abd al-Karīm ibn Muḥammad al-Ḥamawī (13-14), on Jamāl al-Dīn Muḥammad ibn 'Imād al-Ḥamawī (29); or omitted; e.g., on Ḥasan ibn 'Alī Ibn al-Ḥarīrī (17), on shaykh Shihāb al-Dīn Aḥmad ibn 'Uthmān (18), on Shams al-Dīn Muḥammad ibn Abī Bakr al-Fārsī (19), on the aforementioned Jamāl al-Dīn Muḥammad ibn 'Imād al-Ḥamawī (28), on Shihāb al-Dīn Aḥmad ibn 'Abd al-Raḥmān al-Maqdisī (29), on the death of Amīr Shihāb al-Dīn Aḥmad ibn Muḥammad al-'Uqaylī (31).

---

[72] In al-Jazarī's version, these two events follow the paragraph on the arrest of Amīr Badr al-Dīn Baysarī (5).

[73] In al-Jazarī's version, these follow the confiscation of Bahā' al-Dīn Ibn al-Ḥillī's fortune in Cairo (10). The order of these two paragraphs is also different in al-Jazarī's version, in that the Nile flooding is mentioned first.

[74] The event was dated on the 29th of Ramaḍān; since this paragraph was removed from al-Yūnīnī's text, the date of the following paragraph "on the same day" (6) is confusing.

3) Al-Yūnīnī's interest in verifying and adding geographical facts is also seen in his effort to point out the location of a ṣūfī cemetery at al-Mizza (19).

4) A very important aspect for consideration in this collation between the two versions is the poetry they preserve, given that one of the functions of the *wafayāt* section is, as will be discussed below, to preserve poetry produced during that time in Egypt and Syria. Variant readings[75] are remarkable in this year's *wafayāt* section (21, 22, 26, 32, 33, 34, 36). In addition, an enormous number of poems, or lines, are missing from Ms. Paris, and have survived only in al-Yūnīnī's version (e.g., 24, 26, 27, 28, 32, 36, 37, 38, 39, 40, 42, 42-43, 43, 44, 45-46).[76] Al-Yūnīnī's version also contains some additional details about the transmission of these poems (30, 32-33).

As briefly stated above, there is a high degree of agreement between al-Jazarī's manuscript and one of al-Yūnīnī's manuscripts (Ms. Ahmet III 2907/e. 3) as opposed to al-Yūnīnī's other manuscript (Ms. Landberg 139); the most fascinating example is found in a case where Ms. Landberg 139 reads *fa ṣirtu* muḍnan *li-faqd dīnī* vs. al-Jazarī's *fa ṣirtu* abkī *li-faqd dīnī*, while Ms. 2907/e. 3 has *fa ṣirtu* muḍnan abkī *li-faqd dīnī* (21); other interesting instances include: Ms. Landberg 139 has *min riḍāka* as opposed to both Ms. 2907/e. 3 and al-Jazarī's *min wiṣāli* (26); *layl* vs. *dalīl* (31); *al-zamān* vs. *al-manūn* (34), to cite just a few.

Indications that al-Jazarī is the source of the poetry are found also in 41, 43, and 44 where the phrase *anshadanī* (the poet recited to "me," i.e., to al-Jazarī) was altered to *unshida lahu* (a poem is attributed to so-and-so).

In sum, al-Yūnīnī's version is more complete in terms of the poems it recorded. It may be that a better exemplar of al-Jazarī's text was in al-Yūnīnī's hands at the time, or it may be that as far as the poetry is concerned, better versions (some individuals' anthologies, not necessarily from al-Jazarī's version) may have been available in circulation which could be cross-checked easily by later scribes.

[75] These variations were made on purpose, i.e., they are unlikely to have been scribal errors.

[76] There are also a few cases in which al-Jazarī's version contains some poems that are not found in al-Yūnīnī's text; see above, 47.

A.H. 698

Ḥawādith: Aside from minor variations (many of which may well be scribal errors), there is a continuity in all of the peculiarities that occurred in the text for the previous years:

1) A number of details were added to al-Yūnīnī's version, such as place names of the Mamluk sultanate (48), rulers outside Egypt and Syria (48-49), the general situation concerning the Crusaders (49), the participants in last year's pilgrimage (51), the names of the amīrs who came to arrest Baktimūr al-Silāḥdār (52), Qibjāq's party (54), the coming of the viceroy's family to Damascus (67), the source for the Cairo earthquake (69), appointments in Damascus and Cairo (72), the background information that one Amīr Nakhiya was Qalāwūn's father in-law (72), the conversation between Jāghān and Fakhr al-Dīn al-A'zāzī after the former learned that the missing treasure was actually deposited with the latter (74), and this year's pilgrimage (75).

Some other details were omitted in al-Yūnīnī's version; e.g., Qibjāq's defection (55), an anecdote about Qibjāq's father (56), the name of the amīr who brought the news of the sultan's assassination (59), the information that Amīr Sayf al-Dīn Quṭlū was Amīr Salār's brother (61), the itinerary of Ghazān's army (64), the Cairo earthquake (69), etc.

2) Al-Yūnīnī's effort to verify and change official titles and technical terms given in al-Jazarī's version; e.g., *wilāyat al-barr* instead of al-Jazarī's *barr Dimashq* (50), *barr wa-al-madīna* instead of *wilāyat al-barr wa-Dimashq* (61), *bāb al-sirr* instead of *bāb al-qal'a* (63), etc.

3) The phrases indicating al-Jazarī's direct sources have been changed to rather neutral ones such as *dhakara lī* (I [i.e., al-Jazarī] was told that . . .) to *qāla* (he said that, 50), *sa'altuhu* (I asked him . . .) to *akhbara* (he mentioned that, . . . 63), *ḥakā lī* to *ḥakā* (70), etc.

4) The tendency to alter verbs continues; e.g., *raja'ū* instead of al-Jazarī's *'ādū* (51), *yub'athu* instead of *yusayyaru* (55), *ijtama'ū* instead of *khada'ū* (55), *yakhruju* instead of *yaṭla'u* (58), *qabḍ* instead of *mask* (59), *ḥaṣala lahu* instead of *thāra 'alayhi* (61), *nafaqa* instead of *anfaqa* (64), *ṣa'adū ilā* instead of *laḥiqū bi* (65), *waṣala* instead of *dakhala* (67); and other synonyms, e.g., *al-ḥabs* instead of *al-jubb* (58), etc.

5) Al-Yūnīnī also seems to be interested in showing off his knowledge; e.g., an explanation of the exchange rate of currency (55-56), the adding of the Coptic calendar to the narrative (69, 71).

6) The text also contains some syntax alterations; compare the two versions of Ḥusām al-Dīn's account of the sultan's assassination (57).

7) There is one very interesting instance in which the change of phrases indicating the involvement of the original author (namely, al-Jazarī) must be interpreted differently from all other cases. This time, al-Yūnīnī appears in the first person and al-Jazarī's version contains a neutral tone: in a report of the comet observed in Damascus, the text reads *li-anna kunnā narāhu* (because we looked at it [i.e., the comet]) "at the Damascus Mosque," while al-Jazarī's text gives *li-annahu kāna yurā* (because it [i.e., the comet] was seen . . .). This rare case raises an intriguing question: although nearly all evidence has pointed to al-Yūnīnī's copying from al-Jazarī, here we see evidence that al-Yūnīnī was in Damascus and saw the comet while al-Jazarī was not. In other words, al-Yūnīnī's stamp is still, somehow, left within the textual fabric.

Wafayāt: This year's *wafayāt* section is relatively short, and it continues all the features discussed above:

1) Five obituaries are omitted while 12 are added by al-Yūnīnī.

2) Some details were added by al-Yūnīnī; e.g., the tariff charged on the Mecca route (78-79), on one Zayn al-Dīn Muḥammad ibn Aḥmad's birth date (79), the death of Amīr Badr al-Dīn Baysarī in Cairo (89), the date of receiving the news of al-Malik al-Muẓaffar in Damascus (90); while some others were omitted by al-Yūnīnī; e.g., on Amīr Shams al-Dīn Sunqur (77), a lengthy biography of Taqī al-Dīn Tawba ibn ʻAlī al-Takrītī (85-86), on Amīn al-Dīn Salīm ibn Muḥammad's career (91), on Amīr Jamāl al-Dīn Āqqūsh (92).

3) Revised syntax; e.g., 78, note to line 3; 89, note to line 14-90, line 2, etc.

4) Alteration of verbs; e.g., *yulḥaqu* instead of al-Jazarī's *yujbā min* (78), *yataqanna'u* instead of *yaqna'u* (95).

5) Variant readings in poetry (81, 84, 85); and some poems, or lines, that are missing from al-Jazarī's version (82, lines 8-12).

A.H. 699 (fragment)

Ms. Paris ends at the beginning of this year (99), and our collation, therefore, is confined to these limited folios. The basic features displayed in the previous years' sections are also to be seen here:

1) The adding of place names in the list of rulers section (96).

2) The alteration of synonymous verbs or nouns; e.g., *dakhala* instead of al-Jazarī's *waṣala ilā* (97), *yamna'u* instead of *yaṣrifu* (97), *tabi'ahum* instead of *mana'ahum* (97), *al-naw'* instead of *al-ḍarb* (98), *akhraqa* instead of *naqaba* (99), etc.

3) Some trivial details were omitted in al-Yūnīnī's version; e.g., 97, note to lines 5, 6.

4) The syntax is corrected; e.g., 98, note to line 13.

The above collation reveals that:

1) This portion of the *Dhayl*, which only survives in two manuscripts (Ms. Ahmet III 2907/e. 3 and Ms. Landberg 139) and constitutes the bulk of the "third volume" of the Buhūtī Set and the "18th volume" of the Nastarāwī Set (a *Mukhtaṣar* and *Dhayl* collection), is essentially a synthesis of al-Jazarī's *Ḥawādith* edited by al-Yūnīnī. This fact is partially acknowledged by al-Yūnīnī himself. On several occasions, he mentions al-Jazarī as his source.

2) In quoting nearly verbatim from al-Jazarī's account, al-Yūnīnī omitted some materials and added some others which were either his own or taken from another ancestral manuscript of al-Jazarī's chronicle. Some accounts missing from Ms. Paris, the only extant codex of this part of al-Jazarī's work, are also found in al-Yūnīnī's version.

3) Al-Yūnīnī's editing is obvious throughout the text in that he fixed the syntax, verified certain facts, altered some technical terms and verbs, and rearranged some paragraphs.

The remaining text (A.H. 699-711)

Now we turn to the remaining portion of the *Dhayl* to which no parallel text from al-Jazarī's version has survived. Keep in mind that al-Jazarī's authorship of the preceding years of A.H. 697 and 698 is reasonably well established; now we come to the year 699/1299-1300, a year full of events marked by the Mongol occupation of Damascus and its impact on political, social, and religious life in Syria. Little, who examined both al-Jazarī's and al-Yūnīnī's versions of this year, has convincingly pointed out that these are al-Jazarī's accounts, copied by al-Yūnīnī.[77] Among these accounts, the most fascinating one is a "Damascus diary," which offers a vivid description of what happened to Damascus and its residents under the Mongol occupation. Al-Yūnīnī, a resident of Ba'labakk, does not tell us whether this extraordinary eye-witness "diary" was drawn from his own observations or was taken from al-Jazarī, a native of Damascus. Nevertheless, there is a clue: al-Jazarī's name is mentioned at the end of this year's *ḥawādith* section as the author of a concluding poem lamenting the suffering of Damascus (132-33). This reference may not

[77] *Introduction*, 57-61.

be sufficient to prove that al-Jazarī should necessarily be considered the author of the text that precedes the poem, but it still suggests it.[78]

Al-Jazarī's name is mentioned again in the *wafayāt* section of the year A.H. 700 as the source of a biography (233). Since al-Jazarī is only named in the middle of a biographical sketch, it is hard to tell whether he is also responsible for the accounts that precede and follow.

The most striking and suggestive case, though, is found in the text of the year A.H. 701 where a lengthy quotation obviously from one of al-Jazarī's collections of miscellaneous pieces is found to have been inserted in the middle of the narrative of this year's events, and is, surprisingly, totally out of context. It occurs between the report (which ends with *wa-sāfara ilā Dimashq*) on two Syrian learned men's return to Damascus in this year from an exile in the "land of the Mongols," and an anecdote (which begins with *wa-fī muntaṣafi rabī' al-awwal* . . .) about a strange hailstorm that had hit the region of Bārīn, Hama.[79] This cluster of text (approximately 20 folios, perhaps originally a quire in manuscript) begins with *qāla al-shaykh . . . al-Jazarī raḥimahu Allāh yadhkuru* . . . (note that al-Jazarī died after al-Yūnīnī and it is therefore chronologically impossible for the latter to refer to the former with such a phrase), and is followed by a variety of treatises which can be roughly classified into three parts:

First is the *manāqib*-hagiographal materials about Egyptian ḥadīth teachers with whom al-Jazarī met in Cairo and Alexandria and from whom he received ḥadīths during the months Muḥarram to Jumādā II A.H. 701; among them were Sharaf al-Dīn 'Abd Allāh al-Mu'min al-Dimyāṭī, the Shāfi'ī chief judge Taqı al-Dīn Muḥammad ibn 'Alī al-Qushayrī, well known as Ibn Daqīq al-'Īd (d. 702/1303),[80] Shihāb al-Dīn Aḥmad ibn Isḥāq al-Ḥamdānī al-Abraqūhī (d. 701/1301),[81] 'Alā' al-Dīn 'Alī ibn 'Abd al-Ghanī Ibn Taymīya al-Ḥarrānī, and

---

[78] That an author concludes his text with verses is not an unfamiliar device in medieval Arabic writings; moreover, this pattern (that al-Jazarī opens a chapter and concludes with a poem) is repeated in the text for A.H. 701 where an independent collection of miscellaneous texts compiled and edited by al-Jazarī (to be discussed below) is wrongly inserted. More interestingly, this "Damascus diary" is ascribed to al-Dhahabī as well; cf. Somogyi, "Adh-dhahabī's Record." The authorship of this "diary" needs to be investigated further.

[79] Ms. Landberg 139, ff. 274b-277b (where the manuscript ends, in the middle of the *majmū'a*) and Ms. Ahmet III 2907/e. 3, ff. 216a-236a. The insertion, which is omitted in the present edition, occurs between 253, line 21 and 254, line 1.

[80] For his biography see al-Dhahabī, *Tadhkirat al-ḥuffāẓ*, 4:262-64.

[81] For his biography see Ibn al-'Imād, *Shadharāt*, 6:4; he is also mentioned in al-Birzālī's *al-Muqtafā* (Ms. Ahmet III 2951, 2:228a) as an important ḥadīth transmitter.

Tāj al-Dīn 'Alī ibn Aḥmad al-Ḥusayn al-'Irāqī.[82] The emphasis of the quotations is clearly on the ḥadīths transmitted to al-Jazarī on the authority of these shaykhs. It is also important to recognize that one of the key figures in our following source criticism, i.e., al-Dimyāṭī, was evidently al-Jazarī's direct informant and that al-Jazarī's trip to Egypt in 701/1301 can be used to connect al-Jazarī with the sources and events in certain portions of the text.

Second is a collection of *faḍā'il* works, namely panegyrics on the merits of certain cities and historical sites, written by, or transmitted on the authority of, al-Jazarī. These include a description of his visit to the Giza pyramid in Rajab A.H. 701,[83] the tale of the Lead Dome (*al-qubba allatī min al-raṣāṣ*) which al-Jazarī claimed that he copied from a manuscript written by a scholar from Ḥarrān (Hellenopolis), a list of the ancient Egyptian kings quoted from al-Ṭabarī, a treatise entitled *Dhikr 'ajā'ib Miṣr* (The Wonders of Egypt), and another entitled *Dhikr aṭā'ib Miṣr* (The Beauties of Egypt), a title (without text) of *Dhikr jabal al-Muqaṭṭam* (On the Muqaṭṭam Mountain at Cairo), and several notes about Egypt quoted from different books.

Third is the *manāqib*-hagiography of Shams al-Dīn Abū al-Nidā' Ma'aḍḍ ibn Naṣr Allāh, well known as Ibn al-Ṣayqal al-Jazarī (d. 701/1301).[84] It contains a substantial portion of his famous 50 *maqāmāt*, well known as *al-Maqāmāt al-zaynīya*. All of the *maqāmāt* follow the model set by al-Ḥarīrī and are of the *faḍā'il* genre, namely descriptions of cities or historical sites in Syria, Egypt, and the Jazira.[85]

The entire segment concludes with al-Jazarī's verses.

It is evident that: 1) these quotations appear to have come from an independent *majmū'a*-collection compiled and edited by al-Jazarī; 2) they do not fit into the context in which they were inserted (the middle of the *ḥawādith* section of the year A.H. 701); and 3) since al-Jazarī is referred to as deceased (*raḥimahu Allāh*), the inappropriate insertion was certainly made by a later copyist or editor. This instance warns us about the high possibility of a con-

[82] All are unidentified.

[83] This is again a key event attesting to al-Jazarī's presence in Egypt in 701/1301.

[84] The manuscripts of his collection of 50 *maqāmāt* are found in Ms. Bankipore (Arabic 2593), British Library (Nos. 669, 1403), and Istanbul, Nuruosmaniye (4273); see Nadwi, 23:102-4; also Ḥājjī Khalīfa, 1785; *GAL*, II:159.

[85] The text presented in the manuscript as quoted on al-Jazarī's authority is slightly different from Ms. Bankipore 2593 (Nadwi, 23:102-4); for instance, the order of the 19th *maqāma* (*al-Iskandarīya*) and the 29th (*al-Qudsīya*) is inverted in Ms. Bankipore, the unnamed 25th *maqāma* is entitled *al-Malṭīya* in Ms. Bankipore and the title of the 32nd (*al-Wāsiṭīya*) is given as *al-Ḥimṣīya* in Ms. Bankipore. Ms. Bankipore is not dated (the catalogue has "probably 13th century").

flation of al-Jazarī's and al-Yūnīnī's texts by later hands. It also shows that al-Yūnīnī's borrowing from al-Jazarī's accounts was taken for granted by this later editor (or scribe) who knew the two authors' works and hence the chance of such misplacement.

The above textual notes, though very slim, suggest a continuation of the basic nature of the "Jazarī-Yūnīnī tradition," and that is, a synthesis of al-Jazarī's *Ḥawādith* edited by al-Yūnīnī or some later editor in his name.

The last "volume" of the *Dhayl*, which only survives in the Buhūtī Set (Ms. Ahmet III 2907/e. 4), deserves our special attention for it is the only extant textual testimony to this part of the "Jazarī-Yūnīnī tradition." Starting from the year A.H. 702 and ending with the year A.H. 711, this portion of the text constitutes, as the colophon of the manuscript states, the "fourth volume" (*mujallad*) of al-Yūnīnī's *Dhayl*. The manuscript contains some textual notes which require discussion:

First, the textual basis of this "volume" proves to be a problematic one: a great number of blank spaces left deliberately by the scribe of the manuscript[86] reveal that the parent codex from which this volume was copied was itself a defective codex that contained, in its turn, numerous lacunae. There is also some evidence of misplacement or contamination: the *wafayāt* section of A.H. 710 ends abruptly with "some poetry [handed down] by our shaykh . . . 'Abd al-Mu'min al-Dimyāṭī in his *al-Mu'jam* (i.e., *Mu'jam al-shuyūkh*)[87] as follows . . ." (*fī-hā shay' min anāshīd shaykhinā . . . al-Dimyāṭī min Mu'jamihi fa-min dhālika qawluhu* . . .). A total of approximately 80 poems attributed to some 40 authors are recorded (ff. 201b-212a). However, none of these authors or poems appear to have any relevance to this particular year: all the authors were 'ulamā' who lived in the 6th/12th or 7th/13th centuries, namely, during the Ayyubid period; nor is this the right place for al-Dimyāṭī's own obituary. He died in 705/1306.[88] Notice the strange wording of *wa-fī-hā*, which is a typical introductory phrase of an obituary note in the *Dhayl* (*wa-fī-hā tuwuffiya* [so-and-so] . . .). Apparently some obituaries are missing here and are replaced, instead, by quotations (perhaps a quire in the original codex) from al-Dimyāṭī's *Mu'jam al-shuyūkh*.

Second, al-Jazarī's name is not mentioned in the manuscript at all, nor is al-Yūnīnī's (except on the title page and in the colophon). There are a great

---

[86] Cf. above, 26.

[87] The work has been published under the title of *Le Dictionnaire des Autorités* (ed. G. Vajda, Paris, 1962); for al-Dimyāṭī and his *Mu'jam* also cf. below, 74, 77-78.

[88] For al-Dimyāṭī's biography see "al-Dimyāṭī," *EI²*, by G. Vajda.

number of passages where the author refers to himself with such phrases as *qultu* (I said) (56b, 72b, 83b, 95a, 115b, 132b, 141a, 200a, b, 211a), *sa'altu* (I asked) (141a), *aẓunnu* (I think) (188a), *naqaltu* (I copied from [a manuscript]) (13b), *anshadanī* (he recited to me [the following poem]) (32b, 42a, 188a, 192b, 223b), *akhbaranī* or *akhbaranā* (I was told; or we were told) (16b, 29b, 56b). These are left unidentified and are attributed to an obscure "*mu'allif*" (author) who appears once in the text (185b) in the following quotation: *qāla al-mu'allif wa-anshadanī al-shaykh Athīr al-Dīn Abī* [sic] *Ḥayyān bi-al-Qāhira fī Dhū al-Qa'da sanat ithnay 'ashara* [sic] *wa-sab'imi'a qāla* (the author said: Shaykh Athīr al-Dīn Abū Ḥayyān recited to me the following poem in the month of Dhū al-Qa'da, A.H. 712, in Cairo . . .). Given that this Athīr al-Dīn Abū Ḥayyān was, as will be discussed below,[89] most likely al-Jazarī's direct informant and that the latter's visit to Cairo during the year 712/1312 was well documented, this "author" can be no one else but al-Jazarī, not al-Yūnīnī.

Third, another suggestive instance is found in 218b-219b where the text states that the dispute between two Damascene leading religious figures, 'Izz al-Dīn Ibn al-Qalānisī and the chief judge Najm al-Dīn Ibn Ṣaṣrā, was settled through the mediation of one "shaykh Quṭb al-Dīn al-Yūnīnī." Such a wording hardly sounds like an author's tone; here al-Yūnīnī appears as the *subject* of the narrative rather than the *narrator*. In this connection, his father Muḥammad is referred to as a totally strange person, not as "my father" (50b, 142b, 194b).

Fourth, from the historical evidence, we continue to see the familiar signals: Abū Ḥayyān continues to be one of the major sources for poetry and biographical information (36b, 42b, 147a, 185b). The obvious clue to his contact with al-Jazarī is further attested by their meeting in Cairo in the year 712/1312 (42b, 185b). Similarly, al-Dimyāṭī's connection to al-Jazarī is reflected in the events of the year 701/1301 when al-Jazarī attended his ḥadīth sessions at the Ẓāhirīya Madrasa in Cairo (56b); his *Majmū'* is also quoted (201b). We also hear from the Mamluk amīr Najm al-Dīn Ibn al-Miḥaffadār, mentioned above, a direct informant of al-Jazarī's, a report on the earthquake that hit Syria in the year 702/1302 (72a).

All these direct and indirect pieces of evidence indicate that: 1) the last "volume" of the *Dhayl* clearly shows the main feature of the previous text, namely, that it is basically al-Jazarī's account with possibly some later editing, but 2) unlike the previous text, the editing of this volume does not seem

---

[89] Cf. below, 74-75.

to have been done by al-Yūnīnī, who is mentioned in the text as a third person and not as the author, or even the editor. My suggestion would be that this "volume" contains basically al-Jazarī's work and that it was wrongly attributed to al-Yūnīnī by a later editor. Since this part of al-Jazarī's original chronicle is lost today anyway,[90] the question of the authorship of this precious textual tradition thus becomes of less significance.

The reason why al-Yūnīnī chose to quote from al-Jazarī nearly verbatim, and thus opened the door to misplacement and confusion, is unknown. In my opinion, this perhaps has to do with: 1) al-Jazarī's reliable sources, especially those from his native Damascus, and from his Egyptian connections. In this regard, we might recall that al-Yūnīnī began to lead a secluded life at some point in his later years, devoting himself to piety and mysticism and therefore being more remote from centers of events such as Damascus and Cairo;[91] and 2) al-Jazarī's better writing in which all the *ḥawādith* and *wafayāt* sections are equally divided and the materials evenly presented. However, since these speculations are quite limited, it appears that we might be better off by going beyond the textual aspects and looking at other factors, such as the historicity of both al-Yūnīnī's and al-Jazarī's references to their sources, the dynamics of information exchange among Damascene 'ulamā' at the time, and the mechanism of medieval Muslim scholarship that involves certain technical procedures in handing down a given text. In other words, we need to scrutinize not only the authors in question but also those other central figures—sources, editors, and copyists—that are known as having been directly or indirectly involved in the shaping and handing down of the entire text of the *Dhayl* in the form in which we now know it.

---

[90] In addition to Ms. Paris 6739 and al-Dhahabī's *Mukhtār* version, the only extant fragment of the *Ḥawādith al-zamān* that covers the years after A.H. 699 is Ms. Istanbul, Köprülü 1037 (covering A.H. 725-738), which is not of the "Jazarī-Yūnīnī tradition" at all; al-Yūnīnī, for one thing, died in A.H. 726, and his *Dhayl* was perhaps never meant to go beyond A.H. 711.

[91] Cf. above, 14-16.

CHAPTER THREE

THE SOURCES

1. Al-Yūnīnī's Sources

A scholar trained in ḥadīth transmission, al-Yūnīnī was meticulous in establishing the authenticity of his stories. This is particularly true of the first part of the text (A.H. 654-690) which, as discussed in the previous chapter, is al-Yūnīnī's original writing. Thanks to al-Yūnīnī's relatively consistent terminology, we are able to classify all of his sources roughly into the following categories: 1) his own eye-witness records of the events and people, which he had written down in his notebooks (*muswaddāt*); 2) written sources: those include original documents or manuscripts in the possession of al-Yūnīnī, often introduced by phrases like *ra'aytu khaṭṭahu* (I saw his autograph), *waqaftu 'alā khaṭṭihi* (I obtained his manuscript), etc., and citations from "published," that is, circulated, works, usually referred to by such phrases as *qāla [fulān] fī* or *dhakara [fulān] fī* (both meaning: he said in [his book] . . .); and 3) oral informants: they are always quoted as *ḥakā lī*, *ḥaddathanī*, *akhbaranī* (all meaning: he told me), *anshadanī* (he recited poems to me), and occasionally, *qāla lī* (he said to me).

A Syrian scholar's library: al-Yūnīnī's written sources

A number of Egyptian and Syrian sources are used intensively by al-Yūnīnī for the years 654/1254-690/1291, the years of the late Ayyubids and early Mamluks. Among them Ibn Khallikān (d. 681/1282)[1] was the most important. Apart from Ibn Khallikān's acclaimed *Wafayāt al-a'yān* from which al-Yūnīnī draws heavily for biographical information,[2] a considerable amount of "archival" materials reported on Ibn Khallikān's authority, which are not found elsewhere today, have survived through al-Yūnīnī; these include the official correspondence (*mukātabāt*) and reports of military campaigns with the

[1] See "Ibn Khallikān," *EI*², by J. U. Fück; also *GAL*, I:326-28; *GALS*, I:561.

[2] *Dhayl*, 1:19, 38-39, 42, 144, 183, 337-40; 2:19, 27, 166, 225, 309-10, 328-29, 421, 441.

Crusaders and Mongols (*kutub al-bashā'ir*) drafted by the chanceries (*kuttāb dīwān al-inshā'*).[3] Ibn Khallikān's access to these materials was unique: being in charge of the office of judge (*al-qaḍā' wa-al-ḥukm*) in Damascus (A.H. 659-669, A.H. 676-680), many such documents were themselves addressed to, and received by, him in person; e.g., the *kutub al-bashā'ir* during the 664/1265-666/1267 war with the Crusaders and Mongols. Ibn Khallikān's political career came to an end around the years 679/1280 and 680/1281,[4] and so did his access to these archives. However, as far as the years A.H. 654 to 680 are concerned, he was without question al-Yūnīnī's most often quoted source for events as well as biographical information (his *Wafayāt* was finished a little earlier, in A.H. 672). It is evident that some of Ibn Khallikān's manuscripts were at al-Yūnīnī's disposal[5] and they contain a lot of biographical notices and poetry.[6] Nonetheless, al-Yūnīnī does not say where he got the archival materials under Ibn Khallikān's name. Ibn Khallikān also appears as the subject of the narrative: his biography, perhaps one of the earliest of its kind, is presented by al-Yūnīnī[7] along with many details about his career.[8]

Other major sources for the Ayyubids and early Mamluks used by al-Yūnīnī are:

Abū Shāma (d. 665/1268):[9] Al-Yūnīnī acknowledged that he had used Abū Shāma's *Dhayl Ta'rīkh*, apparently referring to his *Dhayl al-Rawḍatayn*,[10] for information on certain events such as the Medina fire in A.H. 654,[11] the Mongol occupation of Damascus in A.H. 657,[12] and some biographical data.[13] Yet in comparison with Ibn Khallikān, Abū Shāma's accounts were not thoroughly utilized by al-Yūnīnī. In this connection, one finds that among Abū Shāma's works mentioned by al-Yūnīnī in the former's biography,[14]

---

3 *Dhayl*, 2:338-43, 375, 377-81, 382-84, 445-46, 448-49; M:32.

4 He was arrested and dismissed by sultan Qalāwūn.

5 *Dhayl*, 3:189.

6 *Dhayl*, 2:392-94; 3:71, 221-28; 4:18, 61, 207.

7 *Dhayl*, 3:153-66.

8 *Dhayl*, 2:456; 3:41, 43, 53, 87, 142, 237, 293-94; 4:37.

9 For his biography, see "Abū Shāma," *EI²*, by H. Ahmad; for his historical works, see Cahen, *Syrie*, 66-67; Humphreys, *Ayyubids*, 397-98; Thorau, *Baybars*, 269; al-Munajjid, *Mu'jam al-mu'arrikhīn*, 100-3.

10 The work was published under the title of *Tarājim rijāl al-qarnayn al-sādis wa-al-sābi'* (ed. M. Z. al-Kawtharī, Cairo, 1947).

11 *Dhayl*, 1:11.

12 *Dhayl*, 1:367.

13 *Dhayl*, 1:73; 2:223.

14 *Dhayl*, 2:367. Fifteen titles are ascribed to Abū Shāma; some of them are not found in *GAL*; cf. *GAL*, I:386f; *GALS*, I:550f.

there is one entitled *al-Wāḍiḥ al-jalī fī al-radd 'alā al-Ḥanbalī* (A Manifest Refutation of the Ḥanbalī),[15] which may have disturbed al-Yūnīnī, an ardent Ḥanbalī.

Ibn Ḥamawayh al-Juwaynī (d. 674/1275):[16] He is considered an important source for the late Ayyubids,[17] and yet none of his works has survived. According to Cahen, some of his accounts were preserved by Sibṭ Ibn al-Jawzī and al-Dhahabī.[18] We are indebted to al-Yūnīnī for preserving some other passages in the *Dhayl*, which are mainly biographical data.[19]

Ibn Shaddād (d. 684/1285):[20] He was al-Yūnīnī's major source on Mamluk sultan Baybars.[21] According to Peter Thorau, some of Ibn Shaddād's accounts are quoted by al-Yūnīnī anonymously.[22] Ibn Shaddād's other accounts, e.g., those on Hülegü's combat,[23] and on Ibn Khallikān,[24] are quoted in the *Dhayl* as well. Two titles attributed to Ibn Shaddād are mentioned by al-Yūnīnī: his *Ta'rīkh Ḥalab*[25] and *Sīrat al-Malik al-Ẓāhir Rukn al-Dīn.*[26] Of the latter, the second volume was published under the title *Ta'rīkh al-Malik al-Ẓāhir*;[27] and al-Yūnīnī is credited with preserving in the *Dhayl* some passages from the lost first volume.[28] It is worth noting here that, besides Ibn Shaddād's authoritative accounts on Baybars, al-Yūnīnī also distinguished himself with his exclusive materials on this most famous Mamluk sultan;[29] he must have had some other sources that are not known to us.

---

[15] This title is not listed in *GAL*. From Louis Pouzet we know that Abū Shāma used to teach at the Shāfi'ī madrasas in Damascus, but there is no clue about the possible antagonism between him and the Ḥanbalīs; cf. Pouzet, *Damas*, index.

[16] The full name given in the *Dhayl* is Sa'd al-Dīn Mas'ūd ibn 'Abd Allāh ibn 'Umar, but al-Munajjid, *Mu'jam al-mu'arrikhīn* (112), has Sa'd al-Dīn al-Khaḍir ibn 'Abd Allāh.

[17] Cahen, *Syrie*, 63-64; Humphreys, *Ayyubids*, 398.

[18] Cahen, *Syrie*, 64, note 3.

[19] *Dhayl*, 1:24, 37 (his *laqab* here is wrongly given as Sayf al-Dīn), 79; 3:278-79.

[20] For his biography, see "Ibn Shaddād," *EI²*, by D. Sourdel; Cahen, *Syrie*, 56, 75-76; Humphreys, *Ayyubids*, 398-99; Thorau, *Baybars*, 270-71. He should not be confused with Bahā' al-Dīn Ibn Shaddād (d. 632/1235), the famous biographer of Saladin.

[21] *Dhayl*, 3:239-62, 266ff.

[22] E.g., the account of the battle of Albistān (3:176-77); see Thorau, *Baybars*, 267.

[23] *Dhayl*, 2:161-62.

[24] *Dhayl*, 4:152.

[25] This is not found in *GAL*. It perhaps refers to the part that deals with Aleppo from his famous historical topography entitled *al-A'lāq al-khaṭīra fī dhikr umarā' al-Shām wa-al-Jazīra*; cf. *GAL*, I:634; *GALS*, I:883. The part that deals with Aleppo was published by D. Sourdel (Beirut, 1953).

[26] *Dhayl*, 4:270.

[27] Ed. A. Hutait (Wiesbaden, 1983).

[28] See Thorau, *Baybars*, 271.

[29] Cf. Thorau, *Baybars*, 241-42, 265-66 (has *Dhayl* II, 45 for II, 445), 267.

Ibn 'Abd al-Ẓāhir (d. 692/1293):[30] The author of the famous biography of Baybars, *Sīrat al-sulṭān al-malik al-Ẓāhir Baybars*, and a historical topography of Cairo, *al-Rawḍa al-bahīya al-zāhira fī khiṭaṭ al-mu'izzīya al-Qāhira*. Al-Yūnīnī quoted both from his historical works and from the official communiqués he wrote in his capacity as the confidential secretary (*kātib al-sirr*) to sultan Qalāwūn. For example, Qalāwūn's appointment of his son Khālid (i.e., al-Malik al-Ashraf) as his successor was, as al-Yūnīnī tells us, drafted by Ibn 'Abd al-Ẓāhir; and the text based on his handwritten copy is reproduced in the *Dhayl*.[31]

Ibn Wāṣil (d. 697/1298):[32] Ibn Wāṣil is of special interest to us because, as discussed above,[33] his work was quoted at length by al-Yūnīnī in the first draft[34] and then replaced by al-Jazarī's account in the "revised draft" (Version II). Although al-Yūnīnī failed to name the title, the work of Ibn Wāṣil he refers to is most plausibly the *Mufarrij al-kurūb*, which was planned to reach A.H. 680[35] and was completed in A.H. 683. Since al-Yūnīnī's first draft was finished in 690/1291, Ibn Wāṣil's work seems to have served as a reference for cross-checking contemporary events.

In addition to these sources which are relatively well-known, the writings by chancery secretaries (*kuttāb dīwān al-inshā'*) constitute a mine of information that has been largely overlooked by modern researchers. Unlike some prominent senior secretaries like Ibn 'Abd al-Ẓāhir, most of these clerks were rarely identified as the authors of a tremendous body of writings: letters (*mukātabāt*), reports of military victory (*kutub al-bashā'ir*), and other kinds of official documentation. This kind of original and valuable material apparently drew al-Yūnīnī's attention, perhaps through Ibn Khallikān, Ibn 'Abd al-Ẓāhir, and other sources. Some of these authors' names are occasionally recorded. Among them the most frequently quoted is an obscure figure called Shihāb al-Dīn Maḥmūd al-Kātib, a low-ranking clerk (*kātib al-durj*) in Damascus[36] whose official writings in the name of Ḥusām al-Dīn Lājīn, then

---

[30] For his biography, see "Ibn 'Abd al-Ẓāhir," *EI*², by J. Pedersen; also *GAL*, I:318f; *GALS*, I:551; Cahen, *Syrie*, 74; Thorau, *Baybars*, 269-70.

[31] *Dhayl*, 4:47ff.

[32] See *GAL*, I:323; *GALS*, I:555; Cahen, *Syrie*, 68-70; Humphreys, *Ayyubids*, 395-96; Thorau, *Baybars*, 269.

[33] Cf. above, 31.

[34] *Dhayl*, 1:19, 73; 2:9, 114-25, 205f.

[35] See El-Shayyal's introduction to the 1953 Cairo edition, 10.

[36] His biography is not found; from al-Munajjid, *Mu'jam al-mu'arrikhīn* (178), we know that at least in 753/1252 he was alive; also cf. *GALS*, II:54. According to al-Qalqashandī, the *kātib al-durj* was the second-rank clerk in the *dīwān al-inshā'* under the

the viceroy of Syria, are abundantly quoted by al-Yūnīnī for the years after A.H. 679: e.g., his poems describing the combat with the Mongols on the Euphrates in A.H. 671,[37] official letters on Lājīn's behalf in A.H. 683,[38] reports and poems on the Mamluk conquest of al-Marqab in A.H. 684,[39] reports on Qalāwūn's combat with the Mongols,[40] and the Mamluk conquest of Tripoli in A.H. 688.[41] An enormous amount of poetry composed by him or presented to him on a variety of themes is also meticulously recorded.[42] Recorded also are some events witnessed by this clerk, e.g., the fire at the Horse Market of Damascus in A.H. 687.[43] This unidentified Maḥmūd al-Kātib is without doubt one of al-Yūnīnī's major Damascene sources for the events of the A.H. 670s and 680s, especially after Ibn Khallikān's death. Ḥusām al-Dīn Lājīn's other secretary, Kamāl al-Dīn Aḥmad Ibn 'Aṭṭār is also mentioned by al-Yūnīnī as having written official letters in Lājīn's name.[44]

Among the kātibs of Egypt, we hear about one Tāj al-Dīn Aḥmad Ibn al-Athīr who was in charge of drafting sultan Qalāwūn's letters and other communiqués.[45] This Ibn al-Athīr was probably brought to al-Yūnīnī's attention by an Egyptian Amīr 'Alam al-Dīn al-Dawādārī who told al-Yūnīnī about his encounters with this high-ranking clerk on some occasion.[46]

Other kinds of official documents also caught al-Yūnīnī's eye. For instance, the court records (*isjālāt*)[47] issued, or held, by one shaykh Badr al-Dīn Yūsuf ibn al-Ḥasan al-Sinjārī, the magistrate (*mutawallī*) of the county of Ba'labakk, were made available for al-Yūnīnī's view.[48]

To the Egyptian and Syrian sources should be added certain minor chronicles and biographical dictionaries dealing with specific cities and regions.

---

kātib al-sirr or *ṣāḥib dīwān al-inshā'*; his duties included drafting letters and documents on behalf of the viceroy and vizier; see *Q2*, 280-81.

[37] *Dhayl*, 3:3-4.

[38] *Dhayl*, 4:202.

[39] *Dhayl*, 4:248-53, 256-59.

[40] *Dhayl*, M:75.

[41] *Dhayl*, M:20-28.

[42] *Dhayl*, 3:386-405; 4:113-19, 187-90, 311; M:1-2, 6-10, 71-73.

[43] *Dhayl*, M:152.

[44] *Dhayl*, 4:253-56.

[45] *Dhayl*, 4:9, 241-48; M:16-17.

[46] *Dhayl*, M:83.

[47] For *isjālāt*, legal certificates issued by, and registered with, a judge (*ḥākim*), see *Q1*, 14:346-49 (the term is given its full form as *isjālāt al-'adāla*, or *al-isjālāt al-ḥukmīya*, and has more specific meaning). Al-Yūnīnī only mentions *isjālāt*, which might be a general reference to "court records."

[48] *Dhayl*, 2:332.

These were used by al-Yūnīnī for information on events or figures connected with these places:

Ibn al-Mustawfī, Sharaf al-Dīn al-Mubārak (d. 637/1239): The vizier of Irbil and author of *Ta'rīkh Irbil,*[49] he was used as the main source on Irbil and the Jazira area.[50]

Ibn al-Najjār al-Baghdādī, Abū 'Abd Allāh Muḥammad (d. 643/1245): His *Ta'rīkh li-*[sic]*Baghdād*[51] was cited for information on Baghdad.[52]

Ibn al-'Adīm (d. 660/1262):[53] Al-Yūnīnī mentions that he had obtained "the third volume" of Ibn al-'Adīm's *Ta'rīkh Ḥalab*[54] and relied on it for information connected with Aleppo.[55] Though he did not indicate which one of Ibn al-'Adīm's two famous histories of the city of Aleppo (*Bughyat al-ṭalab fī ta'rīkh Ḥalab* or *Zubdat al-ḥalab fī ta'rīkh Ḥalab*) he was using at the time, the former appears to be the one in question.[56] Of special interest are al-Yūnīnī's lengthy quotations from Ibn al-'Adīm on Nizārī Ismā'īlism and related matters. A good portion of Ibn al-'Adīm's accounts on the subject, which have been lost today, can be retrieved from al-Yūnīnī's quotations. Among those quotations is Ibn al-'Adīm's unique biography of Rāshid al-Dīn Sinān, the grand master of the Assassins in Syria. Bernard Lewis is of the opinion that al-Yūnīnī's version is "the fullest of the surviving recensions, and may well contain the full text as written in the Buġya."[57]

Manṣūr ibn Sālim (d. 673/1274):[58] He was used as the source about Alexandria.[59] Two titles ascribed to him, along with his biography, are mentioned by al-Yūnīnī: 1) *Ta'rīkh al-Iskandarīya*; and 2) *Ta'rīkh li-*[sic]*manārat al-Iskandarīya*;[60] the latter is not listed in *GAL*.

---

[49] In four volumes; see *GALS,* I:496.

[50] *Dhayl*, 1:65, 75, 337; 2:481; 4:153, 321-23.

[51] *GALS,* I:360 gives *Ta'rīkh madīnat al-salām*; also see Cahen, *Syrie*, 36.

[52] *Dhayl*, 1:65-70.

[53] For his biography, see "Ibn al-'Adīm," *EI*[2], by B. Lewis; also Cahen, *Syrie*, 62-63; Humphreys, *Ayyubids*, 396-97. His *laqab* is sometimes wrongly given as Jamāl al-Dīn in the *Dhayl* (1:108). For the most recent comprehensive study of Ibn al-'Adīm's life and his principal work *Bughyat al-ṭalab*, see Morray.

[54] *Dhayl*, 1:199.

[55] *Dhayl,* 1:108-11; 3:39-40; 4:149-50, 327.

[56] Cf. Morray, 145, note 5.

[57] Lewis, "Rāšid al-Dīn Sinān," 225-67, in which he presented an edition and English translation of this part of the *Dhayl*. Compare Lewis's edition (260-67) with that of Melkonian; see *Dhayl,* M:47-54.

[58] *GALS,* I:573-74.

[59] *Dhayl*, 2:132-33, 356-57.

[60] *Dhayl*, 3:103.

Some fragmentary materials, many of which may well be unfinished manuscripts, were also used by al-Yūnīnī to supply additional information, or anecdotes, for certain events:[61] thus we have the accounts by Ḥusām al-Dīn Ibn Abī 'Alī (d. 658/1260), an Egyptian amīr, on the Franks in Egypt;[62] one shaykh Shams al-Dīn Abū al-Muẓaffar on the Franks in Dimyāṭ;[63] Naṣīr al-Dīn Ḥasan ibn al-Naqīb al-Kinānī's poem describing the Euphrates combat in 671/1272;[64] and the eye-witness account by one Muḥammad ibn Mūsā al-Maqdisī, a kātib on the Egyptian expedition, of the siege and conquest of Tripoli in 688/1289.[65]

A substantial number of al-Yūnīnī's sources deal exclusively with the biographies of learned persons. In this connection, it is striking that al-Yūnīnī mentions his sources frequently in the *wafayāt* sections but relatively infrequently in the *ḥawādith* sections, although the two are, for the most part, evenly divided and given equal importance. This tendency is seen very clearly in the years A.H. 658, 661-666, 667-668, 670, 680-682, 685-686 and A.H. 689, in which not a single source is mentioned by name in the *ḥawādith* sections, while an average of 20 or 30 names are acknowledged as the sources for each year's *wafayāt* sections. Curious as it may be, al-Yūnīnī's strength and originality in the biographical information of Syrian learned persons are self-evident. Another point that can be made is that in addition to his own observations, the *ḥawādith* sections may contain some kind of "official version" of reports from Egypt which were thought to be common knowledge and needed no further authentication. The text shows that Egyptian events, though narrated in detail, are often given without sources, while events outside of Egypt, especially those concerning the Franks and Mongols, are always supplied with background information and source references.

Following a long-cherished Muslim scholastic tradition, these biographies usually include the achievements of these persons in all fields of higher learning: the ḥadīths they transmitted, the historical accounts they handed down, and all kinds of literary products they composed. Al-Yūnīnī made it clear that during his career he had read a vast number of manuscripts of this *manāqib*-hagiography-anthology type. Sometimes not only the deceased person's biography and literary works are recorded in great detail, but also information con-

[61] Such additional information is usually introduced by a phrase like *wa-dhakara fulān mā ma'nāhu* (so-and-so mentioned an analogous story about [the aforementioned event]).

[62] *Dhayl*, 2:174, 213.

[63] *Dhayl*, 2:202ff.

[64] *Dhayl*, 3:4.

[65] *Dhayl*, M:28-31.

cerning those who were connected with him, e.g., his father, son, teachers, or friends. As a result, an immense body of biographical material as well as literary texts, prose and verse, often with their sources, have been included in each year's *wafayāt* section, providing a general anthology of Syrian literary works of the time.[66]

Some of these *manāqib-rijāl* materials are originally grouped according to profession and fields, or schools and sects, with which the men were affiliated in their lifetime. As such, al-Yūnīnī's sources for the 'ulamā' in general were naturally those mainstream *ṭabaqāt* authors, such as Zakī al-Dīn Ibrāhīm ibn 'Abd al-'Azīz al-Mālikī (d. 687/1288),[67] the author of the *Ikhtiṣār Wafayāt al-a'yān*, an abridged version of Ibn Khallikān's work.[68] As regards Shāfi'ī jurists, al-Yūnīnī had plenty of references: the accounts[69] by Tāj al-Dīn 'Abd al-Raḥmān al-Fazārī (d. 690/1291)[70] and his son Burhān al-Dīn Ibrāhīm (d. 729/1328);[71] the famous Najm al-Dīn Aḥmad Ibn Ṣaṣrā (d. 723/1322);[72] Yāsīn ibn Yūsuf al-Zarkashī (d. 686/1287)[73] and his student Muḥyī al-Dīn al-Nawāwī (d. 676/1278);[74] to this list should also be added Kamāl al-Dīn 'Umar al-Taflīsī (d. 672/1273).[75] For Mālikī scholars and ṣūfīs, especially those from North Africa, he cited, curiously, from the famous ṣūfī saint Abū al-Ḥasan al-Shādhilī (d. 656/1258).[76] For poets, al-Yūnīnī consulted Ḍiyā' al-

---

[66] For al-Yūnīnī's methodology of arranging *adab* materials, especially poetry, in the *Dhayl*, also cf. below, 89-91.

[67] His *nisba* is given as al-Lūrī in al-Sakhāwī, *I'lān*, 153 (Rosenthal's translation, *Historiography*, 500), instead of al-Kūrī in the *Dhayl*; Ibn al-'Imād, *Shadharāt*, 5:400, also gives al-Lūrī.

[68] *Dhayl*, 4:190-91.

[69] *Dhayl*, 2:168-69; 3:191-92; 4:78-79, 141; M:61 (al-Yūnīnī states that he quoted from Tāj al-Dīn's autograph), 68, 69.

[70] For his life and career, see al-Subkī, *Ṭabaqāt al-Shāfi'īya*, 8:163-64; al-Munajjid, *Mu'jam al-mu'arrikhīn*, 122.

[71] For his biography, see Ibn Kathīr, *Bidāya*, 14:146; al-Subkī, *Ṭabaqāt al-Shāfi'īya*, 9:312-98; al-Munajjid, *Mu'jam al-mu'arrikhīn*, 138.

[72] *Dhayl*, 2:169; 4:127-28, 320; for his biography, also see "Ibn Ṣaṣrā," *EI²*, by W. Brinner.

[73] *Dhayl*, 3:284; his name is given as Yāsīn ibn 'Abd Allāh in Ibn Kathīr, *Bidāya*, 13:312; Ibn Kathīr's account does not seem very accurate for: 1) the name Yāsīn ibn Yūsuf has been attested by many other references such as al-Subkī, *Ṭabaqāt al-Shāfi'īya*, 8:396-97; Ibn al-'Imād, *Shadharāt*, 5:403; and 2) the text of *Bidāya* appears to be corrupt in that it suggests that Yāsīn was the same person as shaykh al-shuyūkh Muḥyī al-Dīn al-Nawāwī, who was in fact Yāsīn's student.

[74] *Dhayl*, 4:190; his name was Yaḥyā ibn Sharaf al-Ḥurrānī al-Shāfi'ī; see *GAL*, I:496; *GALS*, I:680; al-Subkī, *Ṭabaqāt al-Shāfi'īya*, 8:395-400; Ibn Taghrībirdī, *Nujūm*, 7:278.

[75] *Dhayl*, 4:308-9; for his biography, see al-Subkī, *Ṭabaqāt al-Shāfi'īya*, 8:309-10.

[76] *Dhayl*, 4:318; al-Yūnīnī did not mention the title of al-Shādhilī's work. It is to be noted that so far there is no record of the existence of any biographic or hagiographic

Dīn Ibn al-Athīr's (d. 637/1239)[77] *Mathal al-sā'ir fī adab al-kātib wa-al-shā'ir*[78] and al-Mubārak ibn Abī Bakr Ibn Ḥamdān's (d. 654/1256) acclaimed *Qalā'id al-jumān fī farā'id shu'arā' hādhā al-zamān*[79] (also known as *Qalā'id al-farā'id,*[80] *Qalā'id al-jumān,*[81] and *'Uqad al-jumān fī shu'arā' hādhā al-zamān*[82]). As for physicians, al-Yūnīnī often quoted from Ibn Abī Uṣaybi'a's[83] famous *Ṭabaqāt al-aṭibbā'*.[84]

Poetry occupies a significant portion of the entire text of the *Dhayl.*[85] Of special value are the verses attributed to the indigenous 'ulamā' of Damascus and Ba'labakk, many of whom were the acquaintances of al-Yūnīnī or of his father and brother. Al-Yūnīnī stresses repeatedly the fact that many of these verses were quoted by him directly from the authors' autographs or the manuscripts dictated by the authors to their family members or fellow students. For instance, there is the mention of one Jamāl al-Dīn Yaḥyā al-Ṣarṣarī's (d. 656/1258)[86] *Dīwān* in 20 volumes which was presented, along with ḥadīth collections, by the author to al-Yūnīnī's father.[87] In another case, al-Yūnīnī tells us that one Sharaf al-Dīn 'Abd al-'Azīz al-Anṣārī (d. 662/1264)[88] "has written a vast number of verses that have not been collected in a *dīwān* yet; and I have obtained a collection copied by the author himself," which includes poetry and anecdotes as well as the author's father's *manāqib-*

works by al-Shādhilī, except for some letters, litanies, and prayers; see "Shādhilī," *EI*[2], by P. Lory. For more details on al-Shādhilī, see *GALS*, I:804-6; Ḥājjī Khalīfa, 404, 661-2; al-Baghdādī, *Hadīyat al-'ārifīn*, 1:709-10; and most recently, Richard J. A. McGregor, "A Sufi Legacy in Tunisia: Prayer and the Shadhiliyya," *IJMES* 29/2 (1997): 255-77, with up-to-date bibliography.

[77] "Ibn al-Athīr," *EI*[2], by F. Rosenthal. He should not be confused with his brother, the historian 'Izz al-Dīn 'Alī Ibn al-Athīr.

[78] *Dhayl*, 1:64, 178; see Bonebakker's edition and study in *Oriens* 13-14 (1961): 186-94; there is also an edition by M. M. 'Abd al-Ḥamīd (Cairo, 1939).

[79] *Dhayl*, 1:77-78; 2:369; see *GAL*, I:357ff; *GALS*, I:521; it has now appeared in a facsimile edition in ten volumes (Frankfurt, 1990).

[80] *Dhayl*, 1:334-37.

[81] *Dhayl*, 2:305-307; 3:277-78; 4:193.

[82] *Dhayl*, 3:41.

[83] For his biography, see Hamed Waly, *Drei Kapitel aus der Arztegeschichte des Ibn Abī Oṣaibi'a* (Berlin, 1910).

[84] *Dhayl*, 1:93; 3:194; M:97.

[85] Cf. chapter 4 below, 87-94.

[86] A blind Iraqi poet; his *Dīwān* is said to have contained the *qaṣīda dālīya* on Ḥanbalī *fiqh* consisting of 2,774 verses; see *GAL*, I:290; *GALS*, I:443.

[87] *Dhayl*, 1:257-332.

[88] His biography is found in al-Kutubī, *Fawāt al-wafayāt*, 1:289-94; Ibn Taghrībirdī, *Nujūm*, 7:214.

biography; all were copied by al-Yūnīnī.[89] An unidentified Mukhliṣ al-Dīn al-Mubārak al-Ghassān al-Ḥimṣī's abridged edition of Ibn Kalb's genealogical work on the Arab tribes *Kitāb al-jamhara fī al-ansāb* and his manuscripts of poetry were also recorded by al-Yūnīnī.[90]

Many of the verses presented in the *Dhayl* are al-Yūnīnī's exclusive materials: e.g., Zayn al-Dīn 'Abd al-Ṣamad (d. 686/1287)[91] wrote his poems and sent them from Medina to al-Yūnīnī;[92] the poems by shaykh Zakī al-Dīn Muḥammad, the qāḍī of Ba'labbak, were handed over by his son to al-Yūnīnī upon the latter's request;[93] the poems by Muwaffaq al-Dīn 'Abd Allāh al-Anṣārī, a friend of al-Yūnīnī, were recorded at length.[94] Other poets whose autographs were used by al-Yūnīnī are: Ṣadr al-Dīn 'Abd al-Raḥmān (d. 656/1258), the Shāfi'ī qāḍī of Ba'labakk and al-Yūnīnī's father's former student;[95] Najm al-Dīn Muḥammad Ibn Siwār al-Shaybānī (d. 677/1278);[96] Shams al-Dīn Muḥammad al-Ba'labakkī, a historian whose death in battle was witnessed by al-Yūnīnī;[97] and Mu'īn al-Dīn 'Uthmān al-Fahrī (d. 685/1286).[98]

It is very interesting to note that al-Yūnīnī's sources for poetry also include some Mamluk amīrs such as Amīr 'Alam al-Dīn al-Dawādārī (also known as al-Duwaydārī, d. 699/1299), who was famous for his military accomplishments as well as for his achievements in learning.[99]

---

[89] *Dhayl*, 2:240-95.

[90] *Dhayl*, 3:37-38.

[91] He was known as Ibn 'Asākir al-Dimashqī al-Makkī, a ḥadīth scholar based in Mecca; for his biography, see al-Kutubī, *Fawāt al-wafayāt*, 1:275; also *GAL*, I:450, II: 123. He should not be confused with the historian Ibn 'Asākir.

[92] *Dhayl*, M:10-13.

[93] *Dhayl*, 2:74-75.

[94] *Dhayl*, 3:322-28.

[95] *Dhayl*, 1:247ff.

[96] *Dhayl*, 3:405-32; a Damascene ṣūfī poet; for his biography, see al-Kutubī, *Fawāt al-wafayāt*, 2:216-20; Ibn al-'Imād, *Shadharāt*, 5:359; al-Ṣafadī, *al-Wāfī*, 3:142; also *GAL*, I:299.

[97] *Dhayl*, 4:121-22.

[98] *Dhayl*, 4:286-89, where his obituary is presented.

[99] *Dhayl*, M:3, 79-81; the amīr was the commander (*nā'ib*) of the Damascus Citadel around A.H. 678; cf. Ibn al-Dawādārī, *Kanz*, 8:230-31, 307-8, 361-62; 9:40. He was also credited with showing interest in ḥadīth and learning. The amīr is not related to Sayf al-Dīn Ibn al-Dawādārī, the author of *Kanz*. For a general discussion of non-Arab Mamluks' involvement in intellectual and literary life of 14th century Egypt and Syria see Haarmann, "Arabic in Speech, Turkish in Lineage."

A Ba'labakki learned man's world: al-Yūnīnī's oral sources

As remarked above, the *Dhayl* is particularly rich with sources from the indigenous learned communities, especially those of Damascus and Ba'labakk. In this regard, al-Yūnīnī's first-hand information not only came from his personal observations and experiences, but also from his father and brother who were highly respected in these communities. There were also a great number of fellow scholars with whom al-Yūnīnī had very active and close contacts—some of them through his father's and brother's connections—and from whom he received a large amount of information. Al-Yūnīnī's meticulous use of these orally-transmitted materials, combined with written sources, makes the *Dhayl* especially valuable in terms of its coverage of contemporary religious life in Syria, and of Ḥanbalism in particular. In this sense, the *Dhayl* itself, especially the *wafayāt* sections, can virtually be read as a Who's Who of Damascene and Ba'labakki 'ulamā' during the second half of the 7th/13th and first half of the 8th/14th centuries.[100]

We can organize al-Yūnīnī's direct informants roughly into three groups, as follows:

1. Dignitaries (a'yān) *of Ba'labakk and Damascus.* The majority of them, especially those who lived in Ba'labakk, are not well known to us, except for a few such as 'Abd al-Raḥmān ibn Muḥammad al-Ba'labakkī al-Yūnīnī (d. 732/1331),[101] Najm al-Dīn Mūsā ibn Ibrāhīm al-Shaqrāwī (d. 702/1302),[102] Muḥammad ibn Riḍwān (d. ca. 700/1300),[103] and Muḥammad ibn 'Abbās al-Rabī' al-Dunayṣarī (d. 686/1287).[104] A list of these indigenous 'ulamā' who were not famous includes: shaykh 'Īsā ibn Aḥmad al-Yūnīnī,[105] Abū Ṭālib ibn Aḥmad al-Yūnīnī,[106] one shaykh 'Imrān,[107] 'Alī ibn Abī Bakr al-Yūnīnī,[108] Shihāb al-Dīn Muḥammad Ibn al-'Ālima,[109] al-'Imād Muẓaffar ibn Sanī al-

[100] It is noteworthy that these do not belong only to the Sunnī establishment; Shī'ī figures are also included in the *Dhayl.*

[101] *Dhayl*, 2:303; for his biography, see al-'Asqalānī, *Durar*, 2:451.

[102] *Dhayl*, 2:9-10, 169; for his biography, see al-'Asqalānī, *Durar*, 5:141-42.

[103] *Dhayl*, 3:19-25; for his biography, see al-'Asqalānī, *Durar*, 4:60-61.

[104] *Dhayl*, 4:329; for his biography, see al-Kutubī, *Fawāt al-wafayāt*, 1:122; Ibn Abī Uṣaybi'a, *Ṭabaqāt al-aṭibbā'*, 2:267-72; al-Ṣafadī, *al-Wāfī*, 3:200.

[105] *Dhayl*, 1:26-28.

[106] *Dhayl*, 1:29-30.

[107] *Dhayl*, 1:30.

[108] *Dhayl*, 1:30-31.

[109] *Dhayl*, 1:95; his brother Aḥmad ibn As'ad (d. 656/1258) was a famous Damascene physician whose biography is found in *Dhayl*, 1:92-95.

Dawla,[110] al-Jamāl Naṣr Allāh,[111] 'Alā' al-Dīn 'Alī ibn Ghānim,[112] Muḥammad ibn 'Abd al-Wāḥid,[113] Naṣr al-Dīn 'Alī Ibn Qarqīn,[114] Bahā' al-Dīn 'Abd Allāh (known as Ibn Maḥbūb),[115] Fakhr al-Dīn Ayāz,[116] Ghānim Ibn al-'Ashīra,[117] Fakhr al-Dīn al-Ḥasan ibn 'Alī,[118] Ḥusām al-Dīn Lu'lu' ibn 'Abd Allāh,[119] and al-Shams Muḥammad ibn Khālid.[120]

As we have learned from the above sketch of al-Yūnīnī's life, his pilgrimage to Mecca in 673/1275 was accompanied by a group of Damascene and Ba'labakki learned men who handed down an abundance of information, ḥadīth, history, anecdotes ranging from the marvelous (*al-'ajā'ib*) to the bizarre (*al-gharā'ib*), poetry, etc., to al-Yūnīnī and whose friendship al-Yūnīnī was to keep later in his life. Among these were: Ibrāhīm ibn Sa'd Allāh,[121] a ḥadīth scholar and the father of the chief judge Badr al-Dīn Muḥammad; Majd al-Dīn Muḥammad ibn Aḥmad,[122] a ṣūfī poet and jurist; Muḥammad ibn 'Alī,[123] a ḥadīth transmitter and a well-known dream interpreter; Kamāl al-Dīn Muḥammad ibn 'Abd al-Raḥmān,[124] a famous physician; Fakhr al-Dīn 'Abd al-Raḥmān ibn Yūsuf,[125] a veteran Ḥanbalī teacher and an old friend of al-Yūnīnī's father; and Najm al-Dīn Aḥmad ibn 'Abd al-Raḥmān,[126] the Ḥanbalī chief judge in Damascus, among others.

2. *The 'ulamā' of Egypt and other places.* Among them, Shaykh Khaḍir ibn Abī Bakr is perhaps the most intriguing; al-Yūnīnī reported that he had

---

[110] *Dhayl*, 2:22.

[111] *Dhayl*, 2:22-23.

[112] *Dhayl*, 2:30-32; he met with al-Yūnīnī in A.H. 691 in Ba'labakk. According to Krenkow, he died in A.H. 737; *Dhayl*, 2:30, note 1.

[113] *Dhayl*, 2:74; he was the qāḍī of Ba'labakk and died in A.H. 658. Al-Yūnīnī claimed that the shaykh used to recite poems to him but he was "unable to memorize any of them" and thus asked the shaykh's son to write down his father's poems for the record.

[114] *Dhayl*, 2:79, 485-86; 4:126. According to Krenkow, he died in A.H. 692; *Dhayl*, 2:79, note 1.

[115] *Dhayl*, 2:141.

[116] *Dhayl*, 2:488.

[117] *Dhayl*, 3:90.

[118] *Dhayl*, 3:134; he was the head of the 'Alids (*naqīb al-ashrāf*) of Ba'labakk and died in A.H. 674.

[119] *Dhayl*, 4:32; he was a *kātib al-jaysh* in Damascus and died in A.H. 678.

[120] *Dhayl*, 4:126.

[121] For his biography, see *Dhayl*, 3:187-89.

[122] For his biography, see *Dhayl*, 3:386-400, where a number of his poems are also recorded.

[123] For his biography, see *Dhayl*, 3:137.

[124] For his biography, see *Dhayl*, Ms. Landberg 139, f. 2a.

[125] For his biography, see *Dhayl*, M:34f.

[126] For his biography, see *Dhayl*, M:59-60.

heard this legendary figure[127] talk about the Mamluk conquest of Ḥiṣn al-Akrād in 665/1266.[128] Al-Yūnīnī's other informants include Bahā' al-Dīn al-Fā'izī, who met al-Yūnīnī in Mecca in A.H. 673 and then in Cairo in A.H. 675-76, and A.H. 689;[129] 'Uthmān ibn 'Abd Allāh al-Āmidī, a Ḥanbalī teacher in Mecca who also met with al-Yūnīnī during the 673/1275 pilgrimage;[130] 'Āmir ibn Yaḥyā, a Qur'ān reciter who met with al-Yūnīnī in A.H. 692 in the village of Yūnīn;[131] 'Izz al-Dīn 'Abd al-'Azīz ibn 'Abd al-Salām (d. 660/1261),[132] from whom al-Yūnīnī received a number of ḥadīths in A.H. 659 in Cairo;[133] and Naṣr al-Dīn Ḥasan Ibn Shāwir (d. 687/1288),[134] who recited his verses to al-Yūnīnī in Cairo.[135]

3. The Mamluks. Most of them were low-ranking officers from whom al-Yūnīnī managed to gain some inside stories. Among these Mamluks are: Ḥusām al-Dīn Ātish al-'Izzī—the *ustādhdār* of 'Izz al-Dīn 'Abd al-'Azīz Ibn Waddā'a, the commander (*mutawallī*) of the Ba'labakk Citadel—who tried very hard to prove his master Ibn Waddā'a's innocence in the death of Amīr Sayf al-Dīn Baktūt ibn 'Abd Allāh;[136] and Amīr Najm al-Dīn al-Ḥasan ibn Muḥammad al-Anṣārī, who used to serve Amīr 'Izz al-Dīn Aybak al-Mu'aẓẓamī, the ruler of al-Ṣarkhad, and was himself the commander of the Ba'labakk Citadel at the time he spoke to al-Yūnīnī.[137] One unidentified Asad al-Dīn Ibn al-Ṣu'lūk related some anecdotes about al-Malik al-Ṣāliḥ Ismā'īl to al-Yūnīnī in A.H. 691 at the Ba'labakk Citadel;[138] and one Amīr 'Alā' al-Dīn Aydak ibn 'Abd Allāh al-Ṣāliḥī (d. A.H. 690)[139] told stories about sultan Qalāwūn to al-Yūnīnī.[140]

---

[127] Cf. above, 11, note 41.
[128] *Dhayl,* 3:265-66.
[129] *Dhayl,* 1:82; 4:208.
[130] *Dhayl,* 3:137.
[131] *Dhayl,* 1:31-32.
[132] A Shāfi'ī jurist born in Damascus and later lived in Cairo; for his biography, see al-Kutubī, *Fawāt al-wafayāt*, 1:287; al-Subkī, *Ṭabaqāt al-Shāfi'īya*, 8:209-55; also *GAL*, I:554; *GALS*, I:766.
[133] *Dhayl,* 3:137-38.
[134] Known as al-Nafīsī, an Egyptian poet; for his biography, see al-Kutubī, *Fawāt al-wafayāt*, 1:118.
[135] *Dhayl,* M:6.
[136] *Dhayl,* 1:124.
[137] *Dhayl,* 4:265.
[138] *Dhayl,* M:45.
[139] He is perhaps the one named Aydakīn al-Ṣāliḥī in Ibn al-Dawādārī, *Kanz*, 8:31.
[140] *Dhayl,* M:99.

2. The Sources of the Jazarī-Yūnīnī Tradition

Having concluded a general survey of al-Yūnīnī's sources and informants, attention will now be directed to some specific names which are significant not only for the accounts they provide but also for the investigation into the authorship of the later part of the *Dhayl*, namely, the "Jazarī-Yūnīnī tradition," and related matters. My method is to target *key figures* and *key events*; the former I define as al-Yūnīnī's direct sources or informants who continue to function as sources in this part of the text; and the latter as the events in which these figures were all involved together with al-Yūnīnī. For example, one of the key events mentioned most often is al-Yūnīnī's pilgrimage to Mecca in the year 673/1275 during which he was able to befriend a large number of fellow 'ulamā' and establish long-term friendships with some of them. The significance of this event lies in that it can be used to attest al-Yūnīnī's authority on certain events he describes, i.e., anybody mentioned as having met with "me" during the 673/1275 pilgrimage is evidently al-Yūnīnī's informant and it follows that the account in question is on al-Yūnīnī's authority. The same method is applied to confirm al-Jazarī's authenticity.

Some figures who are frequently cited in both al-Yūnīnī's and al-Jazarī's versions as primary sources and thus deserve our special attention are the following:

'Izz al-Dīn Muḥammad Ibn Abī al-Hayjā' (d. 700/1301): A Mamluk amīr of whose career and life little is known to us.[141] A vast amount of information, written and oral alike, was passed on by him to al-Yūnīnī. Al-Yūnīnī confirms that he met with the amīr on Rabī' II 5, A.H. 692 in Damascus[142] and heard the amīr's accounts on a variety of important issues and persons;[143] that he not only copied poems from the amīr's manuscripts,[144] but also received, orally, biographical data as well as poetry from him.[145] Moreover, al-Yūnīnī tells us that he used to discuss with the amīr various topics such as dream interpretation, and so forth.[146] This amīr continues to be mentioned as

[141] His obituary is in *Dhayl*, the present edition, 238, where his *ta'rīkh* is mentioned as well.

[142] *Dhayl*, 2:32-33.

[143] *Dhayl*, 1:123, 176-78; 2:77-79, 398-99.

[144] *Dhayl*, 2:83-84; 3:204.

[145] *Dhayl*, 2:168-69; 4:323-27.

[146] *Dhayl*, 2:441.

a source for the revised draft (Version II). Since Version II is believed to have mixed many of al-Jazarī's accounts, the existence of this Amīr Ibn Abī al-Hayjā' is a proof of al-Yūnīnī's authority on certain accounts in the text.[147]

Sharaf al-Dīn 'Abd al-Mu'min Ibn Khalaf al-Dimyāṭī (d. 705/1305):[148] Though one of the most important figures of the last third of the 7th/13th century in the transmission of ḥadīth, he is mainly mentioned in the "Jazarī-Yūnīnī tradition" as the source for Egyptian poetry.[149] His famous biographical dictionary *Mu'jam al-shuyūkh*[150] was a major written source for both al-Yūnīnī and al-Jazarī.[151] The text of the *Dhayl*, though, does not supply any evidence that al-Yūnīnī ever met with al-Dimyāṭī. On the other hand, we know for sure that he was al-Jazarī's teacher in Cairo, and accordingly, the latter's direct informant.[152] In addition, there is a mention in the text that al-Jazarī met al-Dimyāṭī at Cairo in A.H. 701 and received some ḥadīths from the latter.[153] And furthermore, al-Dimyāṭī's close relationship with Athīr al-Dīn Abū Ḥayyān, who will be discussed below, was confirmed by medieval Muslim writers.[154] The frequently cited phrase of *anshadanā* (he recited to us a poem), which only occurs in Version II,[155] also implies al-Jazarī's direct involvement, rather than that of al-Yūnīnī.

Athīr al-Dīn Abū Ḥayyān, Muḥammad ibn Yūsuf al-Gharnaṭī (d. 745/1344):[156] Well-known as one of the greatest Arab grammarians, he appears for the first and only time in the revised version of the *Dhayl* (Version II) and is said to have met with "me" in Dhū al-Qa'da, A.H. 712 in Cairo.[157] That he is the major source of poetry for al-Jazarī, not al-Yūnīnī, is attested in the text that is to follow, namely, the "Jazarī-Yūnīnī tradition"; in al-Jazarī's version, the provenance is once given as: *anshadanī Athīr al-Dīn* (Athīr al-Dīn recited to me the following poem . . .) while al-Yūnīnī mentions him as an in-

---

[147] E.g., *Dhayl*, 3:383, 502.

[148] *GAL*, II:88; *GALS*, I:79; for his biography, see "al-Dimyāṭī," *EI²*, by G. Vajda.

[149] *Dhayl*, 3:38, 71-72.

[150] For al-Dimyāṭī and his *Mu'jam*, also cf. above, 57-58.

[151] Compare Ms. Landberg 139, f. 91a, 152a, 166a with Ms. Paris arabe 6739, p. 216, 386, 435, respectively.

[152] See "al-Djazarī," *EI²*, by A. S. B. Ansari.

[153] See *Dhayl*, the present edition, 254-55.

[154] E.g., al-Ḥusaynī al-Dimashqī, *Dhayl Tadhkirat al-ḥuffāẓ*, 24-25.

[155] *Dhayl*, 1:432, 433, 434, 504, 524, 525-26.

[156] For his biography, see "Abū Ḥayyān," *EI²*, by S. Glazer; al-Ḥusaynī al-Dimashqī, *Dhayl Tadhkirat al-ḥuffāẓ*, 23ff.

[157] *Dhayl*, 1:482.

direct source: *qāla . . . Athīr al-Dīn . . .* (Athīr al-Dīn quoted . . .).[158] This provenance has been repeated throughout the text for the years A.H. 699 and 700.[159] In addition, we have seen many other indications that al-Jazarī was certainly in Cairo during A.H. 712-713.[160]

Another important figure is an unidentified Mamluk amīr named Sayf al-Dīn Ibn al-Miḥaffadār.[161] First mentioned as a source for the events of A.H. 691,[162] this amīr was obviously al-Jazarī's informant: he is said to have met with al-Jazarī at the Damascus Citadel; and many of his first-hand accounts on Mamluk politics and military campaigns have been recorded in the text; they include the conflict between al-Malik al-Ashraf and other amīrs, the death of al-Malik al-Ashraf, and Amīr 'Izz al-Dīn al-Afram's career.[163] It is quite suggestive that in a portion of the text which proved to be al-Jazarī's own, i.e., the fact mentioned above about al-Jazarī's *majmū'a* being wrongly inserted into the *Dhayl*, this amīr is credited with reciting al-Ṣanawbarī's famous poem in describing Damascus to "us," namely, to al-Jazarī and his friends.[164] Aside from this Ibn al-Miḥaffadār, there is another Mamluk amīr Najm al-Dīn Ḥamza Ibn al-Miḥaffadār who described to al-Jazari the earthquake that had hit Cairo in 698/1298. This Ibn al-Miḥaffadār is frequently cited as a source for the Egyptian events in the last "volume" of the *Dhayl*, which has, as discussed above, proved to be al-Jazarī's chronicle but has been mistakenly ascribed to al-Yūnīnī.

3. Al-Birzālī: Source and Editor

Finally, we should now turn to the most significant and central figure in the shaping and transmission of both al-Jazarī's and al-Yūnīnī's chronicles: 'Alam al-Dīn al-Qāsim al-Birzālī.[165]

---

[158] See Ms. Paris arabe 6739, p. 207 (al-Jazarī's version) and Ms. Landberg 139, f. 86b (al-Yūnīnī's version).

[159] See *Dhayl*, the present edition, 139, 155, 236.

[160] Ms. Ahmet III 2907/e. 4, f. 192a.

[161] We only know that he was the son of Amīr-Jānidār Shams al-Dīn Abū al-Bayān Bannā'; see Ms. Landberg 139, f. 55a.

[162] Ms. Landberg 139, f. 55b (al-Yūnīnī) vs. Ms. Paris 6739, p. 119 (al-Jazarī).

[163] Cf. Ms. Landberg 139, ff. 92b-93b, 101a-b, 139a (al-Yūnīnī) vs. Ms. Paris 6739, pp. 221f, 245f, 355 (al-Jazarī), respectively.

[164] Ms. Ahmet III 2907/e. 3, f. 235b.

[165] The most comprehensive biography and bibliography of al-Birzālī is still "al-Birzālī," *EI*², by F. Rosenthal; also cf. 'Abbās al-'Azzāwī, "al-Birzālī," 519-27; al-Munajjid, *Mu'jam al-mu'arrikhīn*, 142-44. I wish to thank Franz Rosenthal who kindly

Al-Birzālī was cited as a source for the first time in the year 684/1284-85 in connection with biographical information and poetry.[166] As mentioned above,[167] a parent codex (Ms. Bodleian) for the first draft of the text (perhaps covering years A.H. 654-690) was in fact dictated by al-Yūnīnī to al-Birzālī and was eventually transmitted under al-Birzālī's supervision. However, this part of the text does not show that al-Yūnīnī learned much from the younger al-Birzālī. This is quite in contrast to the later part of the text, the "Jazarī-Yūnīnī tradition," where al-Birzālī becomes the major source, as will be shown in the following.

Al-Birzālī was apparently one of the principal authorities for nearly every year's events and obituaries throughout the entire *second part* of al-Yūnīnī's *Dhayl*, that is, the "Jazarī-Yūnīnī tradition." That al-Birzālī was a direct informant of al-Jazarī is confirmed by the above comparison of al-Jazarī's and al-Yūnīnī's versions (covering A.H. 691-698). In this connection, we have good reason to believe that al-Birzālī met with al-Jazarī in Ṣafar, A.H. 705 (August and September, 1305), and presented to him both historical information and literary works, including the poems by al-Sakhāwī,[168] and the account of Ghazān's conversion to Islam.[169] That al-Birzālī was a direct informant of al-Jazarī is also reflected in the textual alterations made by al-Yūnīnī in the material he copied from al-Jazarī: he changed al-Jazarī's references in the first person to the third, that is, al-Jazarī's *ḥakā lī al-Birzālī* (al-Birzālī told me . . .)[170] is changed by al-Yūnīnī to *ḥakā al-Birzālī* (al-Birzālī said [in his work]), and *mimmā akhbara bihi al-Birzālī* (from al-Birzālī's account it is said that . . .).[171] Al-Birzālī's presence as a source of both events and poetry is pervasive in this part of the text.[172]

---

copied for me some bibliographical materials on al-Birzālī in the summer of 1992. In addition to the works by al-Birzālī mentioned in *GAL* and Rosenthal's article, I have found the following:

1) *Thabt masmūʿāt al-Birzālī ʿalā shuyūkhihi* or *Taʿlīqāt ʿAlam al-Dīn li-samāʿatihi ʿalā mashāʾikhihi min Jumādā I ilā shahr Shaʿbān*, a ḥadīth collection with commentary, Ms. Damascus, al-ʿUmarīya (*Catalog*, 87-88);

2) *Khamsat ʿashar ḥadīthan min al-ʿawālī*, a ḥadīth collection, Ms. Damascus, al-ʿUmarīya (*Catalog*, 319).

[166] *Dhayl*, 4:265-68, 286.

[167] Cf. above, 22, 44, 45-46.

[168] Ms. Landberg 139 (al-Yūnīnī), f. 78a vs. Ms. Paris 6739 (al-Jazarī), p. 189.

[169] Ms. Landberg 139, f. 120a, 212a vs. Ms. Paris 6739, p. 306, 310.

[170] Ms. Paris 6739, p. 335.

[171] Ms. Landberg 139, f. 130a, 130b.

[172] Ms. Landberg 139, f. 125b, 128b (the corresponding paragraph is missing from al-Jazarī's version), 130a, b vs. Ms. Paris 6739, p. 324, 335-36, 343; also *Dhayl*, the present edition, 30, 32-46, 47, 93, etc.

This tendency is continued in al-Yūnīnī's text in which the corresponding part of al-Jazarī's version has no longer survived (A.H. 699-701). It is significant to note here that al-Birzālī, an extremely popular and sociable personage in Damascene learned circles,[173] was perhaps the only one among the three historians who had personal contacts with Ibn Taymīya, a figure always in the center of political, religious, social, and diplomatic events in Damascus at the time. As pointed out above, Ghazān's conversion to Islam was related by Ibn Taymīya's brother Zayn al-Dīn to al-Birzālī; and Ibn Taymīya's accounts of his negotiation with Quṭlū-Shāh and other Mongol generals, including Ghazān himself at one point, were handed down through al-Birzālī as well.[174] Apart from the meeting between al-Birzālī and al-Jazarī in the year 705/1305, al-Birzālī must have run into al-Jazarī in Rabī' II, A.H. 703 and recited to him the poems of one Shams al-Dīn Muḥammad al-Ba'labakkī.[175] Al-Birzālī's ḥadīth teachers are always singled out in obituary notes.[176] Despite the phrases *anshadanī al-Birzālī* (al-Birzālī recited a poem to me) or *ḥakā lī al-Birzālī* (al-Birzālī told me) that may, at the first glance, be confused as referring to al-Yūnīnī, based on our study of the overall nature and authorship of this part of the text, the "me" here ought to be regarded as referring to al-Jazarī.

In the last "volume" of the text (covering A.H. 702-711), al-Birzālī is even more visible; he is mentioned not only as an oral source, but his manuscripts are cited as well. It is apparent that the real author (al-Jazarī?) of this volume relied heavily on al-Birzālī's biographical information concerning the ḥadīth teachers[177] and poetry.[178] In this connection, it might not be out of place to recall that al-Birzālī was also the copyist of the above-mentioned al Dimyāṭī's *Mu'jam al-shuyūkh*, a cluster of whose material was found wrongly inserted into this volume as well.[179] Al-Birzālī functions as a source not only through his first-hand observations, but also through the information he gathered by other means (e.g., al-Birzālī received a letter, at Damascus, from Medina con-

173 According to Ibn Kathīr, al-Birzālī was loved by "people of all groups" in the city of Damascus (cited in Chamberlain, 115, especially note 51).

174 *Dhayl*, the present edition, 119.

175 *Dhayl*, the present edition, 156.

176 *Dhayl*, the present edition, 197, 198, 238.

177 Ms. Ahmet III 2907/e. 4, f. 24a, 25a, 157a.

178 Ms. Ahmet III 2907/e. 4, f. 31b, 54b, 152b, 223b, 225a (this poem was dedicated to al-Birzālī).

179 Georges Vajda mentions a Damascus manuscript (al-Ẓāhirīya, *Majmū'a* 37), which is al-Birzālī's autograph of al-Dimyāṭī's *Mu'jam*; see *Dictionnaire*, 23; also see above, 57-58.

cerning the lanterns in the Holy Shrine, etc.).[180] We also learn that the author of this volume (al-Jazarī?) had used al-Birzālī's manuscripts for biographical data.[181] Al-Birzālī has also merged himself into the narrative; in one case, his participation in a religious ceremony at Damascus in the year A.H. 706 is described vividly and at length.[182]

The relationship between al-Birzālī's and al-Jazarī's writings has been investigated by 'Abbās al-'Azzāwī who, citing medieval authorities, states that al-Jazarī was the earliest Arab historian to quote from al-Birzālī's highly valuable accounts on history and ḥadīth.[183] Our textual analysis and source criticism above further demonstrate that al-Birzālī's historical accounts, biographical notices,[184] and ḥadīths were directly transmitted to al-Jazarī, and that al-Yūnīnī received these from al-Jazarī's work. But this conclusion solves only half of the problem. It is natural for us to ask: Why should al-Yūnīnī, al-Birzālī's former teacher, rely on al-Jazarī, whom he perhaps did not even know in person, for al-Birzālī's accounts? What kind of contacts and interactions existed among the three?

As we have learned above, al-Birzālī used to be a student of al-Yūnīnī and his brother 'Alī[185] and, more significantly, the one who oversaw the copying

---

[180] Ms. Ahmet III 2907/e. 4, f. 49a.

[181] Ms. Ahmet III 2907/e. 4, f. 83a, 137a, 140a.

[182] Ms. Ahmet III 2907/e. 4, f. 122a, 124a.

[183] "Al-Birzālī," 524. Al-Birzālī's position in medieval Syrian historiography is reflected through the fact that his works—none of which is available in print so far (except for the *Mashyakhat Ibn Jamā'a*, which he edited)—were widely quoted by al-Dhahabī, Ibn Kathīr, Ibn Rāfi' al-Salām, al-'Aynī, and Ibn Ḥajar al-'Asqalānī, to name just a few. Ibn Taymīya, who honored al-Birzālī with the title of *mu'arrikh al-'aṣr* (the Historian of the Age), even claimed that it was al-Birzālī who aroused his interest in pursuing ḥadīth studies (*huwa alladhī ḥabbaba ilayya ṭalab al-ḥadīth*) as well as history; see 'Abbās al-'Azzāwī, "al-Birzālī," 522ff. In al-Subkī's assessment, al-Birzālī was one of the Big Four ḥadīth-ta'rīkh scholars and "there is not yet a fifth one in the field (*lā khāmisa lahum fī hādhihi al-ṣinā'a*) [to match them]"; see *Ṭabaqāt al-Shāfi'īya*, 6:246-47.

[184] Al-Birzālī's major biographical work, entitled *al-Mu'jam al-kabīr* (mentioned in al-'Asqalānī, *Durar*, 3:322), is lost today.

[185] Cf. above, 8, note 14. Al-Birzālī also mentions that he came to Ba'labakk "four times to study" with 'Alī and that 'Alī, in his turn, used to come to Damascus and al-Birzālī "attended every one of his sessions to listen to [ḥadīth transmitted by] him and benefited a lot from him" (*wa-fī kull nawba nasma'u minhu wa-nastafīdu minhu*). In A.H. 701, 'Alī came to Damascus twice, once in Ṣafar and again in Sha'bān, and al-Birzālī thus ordered his two sons to study ḥadīth with (*yasma'u*) 'Alī at the time; see *al-Muqtafā*, Ms. Ahmet III 2951, 2:55a-b.

of the first draft of al-Yūnīnī's *Dhayl.*[186] His access to al-Yūnīnī's information must have been direct.[187] It thus appears likely that some of al-Birzālī's accounts, especially those concerning the Ḥanbalī community in Ba'labakk, were derived originally from al-Yūnīnī. A case in point is the biography of 'Alī, al-Yūnīnī's brother. A comparison of al-Birzālī's version[188] with the one attributed to al-Yūnīnī shows clearly that the two texts are actually identical.[189] It is unlikely that al-Yūnīnī should take al-Birzālī as the source for his own brother's biography. What is certain, on the other hand, is that some of al-Birzālī's materials were quoted in al-Jazarī's *Ḥawādith*, upon which al-Yūnīnī, in his turn, relied heavily for his later draft of the *Dhayl* (Version II). We thus have a cycle here: al-Birzālī used some of al-Yūnīnī's accounts in the first place, and then handed those, along with his own stories, down to al-Jazarī; and al-Jazarī used these materials, together with others, to complete his *Ḥawādith* which impressed al-Yūnīnī so much that he decided to use this well-written chronicle as a major reference to finish his own *Dhayl.*

In addition, al-Birzālī's association with numerous medieval Arabic writings can be explained by the fact that he, as Franz Rosenthal has also noted, was well-known at the time in Damascus for his good handwriting.[190] A large number of the works of his fellow 'ulamā' were thus made famous through his "promotion": his hand-written copying (*takhṭīṭ*) or editing (*takhrīj*).[191]

[186] This copy (Ms. Bodleian Pococke 132) was made in the year 709/1309 and therefore the second part, which was to reach the year A.H. 711, had at the time not yet been completed.

[187] There is no direct evidence to attest to such an assertion; however, al-Yūnīnī's father and brother as sources are clearly acknowledged by al-Birzālī in his *al-Muqtafā*; cf. Ms. Ahmet III 2951, 1:21a, 273a, 274a; 2:90a, 123a, 129a, 333a.

[188] See Ms. Ahmet III 2951, 2:55a-56a; his account is so meticulous and detailed as to have surprised the modern editor of Ibn Mufliḥ's *al-Maqṣid* (Riyadh, 1990) who wrote a note that "he (i.e., al-Birzālī) related the information about 'Alī in such a surprisingly detailed way (*bi-tafṣīl gharīb*) the like of which we have not seen often in any medieval *rijāl*-works"; *al-Maqṣid*, 2:260, note 1.

[189] Al-Birzālī's account was quoted in Ibn al-'Imād, *Shadharāt*, 6:3-4. There are some scribal errors in the manuscript; e.g., the name of Sharaf al-Dīn Abū al-Ḥusayn 'Alī ibn . . . is missing (Ms. Ahmet III 2951, 55a). Al-Yūnīnī's version is in *Dhayl*, the present edition, 260.

[190] See "al-Birzālī," *EI*[2].

[191] For instance, Ibn Jamā'a's (d. 733/1332-33) famous *Mashyakha* is known as having been "edited" by al-Birzālī (*takhrīj al-shaykh . . . al-Birzālī*); see the title page of Ms. Istanbul, Süleymaniye, Musalla Medresesi 32 (reproduced in the 1988 Beirut edition, ed. Muwaffaq ibn 'Abd Allāh). A random bibliographical survey reveals that a sizable amount of medieval Arabic works were circulated in copies written by al-Birzālī:

1) *Fawā'id ḥisān* by Aḥmad ibn Muḥammad al-Iṣbahānī (d. 576/1180), Ms. Damascus, al-'Umarīya (*Catalog*, 136);

Both al-Yūnīnī's *Dhayl* and al-Jazarī's *Ḥawādith* should be included in this large body of literature as well. Al-Birzālī's stamp was so deeply marked on these two works[192] that one may wonder whether the insertion of al-Jazarī's collection into al-Yūnīnī's "third volume" of the *Dhayl* and the probable misattribution of the "fourth volume" of the text may somehow be due to al-Birzālī's involvement. After all, al-Birzālī was the only person among the three to have personally known the other two and to have lived long enough to oversee the copying and circulation of their works.

What we can gather from the above textual evidence and source criticism is that al-Birzālī is the most important source for the years from A.H. 695 to the end in al-Jazarī's *Ḥawādith* which, in turn, constitutes the textual basis for the second part of the *Dhayl* (A.H. 690-711) attributed to al-Yūnīnī. Al-Birzālī's role in shaping and transmitting the *Dhayl* and the *Ḥawādith* may be described as that of an editor, a source, and a transmitter.

---

3) *Qaṣīda mīmīya* by 'Alam al-Dīn al-Qāsim ibn Aḥmad al-Andalusī (d. 661/1262-63), Ms. Damascus, al-'Umarīya (*Catalog*, 424);

4) *Muntakhab min Kitāb al-arba'īn fī sha'b* (*shu'ab*?) *al-dīn* by 'Alī ibn al-Ḥasan al-Saffār (fl. A.H. sixth century), Ms. Damascus, al-'Umarīya (*Catalog*, 654).

In addition, al-Birzālī's autograph, entitled *al-Muntaqā min Kitāb al-bukhalā'*, an anthology of selections from al-Khaṭīb al-Baghdādī's *Kitāb al-bukhalā'*, is now preserved in Princeton (Mach 4322). The manuscript was dated on Ṣafar 25, A.H. 736, in Damascus; see Mach, *Catalogue*, 370-71. According to al-Munajjid, a copy of Abū Shāma's *Mukh- taṣar Ta'rīkh Dimashq* (Yahuda 430 [Mach 4619]) was copied by al-Birzālī as well; see al-Munajjid, *Mu'jam al-mu'arrikhīn*, 101; also Mach, *Catalogue*, 397 (which does not give such information).

[192] With regard to al-Birzālī's role in circulating al-Jazarī's works, there is evidence that al-Birzālī was plausibly al-Jazarī's editor as well: on the colophon of a fragmentary manuscript (Ms. Istanbul, Köprülü 1037; Şeşen, *Catalogue*, 1:530) of al-Jazarī's *Ta'rīkh* (covering the years from A.H. 726 on) there is a biography of the author (*tarjamat al-mu'allif*) by al-Birzālī. The colophon claims that the biography was copied directly from al-Birzālī's autograph made in the year A.H. 739; that is to say, al-Birzālī was possibly the one who oversaw the copying of al-Jazarī's work and added a postscript to the manuscript.

CHAPTER FOUR

THE *DHAYL* AND EARLY MAMLUK SYRIAN HISTORIOGRAPHY: THE MAKING OF A MODEL

The relationship between al-Yūnīnī, al-Jazarī, and al-Birzālī forms one of the most fascinating episodes in early Mamluk historiography. Instead of certain conclusions, there is an abundance of observations and hypotheses. In this connection, the present study of al-Yūnīnī's *Dhayl* serves not only as a prolegomenon to a critical edition, but has also tried to shed light on other contemporary Syrian historical writings. This is particularly true in the cases of al-Jazarī and al-Birzālī, for the former's *Ḥawādith* has survived only in part, and largely in the *Dhayl*, while the latter's works have fared even worse: of his *ta'rīkh* writings, only one work, entitled *al-Muqtafā*, has come down to us in a unique, but badly preserved, manuscript (Ms. Istanbul, Ahmet III 2951/1, 2). As it turns out, *al-Muqtafā* is quite different from the works of al-Yūnīnī and al-Jazarī and does not contain al-Birzālī's own accounts which had been used heavily by al-Jazarī and, through al-Jazarī, by al-Yūnīnī. As our above analysis has proved, the *Dhayl* ascribed to al-Yūnīnī in its current form is, in many ways, the best text among the contemporary Syrian historical writings that has survived to cover the period in question. Moreover, with regard to the complex textual relationship in which it was involved, it can be described more accurately as "a Damascus chronicle as witnessed and recorded by a group of Syrian historians."

To claim that there was a kind of "teamwork" among the three Syrian historians may be an unwarranted exaggeration. The fact, as the above study has demonstrated, shows that they often voluntarily quoted, or edited, each other's works, that their writings are similar in content and form and, therefore, could easily be confused with one another, etc., and this strongly suggests the existence of a common practice of borrowing rough material from one another and co-operation among the Syrian authors who might be inclined to consider historical facts as common knowledge for everybody. Our modern concern with original authorship and plagiarism was perhaps not theirs.[1] It

[1] In this connection, Michael Chamberlain's recent study of the common practice among Damascene 'ulamā' in copying or editing each other's works out of the desire for

also points to the development of a generally accepted and commonly followed *model* of historical writing at Damascus that displays some very interesting new elements which had not previously been seen in medieval Muslim historiography. These include the combination of chronicle and biographical dictionary within an annalistic framework, the tendency of "*adab*ization" in historical writing with the inclusion of a vast amount of poetry, anecdotes, and other *adab* material, and the increasing influence of colloquial language.

We must keep in mind that these three Syrian historians not only had a profound impact on early Mamluk historiography and ḥadīth studies but also had a strong influence upon their younger colleague al-Dhahabī, who was, as remarked above, in fact the editor of al-Yūnīnī's and al-Jazarī's chronicles, and under whose stewardship medieval Muslim historiography reached its full maturity. We know, too, that a number of important contemporary and later authors, e.g., Ibn al-Dawādārī, al-Nuwayrī, al-Maqrīzī (d. 845/1442), al-'Aynī (d. 855/1451), and Ibn Taghrībirdī (d. 874/1470), relied mainly on them for the history of Syria, and some of these later historians were evidently influenced by their method. A better understanding of the interaction and relationship among them will, therefore, enrich our knowledge of medieval Muslim ḥadīth and *ta'rīkh* scholarship considerably.

1. *Ta'rīkh* as Biographical Dictionary

The significance of this "Syrian school" for medieval Muslim Arabic historiography does not confine itself to the originality of the information its representative authors provided but extends to technical matters that constitute the *form*, or *model*, of their writing. Much previous research on early Mamluk historiography has concentrated on the historicity of the sources and their relatedness; relatively little work has addressed the development of forms of historical writing during this period which were crucial to the later evolution of pre-modern Muslim historiography.[2] Results from the present study of al-Yūnīnī's text and its relationship to those of al-Jazarī and al-Birzālī thus al-

ifāda (mutual benefit [from each other's knowledge]), *baraka* (blessings), or *ḥubb* or *maḥabba* (love) is very inspiring; see Chamberlain, 79, 111-13, 118, note 74, 135, note 164, 144.

[2] The studies that deal extensively with the subject are Haarmann, *Quellenstudien*, 119-200; "Auflösung und Bewahrung," 46-60; Radtke, *Weltgeschichte*, 139-205 (general discussion of the themes, genres and types in Mamluk historiography) and 206-360 (a case study of Sibṭ Ibn al-Jawzī and Ibn al-Dawādārī's works).

low us to sketch the overall technical development in historical writing under this "Syrian school" as follows:[3]

Inspired by Sibṭ Ibn al-Jawzī's *Mir'āt al-zamān fī ta'rīkh al-a'yān*, al-Yūnīnī undertook to continue his own chronicle. His work is distinguished by its Syrian-centered contents as well as by its form: a combination of history, biographical dictionary,[4] and literary anthology. In doing so, al-Yūnīnī took over Sibṭ Ibn al-Jawzī's format of *ta'rīkh* writing which consisted of a presentation in strict annalistic form in two clearly divided sections: one for events (*ḥawādith*) and the other for obituaries-biographies (*wafayāt*). The extensive treatment of learned persons' biographies, especially those of the prominent ḥadīth transmitters, including their literary products, in a *ta'rīkh* work is, to my knowledge, the innovation of Sibṭ Ibn al-Jawzī's grandfather, Ibn al-Jawzī (d. 597/1200).[5] Sibṭ Ibn al-Jawzī polished and improved the format which, in turn, greatly inspired al-Yūnīnī.

It is true that theoretically the *ḥawādith* and *wafayāt* sections are supposed to enjoy an equal share in the overall composition; in Sibṭ Ibn al-Jawzī's work, however, the obituary section in fact constitutes, as the title itself suggests (*Mir'āt al-zamān fī ta'rīkh al-a'yān*, The Mirror of the Ages with Regard to the Biographies of the Dignitaries), the major part of the chronicle and it always seems to overshadow the event section. This feature was incorporated in al-Yūnīnī's *Dhayl*, inasmuch as sometimes the obituary of a mi-

---

[3] A summary of modern scholarship on the "Syrian school" of historical writing is found in Humphreys, *Islamic history*, 240-41.

[4] For modern scholarship on medieval Arabic biographical writing, see Rosenthal, *Historiography*, 100-6; Young, "Arabic biographical writing," 168-87; al-Qāḍī, "Biographical dictionaries," 93-122; and Khalidi, *Arabic Historical Thought*, 204-10. All these studies focus mainly on biographical dictionaries as well as individual biographies in monograph form, passing over in silence the subject of biographical writing within chronicles.

[5] The structure of *al-Muntaẓam fī ta'rīkh al-mulk wa-al-umam* by Ibn al-Jawzī has been thoroughly studied by Joseph Somogyi; see "The *Kitāb al-muntaẓam* of Ibn al-Jauzī," and "The *Ta'rīkh al-islām* of adh-Dhahabī," especially 817-19. Cahen was of the opinion that it was the "first example of a type which must subsequently have been widely produced . . . consisting of an addition to the events of each year of obituary notes on deceased celebrities"; however, the work lacks coherent organization and is believed somewhat botched and unfinished; see "History and historians," 218. A quick look at the *al-Muntaẓam* reveals that the basic outline for Sibṭ Ibn al-Jawzī's later writing was already established by the grandfather, and these include the clearly divided *ḥawādith* section, headed by the phrase *fa-min al-ḥawādith*, and *wafayāt* section, with the headline *dhikr man tuwuffiya*, that contains detailed obituaries with lengthy quotations of the deceased persons' literary work, especially poetry.

nor learned man, along with his literary output, would exceed a report on a Mamluk battle or an affair of state in terms of detail and length. And among these learned men, great ḥadīth transmitters' lives and achievements are always being highlighted; information about a person's involvement in ḥadīth transmission has constantly been singled out as one of the most important aspects in his intellectual life. Al-Yūnīnī's format must have inspired al-Jazarī, who, in his turn, contributed to this endeavor a well-researched, better-organized, and handsomely presented work, the *Ḥawādith al-zamān wa-anbā'uhu wa-wafayāt al-akābir min abnā'ihi* (Events of the Ages and Biographies of Leading Dignitaries). It is apparent that al-Jazarī had carefully studied al-Yūnīnī's work, perhaps its first draft, and heavily borrowed the accounts it contained for the earlier parts of his own work. His chronicle was well received by the Damascene learned community as well as by al-Yūnīnī, who would decide to revise his own work by quoting al-Jazarī's accounts and, more importantly, reproducing and further smoothing his format.

This kind of interactive effort did not, of course, take a one-way direction. Al-Jazarī also intensively relied on al-Birzālī for all kinds of information. A prominent ḥadīth professor and historian in Damascus, al-Birzālī had studied under and learned a great deal from the two Yūnīnī brothers. Al-Birzālī's role in this group can be, as already remarked above, depicted as a bridge between al-Yūnīnī and al-Jazarī. Al-Birzālī received and transmitted al-Yūnīnī's first draft of the *Dhayl,* provided various kinds of information to al-Jazarī, and perhaps also supervised, though it seems with less skill, the final version of both al-Jazarī's and al-Yūnīnī's works and caused some confusion and conflation between the two.

We have reason to believe that al-Birzālī's vast collection of information, including poetry, was originally written down in some form of monograph, and this may be in the same basic format as that seen in al-Yūnīnī's and al-Jazarī's works: a combination of *ta'rīkh,* biographical dictionary and literary anthology in two equally divided event and obituary sections.[6] Some such monograph, now lost, must have been available to al-Jazarī for quotation.

Curiously, however, the only extant historical work by al-Birzālī, the *al-Muqtafā*, does not contain materials which were used by al-Jazarī and, by extension, by al-Yūnīnī; but it exhibits a new approach to *ta'rīkh*. Al-Birzālī abandoned the customary form of equally divided event and obituary sections

---

[6] Al-Munajjid has pointed out that a manuscript wrongly attributed to al-Birzālī is actually al-Jazarī's work; cf. Little, *Introduction*, 47, note 1. This incident is instructive in suggesting that al-Birzālī's history work (other than *al-Muqtafā*) may be very similar to that of al-Jazarī.

and combined the two indiscriminately into one strictly annalistic form based on a monthly chronological order. A comparison of the *Dhayl*, and more accurately, the sections known to make up the "Jazarī-Yūnīnī tradition," with al-Birzālī's own work *al-Muqtafā*, a continuation of Abū Shāma's *Dhayl 'alā al-Rawḍatayn*,[7] shows that there are certain basic differences between the two. First of all, there is no longer in *al-Muqtafā* any division into *ḥawādith* and *wafayāt* sections for each year as is the case in al-Yūnīnī's and al-Jazarī's works. Instead, as Little puts it:

> It is the most strictly chronological in format, being divided not just into years but into months as well; furthermore, obituaries of obscure scholars and functionaries are interwoven day by day.[8]

The second difference is that all literary products by the deceased scholars, with poetry foremost among them, are no longer included in the chronicle, although al-Birzālī himself was one of the major sources for the poetry quoted by al-Jazarī and al-Yūnīnī. Since al-Birzālī's *al-Muqtafā* was completed later than al-Yūnīnī's and al-Jazarī's works,[9] these differences would seem to indicate that al-Birzālī attempted to develop a new format for *ta'rīkh* writing,[10] an attempt that apparently had not been so successful.[11] His ex-

---

[7] *Al-Muqtafā li-Ta'rīkh al-shaykh al-imām al-'ālim Shihāb al-Dīn Abī Shāma*, Ms. Istanbul, Ahmet III 2951/1, 2. I wish to thank Giuseppe Scattolin, of Cairo for helping me obtain a microfilm of the manuscript.

[8] *Introduction*, 47.

[9] As a rule, al-Birzālī usually does not name his sources in *al-Muqtafā*; however, sometimes he indicates that he checked with al-Jazarī's work (Ms. Ahmet III 2951, 2:264a), or that his source of certain stories was 'Alī, al-Yūnīnī's brother (Ms. Ahmet III 2951, 1:21a, 273b, 274a), and Amīr Najm al-Dīn Ibn al-Miḥaffadār (Ms. Ahmet III 2951, 2:242a).

[10] Little has pointed out that the "very lack of organization and discrimination" in al-Birzālī's *al-Muqtafā* "reveals an inability or disinclination to discern or assign importance to events"; see *Introduction*, 52. This may be the reason behind the unpopularity, and thus obscurity, of al-Birzālī's *al-Muqtafā* among medieval and modern scholars.

[11] Aside from the *Muqtafā*, al-Birzālī is said to have written another history book which was identified by al-Ṣafadī as *Ta'rīkh al-shaykh 'Alam al-Dīn al-Birzālī*; the work is believed to be lost today; see Little, "al-Ṣafadī," 201. However, according to 'Abbās al-'Azzāwī, the *Muqtafā* was also known by the name of *Ta'rīkh al-Birzālī*; see "al-Birzālī," 523. I have come across references to four manuscripts bearing the title of *Ta'rīkh al-Birzālī*:

1) Ms. Gotha, Möll. 268 (Pertsch 1728);

2) Ms. Gotha, Möll. 530 (Pertsch 1569);

3) *Al-Muntakhab min Ta'rīkh 'Alam al-Dīn al-Birzālī*, Ms. Berlin, Sprenger 61 (Ahlwardt 9449);

periment does not seem to have gained much approval, not even from his own student al-Dhahabī, whose monumental work of *Ta'rīkh al-Islām wa-wafayāt* (or *ṭabaqāt*) *al-mashāhīr wa-al-a'lām* (The History of Islam and the Obituaries of Famous Learned Persons) demonstrates, as the title itself clearly claims, precisely a continuation of al-Yūnīnī's and al-Jazarī's form of combined events and obituaries within a chronological framework. Like other branches of Ḥanbalī learning, this method of *ta'rīkh* writing was transferred from Baghdad to Damascus: it was started by the Ḥanbalī Ibn al-Jawzī of Baghdad, transmitted through his grandson Sibṭ Ibn al-Jawzī of Damascus, and was eventually polished in the hands of the Ḥanbalīs al-Yūnīnī, of Ba'labakk, and al-Jazarī, of Damascus.

In this connection, it is generally held by modern scholarship that in the long history of ḥadīth and of the various sciences which evolved from it, *ta'rīkh* being one of them, "two ages of intensity may be distinguished," in Tarif Khalidi's assessment:

> the first in the 3rd-5th/9th-11th centuries, when *Hadith* was classified and edited, and second in the 8th-9th/14th-15th centuries, when the great Mamluk biographical dictionaries of *Hadith* transmitters and related topics were completed.[12]

One of the leading figures of this genre, i.e., al-Dhahabī, was influenced tremendously by al-Yūnīnī's, al-Jazarī's, and al-Birzālī's treatment of biographies of ḥadīth transmitters and other 'ulamā' elite. And in this respect, we do see that a commonly accepted model used by al-Yūnīnī, al-Jazarī and, most likely, al-Birzālī, has been followed later, not only in Damascus but also in Cairo. In this regard, it might be safe to say that al-Dhahabī and other later Mamluk compilers of great biographical dictionaries stand high upon the shoulders of the Syrian ḥadīth scholars and historians under discussion.[13]

---

4) *Ta'rīkh mukhtaṣar lil-mi'a al-sābi'a wa-mā ba'dahā*, ascribed to al-Birzālī, Berlin, We. 288 (Ahlwardt 9448).

Among these, 3) and 4) share the identical colophon that claims to be a continuation (*Dhayl*) of Abū Shāma's chronicle made by al-Birzālī. More research is needed.

[12] *Arabic Historical Thought*, 17.

[13] Al-Dhahabī's new textual device as opposed to that of his Damascene predecessors is seen in his arrangement of *ṭabaqāt*, in that he first listed all the names of the deceased persons at the head of each year's text, but the detailed biographies would be grouped alphabetically and presented in *ṭabaqāt*, i.e., every 10 years as one *ṭabaqa*; also cf. Somogyi, "The *Ta'rīkh al-islām* of adh-Dhahabī," especially 830-31, 846-48.

2. *Ta'rīkh* as Anthology of *Adab*

Another remarkable phenomenon in the overall content of the *Dhayl* is the vast amount of poetry it contains, a literary corpus that has drawn very little attention in modern Mamluk historiographic scholarship. A total of approximately 2,200 poems are found in the voluminous *Dhayl*,[14] the longest among them being an elegy to al-Ḥusayn, the Prophet's grandson, which contains 1,165 lines (in 233 *takhmīs*, or quinary stanzas),[15] while the shortest ones comprise merely a single line.

At first glance, one's impression is that these numerous poems seem to have been disproportionally put together, inasmuch as the vast majority of this gigantic poetic corpus is obviously *not* part of the historical narrative line. For instance, only 63 poems, that is, less than four percent of the total number of verses, occur in the *ḥawādith* sections and are directly related to describing, or commenting on, the "events" of the chronicle *per se*; given that some of these are *madīḥ*s, i.e., panegyric poems in honor of a sultan or a viceroy,[16] the actual number of such narrative verses[17] is even less. In contrast, the entire text of the *Dhayl*, mainly that of its *wafayāt* sections, is re-

[14] My calculation yields 2,117 poems. This figure is of course a preliminary one; it only covers the major available manuscripts as well as the published parts.

[15] *Dhayl*, 3:341-83; by Muwaffaq al-Dīn 'Abd Allāh who died in A.H. 677. It is obvious that biographies of the famous Shī'ī 'ulamā' and poems of Shī'ī sentiments were generally not excluded from the *Dhayl*.

[16] *Dhayl*, 1:465 68 (A.H. 659, a eulogy of al-Malik al-Nāṣir Ṣalāḥ al-Dīn Yūsuf); the present edition, 3-4 (A.H. 697, a tribute to sultan Lājīn); Ms. Ahmet III 2907/e. 4, ff. 165a-166b (in honor of al-Malik al-Nāṣir Muḥammad ibn Qalāwūn).

[17] E.g., poems describing the Baghdad earthquake; the Medina fire that destroyed the Prophet's Mosque (A.H. 654, *Dhayl*, 1:9-11); the Mongols' siege of Damascus (A.H. 658, *Dhayl*, 1:359-67); a flood that caused severe damage to Damascus (A.H. 669, *Dhayl*, 2:451); the Mamluk-Mongol campaign on the Euphrates (A.H. 671, *Dhayl*, 3:3-4); the sultan of Delhi Malik Ghiyāth al-Dīn's battle with the Mongol troops (A.H. 675, *Dhayl*, 3:178f); a fire at Damascus (A.H. 681, *Dhayl*, 4:146); the Mamluk conquest of al-Marqab (A.H. 684, *Dhayl*, 4:356); an incident that involved a Christian's love affair with a Muslim woman and the viceroy Amīr Ḥusām al-Dīn's decree to burn the man to death and cut the woman's nose off (A.H. 687, *Dhayl*, M:1); the Mamluk victory over the Mongols at Tripoli (A.H. 688, *Dhayl*, M:20-26); the Mamluk conquest of the Qal'at al-Rūm (A.H. 691, *Dhayl*, Ms. Landberg 139, ff. 56b-59b); a confrontation between the Christians and Muslims (A.H. 693, *Dhayl*, Ms. Landberg 139, f. 103a); the Mongol occupation of Damascus (A.H. 699, *Dhayl*, the present edition, 112-13, 132-35); the dress code imposed upon the non-Muslim communities in Cairo and Damascus (A.H. 700, *Dhayl*, the present edition, 222); sultan al-Malik al-Nāṣir's triumphal return to Cairo after combat with the Mongols (A.H. 702, *Dhayl*, Ms. Ahmet III 2907/e. 4, f. 8a, 9a-11a), among others.

plete with quotations from every level of traditional Arabic prosodic discourse—from *qaṣīda* (formal classical ode) to a variety of *qiṭ'a* (occasional verse) whose genres range from *madīḥ* (panegyric),[18] *waṣf* (descriptive poetry),[19] *rithā'* (elegy),[20] to *ghazal* (love poetry),[21] *hijā'* (satire),[22] *khamrīyāt* (drinking songs),[23] and *zuhdīyāt* (ascetic poetry)[24]—as well as parodies of the generic characteristics of many of them. For instance, a certain number of

---

[18] *Dhayl*, 1:38, 39, 62, 63-64, 74, 75, 82, 94, 96, 98, 100, 101, 108, 112, 113, 115, 118, 119, 120, 121, 133, 136, 168, 171, 178, 179, 189, 192, 201, 202, 209, 211, 215, 216, 241, 247, 250, 258-328 (in praise of the Prophet, made up of 28 poems whose ending rhymes include the entire Arabic alphabet, from *hamza* to *yā'*), 335, 340, 345, 346, 428, 501, 504, 545; 2:75, 82, 115, 143, 144, 145, 168, 205, 219, 244, 251, 254, 255, 256, 258, 259, 287, 288, 306, 307, 308, 356, 441, 475, 481; 3:9, 17, 45, 62, 63, 71, 74, 138, 140, 143, 155, 156, 158, 163, 219, 227, 312, 386, 406, 414, 426, 441; 4:66, 67, 69, 73, 113, 116, 166, 193, 198, 223, 282, 286, 309, 324; M:3, 10, 12, 65, 71, 72, 74; Ms. Landberg 139, f. 61b, 66b, 68b, 78a, 79a, 86b, 88a, 123b, 138b, 140a, 144a, b, 145a, 165b, 166b, 168b, 169a; the present edition, 19, 27, 30, 81, 95, 137, 167, 168, 169, 173; Ms. Ahmet III 2907/e. 4, f. 15b, 16b, 17b, 33a, 112a, 117b, 118a, 129b, 141a, 142b, 144b, 150b, 154b, 168a, 173a, b, 175b, 176a, 179b, 185a, 211a, b, 225a, 230b, 231a, 233b. The Prophet, the sultans, Mamluk amīrs, and prominent 'ulamā' are the subjects of these poems.

[19] *Dhayl*, 1:66, 68, 69, 78, 84, 102, 105, 108, 111, 114, 123, 142, 149, 189, 190, 191, 198, 199, 211, 244, 247, 333, 386, 412, 418, 419, 423, 428, 476; 2:10, 11, 12, 25, 26, 132, 185, 212, 229, 256, 259, 260, 270, 357, 426, 458, 459, 483, 489; 3:12, 20, 35, 104, 109, 126, 127, 134, 138, 143, 152, 199, 200, 202, 204, 205, 303; 4:65, 127, 278, 279; M:42, 97, 103; Ms. Landberg 139, f. 67a, 68b, 70a, 85b, 88a, 123b, 149a, b, 150a; the present edition, 142, 161, 183, 185, 200, 201, 222, 229; Ms. Ahmet III 2907/e. 4, f. 18b, 21b, 54a, 63b, 66a, 93b, 203a, 234a. The most frequent theme is the description of Syrian cities or towns; other topics range from Mamluk-Mongol battles, historical sites, wedding scenes, flowers, birds, to daily items or handicrafts.

[20] These are usually attached to the corresponding obituaries in the *wafayāt* sections, and are too numerous to count.

[21] The *ghazal* poems constitute the overwhelming share of the poetic corpus in the *Dhayl*, and are too numerous to count.

[22] *Dhayl*, 1:22, 117, 161, 200, 204, 205, 212, 213; 2:419; 3:68, 69, 70, 72, 157, 279; 4:64, 70, 72, 73, 207, 227, 290, 291, 317, 323; M:37, 78; Ms. Landberg 139, f. 62a; the present edition, 84, 112 (on the Mongols' collaborators in Damascus who were nicknamed al-Ḥinn and al-Binn, in *ḥawādith* section, A.H. 699; for al-Ḥinn and al-Binn, also cf. Graf, 97-99, 135-38, 140-42), 143, 156, 172, 210 (on the dress code imposed upon non-Muslims in Damascus, in *ḥawādith* section, A.H. 700), 235; Ms. Ahmet III 2907/e. 4, f. 102b, 118b, 147a, 233a.

[23] *Dhayl*, 1:21, 36, 105, 114(?), 159, 204, 213, 216, 217, 223, 416, 423, 425, 428, 432, 475, 520, 521, 522; 2:246, 281, 282, 283, 465, 482, 483; 3:200, 226, 323, 326, 329, 330, 331, 332, 335, 336, 415, 416, 417; Ms. Landberg 139, f. 65b, 147b; the present edition, 31, 32, 44, 45, 186, 199, 222, 223; Ms. Ahmet III 2907/e. 4, f. 129b.

[24] *Dhayl*, 1:156, 525; 2:12, 167(?), 245, 248, 263, 482; Ms. Landberg 139, f. 62b, 111a; the present edition, 239; Ms. Ahmet III 2907/e. 4, f. 206a.

poems follow the traditional *hijā'* (satire) genre but their purpose appears to be simply a desire to make fun of something "spectacular." For instance, Muḥyī al-Dīn 'Abd Allāh al-Sa'dī, a chancery clerk (*kātib al-inshā'*) in Egypt, once wrote a poem about a person on whose nose was a birthmark (*fī anfihi khāll*); the poet must have enjoyed doing this so much that he eventually came up with nine more poems on the same subject; and all of them are, with an equal enthusiasm, recorded verbatim in the *Dhayl.*[25] A large number of poems contain *alghāz* (sing. *lughz*, riddles), apparently to be exchanged among the learned elite as a popular pastime.[26] In connection with the traditional *ghazal* genre, a considerable number are the so-called *al-ghulāmīyāt*, i.e., poems celebrating the love of male youth, long a favorite topic in classical Arabic poetry since the late Umayyad period and evidently very much alive during the Mamluk period.[27] Ṣūfī poetry also occupies a noticeable portion of the anthology.[28]

The methodology of arranging poetry and other *adab* materials in al-Yūnīnī's and al-Jazarī's texts appears to follow a "radiating circle" centered around the obituaries-biographies of the learned persons, and so the anthology would include:

1) Poems written by the *ṣāḥib al-tarjama*, i.e., the person to whom an obituary-biography is devoted;

---

[25] Ms. Landberg 139, ff. 86b-87b.

[26] Many of these "riddle" poems were part of the correspondence exchanged among the 'ulamā' (*kutiba fī ṣadr kitāb* . . .); the replies by the addressees, also in verse, were usually collected by the later anthologists as well; examples can be seen in *Dhayl*, 1:99-100, 179-80, 182-83, 190, 425, 473; 2:248, 266, 268, 271, 275, 280, 392, 393-94; 3:41, 71, 98, 99, 100, 101, 395; 4:159; M:97; Ms. Landberg 139, f. 85b, 88a, b; Ms. Ahmet III 2907/e. 4, f. 131b, 133b-135a, 176a, b, 183b-184b, 185b.

[27] *Dhayl*, 1:14, 102, 103, 386, 413, 417, 418, 422, 482; 2:25, 37-38; 3:21, 91, 92, 163, 200, 201, 314; 4:128, 134, 154, 276; M:40; Ms. Landberg 139, f. 65b, 85a, b, 86a, 87b, 110b, 116a, 138b, 151a; the present edition, 21, 24, 25, 83, 139-40, 159, 173, 261; Ms. Ahmet III 2907/e. 4, f. 21a, 32a, 209b, 233a. By and large, nearly all these poems are introduced by a phrase of *qāla fī malīḥ* (on a handsome man), or *qāla fī ghulām* (on a young man), or, occasionally, *qāla fī mamlūk ḥasan al-manẓar* (on a good-looking Mamluk; 3:163), *qāla fī azraq al-'aynayn* (on a man with blue eyes; Ms. Landberg 139, f. 87b); these do not include numerous *ghazal* poems addressed to male lovers. According to G. Schoeler, the term *ghulāmīyāt* refers to "a kind of transitional form, . . . addressed to girls who dress and look like boys"; see "Bashshār b. Burd, Abū 'l-'Atāhiyah and Abū Nuwās," 297. I am not sure whether this is the case in a Mamluk context. For homosexual love in classical Arabic poetry in general, cf. Hamori, "Love poetry (*ghazal*)," 208. For handsomeness being one of the factors in a Mamluk's success in his career, cf. Levanoni, *Turning Point*, 34, 38, 40.

[28] E.g., *Dhayl*, 1:247; the present edition, 153-55; Ms. Ahmet III 2907/e. 4, f. 108a, etc.

2) poems on the *ṣāḥib al-tarjama*, written, for the most part, by his fellow 'ulamā';

3) poems transmitted on the authority of the *ṣāḥib al-tarjama*; those occasionally even include some poems by pre-Mamluk-era Arab poets which had not been widely circulated; for instance, three poems attributed to Abū Nuwās were recorded because they were "not included in his *dīwān*;"[29]

4) poems by, or about, or transmitted on the authority of, the people who were associated with the *ṣāḥib al-tarjama*;

5) poems that are relevant, in topic or certain artistic aspects, etc., to the poems cited. In this respect, one can easily sense the role played by the author of the *Dhayl* not only as a historian but also very much as a literary critic. An abundance of evidence in the *Dhayl* shows that al-Yūnīnī was not always content with simply citing the poem but would very often make some comment such as "this is better (or worse) than so-and-so's poem on the same subject," or "the idea (or the image, or the rhetorical device) of this poem was actually taken from (*ma'khūdh min*) so-and-so's writing," or "the meter of these lines is the same as (*'alā wazn*) so-and-so's such-and-such poem," and so forth;[30] and then we are provided with full or partial citations from the examples in question.

Concerning this "radiating circle" of poetry quotations, a question is naturally to be raised: How could any text, not to mention a chronicle, possibly exhaust all the verses of an era well known for its quantities of *adab* output? In other words: What were al-Yūnīnī's, and al-Jazarī's, criteria in selecting materials for an anthology like this?

The very pervasiveness of these verses, and the fact that in the second revised draft al-Yūnīnī put even more verses into the text while cutting the historical narrative,[31] have led us to believe that they are an essential and deliberate part of the author's composition strategy. A careful reader would realize that al-Yūnīnī's preface to the *Dhayl* was actually written, for the most part,

[29] *Dhayl*, the present edition, 223. The three poems were transmitted on the authority of the *ṣāḥib al-tarjama* Shams al-Dīn Ibrāhīm al-Jazarī al-Kutubī, well known by the name of Ibn Sham'ūn (d. A.H. 700). Of the three, only one is found in several editions of the *Dīwān Abī Nuwās* with slight variations; see *Dīwān Abī Nuwās* (ed. Aḥmad 'Abd al-Majīd al-Ghazzālī, Cairo, 1953), 221; *Dīwān Abī Nuwās* (editor unknown, Beirut, 1962), 372; *Dīwān Abī Nuwās, Khamrīyāt Abī Nuwās* (ed. 'Alī Najīb 'Aṭawī, Beirut, 1986), 1:234. None of the three poems are found in Ewald Wagner's edition (3 vols., Wiesbaden, 1958; vol. 4, ed. G. Schoeler, 1972).

[30] E.g., *Dhayl*, 1:84, 188-89, 199, 219-20, 418, 501, 503, 518; 2:249, 250, 307, 356, 418; 3:153, 225; 4:136.

[31] Cf. above, 30-31.

in *maqāmāt*-like rhyming prose,[32] which sets the tone for a chronicle whose goal seems as much to entertain the reader with a variety of high quality belles-lettres writing, especially verse, as to report historical facts. A close reading of the poetry collected in the *Dhayl* has shown that as far as the classical Arabic formula is concerned, the criterion for compiling an anthology remains largely unchanged in the early Mamluk period. In discussing late 'Abbasid *adab* anthologies, Seeger Adrianus Bonebakker observed that in them,

> verse and prose, anecdote and aphorism were drawn from the fields of political, ethical and religious thought, and from many other areas of learning as these multiplied, the anthologists' aim always being to stress the curious, the entertaining and, above all, *the linguistic and literary* merits of the material presented (italic mine).[33]

Exactly the same can be said about the *adab* materials in al-Yūnīnī and al-Jazarī's works. Al-Yūnīnī and al-Jazarī made it clear that most of the poems were chosen because they were "good poems" (*naẓm jayyid*, or *naẓm ḥasan*), that is, it was strictly an "art for art's sake" enterprise, so to speak. This commitment to pure aesthetic values is so strong that sometimes al-Yūnīnī would insist on citing some well-written but perhaps indecent erotic poem written by some "virtuous" (*fāḍil*) religious scholar, acknowledging that doing so might damage the shaykh's image as a religious figure.[34] It is very interesting to observe such cases in which the consideration of pure artistic value outweighs the concern for moral responsibility.

A modern historian seriously looking for the "hard data" of historical facts might find the bulky poetry section in al-Yūnīnī's and al-Jazarī's texts very much of a distraction. A literature scholar, on the other hand, may be ready to conclude that the poems preserved there are, for the most part, mediocre, to say the least. By today's standards, these 14th-century Syrian historians' editing skills seem inconsistent and unbalanced, in that the *adab* materials are not always carefully used for maximum effect, not to mention the cases in which *adab* items or groups are inserted in obviously wrong contexts. However, one does sense that there was some kind of editorial planning, and many

---

[32] *Dhayl*, 1:1-2.

[33] "*Adab* and the concept of belles-lettres," 27-28.

[34] E.g., *Dhayl*, 4:418-19; introducing 'Abd al-Majīd Ibn Abī al-Faraj al-Rūdhrāwī's (d. A.H. 667) erotica, al-Yūnīnī stated that the shaykh "wrote beautiful poems although they may undermine his moral excellence" (*la-hu naẓm jayyid lākinnahu munḥaṭṭ faḍīlatihi*).

of the poems quoted were indeed the ones appreciated or admired by al-Jazarī and al-Yūnīnī and were popular in *their* time. And after all, one is certainly able to gain insight into, to borrow Haarmann's words, "*ṣuwar min adab al-'aṣr*,"[35] that is, an overview of the literary output at the time, which represents exactly one of the major goals set forth by these Syrian historians-anthologists.

On the other hand, a careful researcher may elicit from some of the poems and other *adab* materials valuable sources for the study of the history, especially the social and intellectual history, of the period. In this respect, certain genres of poems deserve our special attention. One is the so-called *badīh*, poems inspired by, or commenting on, some unexpected events or occasions which were not included in the *ḥawādith* sections. The term *badīh* derives from the phrase most often used to introduce the poems, as in *qāla badīhan*, . . . or *qāla irtijālan*. . . . We find, for instance, poems describing a particular Mamluk-Mongol combat,[36] or a particular confiscation of some Mamluk amīrs' or 'ulamā's household properties (*al-ḥawṭa*),[37] or of granting land tenure (*iqṭā'*) to an amīr,[38] and so forth. Another genre is the poems written as part of the correspondence among the 'ulamā' and Mamluk amīrs on the occasion of the addressee's promotion to a prestigious position, or receiving a robe of honor (*khil'a*) from the sultan, or the like.[39] Some of these poems not only give us a tracing of the actual events of the personnel changes and power struggles that took place in the Mamluk political arenas in Cairo and Damascus but also shed light on the psyche of the era. For instance, Nāṣir al-Dīn Aḥmad ibn Muḥammad (d. 683/1284), the qāḍī of Alexandria, first wrote a poem congratulating one Zayn al-Dīn Ibn Abī al-Faraj for his promotion to the judgeship (*al-ḥukm*) in Alexandria, but soon wrote a poem ridiculing the same person after he was dismissed from the position.[40] In this connection, noteworthy also are the satirical poems depicting the atmosphere of jealousy and animosity among the Cairene and Damascene 'ulamā' over seeking attention, power or influence or simply over material benefits. We thus find an Egyptian 'ālim Mu'īn al-Dīn 'Uthmān Ibn Sa'īd's (d. 680/1281) bitter complaint about the decision made by the chief judge in Cairo to cut off all the

[35] Cf. the headings in Ibn al-Dawādārī, *Kanz al-durar* (ed. Ulrich Haarmann), 9:384.
[36] *Dhayl*, 1:141, 142; 2:212; 4:222; Ms. Ahmet III 2907/e. 4, f. 22a.
[37] *Dhayl*, 4:197.
[38] *Dhayl*, 2:215.
[39] *Dhayl*, 4:320; Ms. Landberg 139, 167a; Ms. Ahmet III 2907/e. 4, f. 167b, 223a.
[40] *Dhayl*, 4:207.

poets' pensions (*qaṭ' arzāq al-shu'arā' min al-ṣadaqāt*);[41] we also see several lampoons attacking a promotion which was widely perceived as a typical case of nepotism in Cairo.[42]

Curiously, many of the features of the above-discussed model shared by al-Yūnīnī and his Syrian colleagues are generally not seen in the writings of their contemporary Egyptian counterparts such as Baybars al-Manṣūrī (d. 725 /1325), al-Nuwayrī, and to a certain extent, Ibn al-Dawādārī. Among these Egyptian writings, al-Nuwayrī's *Nihāyat al-arab* belongs to an entirely different genre, the so-called *adab al-kātib,* i.e., manual for Mamluk civic clerks, wherein "history" (*al-ta'rīkh*) occupies a position as the fifth, and last, "art" (*al-fann*), while poetry is the second.[43] As for the major Egyptian chronicles in the strict sense of the word, such as Baybars al-Manṣūrī's *Zubdat al-fikra*[44] and his *al-Tuḥfa al-Mulūkīya*,[45] and the famous "anonymous" Chronicle,[46] all of these evidently followed what may be called "the Ibn al-Athīr model,"[47] i.e., basically an annalistic form following that of al-Ṭabarī, with a few obituaries of rulers or statesmen attached at the end of the text for each year. Among these, Ibn al-Dawādārī's *Kanz al-durar* is a work that has attracted much attention from modern scholarship for it is believed to represent a trend in Mamluk historical writing. Ibn al-Dawādārī's work is also of special interest for our current study because it is believed to have taken al-Jazarī's chronicle as model. However, Ibn al-Dawādārī's work still reveals more similarities related to the contemporary Egyptian chronicles than to al-Jazarī's writing. The brief obituary notes in these Egyptian chronicles usually contain neither biographical details nor literary products, nor were they intended to focus on prominent ḥadīth transmitters. Moreover, poetry occupies a very limited portion of these Egyptian chronicles, if it is not totally absent. More interestingly, unlike the Syrian works, poetry in Egyptian chronicles, to a large extent, *is* part of the historical narrative line.[48] A vast

---

[41] *Dhayl*, 4:290-91.

[42] *Dhayl*, 4:312.

[43] *Nihāyat al-arab fī funūn al-adab*, 31 vols. (Cairo, 1923-1990).

[44] The work is still in manuscript form (Ms. British Museum Or. add. 23325); cf. Little, *Introduction*, 4-10. A partial edition (covering 693/1293-698/1298) is presented in Elham, (Arabic text) 1-30.

[45] *Kitāb al-tuḥfa al-mulūkīya fī al-dawla al-Turkīya* (Cairo, 1987).

[46] Ed. K. V. Zetterstéen (Leiden, 1919).

[47] 'Izz al-Dīn Ibn al-Athīr, *Kāmil fī al-ta'rīkh*, 14 vols., ed. C. J. Tornberg (Beirut, 1965-1967 [reprint]).

[48] I have sampled a portion (i.e., A.H. 654-711, the years that have been covered by the *Dhayl*) from the *Kanz al-durar*, the only Egyptian chronicle that contains a substantial amount of poetry, to compare it with the *Dhayl*. It shows that less than 15 poems

majority of these poems are the *madīḥs* (panegyrics) by Egyptian court clerks, dedicated to the Mamluk sultans,[49] an enthusiasm certainly not shared by Syrian 'ulamā' under whose editorship the lengthy panegyrics selected are instead the ones dedicated to the Prophet and his family, great ḥadīth transmitters, and prominent learned men of the era. In other words, while the heroes of the Egyptian chronicles and manuals were the Mamluk sultans and statesmen, the attention of Syrian historians was focused on their fellow *a'yān*, the notable learned men, especially those prominent ḥadīth scholars.

3. Language and Style

The increasing use of colloquial in the language of historical narrative during the Mamluk period has long been noticed by modern scholars. It is commonly believed that Ibn al-Dawādārī, a non-Arab Mamluk resident in Cairo, was perhaps one of the leading representatives of this trend which later reached its fullest expression in the historical romances by such popular authors as Ibn Iyās (d. 930/1524) and others.[50] However, very little attention has been given to Ibn al-Dawādārī's model, the Syrian historian al-Jazarī who, in his turn, had been profoundly influenced by al-Yūnīnī. If we firmly believe that al-Jazarī was indeed the model for Ibn al-Dawādārī, it is clear that we may well consider that this trend had actually started in Syria, at the hands of al-Jazarī, al-Yūnīnī, and al-Birzālī, among others.

A quick look at the language and style of the *Dhayl* shows that attempts have been made by the author(s) to introduce to the classical Arabic language some variants with a provincial vernacular twist. If the pervasive use of Syr-

are attached to the few obituaries at the end of some years (8:37, 181-82, 226, 279, 287, 360); the only exception being A.H. 698 (8:384-99), where a collection of approximately 27 poems by prominent 'ulamā' are recorded. However, the compiler, Ibn al-Dawādārī, apparently hesitated to call the authors of these poems "poets," "because their status was much higher than poets" (*yajlū an yuṭlaqa 'alayhim ism al-shu'arā' li-kawn maḥallihim ya'lū 'alā al-shu'arā'*); see *Kanz al-durar*, 8:483. This perhaps reveals a certain attitude held by Egyptian Mamluks towards poetry and related fields of Arabic culture. For the poems as part of the narrative, see *Kanz al-durar*, 8:48, 51, 57-59, 91, 111, 157, 212, 214, 215-18, 270, 292-99, 315-20, 321, 334-38, 353, 357, 371-72; 9:6, 30-31, 78, 86, 87, 89-100, 122-24, 142, 165-66, 174, 190-95, 205, 208, 235, 236, 240-41.

[49] E.g., *Kanz al-durar*, 8:215-18, 292-99, 315-20, 334-38; 9:89-100, among others.

[50] Cf. Haarmann, *Quellenstudien*, 175-80; a summary of modern scholars' discussion of this topic, especially Ibn al-Dawādārī's language and style, is found in Haarmaan's review of Radtke's *Weltgeschichte*, *JAOS* 115/1 (1995): 134-35.

ian expressions such as *êš* (what's that? why's that?), among others, found in the less formal *dialogue quotations*[51] is more or less reminiscent of an early tradition that can be traced back to al-Ṭabarī's time, what is new here are the numerous cases, within the formal *narrative line*, that deviate from classical written Arabic norms. For instance, the nominative masculine plural ending *ūna* has totally disappeared and is replaced by the colloquial *īna*, so *al-muqaddamūna* is always given as *al-muqaddamīna*, and so forth;[52] the ending *nūn* in an imperfect indicative plural verb is dropped altogether, so we have *yukhbirū* instead of *yukhbirūna*, and so forth;[53] and most amazingly, this irregularity even went so far as to have extended to the ḥadīths transmitted in the *Dhayl*; in one case the Prophet Muḥammad uttered a colloquial *yakūnū* instead of the normal form of *yakūnūna*.[54]

Along with this linguistic awareness of popularizing historical writing was a composition strategy of devoting some, though not substantial, space to wondrous anecdotes and exotic stories whose linguistic vehicle appears to be largely the vernacular. We thus find in the *Dhayl* a considerable number of the so-called *amr 'ajīb* (wondrous stories) or *'ajā'ib* (unusual phenomena) full of vernacular vocabulary and colloquial syntax. For instance, a report from Cairo about sultan Lājīn's recovering from a horse riding incident is narrated with some Cairene colloquial syntax;[55] and an erotic story, narrated in largely colloquial language, of an adulterous affair is followed by a tale that involved two homosexual men and a caliph who was at first stunned and then became sympathetic;[56] a dramatized anecdote about a missing gold treasury is reported at length and the characters' conversations convey a full measure of colloquial peculiarities;[57] and there is always an ardent interest in bizarre stories: in one case al-Yūnīnī reported the "disappearing" of two mountains in Hama, Syria, in the year 700/1301;[58] and in another case, a hailstorm that had hit Hama in the year 701/1302 was reported because "the hailstones took various shapes of animals . . . and man-like," and the language of the narra-

---

[51] E.g., *Dhayl*, 1:139; 2:61, 62, 67, 69; 3:58, 205.

[52] For details, see "Description of the Manuscripts and the Edition," volume two of the present study.

[53] For details, see "Description of the Manuscripts and the Edition," volume two of the present study.

[54] *Dhayl*, the present edition, 178.

[55] *Dhayl*, the present edition, 3.

[56] *Dhayl*, the present edition, 170-72.

[57] *Dhayl*, the present edition, 194-95.

[58] *Dhayl*, the present edition, 221.

tive remains largely in the colloquial form in which it was first reported, perhaps orally.[59]

Considerable numbers of examples notwithstanding, the introduction of entertaining stories in a *ta'rīkh* work and the use of colloquial language in its narrative were, to be sure, still far from being fully developed in al-Yūnīnī's and al-Jazarī's works, compared to later Egyptian chronicles and historical romances, such as those of Ibn al-Dawādārī and Ibn Iyās,[60] wherein such a "literarized" trend, to use Haarmann's term again,[61] appears to be quite overwhelming. If we bear in mind these Syrian authors' painstaking efforts to record high *adab* materials (their poetry selections in classical form being *par excellence*), it is thus not surprising to see a struggle, with regard to language and style, in the *Dhayl* and in al-Jazarī's *Ḥawādith*, to balance the need to make a readable chronicle and the intention to preserve an anthology of high culture *adab*.

The form, or model, cherished by al-Yūnīnī and al-Jazarī went on to become customary in Syrian historical writing in the later Mamluk period and eventually contributed its share, largely through al-Dhahabī's introduction, to the later development of medieval Arabic historiography in the Islamic East.[62] The labor of generations of these Syrian historians, sometimes in an unknowingly collaborative effort as our present case shows, has delivered an explicit message concerning *ta'rīkh* writing: a good *ta'rīkh* (history) is not only a record of factual events, but a register of Muslim religious learning (with ḥadīth and related sciences, especially *rijāl* biographical materials, at its crown), and a selective anthology of Arabic cultural and literary heritage.

---

[59] *Dhayl*, the present edition, 254.

[60] E.g., his *Badā'i' al-zuhūr fī waqā'i' al-duhūr* (Cairo and Wiesbaden, 1960-1963). For a discussion of the so-called "Cairo narrative style" represented by Ibn Iyās and others, see Petry, *Twilight of Majesty*, 7, 9-10. A book-length analysis of Ibn Iyās's language and style in the *Badā'i'* is found in A. M. al-Baqarī, *Ibn Iyās wa-al-lugha min kitābihi Badā'i' al-zuhūr fī waqā'i' al-duhūr* (Alexandria, 1989).

[61] *JAOS* 115/1 (1995): 134.

[62] Cf. William Brinner's discussion of the method of historical writing in Muḥammad ibn Muḥammad Ibn Ṣaṣrā's (fl. ca. 800/1298) time; *Damascus*, xv; also Humphreys, *Islamic History*, 240-41.

CHAPTER FIVE

TRANSLATION: THE *DHAYL* AND AL-JAZARĪ'S *ḤAWĀDITH*[1]

1. The Year of 697/1297-98

The appointment of Jalāl al-Dīn Aḥmad to the office of judge: In this year, on the eve of Wednesday, Ṣafar 10 (November 27, 1297), Qāḍī Jalāl al-Dīn,[2] the son of the [Ḥanafī] chief judge Qāḍī Ḥusām al-Dīn,[3] rode in procession in Damascus, wearing the robe of the judge—white *jubba*-gown and *ṭarḥa*-headgear. People came over to congratulate him. He was addressed by [the title of] chief judge (*qāḍī al-quḍāt)*. Poems were recited in his presence. Panegyrists presented their tributes to him as well. The diploma of his appointment arrived about one week later and was announced several times.

Lājīn's recovery from an accidental injury: In this year, on Friday, Ṣafar 19 (December 6, 1297), a postman came from Cairo to Damascus to report sultan [Lājīn]'s complete recovery from his fall, the weakness of his leg, and his impaired movement, as well as the recovery of his hand and his ability to ride after that in full health. People rejoiced greatly [over the news]. Orders were issued that the markets were to be decorated; drums were to be beaten at the gates of amīrs' [residences] as well as on the [Damascus] Citadel. The decoration remained seven days.

[The story of the sultan's accident is as follows:] Shortly after the sultan had arrested Amīr Qarā-Sunqur al-Manṣūrī,[4] his horse bucked and threw him

---

[1] Following is a translation of the Arabic text of the *Dhayl*, edited here and collated with the *Ḥawādith* (which ends at A.H. 698). All *ḥawādith* (events) sections are translated fully, while biographies and poems in *wafayāt* (obituaries) sections are omitted. The original paragraphing of the Arabic text—each paragraph in the text being usually marked by the phrase of *wa-fīhā* (and in this year . . .)—is generally respected. All the headlines, in italic, are my own. Parentheses ( ) indicate the translator's explanatory notes while square brackets [ ] include conjectural additions to the original text. The list of rulers, officers, and dignitaries that precedes each year's events is to be found in Appendix III.

[2] Aḥmad ibn al-Ḥasan al-Rāzī, died in 745/1344. He was named the Ḥanafī chief judge later in the year A.H. 700. For his biography, see Ibn Kathīr, *Bidāya*, 14:16.

[3] Al-Ḥasan al-Rāzī. The Arabic text above (the present edition, 2) mentions that the father was "then in Egypt and his son acted as his deputy in Damascus, but without independent authority."

[4] Shams al-Dīn, then the viceroy (*nā'ib*), died in 728/1328. For his biography, see al-'Asqalānī, *Durar*, 3:330. His arrest took place in the middle of Dhū al-Qa'da of A.H.

down (*taqanṭara bihi*). His entire body was smashed, his hand and some ribs were broken. Sayf al-Dīn Mengü-Temür[5] kept being informed about his situation and was in despair [of his recovery]; and so was [the sultan] himself. [However,] God blessed him with recovery and he was able to ride [again] whereupon greater Cairo and Damascus, as well as the whole sultanate, were opulently decorated.

Amīr Shams al-Dīn Sunqur[6] related[7] that when sultan al-Malik al-Manṣūr rode out shortly after his illness, people prayed for him. They, especially the city vagabonds (*al-ḥarāfisha*),[8] broke into joyful cheers. One of the vagabonds cried out to the sultan, "Oh, you the golden dick![9] By God, let me see your hand!" The sultan thus waved to the man while holding a whip that simultaneously hit the neck of the horse he was riding [and hence the accident]. His riding parade [after the recovery] was held on Ṣafar 11 (November 28, 1297). [However,] in his *Chronicle*, Shams al-Dīn Muḥammad, known as Ibn al-Bayyā'a,[10] recorded the following: during a polo game, sultan al-Malik al-Manṣūr's stallion stumbled and threw him [to the ground]. A poem was written on this occasion:

You are full of strength, charity and knowledge;
A horse is therefore unable to bear all of this!

As a result, the sultan withdrew [from public view] for one year. When the day of Ṣafar 11 came, in the morning, he looked as wonderful as the bright moon, as strong as a savage lion, and as vigorous as the vast ocean. What a day! Glorious Islam augmented further glory and all the Muslims were in

---

696 (September 4, 1297); cf. al-Nuwayrī (Elham's edition), 63; Ibn al-Dawādārī, *Kanz*, 8:369; Zettersteen, 33; and al-Maqrīzī, *Sulūk*, 1:829.

[5] A Ḥusāmī Mamluk (after Lājīn's *laqab* Ḥusām al-Dīn), he was the main rival of the Ashrafī amīrs (after Ashraf al-Khalīl). Little is known about his life. For historical background on the conflicts between the Manṣūrīs (Qalāwūn's Mamluks; also called Ḥusāmīs) vs. Ashrafīs during the time, see Irwin, *Early Mamluk Sultanate*, 85-104.

[6] Unidentified. He was perhaps Shams al-Dīn Sunqur al-Kamālī, then a chamberlain at Cairo; see Ibn al-Dawādārī, *Kanz*, 8:index.

[7] Al-Jazarī has "related to me."

[8] On the *ḥarāfisha*, see Brinner, "The Significance of the Harafish and their Sultan," *JESHO* 6 (1963): 190-215; also Lapidus, *Muslim Cities*, 177-83.

[9] The text has *qaḍīb al-dhahab* the reference to which is not clear to me; the only term that is close to it is *qaḍīb al-mulk*, which is, according to al-Qalqashandī, a rod wrapped in a *golden* cover inlayed with gems, to be held by the caliph (but not the sultan, LG) in public appearance; see *QI*, 3:468; also al-Maqrīzī, *al-Khiṭaṭ*, 178, 188, 234. On the other hand, in Egyptian colloquial, *qaḍīb* is used specifically to refer to male genitals. Given the circumstances, such an expression was perhaps not as offensive as it might sound. I thank Farouk Mustafa for a comment on this usage.

[10] The author and the work are not identified.

massive rapture. They all burst into cheers, and the hearts and eyes of the Faithful became more firm and enlightened.

The full moon shines after the joy
Has risen, thanks to the Merciful One!
Blessing flows over Egypt and Syria,
And good omens spread in the whole realm.
The universe is cheerful, all creation is smiling,
The blessing is unceasing and the Faith restored.[11]
Among the people, everybody smiles joyfully
And all of them are delighted with God's feat.
Why not? The enemy of the Faith was defeated[12] *by God.*
And al-Malik al-Manṣūr was victorious.[13]
Polytheism died out of fear as monotheism claimed,
"Here is Ḥusām al-Dīn: the Sword of Islam."[14]

Good news spread all over the country (i.e., Syria). Damascus and other Syrian cities were decorated [in celebration]. The happiness of the Syrians was beyond description. God's mercy be upon him (i.e., the sultan) and us!

Qibjāq's appointment to the office of viceroy at Damascus: In this year, the beginning of Rabīʿ I (December 17, 1297), an edict signed by the sultan was delivered to the viceroy of Damascus Sayf al-Dīn Qibjāq at the afternoon prayer, appointing him to the office of viceroy, for the nomination had not hitherto been confirmed in writing. He was granted the robe of the office and a horse.[15] He took the oath in front of the qāḍīs and amīrs in the evening. The following morning, Thursday, Rabīʿ I (December 18, 1297), he rode [with the procession], wearing the robe of the office, and kissed the doorstep of the Postern Gate (*bāb al-sirr*) [at the Damascus Citadel], in honor of the sultanate.

The promotion of Kamāl al-Dīn ʿAbd al-Raḥmān to the chair at the Grand Mosque, Damascus: In this year, on Rabīʿ II 5 (January 20, 1298), Qāḍī

---

[11] The text has *majbūr*, which seems to be more fitting than al-Jazarī's *maḥbūr* (to be pleased). Ibn al-Dawādārī also has *maḥbūr*; see *Kanz*, 8:372. I thank Franz Rosenthal for a comment on the meanings of these two words.

[12] Perhaps referring to al-Malik al-ʿĀdil Kitbughā's being overthrown; see Irwin, *Early Mamluk Sultanate*, 90-93.

[13] This is a pun between the name of al-Manṣūr and the word *manṣūr* (victorious).

[14] This is a pun between Lājīn's title Ḥusām al-Dīn and the word "sword of Islam." Ibn al-Bayyāʿa's quotation ends here. The same account, notwithstanding slight differences, is also found in Ibn al-Dawādārī, *Kanz*, 8:371-2; Zetterstéen, 44; al-Maqrīzī, *Sulūk*, 1:829-30.

[15] The order of the two sentences here has been reversed so the context would be clearer.

Kamāl al-Dīn 'Abd al-Raḥmān,[16] the son of chief judge Muḥyī al-Dīn [Yaḥyā] Ibn al-Zakī,[17] was named to chair a teaching session (*ḥalqat taṣdīr*)[18] at the Grand Mosque of Damascus with 100 *dirhams* [of salary].[19] He delivered an inaugural lecture[20] in the Ṣaḥāba Miḥrāb[21] in the presence of chief judge Imām al-Dīn,[22] head preacher Badr al-Dīn Ibn Jamā'a,[23] and a large number of learned people and scholars.

The Friday prayer began to be held at Mt. Qāsiyūn: In this year, the Friday prayer began to be held[24] in the Mu'aẓẓamīya Madrasa[25] at the foot of Mt. Qāsiyūn. The chair (*mudarris*) of the madrasa Shams al-Dīn Ibn Sharaf al-Dīn al-Ghurafī (al-'Uzafī?)[26] delivered a congregational sermon on Rabī' II 10 (January 25, 1298). This was [made possible] through the mediation of shaykh Ṣāḥib Shihāb al-Dīn al-Ḥanafī[27] and an agreement by al-Malik al-Awḥad Ibn al-Ẓāhir,[28] the principal (*nāẓir*) of the madrasa.

A purge in Cairo and Damascus: In this year, on Rabī' II 6 (January 21, 1298), the sultan arrested Amīr Badr al-Dīn Baysarī[29] in Egypt. All of his property in Damascus was confiscated as well.

In this year, on Rabī' II 27 (February 11, 1298),[30] Ṣāḥib Fakhr al-Dīn ['Umar] Ibn al-Khalīlī[31] assumed the office of vizier of Egypt, a post he had

---

[16] Unidentified.

[17] He died in 668/1270; he was the Shāfi'ī judge in 650/1260; see Pouzet, *Damas*, 413.

[18] For the word *taṣdīr* see Makdisi, *The Rise of Colleges*, 203-6.

[19] This is most likely the monthly payment. On salaries paid to professors in madrasas at Damascus during the time, see Lapidus, *Muslim Cities*, 138-39; Makdisi, *The Rise of Colleges*, 164ff.

[20] The text has *jalasa . . . wa-alqā darsan*; for the significance of the inaugural lecture (usually mentioned as *jalasa al-tadrīs*), see Makdisi, *The Rise of Colleges*, 154-59.

[21] One of the major *miḥrābs* in the Mosque; see 'A. Bahanasī, "al-Miḥrāb al-awwal fī al-Masjid al-Umawī," 13.

[22] 'Umar ibn 'Abd al-Raḥmān ibn 'Umar ibn Aḥmad al-Qazwīnī, died 699/1299, then the Shāfi'ī chief judge at Damascus. For his biography, see al-Subkī, *Ṭabaqāt al-Shāfi'īya*, 5:31; Ibn Kathīr, *Bidāya*, 13:335, 349.

[23] Abū 'Abd Allāh Muḥammad, died in 733/1333. He was also known as *khaṭīb al-balad* (the head preacher of Damascus). For his biography and his Shāfi'ī family in Syria and Egypt, see "Ibn Djamā'a," *EI²*, by K. S. Salibi; also al-Birzālī, *Mashyakhat qāḍī al-quḍāt . . . Ibn Jamā'a*, Introduction, 11-36 (by Muwaffaq ibn 'Abd Allāh ibn 'Abd al-Qādir).

[24] The text has *tajaddada* (al-Jazarī has *uḥditha*), also meaning "resumed." According to al-Nuwayrī, however, the Friday congregational prayer had never been held there before (see Elham's edition, 67). And for unknown reasons, al-Jazarī mentions this event twice in his *Ḥawādith al-zamān*; see Ms. Paris, 241a and 245a.

[25] A Ḥanafī madrasa; see Pouzet, *Damas*, index.

[26] Unidentified.

[27] Unidentified.

[28] Ibn al-Ẓāhir is added after al-Jazarī.

[29] One of sultan Baybars' closest *khushdāsh*-comrades. He died in prison in 1298; see Ibn al-Dawādārī, *Kanz*, 9:13; Irwin, *Early Mamluk Sultanate*, 87-88.

previously held. He [soon] confiscated the assets of the accomplices of al-A'sar[32] and then tracked them down and issued orders to escort al-A'sar's majordomo (*ustād-dār*) [Badr al-Dīn Kīkaldī][33] from Damascus [to Cairo] after confiscating his property.

Mamluk expansion into Cilicia (Armenia): In this year, on Thursday, Jumādā II 5 (March 20, 1298), Amīr 'Alam al-Dīn Sanjar al-Dawādārī,[34] together with Kurtay[35] and a detachment of Egyptian troops, arrived in Damascus en route to Aleppo. People came out to welcome them and watch their processions (*aṭlāb*). The people of Damascus held celebrations in honor of Amīr 'Alam al-Dīn al-Dawādārī. Many dignitaries went out to al-Kiswa[36] to pay tribute to him.[37] He set off from Damascus on Monday, Jumādā II 8 (March 23, 1298). And then they (i.e., the Egyptian troops) joined the Damascene troops, who had gone to Aleppo previously, and the troops from Hims, the coastal Ṣafad, and Tripoli. The ruler of Hama[38] was then at Aleppo as well. Then the entire [joint] forces advanced from Aleppo towards the land of Cilicia (*Sīs*).

They arrived in the Cilician Gates (*dar-bandāt Sīs*)[39] on Thursday, Rajab 4 (April 17, 1298). Then on Sunday, Rajab 21 (May 4, 1298), news of the capture of Tall Ḥamdūn (Til Hamdoun)[40] and its citadel after a siege was announced by musical bands[41] in Damascus. And on Sunday morning, Ramaḍān

---

[30] Al-Jazarī has, "on the first day of Jumādā I . . . and the event is also said to have taken place on Rabī' II 27, God knows best!"

[31] He died in 711/1312. For his biography, see Ibn Taghrībirdī, *Manhal*, no. 1832; for his previous dismissal and Sunqur al-A'sar's taking over, see the event of A.H. 696 (Mss. Landberg 139 and Ahmet III 2907/e. 3); also al-Nuwayrī (Elham's edition), 62-63.

[32] Shams al-Dīn Sunqur al-A'sar, died in 709/1309. He was a favorite amīr of sultan al-Ashraf al-Khalīl; see Zetterstéen, 56-57; Irwin, *Early Mamluk Sultanate*, 80.

[33] His name is supplied by al-Jazarī. Al-Maqrīzī, however, gave the name as Sayf al-Dīn Kīkaldī; see *Sulūk*, 1:836.

[34] A veteran Syrian amīr; died in 699/1299. He used to be the commander of the Damascus Citadel (around A.H. 678); see Ibn al-Dawādārī, *Kanz*, 8:230 and index; 9:40. His obituary is not found in the *Dhayl*.

[35] Shams al-Dīn Aq-Sunqur. For his career, see al-Maqrīzī, *Sulūk*, 1:838; Elham, *Lāǧīn*, 112, 139, 202; Holt, *Syrian Prince*, 27. His name is given by Elham as Kurtuba and by Holt as Karīta.

[36] A suburb of Damascus; see Pouzet, *Damas*, index.

[37] The text has *dakhalū fī khidmatihi*; for the phrase *fī khidmatihi*, or *ilā khidmatihi*, meaning "to pay tribute to him, to salute him," see Dozy, *Supplément*.

[38] Al-Malik al-Muẓaffar Taqī al-Dīn Maḥmūd ibn Maḥmūd ibn Shādhī ibn Ayyūb; he ruled 683/1284-698/1299; see E. von Zambaur, *Manuel*, 99.

[39] As *dar-band Sīs* in other sources (al-Jazarī, Ms. Paris, 480; al-Maqrīzī, *Sulūk*, 1:83). For details, see Boase (ed.), *Cilician Kingdom*, 2; *Oxford Dictionary of Byzantium*, 464.

[40] Also known as Thila Hamtun/T'il Hamtun/Toprak/Toprakkale in Armenian sources; see Boase, *Cilician Kingdom*, 183-84. For the fortress of Tall Ḥamdūn, also see Edwards, *Fortifications of Cilicia*, 244-53.

[41] For the rendering of *duqqat al-bashā'ir*, see Brinner, *Damascus*, I:74, 97, 98.

12 (June 23, 1298), the news was announced for a second time, on account of the citadel of Tall Ḥamdūn, which was conquered on Wednesday, Ramaḍān 7 (June 18, 1298). A midday prayer was called out on the [Damascus] Citadel by the Khalīlīya Band (*nawbat al-Khalīlīya*).

In this year, on the day mentioned above,[42] news of the capture of the Mar'ash (Marash)[43] Citadel was announced by musical bands [at Damascus]. [It was announced also] that the [Mamluk] troops were besieging the citadel of Ḥumaymiṣ,[44] that Amīr 'Alam al-Dīn al-Dawādārī was hit by a rock on the leg and was incapable of riding thereby, that Amīr 'Alam al-Dīn Sanjar, [known as] Ṭuqṣubā al-Nāṣirī, was killed in the battle, and that a large number of amīrs were wounded and many soldiers killed. The citadel was taken by force indeed.

Lājīn's blame on Jāghān: In this year, on Sha'bān 10 (May 23, 1298), a postman came from Egypt to summon the finance agent (*al-mushidd*) Amīr Sayf al-Dīn Jāghān.[45] He set off on Monday, Sha'bān 14 (May 27, 1298) on the post route. The sultan blamed him for his abuses of the people of Damascus and intended to dismiss him from the post as a punishment. [At this point,] his *khushdāsh*-comrade Amīr Sayf al-Dīn Mengü-Temür came out to plead for him. After all of his *khushdāsh*-comrades guaranteed that he would never hurt any of God's creatures again, he was re-appointed to be the finance agent [of Damascus]. [The sultan] then awarded him the robe of the office and sent him back to Damascus. He left Cairo on the post route and arrived in Damascus on Tuesday, Ramaḍān 6 (June 12, 1298). He corrected previous deviations. His temper gradually calmed down and his tyranny diminished.

Al-Malik al-Mas'ūd's return from Constantinople: In this year, al-Malik al-Mas'ūd Najm al-Dīn Khiḍr,[46] the son of al-Malik al-Ẓāhir Rukn al-Dīn Baybars al-Ṣāliḥī, returned to Egypt from the land of al-Ashkurī (Laskaris).[47] He was received by the sultan in a grand procession and was

---

[42] This is a confusing statement; al-Jazarī's version has another event that took place on "Wednesday, Ramaḍān 29" inserted between the present paragraph and the preceding one. We do not know, therefore, which "day mentioned above" is referred to here. It is noted that Zetterstéen has the same confusing text as al-Yūnīnī.

[43] Also known as Germanica Maras; see Boase, *Cilician Kingdom*, 173; Edwards, *Fortifications of Cilicia*, index.

[44] In Armenian sources, it is called Hamus or Cardak; see Boase, *Cilician Kingdom*, 166; Edwards, *Fortifications of Cilicia*, 110-13; also Le Strange, *Palestine*, 543. Arabic sources, however, give it a diminutive form of Ḥumaymiṣ; cf. also al-Maqrīzī, *Sulūk*, 1:80; and al-Nuwayrī has Ḥumayṣ (Elham's edition, 72).

[45] For his career, see Ibn al-Dawādārī, *Kanz*, 8:index.

[46] He died in 708/1308. For his biography, see Ibn al-Dawādārī, *Kanz*, 9:160; Ibn Taghrībirdī, *Manhal*, no. 980.

[47] I.e., the Byzantine territory. For the Banī al-Ashkurī that ruled Constantinople, see *QI*, 8:43, 14:72; more bibliography is to be found in Thorau, *Baybars*, 122 and note 8.

warmly welcomed. He had been dispatched there by al-Malik al-Ashraf. He asked the sultan [Lājīn]'s permission to go on the pilgrimage and was granted permission. His arrival in Cairo was on Wednesday, Shawwāl 6 (July 17, 1298).[48]

Further Mamluk expansion into Cilicia (Armenia): In this year, on Tuesday evening, Dhū al-Qa'da 3 (August 12, 1298), a pigeon-post (*biṭāqa*) was delivered to the Damascus Citadel with the information about the capture of the Ḥumaymiṣ Citadel and the Nujayma[49] Citadel in Cilicia, Armenia, which were extremely strong and well fortified. So the news of the victory kept being announced by musical bands from the [Damascus] Citadel and in front of gates of amīrs' residences for seven days.

On Tuesday, Dhū al-Qa'da 10 (August 19, 1298), the envoy of the Cilician ruler[50] arrived in Damascus and on the same day journeyed on to Egypt. His mission was to request a truce agreement and the sultan's mercy. On Friday, Dhū al-Qa'da 13 (August 22, 1298), the viceroy issued orders to recruit soldiers, as usual, from all backgrounds to guard the citadels in Mar'ash, Tall Ḥamdūn, and Nujayma.[51] Citadel garrisons were thus recruited and all were well equipped.

Āqqūsh's promotion to amīr: In this year, Jamāl al-Dīn Āqqūsh al-Maṭrūḥī[52] was promoted to amīr. On Monday, Dhū al-Qa'da 9 (August 18, 1298), he rode in procession to announce his investiture.

Egyptian army's movement towards/from Aleppo: In this year, on Tuesday, Dhū al-Qa'da 17 (August 26, 1298),[53] en route to Aleppo, an Egyptian corps arrived in Damascus. It was made up of 3,000 cavalrymen and led by the *silāḥ-dār*[54] Amīr Sayf al-Dīn Baktimur al Ẓāhirī al Manṣūrī.[55] On Friday, Dhū al-Qa'da 20 (August 29, 1298), they continued the journey [to Aleppo].

---

[48] More details about his exile in the Byzantine territory are found in al-Nuwayrī (Elham's edition), 65; al-Maqrīzī, *Sulūk*, 1:831.

[49] The place has not been identified. I doubt it is a translation of an Armenian place name ("little star"?) rather than a transliteration.

[50] I.e., Het'um II, who ruled 1289-1301; see *Oxford Dictionary of Byzantium*, 926.

[51] Al-Jazarī has "and Ḥumaymiṣ."

[52] He died in 736/1335-36; an Ashrafī Mamluk, he was then the viceroy of Kerak. For his biography, see al-'Asqalānī, *Durar*, 1:423ff.

[53] Sauvaget, *al-Jazarī*, has "29 XI" (a misprint?) for the date.

[54] Persian, "armor bearer," a title of the Royal Mamluk regiment whose duties included carrying weapons (*silāḥ*) for the sultan or amīr during the war and supervising arms stores; see *Q2*, 182; also Ayalon, "Studies on the Structure of the Mamluk Army," part I, 214.

[55] He died in 703/1303; he was a mamluk of sultan al-Malik al-Ẓāhir Baybars and then al-Malik al-Manṣūr Qalāwūn. For his biography, see al-'Asqalānī, *Durar*, 2:16; also Irwin, *Early Mamluk Sultanate*, 85, 100-1.

In this year, the majordomo (*ustād-dār*) of the sultan, Amīr Ḥusām al-Dīn Lājīn[56] arrived [in Damascus] from Aleppo on the post route. He was on his way back to Egypt and was accompanied by Akhū-Ṣārūjā.[57]

A change of personnel in the Grand Mosque of Damascus: In this year, a change of personnel took place in the administration of the Grand Mosque of Damascus. The process continued during the middle of the month of Dhū al-Ḥijja (September, 1298). Shihāb al-Dīn Ibn al-Naḥḥās[58] was named to be the manager [of the Mosque], replacing 'Izz al-Dīn Ibn al-Zakī.

New appointment to the office of judge at Hama: In this year, the appointment of the preacher Muwaffaq al-Dīn al-Ḥamawī to the office of judge in Hama was delivered to Damascus on Tuesday, Dhū al-Ḥijja 17 (September 25, 1298). He was to succeed the late Qāḍī Jamāl al-Dīn Ibn Wāṣil. He left Damascus heading for the post in Hama on Saturday, Dhū al-Ḥijja 19 (September 27, 1298).[59]

The arrest of Aybak: In this year, news of the arrest of Amīr 'Izz al-Dīn Aybak al-Ḥamawī[60] in Egypt reached Damascus on Saturday, Dhū al-Ḥijja 26 (October 4, 1298). He used to be the viceroy of Damascus during al-Ashraf's reign. They confiscated all his fortunes [in Damascus]. It was said that a group of amīrs were arrested with him. Among them was Sunqur Shāh al-Ẓāhirī.[61] [This was] because of the exposure of their ulterior motives (*mūjib*) about seizing power.[62]

The lack of snow in Damascus: In this year, there was barely any snow in Damascus [and therefore its price soared].[63] Each *raṭl* was sold for one *dirham* in Ramaḍān, which was in June according to the Roman calendar. This price kept steady until the end of Shawwāl (the beginning of August, 1298). In Dhū al-Qa'da (August and September, 1298), snow was totally out of supply. Beer had been sold without snow until the following year, Rabī' I 7, December 13, when rain fell upon us by God's favor and mercy. Following the rain there was a snow fall. [However,] only four ounces of snow were

---

[56] For his career, see Ibn al-Dawādārī, *Kanz*, 9:index. He should not be confused with sultan Ḥusām al-Dīn Lājīn.

[57] Unidentified.

[58] His name is given by al-Jazarī as "Ibn Muḥyī al-Dīn Ibn al-Naḥḥās."

[59] Both manuscripts of al-Yūnīnī's version have "Dhū al-Ḥijja 14" which is obviously a mistake. The date of Dhū al-Ḥijja 19 is according to al-Jazarī.

[60] He died in 703/1303. For his biography, see al-'Asqalānī, *Durar*, 1:451f.

[61] For Sunqur Shāh's arrest with Aybak, cf. al-Maqrīzī, *Sulūk*, 1:829.

[62] This arrest is not mentioned in contemporary Egyptian sources (e.g., Ibn al-Dawādārī, *Kanz*, 8:370), which merely states that "there have been some clashes between the Manṣūrī and the Ashrafī Mamluks, . . ." namely, Mengü-Timür vs. Baysarī. A detailed account of this power struggle is found in al-Maqrīzī, *Sulūk*, 1:833ff.

[63] The content between the brackets is added after al-Jazarī.

found at [the market of] Damascus in the aftermath. They were sold to patients for five *dirhams*. So some [brokers][64] went to Tripoli searching [for snow] in the mountains. They found some old cisterns which had been left from the Frankish reign—and that was 20 years prior to the Muslim conquest of Tripoli—and which had never been opened since. They found in those cisterns blocks of ice and took them to Damascus and sold them at the price of 50 to 70 *dirhams* each *qinṭār*.[65] [However, the ice did not refrigerate the beer as well as the snow they used to have in Damascus did,][66] so beer sellers would put beer on rooftops at night, letting it cool and then took it down before sunrise. In this way beer was kept cold [and tasted good].[67]

In this year, springs, wells, and rivers in Damascus [all] dried up. The Thawrā river was merely two *shibrs*[68] knee-deep while the Baradā river ceased to reach Jisrayn.[69] Most farms in Damascus and the countryside *(al-ṣayyāfī)* and grain farms *(al-maqāṭī)* suffered damage. In the Ghūṭa area, most trees died. The price of flour soared. One sack of flour sold for 15 to 20 *dirhams*.[70]

The arrest of Ibn al-Ḥillī: In this year, Bahā' al-Dīn Ibn al-Ḥillī,[71] the army controller (*nāẓir al-juyūsh*) in Egypt, was arrested. His million-*dirham* fortune was confiscated. Later, Ṣāḥib 'Imād al-Dīn Muḥammad ibn Fakhr al-Dīn 'Alī Ibn al-Mundhir al-Ḥalabī, then the army controller in Syria, was called upon to take over Ibn al-Ḥillī's post in Egypt. His position in Damascus was filled by Ṣafī al-Dīn.[72]

Al-Malik al-Nāṣir's exile to Kerak: In this year, on Rabī' I 4 (December 20, 1297), al-Malik al-Nāṣir Nāṣir al-Dīn Muḥammad, the son of sultan al-Malik al-Manṣūr Sayf al-Dīn Qalāwūn al-Ṣāliḥī, arrived from Egypt to Kerak to stay there. He settled down and was attended to by Amīr Jamāl al-Dīn Āqqūsh,[73] a Manṣūrī majordomo.[74]

---

[64] Added after al-Jazarī.
[65] One *qinṭār* equals 100 *raṭl*s, or 256.4 g.
[66] Added after al-Jazarī.
[67] Added after al-Jazarī.
[68] *Shibr*, the span of a hand.
[69] "Two Bridges," a village in the Ghūṭa area, the suburb of Damascus; cf. Le Strange, *Lands*, 464.
[70] Al-Jazarī has "20 to 25 *dirhams*."
[71] Unidentified. The name is read by Sauvaget as "al-Jillī."
[72] For this event, cf. Ibn al-Dawādārī, *Kanz*, 8:371; Zetterstéen, 45. The event is described by al-Maqrīzī (*Sulūk*, 1:836f) as part of Mengü-Temür's plot. Ṣafī al-Dīn cannot be identified.
[73] He was then the viceroy at Kerak.
[74] For the young prince's exile at Kerak under the orders of Lājīn, cf. Ibn al-Dawādārī, *Kanz*, 8:371; al-Maqrīzī, *Sulūk*, 1:832-33.

The land redistribution in Egypt: In this year, on Saturday, Jumādā I 16 (March 1, 1298), the land redistribution (*al-rawk*) came into effect.[75] Amīrs began to be granted fief lands (*iqṭā'*), while the non-Mamluk *ḥalqa* troopers and all Egyptian soldiers received their fief-related allowance (*akhbāz*). It was an extremely foolish action. And it caused, as will be expounded below, the decline of the Egyptian army, especially the non-Mamluk *ḥalqa* troopers. On Monday, Rajab 8 (April 21, 1298), fief charters (*mithālāt*) were distributed among amīrs in order to divide the *rawk* portions on the basis of a pre-estimation. On Rajab 9 (April 22, 1298), fief charters were distributed among generals (*al-muqaddamīn*). On Rajab 10 (April 23, 1298), the then viceroy Amīr Sayf al-Dīn Mengü-Temür began to distribute charters upon the *ḥalqa* regiment, the Baḥrī regiment, and the Royal Mamluks as well as others. [Later] in the year A.H. 700 (1330-31), some clerks who served in the Egyptian army during that time related to me the following, "I worked for the bureau of the army (*dīwān al-jaysh*) in Egypt for 40 years. The land of Egypt," he continued, "used to be divided into 24 units (*qīrāṭ*): four of these were allotted to the sultan, from which he extracted the cost of his daily needs, expenses and the like; 10 were allotted to amīrs, for their allowances and bonuses; and the remaining 10 units were given to the *ḥalqa* regiment. [Nevertheless,]" he went on, "some people suggested to the sultan and Mengü-Temür that 10 or 11 units would be sufficient for the amīrs and [Mamluk] soldiers and the remaining nine units would be put for the use of (*yastakhdimu 'alayhā*) the [non-Mamluk] *ḥalqa* troopers at the same rate as that of [Mamluk] troops.[76] They then began to carry out this proposal and asked us and [other] clerks who were experts in this business to help. We thus allotted 10 units to amīrs and soldiers; one unit was added to those who suffered hardship; and nine units were left over. After the unexpected assassination of the sultan and Mengü-Temür, great concerns emerged among the amīrs with regard to that [portion of fief lands]. So each amīr was given one or two villages from these nine units. [However,] the army remained too weak to handle the management of peasants (*al-fallāḥīn*).[77] As a matter of

[75] For the so-called "Ḥusāmī *rawk*" of this year, also cf. al-Maqrīzī, *Sulūk*, 1:841, note 3. For the political and military background of this *rawk* and its impact on Lājīn's reform, see Poliak, *Feudalism*, 23-24; Ayalon, "Studies on the Structure of the Mamluk Army," part II, 451ff; Irwin, *Early Mamluk Sultanate*, 92-94.

[76] The text has *'alā miqdār al-jaysh*, the exact meaning of which is not very clear to me.

[77] I.e., "peasants living on the fief lands"; see Poliak, *Feudalism*, 19f; also Brinner, *Damascus*, 1:12, note 79.

fact, the reserved nine units were much better than the 11 units of the fief lands." God knows best.

Personnel changes in the office of finance in Egypt: In this year, Shams al-Dīn Shalḥūnah[78] assumed the post of finance agent (*shadd al-dawāwīn*) in Egypt, replacing Nāṣir al-Dīn Muḥammad al-Shaykhī. He remained in the post until Ramaḍān and was replaced by Ḥusām al-Dīn Ibn Bākhil.[79]

The annual rise of the Nile: The blessed Nile increased [on the scale of the Nilometer by] 17 cubits (*dhirā'*) and nine fingers (*iṣba'*) above [the old water level of] 18 cubits.[80]

The pilgrimage: In this year, the Damascene pilgrims were led by Amīr 'Izz al-Dīn Aybak al-Ṭawīl al-Manṣūrī,[81] and the Egyptian by Amīr Sayf al-Dīn Ṭughjī al-Ashrafī. The 'Abbāsid caliph al-Imām al-Ḥākim bi-amr Allāh Abū al-'Abbās Aḥmad went from Egypt on the pilgrimage with his sons, his entire family, and retinue. The sultan [Lājīn] gave him 700,000 *dirhams*. He was escorted by al-Malik al-Mas'ūd Najm al-Dīn Khiḍr ibn al-Malik al-Ẓāhir and, from Syria [onward], by Amīr Ḥusām al-Dīn Muhannā, the son of Amīr Sharaf al-Dīn 'Īsā ibn Amīr al-'Arab Muhannā,[82] and the qāḍī of the Syrian pilgrim caravan Jamāl al-Dīn al-Raḥbī al-Shāfi'ī.

2. The Year of 698/1298-99

The Mongol attacks on Syria and the preparation for war in Damascus: In this year, on Wednesday, Muḥarram 7 (October 15, 1298),[83] Amīr Jamāl al-Dīn Aqqūsh al-Afram[84] and Amīr Sayf al-Dīn Ḥamdān[85] arrived from Egypt to Syria on the post route. They carried with them the royal edict (*marsūm*) ordering the remaining Damascene troops, [under the command of] the vice-

[78] Unidentified.

[79] Unidentified.

[80] For the annual rise of the Nile in general, see Popper, *The Cairo Nilometer*, especially v-vii, (the scales of measurement in general), 69-73, 87-90, 191 (the plenitude), 102f. (the old water level and the additional increase), 195, Table 32 (the rise of the Nile in the year A.H. 697). The text *"intahat ziyādat al-Nīl . . . min thamāniyat 'ashar . . ."* makes it clear that the 17 cubits and nine fingers was an "additional increase" over the 18 cubits.

[81] Unidentified.

[82] For information on his career, see Ibn al-Dawādārī, *Kanz*, 9:42, 218-27.

[83] Sauvaget, *al-Jazarī*, 75, has 9.I for Muḥarram 7.

[84] He died in 736/1336, and was at this time the viceroy of Kerak. He was later appointed to be the viceroy of Damascus after Qibjāq's defection to the Mongols in 699/1299-1300. For his biography, see al-'Asqalānī, *Durar*, 1:423f; Irwin, *Early Mamluk Sultanate*, 98, 101-2, 105.

[85] Jamdān in al-Jazarī.

roy Grand Amīr Sayf al-Dīn Qibjāq[86] as well as the troops under Arjuwāsh, then the commander of the [Damascus] Citadel,[87] and some of the Baḥrī regiment to march out to battle. They thus joined together and marched forward. They thought that the Mongols were already advancing towards Syria; and the viceroy [Qibjāq] was therefore on the alert and made himself and the remaining troops prepared. On the eve of Wednesday, Muḥarram 14 (October 22, 1298), the viceroy Amīr Sayf al-Dīn Qibjāq made his way to the Akhḍar Square.[88] At dawn, he paraded on horseback. The qāḍīs came at night to say farewell. His guard of honor (*ṭulb*), all wearing their finest clothes and best weapons, marched out as well. [However,] Wednesday evening, some Muslim secret agents (*quṣṣād*) arrived from the territory of the Mongols and reported that the Mongols were camped in their winter quarters and that their expedition to Syria had been called off. This episode was explained to me[89] by the Māliki chief judge Jamāl al-Dīn al-Zawāwī who said, "On Thursday, when we went to see off the viceroy of Syria (*malik al-umarā'*),[90] the governor of the countryside of Damascus (*wālī barr Dimashq*) Amīr 'Alā' al-Dīn Ibn al-Jākī told me, 'The viceroy Amīr Sayf al-Dīn Qibjāq told me that the agents have come and reported that the Mongols were struck by numerous thunderstorms and were forced to return to their winter quarters.' Their plan before the breakdown was to attack Syria. However, they were struck by thunder on the way and a large number of them were hit. Scattered and frustrated, they gave up the determination to carry on the expedition. Thank God!"

The new governor of the countryside of Damascus: In this year, on Saturday, Muḥarram 17 (October 25, 1298), three amīrs came from Cairo to Damascus. Among them was Amīr Ḥusām al-Dīn Lājīn al-Ḥusāmī al-Manṣūrī, who was [to be] the governor of the countryside of Damascus (*wilāyat al-barr*), replacing Amīr 'Alā' al-Dīn Ibn al-Jākī.

---

[86] He was of Mongol origin and died in 701/1301. For his biography and career, see al-'Asqalānī, *Durar*, 3:325ff; Irwin, *Early Mamluk Sultanate*, passim.

[87] 'Alam al-Dīn, died in 701/1301. For his biography, see Ibn Taghrībirdī, *Manhal*, no. 353.

[88] A race course west of the Damascus Citadel; see Brinner, *Damascus*, 1:36, note 215.

[89] The first person "me" here probably refers to al-Jazarī, not al-Yūnīnī; see chapter 3 above, especially 73ff.

[90] *Malik al-umarā'* is a title given to viceroys and governors of Syria (*Q2*, 327) and, according to Ayalon, to those of Alexandria and Upper Egypt as well; see Ayalon, "Studies on the Structure of the Mamluk Army," part III, 65-66.

The royal pavilion made in Damascus, to be sent to Cairo: In this year, on Wednesday, Muḥarram 21 (October 29, 1298), a superb royal pavilion (*dihlīz*), requiring 30 camel-loads, was set up on the Akhḍar Square in honor of sultan al-Malik al-Manṣur Ḥusām al-Dīn Lājīn. The pavilion was extremely marvelous and beautiful. Syrian common people were allowed to see the pavilion and to sit in it. The pavilion remained there for three days for public view. I asked Shaykh Rashīd [al-Dīn, nicknamed] Awḥashtanī,[91] an accountant in the bureau of construction (*'āmil dīwān al-buyūt*), "How much does the pavilion cost?" He told me, "Over 70,000 *dirhams*. In the years A.H. 687 and 688, during the reign of sultan al-Malik al-Manṣūr Sayf al-Dīn Qalāwūn al-Alfī, a pavilion was built and it cost 300,000 *dirhams*. The current one is more splendid and elegant but also much lighter because the pillars of the previous one were 35 cubits (*dhirā'*) high while those of the current one merely 20.[92] The previous pavilion was carried to the Marj[93] during al-Shujā'ī's[94] time and had been set up twice [for public view]. However, a gale had blown it down. God never let sultan [Qalāwūn] see the erected pavilion. He foiled al-Shujā'ī's plan." This [recent] modest pavilion was set up on a large open space, so that even ordinary folks (*al-muta'ayyishūn*)[95] were able to enjoy it. The access to the square had been blocked entirely for a long time. On Sunday, Muḥarram 25 (November 2, 1298), the pavilion was ready to be shipped to Egypt, to the sultan. The bureau of construction [at Damascus] was awarded a robe of honor for this.

The return of last year's pilgrims to Damascus and their complaints: In this year, on Wednesday, Muḥarram 28 (November 5, 1298), the pilgrims led by Amīr 'Izz al-Dīn Aybak al-Ṭawīl returned to Damascus. Among them were Ṣadr Amīn al-Dīn Ibn Ṣaṣrā and Nāṣir al-Dīn Ibn al-Nashshābī. The pilgrims complained about Amīr [Aybak]'s recklessness. He had abused them on the journey. A large number of pilgrims died due to his haste, ill-natured temper, and brutal personality. Amīr Ḥusām al-Dīn Muhannā ibn Amīr Sharaf al-Dīn 'Īsā Ibn Muhannā returned to his homeland after accomplishing

---

[91] Faraj Allāh al-Muslimānī, died in 699/1299. His biography is found in the present edition, 194. The nickname means "I Miss You."

[92] Al-Jazarī has "11."

[93] Perhaps Marj Rāhiṭ, to the east of Damascus and south of the river Baradā; see "Mardj Rāhiṭ," EI^2, by N. Elisseeff; Wulzinger, *Damaskus die islamische Stadt*, 103.

[94] 'Alam al-Dīn Sanjar, the vizier under Qalāwūn. His biography is not found. For information on his career, see Ibn al-Dawādārī, *Kanz*, 8:index; Elham, *Lāğīn*, index; also Irwin, *Early Mamluk Sultanate*, 70-91.

[95] The term has been translated as "boutiquiers et artisans" (Sauvaget, *al-Jazarī*, 76) and "peddlers" (Lapidus, *Muslim Cities*, 82 and note 82).

his duty of pilgrimage and fulfilling his wish. His deeds were greatly appreciated. He had generously donated to charity, taken care of those left behind and [made an effort] to feed people. He had also given charity to the inhabitants of Mecca and Medina as well as to residential religious students (*al-mujāwirūn*)[96] there. May God do good to him!

Rain and snow in Damascus: In the beginning of this year, there had been no rain during the period from Tishrīn I (October, 1298) to Tishrīn II (November, 1298). This situation continued until Saturday, Rabī‘ I 7, Kānūn I 13 (December 13),[97] when rain and snow—by God's blessing and mercy—fell upon us for seven days. Prior to that, people had despaired and had almost given up hope. Thank God! On Wednesday, Rabī‘ II ((January, 1299), heavy snow fell upon Damascus. Roofs and alleys were all covered with snow. The snow remained on [the ground of] alleys for half a month. God knows best![98]

Baktimur's rebellion: In this year, Saturday morning, Rabī‘ II 5 (January 10, 1299), General Sayf al-Dīn Balqāq, the son of Amīr Badr al-Dīn Kūnjak al-Khuwārizmī,[99] arrived in Damascus. He was sent by the viceroy of Syria Amīr Sayf al-Dīn Qibjāq to Egypt to report to the sultan what had happened to them at Hims on account of a group of amīrs coming from Aleppo.

The story is as follows: Ḥamdān had delivered an edict to the *silāḥ-dār* Amīr Sayf al-Dīn Baktimur, who was then stationed at Aleppo. The edict ordered him to dispatch his guard of honor (*ṭulb*) to Tripoli while he himself ought to come [to Cairo] to meet with the sultan to receive the appointment to the office of viceroy in charge of Tripoli and all the fortresses there, succeeding the late ‘Izz al-Dīn al-Mawṣilī. The edict was read to the amīrs at the Horse Market in Aleppo. Baktimur was grateful for that and was delighted. However, [at the same time,] another edict was brought secretly to Amīr Sayf al-Dīn Kūnjak[100] and Amīr Sayf al-Dīn al-Ṭabbākhī, then the viceroy of Aleppo,[101] ordering them to arrest the *silāḥ-dār* Baktimur and al-Albakī, who was then the viceroy of Ṣafad.[102] So when night fell, Amīr Sayf al-Dīn

---

[96] Literally, "neighbors," i.e., "the protected clients of the sanctuary" in Mecca and Medina.

[97] Al-Jazarī has "Kānūn I 3."

[98] I.e., "That's unbelievable!"

[99] He died in 709/1309. For his biography, see al-‘Asqalānī, *Durar*, 2:28. His name is given by Ibn al-Dawādārī (*Kanz*, 8 and 9:index) as Balghāq.

[100] He died in 739/1338. For his biography, see Ibn Taghrībirdī, *Manhal*, no. 1895.

[101] He died in 700/1301. For his biography, see Ibn Taghrībridī, *Manhal*, no. 692.

[102] Fāris al-Dīn al-Albakī/Bakī/Ilbakī in different sources. For his career, see Elham, *Lāğīn*, 217, 220; Brinner, *Damascus*, 1:240, note 1438. After his name, al-Jazarī also has "and Kitbughā."

Kūnjak, Amīr Jamāl al-Dīn Aydughdī Shuqayr, a mamluk of the sultan [Lājīn], and al-Ṭabbākhī, together with a number of amīrs rode out and sent for (*sayyarū khalfa*) the *silāḥ-dār* Amīr Sayf al-Dīn Baktimur and al-Albakī. They claimed that a pigeon-post had been sent from al-Bīra[103] that night with the information of the Mongols' attack. They urged them (i.e., Baktimur's party) to come over to discuss countermeasures. However, earlier that night, they (i.e., Baktimur and his party) had already learned that they (i.e., Kūnjak and his party) planned to arrest them. So they told the messenger, "We will catch up with you soon." The *silāḥ-dār* Amīr Sayf al-Dīn Baktimur, Amīr Sayf al-Dīn al-Albakī, Amīr Jūbān, Tabghāz, and Amīr Buzlār rode on with fury and led their adherents (*a'zāz*) and slaves, heading for the Euphrates. As for 'Azzāz al-Tatarī,[104] he also rode on with fury and led five men, heading for the Euphrates. He arrived at Mārdīn and then died in Sinjār[105] before reaching Ghāzān. Meanwhile, the *silāḥ-dār* Baktimur, al-Albakī, Tabghāz, and other generals reached Qibjāq, who was then stationed with the Damascene army at Ḥims as mentioned above. They wrote to him asking for his protection (*amān*). He guaranteed their safety and swore not to harm them. He also rode out to meet with them and arranged for their accommodations. Then he asked all of them to swear allegiance to the sultan and, next to the sultan, to himself, and to swear not to do any harm to him, to listen to him, and to obey his command. They did so. He then dispatched Balqāq to seek the promise of protection from the sultan on their behalf. Balqāq met with Amīr Sayf al-Dīn Jāghān [at Damascus] and informed him about the situation, telling him that [Qibjāq's] army was still staying in Ḥims. He left for Egypt on the post route the same day.

Qibjāq's defection to Ghāzān: On Monday, Rabī' II 7 (January 12, 1299), Amīr 'Alā' al-Dīn Ibn al-Jākī arrived in Damascus. He was sent by Qibjāq to Amīr Sayf al-Dīn Jāghān to ask the latter to supply money and robes from the warehouse for [the use of] the troops. His request received no answer. Then they sent postmen to explain the situation. Amīr Sayf al-Dīn Jāghān thereupon dispatched [an envoy] from Damascus to condemn Amīr Sayf al-Dīn Qibjāq for his protection of the sultan's enemies and his failure to arrest them despite his capability of doing so. On the other hand, Sayf al-Dīn Kūnjak and Jamāl al-Dīn Aydughdī Shuqayr also sent [envoys] to Qibjāq declaring, "If you have not captured them yet, we will come from Aleppo to

[103] To the northeast of the Euphrates; see *Q1*, 4:137-38.
[104] Unidentified.
[105] To the west of Mosul; see *QI*, 4:322. According to al-Nuwayrī (Elham's edition, 78), it was Buzlār that led five men to Ra's al-'Ayn and died in Sinjār.

get them and you!" At this point, Qibjāq began to realize that he was in trouble for his promise to protect them (i.e., Baktimur's party), and that if he did not capture them, then those [amīrs] would arrest him instead. Damascene troops started to defect from him, fleeing back to Damascus. Sayf al-Dīn Jāghān appreciated that and did not turn them down. Qibjāq then sent [an envoy] to Jāghān, [saying,] "There are no troops remaining with me except for some amīrs. Send me money and troops!" [However,] Jāghān continued to deceive him. Qibjāq saw his troops running away, and heard that the army in Aleppo was coming to get him; and meanwhile the sultan was tardy in response. He realized that his position was in danger. Thereupon Qibjāq, together with Baktimur, al-Albakī, Tabghāz,[106] 'Azzāz, and 500 horsemen, rode out Tuesday night, Rabī' II 8 (January 13, 1299), declaring that he would be marching to Salamīya, [but in fact he] headed towards the Euphrates to join the ruler Ghāzān. Amīr 'Izz al-Dīn Ibn Ṣabra, al-Malik al-Awḥad [Ibn al-Ẓāhir][107] and a group of leading amīrs ran after them in an attempt to appease him. But he did not come back. He was bent on following his own whim, as well as that of the amīrs who obeyed him.

On Tuesday, Rabī' II 15 (January 20, 1299), Amīr Jamāl al-Dīn [Āqqūsh] al-Maṭrūḥī arrived [in Damascus] to report Qibjāq's defection to Jāghān. The latter thus issued a decree to 'Imād al-Dīn [Ibn al-Nashshābī], then the governor of Damascus,[108] to put Qibjāq's house under surveillance but without sequestering his property, and to take his son and followers into custody. Every day some soldiers [of Qibjāq] would return [to Damascus] until Rabī' II 17 (January 22, 1299) when the entire army [of Qibjāq] was back in Damascus.

As for Qibjāq, he arrived at the Euphrates. Sayf al-Dīn Kūnjak and 'Alā' al-Dīn Aydughdī Shuqayr had made their way from Aleppo in pursuit of Qibjāq and his party. Then they found out he had already crossed the Euphrates [and arrived at Ra's al-'Ayn.][109] So they were [only able to] recover some heavy equipment [of his]. In the middle of their chase, they heard the news of the sultan's assassination. Their enthusiasm for capturing Qibjāq therefore diminished.

Qibjāq arrived in Mārdīn and was received by General Būlāhim[110] and the ruler of Mārdīn. The latter met with them (i.e., Qibjāq's party) and treated

---

[106] Al-Jazarī has "Buzlār" instead.

[107] Added after al-Jazarī.

[108] He died in 699/1300. For his biography, see Ibn Kathīr, *Bidāya*, 13:348; al-Dhahabī, *al-'Ibar*, 5:397.

[109] Added after al-Jazarī.

[110] According to al-Jazarī, two Mongol generals, Būlāhim and Ibn al-Bābā, received Qibjāq.

them very well in the hope that they would not reveal his [secret] correspondence with the Muslims. General [Būlāhim] wanted to send Qibjāq and his followers on the post route to join Ghāzān's service but they turned him down and claimed, "We won't go unless we are escorted by guards." Some other [sources] said that there was hostility and rivalry [between the two sides]. Qibjāq placed a big hollow Mongol gold coin (*bālisht*) in front of Būlāhim. And he also displayed a letter by Ghāzān [to him]. At this point, the Mongols were convinced of his credibility. They set out, escorted by their own guards. They passed by Mosul and were welcomed by its inhabitants. From Mosul they headed for Baghdad where they were well received by the Mongol troops as well as the townspeople. Then from Baghdad, they went ahead to join Ghāzān, who was then staying at al-Sīb[111] in the Wāsiṭ Province. Ghāzān welcomed them warmly and treated them with hospitality and plenty of promises and presents. He gave each amīr 10,000 *dīnārs*, each Mamluk 100 *dīnārs*, and each junior Mamluk at the rank of *Rakbdārīya* 50 *dīnārs*. One *dīnār* was equal to 12 *dirhams*. He bestowed upon Qibjāq the region of Hamadān as a fief. [Nevertheless,] Qibjāq graciously declined the offer with the excuse that he had no intention but to escort the ruler Ghāzān so that he would be able to see his face at every single moment. His demand was approved, and his speech was highly admired.[112]

The assassination of sultan Lājīn: As for sultan al-Malik al-Manṣūr Ḥusām al-Dīn Lājīn, he was at that time living inside the Cairo Citadel. Being cautious and seldom riding out, he was afraid of the amīrs' [plots against him]. When Thursday, Rabī' II 10 (January 15, 1299) came, he rode out early in the morning as usual. He was fasting at the time as well. When the evening prayer was over, Amīr Sayf al-Dīn Kurjī,[113] the head of the Burjī regiment, came in. The Ḥanafī chief judge Ḥusām al-Dīn[114] happened to be present there as the sultan was playing chess with Ibn al-'Assāl, a Qur'ān reciter. Prior to that, Kurjī had reached a secret agreement with the *silāḥ-dār* Nughiyah [al-Karmūnī],[115] the head of the royal bodyguards (*ṣāḥib al-nawba*). The

[111] A small town on the east bank of the Tigris below Madā'in; see Le Strange, *Lands*, 36.

[112] Al-Jazarī has "and it is said that Qibjāq then stayed there in the capacity of a *silāḥ-dār*, serving Ghāzān and his Mongol amīrs."

[113] He was killed later this year. For his biography, see Ibn Taghrībirdī, *Manhal*, no. 1900.

[114] Abū al-Faḍā'il al-Ḥasan al-Rāzī; he died in 699/1300. For his biography, see Ibn Kathīr, *Bidāya*, 14:4; also above, 97, note 3.

[115] His biography is not found. The name Nughiyah is also given as Nukiyah, Nogay or Nogai; e.g., Howorth, *The Mongols*; *CHIr*.

sultan asked Kurjī, "How is every thing?" He replied, "I went to the barracks of the Burjī regiment and locked them all in." [But the truth was,] he had put most of the Burjī soldiers along the corridors (*dihlīz*)[116] of the sultan's residence. The sultan thanked him and praised him in front of these present, saying, "Without Amīr Sayf al-Dīn, I would not have been able to become the sultan." Kurjī kissed the ground before the sultan and then rose to his feet, holding a candle which shone with a dazzling light. The royal sword (*al-nimjā)* was next to him. He threw a curtain (*būsheh*) on the sword [to cover it up] and left it aside. Then he said, "Your Majesty has not prayed yet." The sultan said, "Oh yes." The sultan thus stood up to pray and Kurjī struck him with the sword on the shoulder. The sultan at once tried to get the sword but could not find it, though he rose up after the shock of the blow, grabbed Kurjī and threw him on the floor. At this moment, the *silāḥ-dār* Nughiyah took the sword and hit the sultan on his leg and cut it off. The sultan fell down, struggling in a pool of blood, and died. Qāḍī Ḥusām al-Dīn [later] recalled, "I was with the sultan at the time. All I was conscious of was six or seven swords descending upon the sultan while he was concentrating on the chess game." They killed him and then left the [dead] sultan and Qāḍī Ḥusām al-Dīn [in the room] and locked the door behind the two.

[On the other hand,] Sayf al-Dīn Ṭughjī[117] had the remaining Burjī regiment soldiers, who had previously made an agreement with him and Kurjī, waiting at the court gate (*al-darkāh*) [of the Cairo Citadel].[118] So he asked them (i.e., Kurjī and his party), "Is your job done?" They said, "Yes." Then all of them wended their way to Amīr Sayf al-Dīn Mengü-Temür's house. They knocked on the door and said, "The sultan wants to see you now." He did not believe them, and said, "You killed the sultan?" Kurjī thus replied, "Yes, you sissy (*ma'būn*)![119] We came here to kill you too!" Mengü-Temür said, "I will never submit myself to you! I am protected by a contract (*fī jīra*) with Amīr Sayf al-Dīn Ṭughjī." The latter thereupon confirmed his promise of protection and swore neither to harm nor to allow any one else to harm him. Mengü-Temür opened the door. They caught him and took him to the jail. He was imprisoned with [other] captured amīrs. It was said by some [sources] that Amīr Shams al-Dīn al-A'sar stood up to salute him and Amīr

[116] For *dihlīz* meaning "corridor," see Amin et al., *Mamluk Architecture*, 49.

[117] He was killed later this year. For his biography, see Ibn Taghrībirdī, *Manhal*, no. 1243.

[118] Added after al-Jazarī.

[119] For the use of the expression *ma'būn* and its implication, see E. Rowson, "The Effeminates of Early Medina," *JAOS* 111/4 (1991): 695.

'Izz al-Dīn al-Ḥamawī came to scold him and wanted to kill him. That is because Mengü-Temür was the reason for the arrest of those amīrs and the upheaval in the state, in that he had been insisting on controlling all the state affairs. Amīr Sayf al-Dīn Ṭughjī stayed [at the jail] for an hour and then went home for some [other] business. Kurjī seized the opportunity of Ṭughjī's absence and led a group to the gate of the jail and ordered Mengü-Temür to be brought out ostensibly in order to have him shackled according to custom. Mengü-Temür refused to be taken out, but they urged him to follow instructions. They took him out and killed him at the door of the cell. They also looted his house and seized his property.

Al-Malik al-Nāṣir was chosen as the sultan: The same night, they reached an agreement on choosing al-Malik al-Nāṣir Nāṣir al-Dīn Muḥammad, the son of the martyr al-Malik al-Manṣūr [Qalāwūn], to be the sultan, for he was the son of their master. They also agreed on appointing Sayf al-Dīn Ṭughjī to be the viceroy. The amīrs finally came to an agreement and formed an alliance that night. On the following Friday morning (January 16, 1299), the amīrs, generals and soldiers swore allegiance to al-Malik al-Nāṣir and the viceroy Ṭughjī. They then sent an invitation to al-Malik al-Nāṣir to come back from Kerak. On Saturday (January 17, 1299), with a host of troops crowding around, al-Malik al-Nāṣir rode in a royal procession and came up to the [Cairo] Citadel. A lavish banquet was held as usual as if nothing had happened.

Power struggle: Manṣūrī amīrs fought back and gained power: On Monday, Rabī' II 14 (January 19, 1299), the *amīr-silāḥ*[120] Amīr Badr al-Dīn Baktāsh[121] returned, via Syria, from the Cilicia expedition. Before [his arrival in Cairo,] a group of amīrs had gone to Bilbays to inform him about what had happened and to tell him that the whole situation occurred without their consent or knowledge. They agreed with Baktāsh to kill Ṭughjī. These amīrs had also told Ṭughjī to come out to welcome the *amīr-silāḥ* [Baktāsh]. So on Monday morning,[122] he (i.e., Ṭughjī) rode out. The two men looked at each other sternly, and then the *amīr-silāḥ* [Baktāsh] asked Ṭughjī, "We used to have a custom that every time we returned from an expedition the sultan would come out to receive us in person. Don't you know what's wrong with

[120] "Grand master of the armor" whose duty was to bear the sultan's arms during public appearances; the office, which was called *silāḥdārīya*, was held by an Amīr of Thousand; see *Q1*, 4:46, 188.

[121] He died in 706/1306; he was one of the last surviving Ṣāliḥī Mamluks (after sultan al-Ṣāliḥ Ayyūb). For his biography, see al-'Asqalānī, *Durar*, 2:14-15.

[122] Al-Jazarī has "and other said on Tuesday."

me this time that the sultan doesn't come out to see me?" Ṭughjī said, "I don't know what happened to the sultan. The sultan was murdered." Baktāsh said, "Who killed him?" Some amīrs said, "Sayf al-Dīn Ṭughjī and Kurjī!" Baktāsh condemned the man, saying, "Every time the Muslims have a king you kill him! Get out of here and stay away from me!" Then he turned [his horse] away from him. Ṭughjī was certain that he would be killed, so he spurred his horse forward [to fight]. Amīr [Baktāsh] suddenly swooped down on him, grabbed him by his plait of hair (*dabbūqa*),[123] and raised his sword over him. Other amīrs helped him in killing Ṭughjī. Three [other] riders were killed along with him.

In the aftermath, they came to the foot of the Citadel where Kurjī was stationed to guard it. When the news of his comrade Ṭughjī's death reached him, Kurjī ordered the Burjī regiment to put on their weapons and rode out with 2,000 horsemen to defend himself. [On the other hand,] all the *ḥalqa* troopers, amīrs and generals loyal to the *amīr-silāḥ* [Baktāsh] rode out as well at four [o'clock] in the morning. The victorious troops launched an attack on Kurjī's party and defeated them. Some [sources] mentioned that Sayf al-Dīn Kurjī rode by himself, assuming that his party would either march with him or follow him. [However,] they remained behind. And one of his comrades approached him and struck him with the sword, piercing his shoulder. The *silāḥ-dār* Nughiyah al-Karmūnī, who has been mentioned above, was killed with him. A total of 12 persons were killed as well. The situation was thus settled. There was also an agreement on al-Malik al-Nāṣir's succession. They, too, sent an invitation to him to come back and urged him to join them. The official communiqués sent to the provinces were signed by eight amīrs, who were: Amīr Sayf al-Dīn Salār, Amīr Sayf al-Dīn Kurt,[124] Amīr Rukn al-Dīn Baybars al-Jāshankīr, the treasurer (*khazindār*) 'Izz al-Dīn Aybak, Amīr Jamāl al-Dīn Āqqūsh al-Afram, the majordomo (*ustād-dār*) Amīr Ḥusām al-Dīn Lājīn, the *amīr-jānidār*[125] Sayf al-Dīn Baktimur, and Amīr 'Abd Allāh.[126]

---

[123] According to al-Qalqashandī, the Mamluks used to grow their hair long and braid it up into several plaits with red and yellow silk bands. Each such plait was called one *dabbūqa*; see *Q2*, 133.

[124] He was a chamberlain (*ḥājib*) and the head of royal stables (*amīr-ākhūr*) during the time. His biography is not found. For information on his career, see Zettersteen, 24, 37, 57, 81.

[125] *Jān-dār*, Persian, "sword bearer," whose duties included calling on amīrs and escorting them into the *dīwān* as well as presenting correspondence to the sultan; see *Q2*, 48.

[126] Perhaps 'Abd Allāh ibn Aybak al-Dawādārī, the father of the author of the *Kanz*. He was the protocol officer (*mihmandār*) of Syria around 701/1301-2. The *Kanz* contains a great deal of eye-witness accounts for the events during the first decade of the 8th/14th century.

All of them were Manṣūrī Mamluks.[127] They issued declarations to all provinces. This is what happened in Egypt.

Syrian reaction to al-Malik al-Nāṣir's succession: As for the events in Damascus, as mentioned above, Sayf al-Dīn Balqāq had gone from Syria to Egypt to deliver Qibjāq's message. He arrived in Cairo on Saturday, Rabī' II 12 (January 17, 1299). At that time, Ṭughjī, as mentioned above, was still riding in procession and was still in power (*al-mushār ilayhi*). Balqāq made the report to him. He said, "We will issue communiqués to you to put the minds of your amīrs at rest." However, on Monday, Ṭughjī and Kurjī were killed. [Despite that,] the [Manṣūrī] amīrs [in Cairo], as had previously been agreed upon by the two parties,[128] unanimously agreed to issue an edict in his (Ṭughjī's?) name[129] to Amīr Sayf al-Dīn Qibjāq and those amīrs following him, [stating that] everybody should keep his current status and feel at ease. The same edict was also addressed to all the amīrs in Syria; each of whom received a copy of it with the signatures of the eight [Manṣūrī amīrs].

Sayf al-Dīn Balqāq returned to Damascus on Saturday morning, Rabī' II 19 (January 24, 1299), bringing back the news of the assassination of the sultan, Mengü-Temür, Ṭughjī, Kurjī and others. [He also reported that] the amīrs [in Cairo] had agreed on al-Malik al-Nāṣir's [succession]. At that time, the person in charge [in Damascus] was Amīr Sayf al-Dīn Jāghān.[130] [Upon learning the news,] Amīr Sayf al-Dīn Qarā-Arslān[131] jumped up at once [out of jubilation] and appeared to be greatly relieved. He thus took power. He issued orders to closely watch deputies of Sayf al-Dīn Ṭughjī and Amīr Ḥusām al-Dīn [Lājin], the governor of the countryside of Damascus, and put other Royal Mamluks under surveillance. He began to deploy forces and swore allegiance to al-Malik al-Nāṣir. With full powers to command and prohibit, he ruled [Syria].

On Tuesday, Rabī' II 22 (January 27, 1299), Sayf al-Dīn Qarā-Arslān arrested Sayf al-Dīn Jāghān and the governor of the countryside of Damascus Ḥusām al-Dīn [Lājin]. He took the two by himself to the gate of the Damascus Citadel and handed them over to 'Alam al-Dīn Arjuwāsh. The latter imprisoned the two in the Pigeon Tower (*burj al-ḥamām*). It was said that he

---

[127] I.e., the Mamluks of al-Malik al-Manṣūr Qalāwūn.

[128] I.e., between Qibjāq's envoy and Ṭughjī.

[129] The text has *'alā yadihi*, literally, "in his hand."

[130] He was on Mengü-Temür's side.

[131] His title is given as Bahā' al-Dīn in Ibn al-Dawādārī, *Kanz*, 8:383, which appears to be more accurate. According to Ayalon (based on al-Qalqashandī), the name Arslān (or Raslān) was usually associated with the title Bahā' al-Dīn during the early Mamluk period; see Ayalon, "Names," 191 and note 8.

treated them very badly. [Meanwhile,] Balqāq set off on a journey to meet with Qibjāq in order to urge him to return. Qarā-Arslān remained in power in Damascus until the beginning of Jumādā I (February 4, 1299) when he came down with colic. Prior to that, he had suffered from poisoning from which he later recovered. [This time around,] he was overwhelmed by the pain and died. He was buried on Monday, Jumādā I 2 (February 5, 1299). Damascus was left with neither viceroy,[132] nor market inspector (*muḥtasib*), nor finance agent, nor governor [of the countryside].[133] People were thus governed and protected by God. Thereupon, Amīr 'Imād al-Dīn Ibn al-Nashshābī, then the governor of the city of Damascus, took over the task. He began to assume responsibility for the administration of both the countryside and the city of Damascus, as well as the office of market inspection. He did a remarkable job in managing and maintaining the well-being of the city and demonstrated a great deal of ability which was unexpected by the townspeople.

New appointments in Syria by al-Malik al-Nāṣir: On Saturday, Jumādā I 4 (February 7, 1299), postmen came from Cairo [to Damascus], carrying with them communiqués dated Rabī' II 26 (January 31, 1299) with the information that the amīrs [in Cairo] had unanimously shown their support for al-Malik al-Nāṣir. [The postmen also carried] an edict appointing Amīr Sayf al-Dīn Quṭlū-Bek[134] to be the finance agent in Syria, replacing Jāghān. He assumed the office in Damascus on Monday (February 9, 1299). He had [previously] been sent by sultan [Lājīn] to Aleppo to assist Amīr Sayf al-Dīn al-Ṭabbākhī in the capacity of finance agent, overseeing all the fortresses in Aleppo. He had been staying in the [Ablaq][135] Palace at the [Akhḍar] Square [in Damascus] since then and was, due to the death of the sultan, unable to continue with the trip [to Aleppo] and hence stuck in the [palace at the Akhḍar] Square. So as soon as his appointment to the office of finance agent was brought over, he immediately assumed the post.[136] He moved to Amīr Shams al-Dīn al-A'sar's mansion. [Amīrs] at Damascus swore allegiance to al-Malik al-Nāṣir while he (i.e., Quṭlū-Bek) remained in charge of state affairs [in Damascus].

---

[132] The text has *mā fī-hā illā*, . . . literally, "except for the viceroy. . . ." This is an error for *mā fī-hā lā*, . . . for, as the text shows well, the viceroy Qibjāq was out of town at the time.

[133] The text has *wālī*, "governor"; in the text below we are told that *wālī al-balad*, "governor of the city of Damascus" Ibn al-Nashshābī, was in fact in town, so the *wālī* here is referring to *wālī al-barr*, namely, the governor of the countryside of Damascus.

[134] He died in 729/1328. For his biography, see al-'Asqalānī, *Durar*, 3:338.

[135] Added after al-Jazarī.

[136] Al-Jazarī has "and some [sources] said he was Amīr Sayf al-Dīn Salār's brother."

Al-Malik al-Nāṣir's investiture: A pigeon-post was delivered to Damascus on Wednesday, Jumādā I 8 (February 11, 1299) with the information of al-Malik al-Nāṣir's investiture at the Cairo Citadel. Music was played by a band in celebration. On Friday, Jumādā I 10 (February 13, 1299), Amīr Sayf al-Dīn Mughalṭāy al-Dimashqī[137] arrived in Damascus. In his hand there was a letter from sultan al-Malik al-Nāṣir with the information that he had arrived in Cairo from Kerak on Saturday night, Jumādā I 4 (February 7, 1299), stayed overnight in the royal stables (*al-isṭabl*), and then went up to the [Cairo] Citadel on Monday morning, Jumādā I 6 (February 9, 1299). He bestowed upon Amīr Sayf al-Dīn Salār[138] the robe of the viceroy, and upon some amīrs robes of honor. On Jumādā I 9 (February 12, 1299), robes of honor were distributed to all the statesmen in greater Cairo who would usually receive robes of honor under such circumstances. The royal military band (*ṭabl-khānāh*) performed[139] to congratulate all those amīrs. On Jumādā I 12 (February 15, 1299) Mamluk amīrs (*al-nās*)[140] all wore the robes of honor. Sultan al-Malik al-Nāṣir, wearing the robe [bestowed by] the caliph, rode with the royal pageantry (*ubahhat al-malik*), parading to the Horse Market, and then from there he returned to the [Cairo] Citadel. All the amīrs and soldiers dismounted to salute him and kissed the ground before him. His reign was thus firmly established. This was his second reign, a return to the throne.[141] Postmen arrived in Damascus on Saturday, Jumādā I 18 (February 21, 1299), reporting the event. Bands played at the Damascus Citadel and the amīrs' residences to celebrate the occasion. The communiqué was read at the Grand Mosque and the people were delighted.

Āqqūsh's appointment to the office of viceroy in Damascus: On Wednesday, Jumādā I 22 (February 25, 1299), Amīr Jamāl al-Dīn Āqqūsh al-Afram arrived [in Damascus] from Egypt, carrying with him the edict of his appointment to the office of viceroy in Damascus. All the amīrs and the townspeople came out to welcome him. He entered [the city] in a splendid procession. On the following Thursday morning (February 26, 1299), wearing the robe of the viceroy, he rode in procession. Following the custom of his predecessors, he kissed the threshold at the Postern Gate [of the Citadel].

---

[137] Unidentified. His title might well be 'Alā' al-Dīn for nearly all the amīrs named Mughalṭāy have the title of 'Alā' al-Dīn; cf. Ibn al-Dawādārī, *Kanz*, 9:index.

[138] He died in 710/1310. For his biography, see Ibn Taghrībirdī, *Manhal*, no. 1062.

[139] For the meaning of the verb *nazala* in this context, see Sauvaget, *al-Jazarī*, 80.

[140] For the term *al-nās*, see Brinner, *Damascus*, 1:157, note 928.

[141] For the background surrounding al-Malik al-Nāṣir's three reigns, see Irwin, *Early Mamluk Sultanate*, 85-124; and most recently Levanoni, *Turning Point*, especially 5-27.

A banquet was held at the Dār al-Sa'āda.[142] He began with his duties on that day. He discovered many unjust verdicts. He also issued an edict stating that Amīr Sayf al-Dīn Quṭlū-Bek was to be summoned back to Egypt and that he was authorized to name [a new] finance agent as well as all the governors in Syria on his own authority. Amīr 'Imād al-Dīn Ibn al-Nashshābī was removed from the office of governor of the city of Damascus to that of the countryside of Damascus, replacing Amīr Ḥusām al-Dīn Lājīn. His former post was filled by Amīr Jamāl al-Dīn Ibrāhīm Ibn al-Naḥḥās, then the agent of almsgiving, trust funds, and escheat estates (*mushidd al-zakā wa-al-wikāla wa-al-ḥashr*).[143] Ibn al-Naḥḥās's sons were appointed to the positions under him. That was on Thursday, the beginning of Jumādā II (March 6, 1299). The two men were awarded the robes of their offices at the same time and assumed their duties in official robes.

The release of Jāghān: In this year, Sayf al-Dīn Jāghān was released in accordance with a decree arriving from Egypt on Wednesday, Jumādā I 29 (March 4, 1299). He was discharged from the [Damascus] Citadel and was ordered to go to Egypt. He packed up and set off on the journey. On the way, he encountered a courier who carried a fief chart (*manshūr*) awarding him 70 horsemen in Damascus as the *iqṭā'* assignment for his comfort. He returned to Damascus on Sunday, Jumādā II 25 (March 30, 1299). He was very happy for God's grace upon him and for his release from prison.

Sülemish's revolt in Anatolia, Ghāzān's retaliation and the Mamluks' support for Sülemish: In this year, in the last 10 days of Jumādā II (end of March, 1299), Shihāb al-Dīn Aḥmad ibn al-'Imād al-Qaṣṣāṣ[144] came to Damascus from al-Bīra and reported the Mongols' [movements]. He said[145] that the ruler Ghāzān had originally determined to attack Syria with his entire army. He had allotted to Sülemish ibn [Bakbū, or Bākū] ibn Bājū[146] 25,000 horsemen and sent them to Anatolia (*Bilād al-Rūm*), so that Sülemish would take up the Anatolian troops and march towards Syria from the direction of

[142] According to Nasser Rabbat, in the Mamluk period, the two terms of the Dār al-'Adl (Palace of Justice) and the Dār al-Sa'āda (Palace of Felicity) were used interchangeably, designating the same complex. For more details on the Dār al-Sa'āda and Dār al-'Adl in Damascus, see Rabbat, "The Ideological Significance of the Dār al-'Adl," 6-9.

[143] For the term *ḥashr*, meaning "heritage, or treasure, that is left without heir," see Dozy, *Supplément*.

[144] He was then the deputy of Sayf al-Dīn Ṭūghān, the commander of the citadel in al-Bīra; see Ibn al-Dawādārī, *Kanz*, 9:8.

[145] Here al-Jazarī has a note of provenance, "I asked him about the Mongols, and he said. . . ."

[146] For his name, cf. Ibn al-Dawādārī, *Kanz*, 9:index. He died in 1299. For his revolt in Asia Minor, see *CHIr*, 5:386-87; Irwin, *Early Mamluk Sultanate*, 100.

Cilicia. Ghāzān himself would march from Diyār Bakr and [eventually,] both of them would encamp at the Euphrates, attacking al-Bīra, al-Raḥba,[147] and Qal'at al-Rūm.[148] They were supposed to meet at Aleppo. If any [Mamluks] happened to encounter them, they would battle [the Mamluks] jointly. And if not, they would enter Syria straightaway. However, Sülemish's ambition for power grew wider as he arrived in Anatolia. He claimed to be the sovereign of Anatolia and refused to obey Ghāzān any more. He appointed officials, attributed stipends, and granted robes of honor.[149] The Qarmanlis,[150] with more than 10,000 horsemen, submitted themselves to his rule and joined into his service. And on the other hand, Sülemish sent envoys to the sultan in Egypt, looking for help and support against Ghāzān. The envoys arrived in Damascus in Rajab (April, 1299) and then were sent to Egypt, to the sultan.

As regards Ghāzān, he arrived in Baghdad. The city magistrates complained to him about the Sibians (*ahl al-Sīb*) and Bedouins (*al-'urbān*) who had plundered merchants from overseas and waylaid transit traders (*al-sābila*). Ghāzān thus led the remaining army, launching an attack on them and taking booty from them. Then he stayed on in Daqūqa[151] for the winter. As the report on Sülemish's revolt reached him, his determination to proceed to Syria dissipated. He began to allocate 35,000 troops to three generals: 15,000 to General Sultāy,[152] 10,000 to Hindū-Ghān, and 10,000 to Būlāhim, who was to be the commander-in-chief of the entire army. The troops were dispatched to Anatolia.[153]

Ghāzān himself moved from the winter quarters to Tawrīz (Tabrīz). Together with him were Qibjāq, Baktimur, and al-Albakī. The Mongols arrived in Sinjār, and then Ra's al-'Ayn, and then Mārdīn. The ruler of Mārdīn[154] accommodated them and provided plenty of gifts to them. He prepared his own

---

[147] It is on the western side of the lower Euphrates. According to al-Qalqashandī (*Ql*, 4:115), its full name was Raḥbat Mālik ibn Ṭawq; also see Le Strange, *Lands*, 105, 124.

[148] "The Roman Fortress," which was later known as Qal'at al-Muslimīn (The Muslim Fortress), a garrison town to the northwest of Aleppo; see *Ql*, 4:154-55.

[149] Which was usually the sultan's duty.

[150] I.e., the Qarmanli Turkman tribesmen who at the time were in revolt against the Mongols in the Taurus region. For more details, see Irwin, *Early Mamluk Sultanate*, 57, 63, especially 100f.

[151] Today's Tauk; see *CHIr*, 5:325.

[152] His name is given as Suntāy by al-Jazarī, and Suktāy by Ibn al-Dawādārī (*Kanz*, 8:188-89).

[153] Al-Jazarī has "at the beginning of Jumādā I."

[154] Al-Malik al-Manṣūr Najm al-Dīn Ghāzī ibn al-Alpī Qarā-Arslān ibn Īlghāzī, of Artuq. The Artuqī dynasty was at the time under the Mongol protection; see "Artuḳids," *EI²*, by Cl. Cahen; "Mardin," *EI²*, by V. Minorsky.

troops to accompany them; meanwhile he himself dared not come out [to receive] them, fearing that Qibjāq might have exposed [to the Mongols] his secret correspondence with the Muslims. He apologized that he was sick and unable to sit or stand. They accepted his excuse because the precious gifts met their eyes on every side. It was said that before the Mongols' coming, he had prepared two years' provisions in the citadel. God, however, made their lives easy in that the Mongols just passed by him and meant not to target him [at this time].

At the beginning of Rajab (beginning of April, 1299), they (i.e., Ghāzān and his army) arrived at Āmid,[155] and from there headed for Anatolia to fight Sülemish. The two parties met and battled in the end of Rajab (end of April, 1299). The people of Sivas (Sebastea)[156] were at the time fighting against Sülemish as he besieged them. By the time [Ghāzān's] army, led by General Būlāhim, approached him, he (i.e., Būlāhim) had already gathered more than 60,000 horsemen. The Mongolian and Anatolian soldiers [in Sülemish's army] thus deserted at night to join Būlāhim's troops. As for the Turkmen [in Sülemish's army], they ascended to their mountains as they usually would do. Having been left behind with less than 500 horsemen, Sülemish set out from Sivas to Cilicia. He arrived in Baghdad at the end of Rajab (end of April, 1299).

During the [first] 10 days of Sha'bān (beginning of May, 1299), the royal decree arrived from Egypt. It ordered five amīrs from Damascus and a total of 15 amīrs from Hims, Hama, and Aleppo[157] to set out to Sülemish's rescue. On Thursday, Sha'bān 5 (May 8, 1299), the news reached Damascus that the defeated Sülemish had already retreated to Bāhasnā. The action of sending troops stopped thereby. On Thursday, Sha'bān 12 (May 15, 1299), Sülemish ibn [Bākū] ibn Bājū ibn Hülegü arrived in Damascus. He was received by its troops and the viceroy [Āqqūsh al-Afram]. Amīr Badr al-Dīn al-Zardkāsh, the viceroy of Bāhasnā,[158] joined his retinue. They (i.e., the Damascene Mamluks) were very concerned about him and attached an extreme importance to his joining them. They ordered whatever residents of Damascus who had horses to ride to come out to welcome him. So all the residents of Damascus showed up for the occasion. Accompanied by a large procession as well as

---

[155] On the upper Tigris; see Le Strange, *Lands*, 4, 80.

[156] Also known as Sebasteia or Megalopolis-Sebasteia, an ancient city in today's central Turkey. It was one of the most important cities of Anatolia under the Saljuqs.

[157] Al-Jazarī has no "Aleppo."

[158] On the right-bank of the Euphrates. For the fortress of Bāhasnā, see Le Strange, *Lands*, 123, 128.

less than 20 of his own Mongolian followers, Sülemish entered [Damascus]. He was accommodated in the Najīb Khānqāh facing the [Akhḍar] Square[159] and was given a lavish stipend. On the night of Sha'bān 15 (May 18, 1299), they (i.e., the Damascene Mamluks) led them to the Grand Mosque to watch the lights in the city (*al-waqīd*),[160] and to perform the Friday prayer as well. After the prayer, a protocol official and the Mosque watchman took them for a tour. They performed prayers in all of the shrines at the Grand Mosque. On the eve of Sunday, Sha'bān 25 (May 28, 1299), they (i.e., the Damascene Mamluks) sent Sülemish to Egypt on post horses. He arrived in Cairo and then returned to Damascus on Sunday, Ramaḍān 21 (June 22, 1299). And afterwards, he, accompanied by Amīr Badr al-Dīn al-Zardkāsh, went to Aleppo.

A comet observed in Damascus: In this year, during the second 10 days of Rabī' II (mid-January, 1299), a comet (*kawkab dhū dhu'āba*) emerged in the sky between the end of Taurus (*burj al-thawr*) and the beginning of Gemini (*burj al-jawzā'*). Its tail was pointing towards the north, because we saw it in the Grand Mosque of Damascus after the sunset prayer, and it was situated to the west side of the Nasr [Cupola of the Mosque].[161] This took place in the last 10 days of Kānūn II (January, 1299) while the sun was then in Aquarius (*burj al-dālī*).[162] The comet continued to appear until the end of the month and then it disappeared.

Egyptian army's moving towards Aleppo: In this year, on Rajab 17 (April 20, 1299), 4,000 cavalrymen arrived in Damascus from Egypt. Each 1,000 were led by a general and they were: Qattāl al-Sab'[163] with 1,000, the *amīr-shikār*[164] al-Mubāriz with 1,000, Amīr 'Abd Allāh with 1,000, and Amīr Sayf al-Dīn al-Ḥubayshī (al-Jayshī?) with 1,000. The latter was the commander-in-chief. They headed for Aleppo.

---

[159] The term *al-maydān* is usually used to refer to the Akhḍar Square; see Brinner, *Damascus*, index.

[160] Also known as *layālī al-waqūd*, a practice started during the Fatimid period in which mosques and streets in Cairo and Damascus were illuminated in celebration of certain Muslim holidays (Muḥammad's birthday, al-Ḥusayn's birthday, etc.); cf. *Q2*, 293; Langner, *Untersuchungen zur historischen Volkskunde Ägyptens nach mamlukischen Quellen*, 42, 59, 84.

[161] [*Qubbat*] *al-Nasr*, "the Eagle Cupola," was the major cupola in the Grand Mosque.

[162] Variant spelling of *al-dalw*, "Aquarius"; see Kunitzsch, *Untersuchungen zur Sternnomenklatur der Araber*, 22.

[163] The name means "Fighter of the Lion." His and the other three generals' (perhaps lower ranking Mamluk amīrs) biographies are not found.

[164] Persian, *amīr-i shikār*, "controller of the hunt"; an officer in charge of the sultan's hunt; see *Q2*, 49.

Aqjubā's promotion to amīr: In this year, on Saturday, Jumādā II 24 (March 18, 1299), Sayf al-Dīn Aqjubā[165] was promoted to the rank of amīr at the royal drum house (*ṭabl-khānah*) and was nominated to be the finance agent [in Syria],[166] following the rules set up by his predecessors.

In this year, on Tuesday, Jumādā II 13 (March 18, 1299), robes of honor were granted upon amīrs, generals, qāḍīs, governors, and statesmen in Damascus. They all wore the robes Wednesday and Thursday mornings. On the same Thursday, the retinue of the viceroy arrived [in Damascus from Egypt].[167] It was made up of his own mamluks, troops, kinsmen, and followers, and was escorted by Amīr Bahā' al-Dīn Ibn Temür-Ṭāsh and Ibn Janidār. When the retinue of the viceroy entered [the city], the amīrs, generals, qāḍīs, and all others who had been granted robes of honor were wearing them. The people of Damascus came out to watch the scene. It was a grand festive day indeed. The viceroy's family arrived in Damascus that night as well.

The arrest of Kūnjak in Damascus: In this year, on Friday, Rajab 22 (April 25, 1299), after the Friday prayer, Amīr Sayf al-Dīn Kūnjak was arrested at the Dār al-Sa'āda. He was brought to the [Damascus] Citadel. Arjuwāsh and the citadel troops took him through the Postern Gate[168] and put him in a tower until Tuesday night, Ramaḍān 2 (June 3, 1299), when they sent him, together with Ḥamdān's brother, to Egypt under the escort of 100 cavalrymen.

A report on Ghāzān: On Friday, Sha'bān 20 (May 23, 1299), one of Qibjāq's mamluks came [to Damascus] and reported that they had arrived in Hamadhān with the ruler Ghāzān, and that upon their arrival the Mongols split up. He also reported other such things which could not be confirmed. They sent him to Egypt.

The arrest of a group of Ḥanafī 'ulamā': In this year, on Thursday, Rajab 27 (April 30, 1299), the viceroy issued an order to the mayor of Damascus to track down Muḥyī al-Dīn Ibn al-Naḥḥās' three sons and their cousin Shaykh Bahā' al-Dīn Ayyūb. He was to bring Shihāb al-Dīn, the imām at the Ḥanafī chamber of the Grand Mosque, Rukn al-Dīn Bārizī, Raḍī al-Dīn al-Khilāfī and a total of 40 Ḥanafīs, including three Persian merchants, to trial. The circular was announced to all. The following Friday (May 1, 1299), after the prayer, they were brought to the viceroy. The amīrs, as well as the chancellery clerks

---

[165] His biography is not found. Perhaps this was the same Amīr Sayf al-Dīn Aqjubā, the viceroy of Gaza in 698/1298; see Ibn al-Dawādārī, *Kanz*, 9:7, 110.

[166] Added after al-Jazarī.

[167] Added after al-Jazarī.

[168] Al-Jazarī has "which was at the corridor of the Naṣr Gate. . . ."

and others who were present, [came to their defense and] spoke of them highly, saying that they were Muslim learned persons, jurists, and Qur'ān reciters. The viceroy said, "Yes, I know them well. I swear by God, I feel embarrassed by what has been done to them." Then he asked the finance agent Amīr Sayf al-Dīn Aqjubā to stand guarantee on their behalf. Aqjubā said, "I so do for all these persons." The viceroy then ordered them released.

The reason for the arrest of this group [of Ḥanafīs] goes back to a man called Fakhr al-Dīn al-Bukhārī who came to Damascus and hoped to stay in one of the Ḥanafī madrasas. He went to the Qulayjīya [Madrasa][169] and met with its chair Bahā' al-Dīn.[170] Bahā' al-Dīn refused to provide him lodging. Four Persian jurists, who were [later] on the wanted list, came to help him. They went to Muḥyī al-Dīn Ibn al-Naḥḥās' sons and asked them to provide the man lodging in their madrasas, but they were unwilling to do so [because] some Persian jurists staying in their madrasas were against that person. So, Fakhr al-Dīn went to the Ibn 'Aqīl Tavern, which was next to the Martyr Nūr al-Dīn Madrasa, and stayed there. However, he soon began to quarrel with some merchants staying in the tavern. He found no way but to pretend to be (*kataba nafsahu*) a secret agent and then made his way to al-Raḥba. He made up a list [and presented it] to the commander of the Raḥba [garrison], claiming that they were spies and had been sending information secretly to the Mongols. He made all the worst charges against those [Ḥanafīs]. The commander of the Raḥba [garrison] thus wrote to the viceroy in Damascus reporting that an agent had come and informed him that in Damascus there was a group of persons—namely those [Ḥanafīs] mentioned above—who had been passing information on to the Mongols. And then the foresaid episode happened. God knows best.

Qarā-Sunqur and al-A'sar's release: On Tuesday, Sha'bān 24 (May 27, 1299),[171] a postman came to Damascus from Egypt and brought the news of Amīr Shams al-Dīn Qarā-Sunqur's release. He was also offered al-Ṣubayba[172] and Bānyās (Belinas)[173] as well as its vicinity as a fief and was allowed to reside there. The acting commander of the Ṣubayba Citadel was ordered to vacate it. And he did so immediately, cleaning up the citadel for Qarā-Sunqur's use. The news of Amīr Shams al-Dīn al-A'sar's release on Monday, Ramaḍān

---

169 For the Qulayjīya Madrasa, see Pouzet, *Damas*, 50, 65, 259.

170 Likely the above-mentioned Bahā' al-Dīn Ayyūb.

171 Al-Jazarī has "Sha'bān 14."

172 To the southeast of Damascus; see *Q1*, 7:170; 11:112; also Thorau, *Baybars*, 306, Map 2.

173 To the southeast of al-Ṣubayba; see *Q1*, 4:83, 104-5; also Thorau, *Baybars*, 306, Map 2.

22 (July 13, 1299), was also brought [to Damascus]. He was appointed to be the vizier of Egypt on Monday, Ramaḍān 29 (July 20, 1299).

The earthquake of Cairo: In this year, on Ṣafar 24, Kiyahk 5, Kānūn I 1 (December 1, 1298),[174] after the last evening prayer, an earthquake struck Egypt. Two quakes occurred. And between the two there was [a pause that was] sufficient to recite five Qur'ānic verses. Then on Rabī' I 3 (December 9, 1299),[175] another earthquake [which was more severe than the previous one][176] occurred. In addition, Egypt suffered an extraordinarily severe cold spell that lasted for three days[177] the like of which had never been seen before in the country. The following was told by Amīr Najm al-Dīn Ibn al-Miḥaffadār,[178] "On Jumādā I 21 (February 24, 1299), there was a heavy rain in Egypt. The flood inundated the Cairo ditch and destroyed many houses in greater Cairo. The mud remained in the city for a long while. Such a scene," he said, "has never happened before."

The Byzantines' request for a shared harbor: In this year, on Thursday, Ramaḍān 4 (June 5, 1299), the envoy of the Franks, sent by the ruler of Constantinople,[179] arrived in Damascus. He was accompanied by the envoy of the ruler of Cilicia.[180] They carried with them many presents: gems, hawks (*bāzāt*), and falcons (*saqūra*). [The Damascenes saw them off] to Egypt on Saturday, Ramaḍān 6 (June 7, 1299). It was mentioned that their mission to the sultan was about the coastal region in that they wanted to have a harbor there to share with the Muslims (*mīnā' munāṣafa*). It was said that their coming was proposed by their emperor and [made possible] through the mediation of the ruler of Cilicia. There are many accounts [about this mission] some of which are detailed and others brief.

In this year, during the last 10 days [of Sha'bān] (the end of May, 1299), a fleet of [Frankish] ships and boats with two masts (*buṭas*; sing. *baṭsa*) approached Beirut. It was said that there were 30 *baṭsa*-boats, each of which car-

[174] Note that in addition to the Muslim calendar, both Coptic and Syrian calendars are mentioned. It is remarkable that all the cases in which the Syrian or Coptic calendars are used deal with natural phenomena.

[175] Al-Jazarī has "Rabī' II," which is obviously wrong.

[176] Added after al-Jazarī.

[177] Al-Jazarī has the date of this cold spell as Rabī' I 11.

[178] For this amīr who was likely al-Jazarī's direct informant, see the source criticism above, 58, 75.

[179] Michael IX Palaiologos, co-emperor (1294-1320); see *Oxford Dictionary of Byzantium*, 1367-68.

[180] Michael IX Palaiologos married Rita, the sister of Het'um II of Armenia (Cilicia), in January 1296 (*Oxford Dictionary of Byzantium*, 1294). This fact is suggestive enough to trace the background of such co-operation between the two.

ried 600 or 700 soldiers. As they were about to land,[181] God sent winds blowing from all different directions against them. They were entirely dispersed, and some drowned. They retreated helter-skelter. By that time, the Mamluks were dispatching troops in order to defend [Beirut] against them, but when the news of the Franks' dispersal arrived, the dispatch of troops was stopped. Shaykh Muḥammad al-Maghribī related[182] on the authority of a man who happened to be present at the viceroy's place in Damascus while a postman was telling what he had heard from a Beiruti officer, "By God, for 40 years I have been working on the sea, and especially in the Beirut harbor. I have never seen such winds that rose and hit those ships. It's not the kind of wind that we are familiar with." God knows best.

The massacre in Sūdāq: In Ramaḍān (June, 1299), some merchants arrived in Damascus from Sūdāq.[183] They related that the ruler Nughiyah (Nogai),[184] the nephew of the ruler Baraka (Berke),[185] led his entire army and his adherents and came to Sūdāq in early spring. He ordered that every Sūdāqi who used to side with him should take with him his family, property, and belongings and get out of the city. All of his former followers thus did so while more than two-thirds [of the entire population] were left behind. Then he ordered the troops to surround the city and look for the townspeople one by one. They tortured them and plundered all of their properties and then slaughtered them. The entire populace was eventually killed. Afterwards, they set fire to the city and leveled it to the ground as if it had never existed.

The cause of this [massacre] lies in that the revenue collected from the city of Sūdāq used to be divided among four rulers (*malik*), one of whom was the ruler Nughiyah. It was said that the deputies of other rulers, namely his (i.e., Nughiyah's) partners [in sharing the revenue] of Sūdāq, had overlooked (*ta'addaw 'alā*) the rights of the deputies of the ruler Nughiyah in matters such as the stamp-tax (*al-ṭamghāh*) and others. Since Nughiyah was at the time the most senior among the rulers, [by doing so] they had infringed upon

---

[181] Al-Jazarī adds "and to launch an attack on Muslim land. . . ."

[182] Al-Jazarī has "related to me. . . ."

[183] Variants Sughdāq/Surozh, a Crimean trading-port. For the principality of Sūdāq, see *QI*, 14:73, 77; also, Thorau, *Baybars*, 28, note 24.

[184] The famous prince and general of the Golden Horde. He was killed in the battle in 699/1299. Scattered information about him can be found in Howorth, *The Mongols*, II/1:123-46; *CHIr*, 5:535, 384; Elham, *Lāǧīn*, 95, 131-33. His name is given by Ibn al-Dawādārī (*Kanz*, 9:index) as Anghāy.

[185] The khan of the Golden Horde, died in 1265 (Howorth) or 1266 (Barthold/Boyle). For his biography, see Howorth, *The Mongols*, II/1:103-25; "Berke," *EI*², by W. Barthold and I. A. Boyle.

his interests and rights. His wrath thus led to such a huge massacre. [The details of] this event will be mentioned below, God willing.[186]

Al-Malik al-Nāṣir and the Egyptian army's march to Syria: In this year, in Dhū al-Ḥijja, the first day of which fell on a Sunday (August 30, 1299)—and it was the *Nawrūz* (New Year's day) in Egypt as well as the first day of the month of Tūt in the Coptic calendar—, sultan al-Malik al-Nāṣir and the victorious Egyptian army left Cairo, marching to Syria. The sultan's departure from Cairo was on Dhū al-Ḥijja 26 (September 24, 1299).

The annual rise of the Nile: The blessed Nile reached [on the Nilometer's scale] 16 cubits and one-third cubit [over the old water level].[187]

The expansion at the Grand Mosque in Damascus: In this year, during his tenure as the manager of the Grand Mosque, Nāṣir al-Dīn Ibn 'Abd al-Salām renovated the shrine in which the Shāfi'ī qāḍīs performed the Friday prayer. A prayer chamber for the eunuchs *(zāwiyat al-khuddām)*[188] was added to the shrine and its annex building. The shrine became a match for the 'Alī Zayn al-'Ābidīn Mashhad.[189] He named [the new shrine] the 'Uthmān Shrine and appointed his son to be its imām. He led a massive congregation on Friday, Shawwāl 24 (July 25, 1299) at the time of the evening prayer.

The Ḥanafī chief judge's return to Damascus: In this year, the Ḥanafī chief judge Ḥusām al-Dīn returned to Damascus from Egypt on Thursday, Dhū al-Ḥijja 6 (September 4, 1299).[190] As usual, people came out to welcome him. He remained in charge of the office of chief judge at Damascus, the lectureship, and other positions. He held a renewed appointment for all this. He also had a robe of honor bestowed by the sultan which he wore on the day he came back. His son Jalāl al-Dīn thus left these posts and the office

---

[186] The event is not mentioned in the text below, however.

[187] The annual rise of the Nile is usually placed at the end of each year's *ḥawādith* section. It seems that the following paragraphs here were perhaps added from other sources. Other observations that support this hypothesis: 1) The sultan and the Egyptian army's movement to Syria has already been mentioned above and is repeated, with more details, below; 2) these passages do not follow the preceding chronological sequence.

[188] For the term *khuddām* (sing. *khādim*), "eunuchs," see Ayalon, "The Eunuchs in the Mamluk Sultanate," 267-68; "On the Eunuchs in Islam," 84-85. The most recent study of the eunuchs in the Mamluk period is found in Marmon, *Eunuchs and Sacred Boundaries*, 28, 43 (the *ḥārat al-khuddām*, i.e., the residential quarter of the eunuchs), 52-53 (the eunuchs' control of the access to the maqṣūra enclosures in the interior of mosques); however, a *zāwiya*, in a mosque, designated for the use of the eunuchs, is not noted in the above-mentioned studies.

[189] The tomb-sanctuary of 'Alī Zayn al-'Ābidīn; see Ibn Kathīr, *Bidāya*, 13:33, 194; also Pouzet, *Damas*, 138, 146.

[190] Cf. above, 97, notes 2, 3.

of judge. Shams al-Dīn al-Sarūjī[190] resumed the office of chief judge in Egypt.

The preparation for war in Damascus: In this year, in Dhū al-Ḥijja (August-September, 1299), reports on the Mongols' movement towards Syria increased. The secret agents constantly brought such reports back and fires were lighted on the sites [to sound the alarm]. Having inspected the arms storage at night, the viceroy of Damascus reviewed the army on the second of the month (August 31, 1299). Torches were burning and the masses got excited. On Monday, Dhū al-Ḥijja 24 (September 22, 1299), troops arrived in Damascus from Cairo. They were led by Amīr Sayf al-Dīn Quṭlū-Bek and a high ranking amīr from the Ẓāhirīya group.[191] His name was Sayf al-Dīn Nukiyah[192] and he was the father-in-law of both al-Malik al-Ṣāliḥ and al-Malik al-Ashraf, the sons of sultan al-Malik al-Manṣūr Sayf al-Dīn Qalāwūn.

New appointment to the office of viceroy in Tripoli: In this year, Amīr Sayf al-Dīn Kurt al-Manṣūrī assumed the office of viceroy in the Tripoli ports and the coastal fortresses in Rajab (April, 1299). Karīm al-Dīn Abū al-Karam, known as Ibn Laqlaq al-Mustawfī,[193] was appointed to be his chief of staff, replacing Majd al-Dīn Yūsuf Ibn al-Qabāqibī.[194] He set off to join him in Dhū al-Qa'da (August, 1299).

An investigation of the missing treasure: In this year, when the expedition (*al-mujarradūn*) returned to Damascus from Aleppo after their separation from Sayf al-Dīn Qibjāq,[195] [former] mamluks of Amīr 'Izz al-Dīn Aydamur al-Janājī were among them. The amīr had died of poisoning and left no heir other than [his responsibility to] the treasury (*bayt al-māl*). [Now] his *ustād-dār*, secretary, and former mamluks came. Horses, weapons, properties, girths, and other equipment were brought back. However, people asked them, "Where is the gold?" And they said, "By God, [before] setting off, he (i.e., Amīr Aydamur) borrowed 5,000 *dirhams* from Amīr Rukn al-Dīn al-Jāliq and

[190] Aḥmad ibn Ibrāhīm, died in 710/1310, a Ḥanbalī-turned-Ḥanafī jurist. The man was famous for his debate with Ibn Taymīya in his book on *'ilm al-kalām* (scholastic theology). For his biography, see al-'Asqalānī, *Durar*, 1:96;97; Ibn Kathīr, *Bidāya*, 14:60.

[191] I.e., the Mamluks of al-Malik al-Ẓāhir Baybars.

[192] His name is given as Nukay (Nogai) by Ibn al-Dawādārī (*Kanz*, 9:13). His being an in-law of Qalāwūn is not mentioned.

[193] Also known as Karīm al-Dīn al-Ṣaghīr al-Nāẓir, to be distinguished from Karīm al-Dīn al-Kabīr al-Qāḍī. His biography is not found. For his career, see Ibn al-Dawādārī, *Kanz*, 9:index.

[194] Unidentified. Pouzet mentions one Yūsuf ibn Qābiq, the master of a ṣūfī zāwiya around 705/1305-6 in Damascus; see *Damas*, 230.

[195] Cf. above, 111-13.

left his [golden] girth as security." When al-Jāliq was asked about that, he said, "Yes, I did take the golden girth. It was sold and I took the portion that covers the debt and put the rest [of the money] in the treasury." Aydamur's *ustād-dār* and secretary said, "We knew that he had two trunks full of gold. After our return from Gaza and the amīr's settling in Mt. Ṣāliḥīya,[197] he deposited the two trunks with the ḥadīth scholar 'Abd al-Ghanī['s sons] and the Ḥanbalīs in Mt. Ṣāliḥīya. On the night he was ordered to march out, he had the two trunks brought to him and then they were brought at night. But in the morning, we did not see them, nor did we know anything about them at all. Apparently he took from the trunks [what he needed for his] expenses and then sent them back to the above-mentioned Ḥanbalīs. That's all we know and, by God, nothing else is within our knowledge." They thus called on the ḥadīth scholar ['Abd al-Ghanī]'s sons and their fellow Ḥanbalīs for questioning. [In fact,] Amīr 'Izz al-Dīn had taken the two trunks from the Ḥanbalīs and deposited them with Fakhr al-Dīn 'Uthmān al-A'zāzī, a merchant at the Sharb Bazaar. He had told him that there was gold in the trunks and that he ought to watch them carefully. Nobody knew about this except Amīr [Aydamur] and his treasurer (*khazindār*).

[In detail:][198] When Amīr 'Izz al-Dīn al-Janāji was called upon to march towards Aleppo, he brought back the trunks from the ḥadīth scholar ['Abd al-Ghanī]'s sons and told his treasurer, "Rent some camels from those who do not know us and carry these two trunks at midnight on camels. Be careful not to let anybody recognize you and know about this. Send them to Fakhr al-Dīn al-A'zāzī and leave them at his house." The treasurer did exactly what he was asked: he took the trunks to Fakhr al-Dīn al-A'zāzī's house at the time of the dawn prayer. When morning came, Amīr [Aydamur] and his treasurer, and no one else, went to his house and saw the two trunks there. Then they entrusted them to him. He (i.e., the amīr) said, "That's [our] deposit with you. [Keep them] until we come back." And then he set off on the expedition. Both Amīr [Aydamur] and the treasurer were killed. When Fakhr al-Dīn al-A'zāzī saw that those Ḥanbalīs, as well as a large number of the amīr's bodyguards, his *ustād-dār*, and secretary, were blamed [for the loss of the treasure], despite their innocence, he said [to himself], "By God, I cannot wait to tell the truth. How could I bear to let these virtuous men be arrested and frightened on account of something that is stored with me while I myself am in a safe position?" So he got up and went to see Amīr Sayf al-Dīn Jāghān,

[197] At the foot of Mt. Qāsiyūn, to the north of Damascus; see *Q1*, 4:94-96.

[198] The narrative here is repetitious. I use square brackets to distinguish the different narrative lines of the story.

then the finance agent and the executive of the viceroy's office, and told him that he had the two trunks deposited by the late Amīr 'Izz al-Dīn Aydamur al-Janājī who had died in Aleppo. As soon as Amīr Sayf al-Dīn Jāghān heard that, he was overwhelmed with joy and said, "May God reward you! Give me your hand and let me kiss it! You have let 50 men enter paradise! I have accused them of such a crime and determined to punish and torture them while I never thought of you! You have proved their innocence and have brought them to paradise. May God reward you!" Then he asked, "Where are the trunks?" He replied, "At my house." So he took inspectors, court witnesses, and the chamberlain of the treasury and the bureau of inheritance with him to bring the trunks to the treasury. Inside the trunks there were 33,000 golden Egyptian *dīnārs*, escheat property (*ḥashr*),[199] jewelry, golden girths, belts (*kamar anāt*), turbans embellished with silver and gold thread (*kilāwat zarkash*), golden and silver vessels, and other items worth 30,000 Egyptian *dīnārs*. The total value was 63,000 Egyptian *dīnārs*.

[As a matter of fact,] upon hearing the news of Amīr 'Izz al-Dīn al-Janājī's death and even before his former followers (*tarkatuhu*)[200] came over, Fakhr al-Dīn al-A'zāzī had asked to meet with the chief judge Imām al-Dīn al-Qazwīnī and his deputy Qāḍī Jamāl al-Dīn al-Zar'ī and told them, "There is a deposit placed with me by some amīr. And I want to return it to its owners." The qāḍīs said, "Keep it with you for the time being until the amīr's death is confirmed and [make sure whether] he has left heirs or not. If he does have one, give it to him; and if not, then bring it to the treasury." So he had waited until the amīr's mamluks came and the above investigation took place. May God reward the man for his virtue and honesty.

This year's pilgrimage and the turmoil in Mecca: In this year, the Syrian pilgrims were led by Amīr Shams al-Dīn al-'Ayntābī, one of the Damascene amīrs. The pilgrims from Egypt were led by the treasurer and *amīr-jānidār* Amīr 'Izz al-Dīn Aybak al-Manṣūrī. On the journey, they suffered hardships of thirst and hunger. They were disturbed at Mt. 'Arafāt and were harassed in downtown Mecca. Many of them were robbed; their clothes were stripped off and taken away. Some of them were killed and others injured. Shaykh Shihāb al-Dīn Aḥmad ibn Ma'īn al-Dīn al-Jazarī had accompanied the pilgrims from Damascus. He then stayed on in Mecca and enrolled in a resi-

---

[199] The word *ḥashr* does not seem to fit the context; it is probably an error for *jashsh* (Persian and Turkish *jesh*), "sky-blue glass bead."

[200] For the meaning of *tarka*, "people that are left," cf. a ḥadīth: *jā'a al-Khalīl ilā Makka yuṭāli'u tarkatahu* (Abraham came to Mecca to get knowledge of his *tarka*, i.e., Hagar and her son Ishmael), quoted by Lane.

dential learning circle near the sanctuary (*jāwara*) until the year A.H. 701, and then returned to Egypt. He mentioned that a total of 11 people, two women and nine men, were killed, and that the ruler of Mecca, Amīr Najm al-Dīn Numayya,[201] received his share of 500 camels that had been plundered from the Egyptian, Syrian, Bedouin, and other pilgrims. He said that after the departure of the pilgrims, camel meat was on sale in Mecca. Most of the residential students in the sanctuary refused to eat meat, protesting the looting.

3. The Year of 699/1299-1300[202]

Al-Malik al-Nāṣir and the Egyptian army's march to Damascus: As this year began, sultan al-Malik al-Nāṣir was on his way [from] Egypt [to Syria].[203] He arrived at 'Asqalān (Ascalon) in Muḥarram (September-October, 1299) and stayed on until Rabī' I (November-December, 1299). He entered Damascus on Friday, Rabī' I 8 (December 3, 1299) and stayed in the Damascus Citadel. Festive celebrations were held on his arrival. Although it had been raining for the previous two days, it did not prevent townspeople from coming out to watch the happy event. His entry into the city was marked by an extravagant military parade (*tajammul*). In this respect, he perhaps exceeded all the other princes (*malik*) before him. He had been preoccupied by affairs in the Gaza region for two months or less.[204] As reports on the Mongols' advance to-

---

[201] Abū Numayya Muḥammad ibn Abī Sa'd ibn Rājiḥ ibn Qatāda al-Ḥasanī (as it occurs in the present edition, 1, 48, 203, 240), died in 701/1301. His obituary is found in Ibn al-Dawādārī, *Kanz*, 9:80, which gives his name as Muḥammad ibn Idrīs ibn Qatāda ibn al-Ḥasanī, or Muḥammad ibn Idrīs ibn 'Alī ibn Qatāda.

[202] For the second Mongol campaign in Syria, see d'Ohsson, *Histoire des Mongols*; Howorth, *The Mongols*; also Somogyi, "Adh-Dhahabī's record of the destruction of Damascus" in which he presented an annotated translation of al-Dhahabī's account from the *Tārīkh al-Islām*, based on a British Museum manuscript. Somogyi is of the opinion that al-Dhahabī was "a witness of the Mongol campaign in his own city" (355, 359) and, therefore, the author of the record. However, as will be seen through a comparison, much of al-Dhahabī's account of this "Damascus diary" is very similar to that of al-Yūnīnī (and al-Jazarī). More research is needed on the sources shared by Syrian historians at the time; cf. above, chapter 3. A bibliography of the Mongol campaigns in 1299-1301 is also to be found in Irwin, *Early Mamluk Sultanate*, 13.

[203] Added after al-Jazarī.

[204] According to Ibn al-Dawādārī, the sultan first came to a place called Manzilat Tall al-'Ujūl to quell the Oriat Mongols' uprising and then he arrived in 'Asqalān and stayed there until Rabī' I 8; see *Kanz*, 9:15; also Somogyi, "Adh-Dhahabī's record," 360, note 23.

wards the Muslim lands were frequent, it was time for him to come [to Damascus]. So he came and brought Egyptian troops with him.

The battle of Wādī al-Khazindār:[205] The Syrian army marched forward and they were followed by the Egyptian army. The sultan himself, with the remaining troops, marched on Sunday midday, Rabīʻ I 17 (December 12, 1299) from Damascus to Hims to [confront] the invaders. The people of Damascus stayed behind praying for them.

On Thursday, Rabīʻ I 29 (December 24, 1299), news circulated in Damascus that the entire [Mamluk] army had been routed. The battle[206] took place on Wednesday (December 23, 1299).[207] The [Mamluk] troops were then at Hims. Fully armed, they had been riding and ready for battle for three nights and days, so they became very tired and irritated. Prices soared and meanwhile fodder was in short supply. They heard that the Mongols had already moved near to Salamīya. They also heard that the [Mongol] troops wanted to retreat and go home when they learned that the [Mamluk] troops were many and were completely loyal to their master. Such information was in fact a trick [by the Mongols]. On Wednesday morning, the [Mamluk] army rode from Hims, closing in on the [Mongol] army near Salamīya, in a place called Wādī al-Khazindār. The Mongols thus mounted and charged head-on. The battle of Wādī al-Khazindār started at five o'clock in the morning,[208] and soon turned white-hot between the two parties. The left wing of Muslim troops launched an attack upon the Mongols. Over 5,000 of them (i.e., the Mongols) were killed while a few of those [Mamluk troops] lost their lives.[209] The center launched an attack as well. Then God left the Muslims in the

---

[205] Also as al-Khazandār; see Somogyi, "Adh-Dhahabī's record," 361, note 28.

[206] For the Mongol side of the story of this battle, especially Haithon's account, see *CHIr*, 5:387-88.

[207] The non-coincidence of the dates of the battle assigned by Arab authors has been noticed by Little (*Introduction*, 15): Rabīʻ 18 or 28 (December 13 or 23, by Baybars al-Manṣūrī), Rabīʻ 29 (December 24, by Ibn al-Dawādārī). The Mongol sources had it that the Mamluks had intended to attack on December 23, but moved it up to December 22; see *CHIr*, 5:387.

[208] Other Arabic sources, e.g., Ibn al-Dawādārī (*Kanz*, 9:16), al-Dhahabī, (Somogyi, "Adh-Dhahabī's record," 361) also give five o'clock as the time when the battle began. However, the Mongol source, e.g., Haithon, claims that the battle lasted from 11 o'clock until nightfall; see *CHIr*, 5:388.

[209] Ibn al-Dawādārī states that it was the Mamluk right wing that attacked the Mongol left (*Kanz*, 9:16), but Baybars al-Manṣūrī gives the same account as al-Yūnīnī. On the other hand, some Mongol sources also report that Quṭlū-Shāh, the commander of the Mongol right wing (i.e., to fight the Mamluk left), ordered the drums to be beaten and the Mamluks, imagining the presence of Ghāzān, charged in great strength upon the right wing, which broke before them; see *CHIr*, 5:387.

lurch. The [Mamluk] right wing was defeated. So were those marching behind the standards of the Mamluk sultanate (*al-sanājiq al-sulṭānīya*). God routed them. At nightfall, things came to an end. The sultan led a small group of soldiers [in retreat] to Ba'labakk. Equipment and heavy weapons were abandoned and scattered everywhere. Somebody reported that he saw lances thrown on roads as if they were reeds and nobody even bothered to look at them. Soldiers took off helmets from their heads and threw their cuirasses (*jawāshin*) and clothing away in order to lighten the burden on their horses, so the horses could carry them to escape [faster]. Most of the defeated troops went along the road to Ba'labakk.

Damascus in the aftermath of the defeat: On Saturday (December 26, 1299), when people in Damascus confirmed the whole story, they stopped performing *qunūt*-prayers[210] and supplicating (*al-du'ā'*), and became silent. They began to mention good things[211] about the ruler of the Mongols (i.e., Ghāzān), saying that he was a Muslim, that the majority of his troops had been converted to Islam, that they did not pursue the defeated [Mamluk] troops, that when the battle was over they did not kill any more, and that whenever they captured someone they just took his arms and horse and then let him go free. Rumors of this kind increased. The best thing of all was that they did not follow the Mamluks to Damascus.[212] People thus came, picked up their families, belongings, and valuables as much as they could and then headed for Egypt.[213]

The [initial] silence [in Damascus] on Saturday had no real reason. As noontime came, a hubbub of cries suddenly emerged. Unveiled women ran out [from their houses] and the streets were jammed with crowds. If one had asked "what's wrong with these folks?" he would have been told that the Mongols had already entered the city. Such rumors were of course groundless. But people ran away, leaving their shops open behind them. After a while, the situation calmed down a little. The turmoil, however, reached the mountain area and its vicinities. About 10 people were killed at the city gates due to the crowds. Among them were the ḥadīth scholar Najm al-Dīn al-Baghdādī

---

[210] The text has *qunūṭ*; the term "usually seems to be connected in meaning with *du'ā*'" at the *ṣalā*; in the oft-quoted ḥadīth Muḥammad continued to appeal (*yad'ū 'alā*), for a month, for God's help against the enemy; see "Ḳunūt," *EI*², by A. J. Wensinck.

[211] The manuscripts have *khayran*, but *khabaran* (information) is also possible.

[212] Ibn al-Dawādārī explains that the reason why the Mongols did not chase the retreating Mamluk troops into Damascus was that they feared that the Mamluk troops' withdrawal might well be a stratagem; see *Kanz*, 9:17.

[213] For the mass flight from Damascus to Egypt in this year, see Ashtor, *A Social and Economic History*, 290.

and a young Qur'ān reciter from the Maghrib. People remained in such a [confused] state all day Saturday. They were saying that the dignitaries of the city were about to meet with Amīr Sayf al-Dīn Qibjāq with presents in order to sue for a [peaceful] settlement. On Saturday night, the [Shāfi'ī] chief judge Imām al-Dīn [al-Qazwīnī], the Mālikī chief judge Jamāl al-Dīn al-Ṣāliḥī, Tāj al-Dīn Ibn al-Shīrāzī,[214] the governor[s] of the city and countryside of Damascus,[215] the market inspector, and a large number of citizens set off for Egypt.

On the eve of Sunday (December 27, 1299), prisoners in the Ṣaghīr Gate[216] jail broke[217] the door and managed to escape. It was said that they were 250 in number.[218] They made their way to the Jābiya Gate,[219] broke the locks, opened the gate and then got out of the city. The people [of Damascus] were in deadly silence and terrible confusion on Sunday morning. They did not know what the outcome of the situation would be. Some of them were panicky. Others were hoping to have their lives spared. And some hoped for more: they expected justice and order. They assembled in 'Alī [Zayn al-'Ābidīn] Mashhad the same day and discussed whether they should send a delegation to the ruler Maḥmūd Ghāzān in hope of gaining an assurance of safety for the sake of the Damascene citizens.[220] Among those who attended the assembly were: the chief judge, then the preacher at the Grand Mosque, Badr al-Dīn Ibn Jamā'a, Shaykh Zayn al-Dīn al-Fāriqī,[221] Shaykh Taqī al-Dīn Ibn Taymīya, the chief judge Najm al-Dīn Ibn Ṣaṣrā, Ṣāḥib Fakhr al-Dīn Ibn al-Shīrajī,[222]

---

[214] He was the market inspector in Damascus in 690/1290, minister of the public treasury (*wakīl al-māl*) and inspector of the Grand Mosque in 694/1294, and head of the chancellery (*nāẓir al-dīwan*) in Cairo in 696/1296.

[215] The text has *walī al-balad wa-al-barr*; however, as the text above shows, the two offices were held by different persons: the governor of Damascus (*al-balad*) was Jamāl al-Dīn Ibrāhīm Ibn al-Naḥḥās and the governor of the countryside (*al-barr*) was 'Imād al-Dīn Ibn al-Nashshābī.

[216] At the southern side of the city; also cf. Wulzinger, *Damaskus die islamische Stadt*, 183.

[217] The text has *aḥraqa* (set it on fire), and so does Ibn al-Dawādārī (*Kanz*, 9:18) and Zetterstéen, 59; but it may well be *akhraqa* (pierced), which is in accordance with al-Jazarī's *naqaba* (broke).

[218] Al-Dhahabī has "about two hundred" (Somogyi, "Adh-Dhahabī's record," 364, note 42), and according to Howorth (*The Mongols*, 3:441), there were 150.

[219] At the southwest side of the city; also cf. Wulzinger, *Damaskus die islamische Stadt*, 185.

[220] Al-Jazarī's version ends here.

[221] 'Abd Allāh ibn Marwān, then the master of the Ashrafīya Dār al-Ḥadīth. He died in 703/1303. For his biography, see al-'Asqalānī, *Durar*, 2:411-12; Ibn Kathīr, *Bidāya*, 14:30; Pouzet, *Damas*, 189, 389-90.

[222] He was then the head of administration (*nāẓir al-dawāwīn*); see the present edition, 96.

Qāḍī 'Izz al-Dīn Ibn al-Zākī, Shaykh Wajīh al-Dīn Ibn Munajjā, Mawlā 'Izz al-Dīn Ibn al-Qalānisī,[223] and his cousin Sharaf al-Dīn, Amīn al-Dīn Shuqayr al-Ḥarrānī, Sharīf Zayn al-Dīn Ibn 'Adnān,[224] Shaykh Najm al-Dīn Ibn Abī al-Ṭayyib, Nāṣir al-Dīn Ibn 'Abd al-Salām, Sharaf al-Dīn Ibn 'Izz al-Dīn Ibn al-Shīrajī, Ṣāḥib Shihāb al-Dīn al-Ḥanafī, Qāḍī Shams al-Dīn Ibn al-Ḥarīrī,[225] Shaykh Muḥammad Ibn Qawām al-Nābulusī,[226] Jalāl al-Dīn, Qāḍī Imām al-Dīn's brother, and Jalāl al-Dīn, Qāḍī Ḥusām al-Dīn al-Ḥanafī's son, as well as a large group of Qur'ān reciters, jurisconsults, and court functionaries.

On Monday (December 28, 1299), after the midday prayer, they set out on the journey. Shortly after their departure, a town crier (*munādin*) of Damascus announced a decree issued by Amīr 'Alam al-Dīn Arjuwāsh:[227] "Not a single item of military equipment is allowed to be put on sale! Your sultan is still in power!" Horses, however, were on sale in Damascus for 50, 40, or 30 *dirhams* each or less. A cuirass worth 100 *dirhams* was sold for 20 or 25 *dirhams*, and a rug worth 100 *dirhams* was sold for 30. There were no longer any markets except those [peddlers] who cried their wares in the city. The city was left with neither mayor, nor viceroy, nor financial agent, nor market inspector, nor judge (*ḥākim*). People began to bully (*akl*) each other. If someone wanted to sell food, he could put any price on it, as high as he chose, and nobody would argue with him. One might be beaten or scolded and would receive no comfort, because people would show neither sympathy nor pity towards him. One could do anything he wished and could occupy any houses he was able to seize. The chaos was bad in Damascus, and it was even worse in the suburbs.

The retreating Mamluk troops: As for the Egyptian and Syrian troops, it is impossible to describe. Most of the amīrs were left alone by themselves and looked feeble and powerless. They had no retinue to execute their command. On the way to al-Kiswa, they were in a great hurry. They were fearful and dared not look at anybody. They were terrified and afraid that the common people would revile them because of the defeat, and that nobody would pay

---

[223] Ḥamza ibn As'ad al-Tamīmī al-Dimashqī, died in 729/1329. For his biography, see al-'Asqalānī, *Durar*, 2:162-63; Pouzet, *Damas*, 43. Zetterstéen has his name as 'Umar Ibn al-Qalānisī (60).

[224] Al-Ḥusayn ibn Muḥammad, died in 708/1310. For his biography, see Ibn Kathīr, *Bidāya*, 14:49.

[225] Muḥammad, died in 728/1328. He was the Ḥanafī chief judge during 699/1300-700/1301. For his career, see Pouzet, *Damas*, 73, 126, 390, 416.

[226] He died in 718/1318. For his biography, see Ibn al-'Imād, *Shadharāt*, 6:49-50; Ibn Kathīr, *Bidāya*, 14:89-90; Pouzet, *Damas*, 243.

[227] He was then the commander of the Damascus Citadel.

attention to their words or follow their orders. A considerable number of troops were unable to continue the return journey to Egypt because their horses either refused to go further or were seized on the way, or simply because they themselves were too weak and poor. They could not even find a place to stay unless they changed their soldiers' uniforms. So some of them were seen wearing officers' uniforms and some shaved their hair[228] or took off the saddle blankets covering their clothes. It is true that God was extremely kind towards them in that He did not let the enemies pursue them and come after them except during the battle and shortly after it. This was God's kindness to them and it was a miracle indeed.

The soaring of prices in Damascus: The price of bread rose. One *raṭl* was sold for two *dirhams*. [The price of] corn flour rose also: a sack of flours cost 40 *dirhams* instead of [the original] 25.[229]

The Mongols in al-Biqāʿ and Wādī al-Taym: On Wednesday (December 30, 1299), a report circulated that a group of Mongols came to al-Biqāʿ and Wādī al-Taym to catch [Mamluk] soldiers. They caused a disturbance by plundering them, arresting them, and things like that.

The Mongols in Damascus: In the suburbs of Damascus, there were many incidents of the destruction of houses, tearing down doors and roofs, and pulling out nails [from buildings]. In the orchards and gardens, the same thing was happening: trees were cut down to be sold as firewood and pigeon houses were dismantled. This situation continued until the end of Thursday, Rabīʿ II 6 (December 31, 1299), when four Mongols arrived [in Damascus]. Together with them was Sharīf al-Qummī[230] who had escaped from [Damascus previously], with two or three other men, before the departure of the delegation of [the above-mentioned] dignitaries. [The Damascenes] took the four Mongols to the Bādharā'īya Madrasa[231] because it was near to the Dār al-Ṣāḥib.[232] It was said that they performed the evening prayer there.

On Friday morning (January 1, 1300), all the city gates remained closed. People were careful not to disturb the Mongols mentioned above. When it

---

[228] According to al-Qalqashandī, only the sultan and amīrs shaved their hair (but not forelocks) in order to wear the so-called *kallūta* head-gear; see *Q2*, 288-89.

[229] For the grain price in Damascus at the time, see Ashtor, *A Social and Economic History*, 293-98.

[230] His name varies as al-Ghutmī (Zetterstéen, 61), al-Qumayy, or al-Qamī (Somogyi, "Adh-Dhahabī's record," 365, note 47).

[231] A Shāfiʿī madrasa in Damascus; see al-Dhahabī, *al-ʿIbar*, 5:293; Ibn Kathīr, *Bidāya*, 13:196-97, 262; Ibn al-ʿImād, *Shadharāt*, 5:331-32. The name is also given as al-Bādarā'īya (Ibn al-Dawādārī, *Kanz*, 9:index; Zetterstéen, 61).

[232] The place is unidentified.

was close to the Friday prayer, the locks on the Tūmā (St. Thomas) Gate[233] were broken. This was done by the deputies of governors (*nuwwāb al-wulāt*) al-Shujā' Humām,[234] Ibn Ḍā'in,[235] who was then the [deputy?] mayor of Damascus,[236] and Ibn al-Dhahabī al-Naqīb.[237] Then the Friday prayer was held, but the sultan's name was not mentioned in the sermon. When the prayer was over, a group of Mongols arrived in the suburbs on the periphery of Damascus. Among them was a general called Ismā'īl who was said to be a relative of the ruler [Ghāzān]. They settled down in the garden area on the edge of the city (*al-ẓāhir*) on the Qābūn road.[238] They brought with them the amnesty firman to the Bādharā'īya Madrasa. The firman, wrapped in leather, was presented and shown to the dignitaries remaining in the city so that they would gather to hear it. People assembled in the Bādharā'īya [Madrasa]. It was proclaimed that the public reading of the firman would take place in the presence of the general [Ismā'īl] who was then in the garden area of the suburbs. So people waited. Then it was said that they (i.e., the Mongols) went to the Grand Mosque and, riding on horseback, passed by the Rawāḥīya Madrasa[239] at around 10 o'clock. They took a town crier with them to call out for the re-opening of shops and business. The ruler [Ghāzān]'s name was cited and blessed by them. They arrived in the Grand Mosque. And people began to gather around until the mosque was almost packed. Then they came out through the Naẓẓāfīn Gate without anything having been read.

The Damascene 'ulamā's meeting with Ghāzān: Friday (January 1, 1300) afternoon, the delegation of dignitaries arrived in Damascus. Some of them came a little later. They had been away for four days. Now they came back and reported that they had met the ruler [Ghāzān] at [the village of] al-Nabk[240]

---

[233] At the northeast side of the city, near the Christian and Jewish district.

[234] The name is read by Somogyi as ash-Shajjā' Himām; see "Adh-Dhahabī's record," 365.

[235] Al-Dhahabī has "Ibn Ṭā'ūn"; see Somogyi, "Adh-Dhahabī's record," 365.

[236] The text has *wālī al-balad*, "the governor of Damascus"; no record, however, shows that he was officially appointed to the office. From the context above, he might well be a *nā'ib al-wālī*, "deputy mayor"; also cf. Somogyi, "Adh-Dhahabī's record," 365.

[237] This name is not mentioned in other sources.

[238] In the northeast suburb of Damascus.

[239] Also as al-Rūḥānīya, a Ḥanafī madrasa. For details, see Pouzet, *Damas*, 49, 52, 65.

[240] The place name is not very clear in either manuscript; in Landberg 139 it appears to be *n-b-k* or *b-n-k* ("the shore" of the Euphrates?) while in Ahmet III 2907 *y-n-k* or *n-y-k*. Ibn al-Dawādārī's *Kanz* and Zetterstéen have *al-layl*, "at night," while al-Dhahabī has al-Nabl (Somogyi, "Adh-Dhahabī's record," 366) which is unidentified. I prefer the current reading of al-Nabk on account of the fact that Ghāzān was then encamped in Marj Rāhiṭ (*CHIr*, 5:388) which was not far away from al-Nabk; for al-Nabk, a village near the Marj of Damascus, see *QI*, 4:97, 112.

while he was marching with his army. They dismounted in front of him and some of them even bent to kiss the ground [before him]. He thus stopped to listen to them. And a contingent of Mongol troops dismounted from horses in front of him. A translator was there to interpret between the two sides. The main message was that "as regards the amnesty decree you requested, we have dispatched it before your coming." The spokesman [of the Damascenes] was Ṣāḥib Fakhr al-Dīn[241] and the appeal was made by the preacher Badr al-Dīn [Ibn Jamā'a]. They then presented the food they brought with them [as presents]. However, his (i.e., Ibn Jamā'a's) appeal appeared to have very limited impact on the ruler [Ghāzān]. They told them that the ruler [Ghāzān] was to stay in the meadows of Marj [Rāhiṭ] and would not enter the city of Damascus until Friday, and that all the city gates should be closed except one in order to avoid turmoil and wrongdoing.[242]

Ghāzān's amnesty firman: Saturday afternoon (January 2, 1300), Amīr Ismā'īl and his colleague Amīr Muḥammad came with a group of Mongols to the sermon chamber (*maqṣūrat al-khaṭāba*).[243] The two amīrs were seated in the seat of honor in the chamber. The preacher at the Mosque [Ibn Jamā'a], Ibn al-Shīrajī, Ibn al-Qalānisī, Ibn Munajjā, and Ibn Ṣaṣrā as well as some others were present at the reading of the amnesty firman. The elite and commoners alike assembled here and filled up the chamber, which was under the Nasr [Cupola]. The firman was read to the public upon the gate (*al-sudda*).[244] He who opened it and read it was one of the collaborators with (*al-wāṣilīn ma'a*) the Mongols. And it was delivered [to the audience] by the muezzin al-Mujāhid.

The text of the firman is as follows:[245]

> By the might of God, the Sublime, the Amīrs of Ten Thousand (*umarā' al-tūmān*),[246] of One Thousand, of One Hundred, and all our soldiers—Mongols, Tajiks(?),[247] Armenians, Georgians, as well as others who obey

---

[241] Al-Dhahabī has "Ibn al-Shīrajī"; see Somogyi, "Adh-Dhahabī's record," 366.

[242] Ibn al-Dawādārī adds "by the Mongol troops"; *Kanz*, 9:20.

[243] Located at the Grand Mosque of Damascus, it was reserved for the sovereign rulers; see Ziadeh, *Damascus*, 71-72.

[244] For *al-sudda*, see Amin, et al., *Mamluk Architecture*, 62.

[245] Several translations of this firman are available; among them are Quatremère, II/II:151-54; Howorth, *The Mongols*, 3:441-43; d'Ohsson, *Histoire des Mongols*, 4:245-49. Slightly varied versions of the Arabic text are found in Ibn al-Dawādārī, *Kanz*, 9:20-23; Zetterstéen, 62-64.

[246] Tūmān, or Ṭūmān, is a Mongol word for ten thousand; see Spuler, *Mongolen*, 399. The title is also given as *amīr al-nuwīn*; see *Q1*, 4:423-24.

[247] The text has *al-bārik*, perhaps an error for *al-tājik*.

us—should be informed that God illuminated our hearts with the light of Islam, and guided us to the religion of the Prophet—upon him be the best blessing and salvation! *Is he whose breast God has expanded unto Islam, so he walks in a light from his Lord . . .? But woe to those whose hearts are hardened against the remembrance of God! Those are in the manifest error.*[248] We heard that the rulers of Egypt and Syria had departed from the path of the Faith. They failed to keep the rules of Islam, broke their covenant [with Islam] and swore wicked oaths. They did not remain loyal [to God] and were thus unable to receive the fulfillment of [God's] promise. Their affairs were in disorder. When one of them assumed power, *he would hasten about the earth, to do corruption there and to destroy the tillage and the stock, and God loves not corruption.*[249] Their trademark became well-known as treating people unjustly, extending aggressive hands to their people's wives and properties, disregarding justice and fairness, and committing oppression and tyranny. When we heard all of this, the wrath of the Faith and the feeling of resentment on behalf of the cause of Islam forced us to come to these lands, in a common effort with our numerous soldiers, to put this aggression to an end and pull this tyranny away. We have made a solemn pledge to ourselves that if God, the Sublime, gave us success in conquering these lands, we would bring this aggression and corruption to an end, and spread justice and charity all over the region, in obedience to the Divine Command. *Surely God bids to justice and good-doing and giving to kinsmen; and He forbids indecency, dishonor, and insolence, admonishing you, so that haply you will remember.*[250] In response to the tasks with which the Messenger [Muḥammad]—God bless him and grant him salvation!—was entrusted, it was said to him that, "*Those doers of justice* (al-muqsiṭūn) *are to be upon pulpits of Light which are located on the right side of the Merciful. And both of His hands are to be at the right side of those who act justly in their rule upon their people and in the way they fulfill their responsibilities.*"[251] Since our sincere intention has included these praiseworthy goals and firm vows, God bestowed upon us the joy of receiving the good tiding of evident triumph and grand conquest. God has completed His grace upon us. He has revealed to us the divine-inspired peace. We have, therefore, defeated the tyrant enemy and

---

[248] *Qur'ān*, 39:22. The translation is that of A. J. Arberry.

[249] *Qur'ān*, 2:205. Arberry translated *tawallā* as "he turns his back." I prefer to render the term, within the context, as "he assumed power."

[250] *Qur'ān*, 16:90.

[251] Muslim, *Imāra*, 18; al-Nasā'ī, *Ādāb al-quḍāt*, 1; Aḥmad Ibn Ḥanbal, 2:160. For the reference to al-*muqsiṭūn*, also cf. *Qur'ān*, 5:42, 49:9, 60:8.

evil army. We made them, like the hands of Sheba, split[252] and *tore them utterly to pieces.*[253] And eventually, *the truth has come, and falsehood has vanished away; surely falsehood is ever certain to vanish.*[254] So, our chests have opened up to Islam, our minds have been strengthened by the true judgment. We have affiliated with a group of people that *God has endeared to* them *belief, decking it fair in* their *hearts, and He has made detestable to them unbelief and ungodliness and disobedience. Those—they are the right-minded, by God's favor and blessing.*[255] So it is our duty to abide by these trusted covenants and confirmed vows. We have, therefore, issued strict regulations that none of our troops, in any rank, should interfere with [the affairs of] Damascus, or its adjacent areas as well as all the rest of the Syrian provinces, that the troops should refrain from assaulting [the civilians'] lives, properties and wives, and that the troops should not loiter around the civilians' sanctuary (*ḥimā*) by any means. Only in this way, would they (i.e., the civilians) cherish with relaxed breasts and have great expectations for the prosperity of the country, in that everybody would be actively engaged in his own business: trade, agriculture, and the like.

As a matter of fact, the tremendous chaos [in Damascus] and the large presence of troops have galvanized the desire of a small number of soldiers, as well as others, to loot and arrest civilians. We have already executed those in the hope that others would learn a lesson and would give up their greedy desire for pillage, arrest, and other wrongdoing. They all ought to know that after the promulgation of this clearly stated decree, we surely will not tolerate [such behavior] any more, and that they must not interfere with the affairs of the people of other religions as well, regardless whether those are Jews, Christians, or Sabians, as long as they pay the *jizya* taxes, fulfilling their legal duties. That is because according to 'Alī—upon him be salvation!—as long as they pay the *jizya* taxes, their properties become like our properties, and their blood becomes like our blood. The sultans are commissioned with the care of those obedient non-Muslims just as they are with the care of Muslims, for they are also their subjects. [The Prophet]—God bless him and grant him salvation!—said, "The imām in charge of people is their guardian. Every guardian is responsible for his subjects."[256]

---

[252] See *Qur'ān*, 27:22, 34:15, "split as the hands of Sheba."
[253] *Qur'ān*, 34:19.
[254] *Qur'ān*, 17:81.
[255] *Qur'ān*, 49:7-8. The words "them" and "their" in the *Qur'ān* read "you" and "your."
[256] Al-Bukhārī, *Aḥkām*, 1; *Istiqrāḍ*, 20; Muslim, *Imāra*, 20; Aḥmad Ibn Ḥanbal, 2, 54, 111.

> So, all the qāḍīs, preachers, shaykhs, 'ulamā', the 'Alids, all the dignitaries as well as commoners ought to celebrate this salubrious victory and splendid triumph and enjoy the grand happiness and jubilee, praying for this invincible dynasty and triumphant empire day and night. This decree was issued on Rabī' II 5, 699 (December 30, 1299) and is made public on the gate of the prosperous Grand Mosque in the capital Damascus on Saturday, Rabī' II 8 (January 2, 1300).

When the reading of the firman was over, people cheered loudly, praising God and wishing good to the ruler [Ghāzān], and as usual, making a lot of noise. The firman made them calm down in relief, assuming that its promises would eventually be fulfilled. After the proclamation of the firman, the Mongols stayed on in the chamber where they performed the afternoon prayer and then went back to their camp.

The continuous disturbances in Damascus: On Sunday, Rabī' II 9 (January 3, 1300), a number of Damascene inhabitants in the Qaymarīya [Madrasa?][257] area suffered damage and humiliation by the Mongols who demanded horses and money.

On Monday, Rabī' II 10 (January 4, 1300), the [Mongol] troops approached Damascus and surrounded the Ghūṭa area. All kinds of evil things: violence, disaster, and pillage, took place. They seized civilians' belongings and slaughtered a number of villagers. The trouble spread and many rumors were reported back in Damascus. However, nobody was able to get out of the city. Some inhabitants [in the city] kept watching, from above the city wall, terrible things—such as plundering, violence, and smashing doors [of houses]—happening in the suburban areas (*al-ḥawāḍir al-barrānīya*), in towns like al-'Uqayba, al-Shāghūr, Qaṣr Ḥajjāj, Ḥikr al-Sumāq, and al-Sab'a. Rumors of the day had it that a large number of Mongols were passing by the periphery of Damascus, heading for the route to al-Kiswa. People thus speculated that they had been ordered to march on Egypt.

The effort to persuade Arjuwāsh to surrender the Damascus Citadel: At the end of this day (January 4, 1300), Sayf al-Dīn Qibjāq, the *silāḥ-dār* Baktimur and others arrived in Damascus and stayed in the [Khāṣṣa] Square.[258]

---

[257] A Shāfi'ī madrasa; see Pouzet, *Damas*, 152-53, 156-58. However, Somogyi suggests that the Alms-House al-Qaymarīya (market) is meant here; see Somogyi, "Adh-Dhahabī's record," 367, note 56.

[258] The word *al-maydān* was usually used in speaking of the *maydān al-khāṣṣa* in Damascus; see Somogyi, "Adh-Dhahabī's record," 367, note 59 and the references given there. However, it was also used, according to Brinner, in speaking of the Akhḍar Square; cf. above, 123, note 159.

On the way they had talked to Arjuwāsh, the commander of the Damascus Citadel. They advised him to surrender the Citadel and said to him, "You are fully responsible for the lives of the Muslims. A tremendous disaster is now facing them." He replied, "It is you that are responsible for such bloodshed. You are the ones who have caused all this. It is because of you that it happened." He was unwilling to comply with their demand.

On Tuesday morning, Rabī' II 11 (January 5, 1300), a memo (*mithāl*) from the viceroy Amīr Ismā'īl was brought over. In the memo, he ordered 'ulamā', learned persons (*ṣulaḥā'*), shaykhs, and notables (*ru'asā'*) to talk to Arjuwāsh and try to convince him to surrender the Citadel; otherwise, the memo claimed, the [Mongol] army would enter the city, and neither the Citadel nor the city would survive. The orders were issued in strong language. Thereupon, a group of these notables met in the Ashrafiya Dār al-Ḥadīth.[259] The ṣūfīs also joined the meeting. They then sent an envoy to Arjuwāsh but the latter did not accede to their requests. He said, "Yesterday Qibjāq and his followers sent messengers to me and I did not even bother to listen to them on the matter, [let alone to you people!]"[260] So the group wended their way from the Dār Ḥadīth to the gate of the Citadel. They stood in front of the gate and begged Arjuwāsh to send out a messenger. He did not comply. Therefore, they sent a messenger to deliver their greetings and message. He was very rude in response and asked, "Who are those guys?" The messenger mentioned their names one by one. He started to curse them and said, "Those are hypocrites and liars. They have let the Muslims down! They have surrendered the city to the enemy!" The messenger explained to him that when they went to the Mongols [asking for a truce], they realized that the Mongols were already marching towards us (i.e., the Muslims). Arjuwāsh said, " The enemy in fact only sent some envoys such as Sharīf al-Qummī and men like him to enter the city, and I don't give a damn about it. And besides, here is a pigeon-post to me from the sultan, the lord of Egypt. It says that they (i.e., the Egyptian army) gathered in Gaza and defeated the Mongol regiment chasing after them. It also contains the commission of the charge of the Citadel." Amongst those who stood at the gate of the Citadel was Badr al-Dīn Ibn Faḍl Allāh. Arjuwāsh recognized the man when the names of the group were mentioned to him. So he said, "Let Ibn Faḍl Allāh come in and take a look at the pigeon-post. It is written by his brother. He must be familiar with his handwriting." A soldier came out to the gate and called for him. However, Ibn

[259] For the Ashrafiya Dār al-Ḥadīth, see Pouzet, *Damas*, 483.
[260] The bracket is added after Zetterstéen, 65, which has [*hal*] *asma'ukum*?

Faḍl Allāh dared not enter. He was so frightened that he simply ran away from his fellow 'ulamā'. The group waited until their messenger came out and told the whole story. Their opinions were divided. They did not wholeheartedly trust the authenticity of that pigeon-post.

On Wednesday, Rabī' II 12 (January 6, 1300), Sayf al-Dīn Qibjāq came to Damascus and was seated in the 'Azīzīya Madrasa.[261] He ordered the 'ulamā' and dignitaries to talk to Arjuwāsh on the issue of the Citadel. So they went back to him. But he refused them and was upset at their presence.

Qibjāq's seizing of power: On this day (January 6, 1300), a large number of firmans were issued to the public from the 'Azīzīya [Madrasa] by the shaykh al-shuyūkh and a general who was said to be a foster brother of sultan [Ghāzān]. Some firmans were issued in the name of Qibjāq. Most of these firmans did not have any effect, however.

On Thursday, Rabī' II 13 (January 7, 1300), people were saying that the ruler [Ghāzān] would perform the Friday prayer in Damascus. Then it was said that he hated to come to the city because of the Citadel's resistance. The townsmen were scared. They began to repair the gates of the streets, and to pile up rocks, mud, and anything available behind those gates. They (i.e., the Mongols) entered buildings and houses frequently, searching for horses and seized a large number of them from civilians.

On the eve of Friday, Sayf al-Dīn Qibjāq stayed overnight at 'Izz al-Dīn Ibn al-Qalānisī's house. On Friday, Rabī' II 14 (January 8, 1300), before the prayer, people were afraid that looting would take place and that disturbances would occur during the prayer. However, such things did not happen. The preacher delivered his sermon at the Grand Mosque with an opening prayer dictated to him which went like this, "Our lord, the greatest sultan, the sultan of Islam and Muslims, the lord of this world and the Faith, Maḥmūd Ghāzān. . . ." A large number of Mongols performed the prayer inside the [sermon] chamber. As the prayer was over, Sayf al-Dīn Qibjāq came to the chamber and mounted, together with Amīr Ismā'īl, the pulpit of muezzins. A host of people gathered beneath the Nasr [Cupola]. 'Abd al-Ghanī[262] announced sultan Ghāzān's official titles and prayed on his behalf, while the audience uttered amen. The appointment of Amīr Sayf al-Dīn Qibjāq to the office of viceroy of all lands of Syria was made public. He was appointed to govern Damascus, Aleppo, Hama, Hims, and other provinces and districts and was entrusted with all the responsibilities, such as to appoint qāḍīs, governors, and preach-

[261] A mixed Shāfi'ī-Ḥanafī madrasa, it was founded by al-Malik al-'Azīz; see Somogyi, "Adh-Dhahabī's record," 368, note 61; Pouzet, *Damas*, passim.

[262] He was then the muezzin of the Grand Mosque.

ers. The muezzin 'Abd al-Ghanī announced this to the public. [Silver] *dirhams* and gold [*dīnārs*] were distributed among the masses. People were pleased with Qibjāq's appointment for they expected that he would treat them gently.

The Ḥanafī chief judge Jalāl al-Dīn mentioned that he had met with Qibjāq and the latter revealed to him the difficulties involved in his job: he was having a very hard time dealing with the Mongols and was in urgent need of 2,000 *dīnārs* in exchange for his appointment. Jalāl al-Dīn said to him, "I have a mare and a she-mule, and I will give them to our lord, the amīr. So he can make use of them [for the payment]." He said, "They have [all] the horses and mules they need. Don't trouble yourself with such a matter. What they really need is gold."

Ghāzān's shaykh al-mashā'ikh comes to Damascus: On the same Friday (January 8, 1300), the shaykh al-mashā'ikh Niẓām al-Dīn[263] arrived in the 'Ādilīya Madrasa[264] and was well received. However, he complained that the Damascenes did not frequent his place [to pay their respects to him]. He claimed that he would settle their problems and find a solution for them on what should be done regarding the matter of the Citadel. Some people in his audience, however, reminded him that Sayf al-Dīn Qibjāq was very familiar with the issue of the commander of the Citadel. The shaykh replied, "Five hundred Qibjāqs are not worth my finger ring." He was extremely arrogant.

The looting at Mt. Ṣāliḥīya: On Saturday, Rabī' II 15 (January 9, 1300), looting began at Mt. Ṣāliḥīya. It started at the tomb of the viceroy 'Izz al-Dīn and the Māridānīya [Madrasa].[265] As time passed, they (i.e., the Mongols) became violent in the mountain area. They entered the Nāṣirīya [Madrasa][266] and the hospital (*al-māristān*)[267] by force. They broke the gates of the tombs and the windows. They climbed up to the Dam Cavern (*Maghārat al-Dam*),[268] the Cave (*al-Kahf*),[269] the Jū' Cavern (*Maghārat al-Jū'*),[270] and other places. They encountered no resistance wherever they went. Then they came

[263] Maḥmūd ibn 'Alī al-Shaybānī. His biography is not found.

[264] One of the most prestigious Shāfi'ī madrasas in Damascus; see Somogyi, "Adh-Dhahabī's record," 369, note 65; Pouzet, *Damas*, index.

[265] A Ḥanafī madrasa; see Pouzet, *Damas*, 60, 66.

[266] It is also called *al-madrasa al-Nāṣirīya al-Jawwānīya*, a Shāfi'ī madrasa; see Pouzet, *Damas*, 158.

[267] For hospitals in Damascus during the time, see Ziadeh, *Syria*, 158-61.

[268] At Mt. Qāsiyūn; see Pouzet, *Damas*, "Carte des environs de Damas."

[269] Perhaps the cave of Jibrīl; see Pouzet, *Damas*, "Carte des environs de Damas."

[270] At Mt. Qāsiyūn; see Pouzet, *Damas*, 82.

down to the mosque.[271] They took away the rugs in it, broke the lanterns and the pulpit, threw away the chest that was used to preserve the Qur'ān (*al-rab'a*), and probably trampled on it. Then they went to the Shaykh Ḍiyā' [al-Dīn] Madrasa[272] while its inhabitants were still inside. They cast stones on them. People inside fought back in self-defense, but later they lost strength and were forced to come out from the madrasa. The Mongols then entered it and sacked it. They broke into the library and threw the books all over the place. They took away an enormous amount of food and grain in the Mt. Ṣā-liḥīya area, and seized many valuables from underground cellars (*al-ṭamā'ir*) and hidden treasures. [They became such experts at this] that if one of them came upon a cellar or hidden treasure, he would quickly locate it as if he had been in charge of digging it in the first place. There is no power and strength save in God, the Exalted, the Glorious!

The last episode [of looting] took place in the Ḥanbalī cloister (*dayr*). People had been gathering there, especially when the turmoil and destruction began to take place in the mountain area, people started to come to the cloister and to seek shelter for the night. Soon it became overcrowded, even the corridors were filled with refugees. On Tuesday (January 12, 1300), the place was surrounded by the Mongols. They came in through the prayer niche (*al-qibla*), violating its sanctity. They plundered the place and entered the halls where civilians took shelter and arrested a number of them. Before that, they had also arrested women, children, and men in the mountain area and killed a few of them.

Ibn Taymīya's effort to rescue the people of Mt. Ṣāliḥīya: When the inhabitants of Damascus heard about what was happening to their brothers [in Mt. Ṣāliḥīya], they were shocked. Shaykh Ibn Taymīya and a group of others made their way to [Ghāzān's] shaykh al-mashā'ikh who happened to be in the 'Ādilīya [Madrasa]. They complained to him about the situation.

On Tuesday (January 12, 1300) midday, he (i.e., the shaykh) went out to talk to the Mongols. Some time between noon and evening, he finally reached them and tried to stop them. As the Mongols heard about the arrival of the shaykh and his companions, they ran away. People in the cloister benefited from this tremendously. The houses of those which had not yet been smashed by the Mongols until the shaykh's arrival were spared. A large number of people from the mountain area had been arrested. People rushed to

---

[271] Al-Ṣāliḥīya had its own assembly mosque (Ziadeh, *Syria*, 87); and it was built by Nūr al-Dīn Maḥmūd ibn Zankī; see, Somogyi, "Adh-Dhahabī's record," 370, note 70.

[272] Also known as *al-madrasa al-Ḍiyā'īya*, a Ḥanbalī institution; see Pouzet, *Damas*, 83, 85, 159.

the cloister almost naked, wearing nothing except rags (*al-akhlāq*), sacks (*al-juwālaq*), saddle-bags (*al-balāshāt*), and the like. They begged for help in rescuing their [captured] wives and children, and in bringing their suffering to an end. Some of the captives were released while the whereabouts of the rest was still unknown.

Looting at al-Mizza and Dārayyā:[273] The situation was still grim. They (i.e., the Mongols) then wended their way to the village of al-Mizza. The majority of the villagers had not been evacuated yet. They (i.e., the Mongols) sacked the village and captured villagers, doing what they had done in the Mt. Ṣāliḥiya area. They also came to the village of Dārayyā. The villagers took shelter in the mosque, but the Mongols broke in and did the same thing that they had done previously. We heard that a group of Dārayyā inhabitants managed to kill nearly 50 Mongol soldiers, and that a number of the villagers lost their lives too.

Ibn Taymīya's effort to gain release of Syrian war prisoners: Shaykh Taqī al-Dīn Ibn Taymīya kept going [to appeal] to those who might be able to mediate or intervene. He visited 'Alam [al-Dīn] Sulaymān al-Hindī,[274] the shaykh al-mashā'ikh Niẓām al-Dīn Maḥmūd ibn 'Alī al-Shaybānī, and Sayf al-Dīn Qibjāq. Then on Thursday, Rabī' II 20 (January 14, 1300),[275] he made his way out [of Damascus] to sultan [Ghāzān]'s campsite which was called al-Ardawā' and located at the foot of the Rāhiṭ hill. He was introduced to Ghāzān but was not given the chance to tell him what had happened. [The only thing] he was allowed to do was to pray for Ghāzān and to leave quickly. He was told that Ghāzān was suffering pain in his leg and was preoccupied [by other matters], and that if he was apprised of what had happened he would be forced to execute a number of Mongol soldiers and this would definitely lead to chaos and dissension that would eventually boomerang for the people of Damascus . . . and so forth. He then met with the vizier Sa'd al-Dīn[276] and Rashīd al-Dīn[277] and talked to them. They pointed out that a

---

[273] Al-Mizza, a suburb which was three miles south-west of the Damascus Citadel; see Brinner, *Damascus*, 1:44, note 268; also Somogyi, "Adh-Dhahabī's record," 370, note 72 (gives the name as al-Mazza). Dārayyā, a village in the Ghūṭa area; see Brinner, *Damascus*, 1:79, note 472.

[274] Unidentified. The *nisba* al-Hindī, however, does not necessarily indicate an Indian origin; see Ayalon, "Names," 219-22.

[275] The text has Rabī' II 25, apparently an error for 20.

[276] The text has *Ibn* Sa'd al-Dīn, an error for Sa'd al-Dīn Savajī who died in 1312. For his career, see *CHIr*, 5:385-86, 396, 402.

[277] Perhaps Rashīd al-Dīn Faḍl Allāh Hamadānī, died in 1318, the author of the *Jāmi'-i al-tawārīkh*. Al-Dhahabī has al-Rashīd al-Yahūdī; see Somogyi, "Adh-Dhahabī's record," 371.

number of top-ranking generals had not yet received any revenue from Damascus up to this point, and that it was necessary to satisfy them. They ordered [soldiers] to bring forth those [Damascene] captives and to launch a search for those who had joined the [Mongol] troops. On Saturday night (January 16, 1300), Shaykh Taqī al-Dīn [Ibn Taymīya] and his companions came back to Damascus.

Damascus on the eve of the Mongol attack on the Citadel: On Saturday (January 16, 1300), people became nervous and the tensions were unbearable. Rumors spread that Damascus was approaching its fate, that the Mongols would ultimately win, that sultan [Ghāzān] had written to Arjuwāsh but the latter had turned him down, that the Mongols would inevitably enter [Damascus] on account of the Citadel, and that what had happened to the mountain area would also befall Damascus. The rumor also had it that whosoever dared to stay in the city would be risking his own life, that if anybody wanted to flee he ought to go to Mt. Ṣāliḥīya, and that it was better that the notables and 'ulamā' would leave the city first. People were scared out of their wits by such rumors, and many of these rumors were blamed on the shaykh al-mashā'ikh [Niẓām al-Dīn]. He was said to have carried his belongings and fled from the 'Ādilīya [Madrasa back to the Mongol camp]. People thus became even more certain about the rumors, arguing that if they were false, why would he have left in such a hurry? It was not until the evening that the shaykh came back with some of his baggage. A group of dignitaries went to see him and told him, "If sultan [Ghāzān] has made any specific demand from the city, we are willing to do our best to comply with it. This ought to be regarded as an offer to buy the city off in exchange for the sultan's granting manumission (*'atq*) to the Muslims."

In one of the preceding nights, two [Mongol] experts in operating mangonels were found killed. A group of soldiers from the Citadel were said to be responsible for the assassination. A report had it that sultan [Ghāzān] was very angry at this incident and flew into a rage. People spent Sunday night, Rabī' II 23 (January 17, 1300), [sleepless,] expecting looting, arrest, and slaughter on the following day. They were desperate as the morning came. And the weather was bitterly cold; that year had never seen such a cold day as this.

It was reported that on the eve of Saturday (January 16, 1300), they (i.e., the city notables) had a meeting at the Grand Mosque. Ibn Munajjā said, "I am willing to give up all my assets (*al-'ayn*). If this still doesn't satisfy [them], here I am, ready to die!" Ibn al-Qalānisī said, "Almost all of our properties have been taken away (*ustu'ṣila*). The only thing left for us is to die in this mosque, one lying next to the other!"

On Sunday morning,[278] the townspeople were saying that the shaykh al-mashā'ikh intended to leave the city [again]. Many people came to the shaykh, seeking protection from him. Those who learned the news were frustrated. He, I mean the shaykh, had already made up his mind not to help the Muslims get out of this crisis. People were really anxious. Rumor reached the Citadel that it would inevitably be put under siege, that combat equipment (*al-ālāt*) had already been installed in the village of Zaydīn, and that it was a life-and-death issue for the Damascenes. It was rumored also that Arjuwāsh received a letter [from Ghāzān] that declared, "If you surrender the Citadel, you will save the Muslims from bloodshed." An enormous number of residences in the city were broken into by the Mongols who were searching for horses. They seized the horses, and, if they found no horses, plundered the places, taking away anything they could by force. More than 10,000 cavalrymen(?)[279] were involved in such [massive] looting.

Heavy levies on Damascene civilians: By the end of the month, the taxes (*al-ṭalab*) imposed on civilians were drastically increased. The amount they used to be taxed was [now] doubled or even manifoldly increased. One hundred thirty thousand *dirhams* were required of [residents of] the Woolcarders Market (*sūq al-khawāṣṣīn*),[280] 100,000 *dirhams* on the Lance Makers [Market?] (*al-rammāḥīn*), 60,000 *dirhams* on the 'Alī Market. And even the Goldsmiths Market (*sūq al-dhahabīyīn*), despite its small size and poor neighborhood, was taxed 2,500 *dirhams*. The amount levied upon the notables and dignitaries was enormous, totaling 30,000 *dīnārs*.[281] According to the account [book], some 400,000 [*dīnārs*] were [planned to be levied]. Notifications of taxes were sent to them and the measure was very tough. A task force made up of Mongol soldiers was in charge of collecting the payment. Each [rich notable] was dealt with by a group [of soldiers]. They were treated harshly and forced to stay overnight at the new shrine wing of the Grand Mosque where the payment (*al-istikhlāṣ*) was supposed to be made. They

---

278 Ms. Landberg 139 has "Saturday," while Ms. Ahmet III 2907 has "Sunday," which is so mentioned in Zetterstéen, 70.

279 The text has *fāris*, "horseman"; I doubt it is a misspelling for *faras*, "horse," as al-Dhahabī's text also shows; thus the sentence should be read as "10,000 horses were seized from the city"; cf. Somogyi, "Adh-Dhahabī's record," 371.

280 For the Woolcarders Market, see Somogyi, "Adh-Dhahabī's record," 371, note 75. The amount of taxes in al-Dhahabī's account was 100,000 *dirhams*.

281 The numbers vary slightly in al-Dhahabī's account; see Somogyi, "Adh-Dhahabī's record," 371-72.

were not allowed to receive visitors, nor provisions. Orders were issued to torture Ibn Shuqayr [by crushing his fingers?] (*'aṣr*).[282] Ibn Munajjā and Ibn al-Qalānisī were threatened to be treated the same way. The Mongols surrounded them, beating them on their backs, clutching their sleeves, and swooping down upon them. Ibn Ṣaṣrā suffered the same [abuse].

The entire Damascene populace was being humiliated and disgraced. Incidents of pillage, robbery, as well as stealing turbans, veils (*al-manādil*), and fur-mantles (*al-farājī*) increased in the city. Whenever they (i.e., the Mongols) saw anybody carrying anything, they would take it away by force. In the suburbs, incidents of smashing doors, climbing up on roofs, plunder, disturbance, and harassment also occurred frequently. The chaos reached its peak on Friday, Rabī' II 28 (January 22, 1300), at the Friday prayer time, when a great clamoring arose from above the houses. People ran from one roof to another. Some of them tried to climb up but fell down to their death. Others broke their ribs. All of them, elite and commoner, wealthy and poor, were scared to death about this taxation and levying which was not only charged upon each person but also upon each household. The demanded amount was so high that the city could never afford it. Even a partial payment covering the main portion of it seemed to be impossible. People were really suffering. The men in charge of this action were Ṣafī [al-Dīn] al-Sinjārī, 'Alā' al-Dīn, an *ustād-dār* of Qibjāq, and Shaykh al-Ḥarīrī's[283] two sons [whose nicknames were] al-Ḥinn and al-Binn.[284] Some poets wrote poems ridiculing them. . . .[285]

The siege of the Damascus Citadel: The month of Jumādā I began with a Monday (January 25, 1300). From the first day of this month, the Mongols

---

[282] The verbal noun *'aṣr* means "to press out" or "to wring out"; the reference to, and descriptions of, it as a means of torture in Mamluk time are also found in some later sources such as Ibn Taghrībirdī's *Ḥawādith al-zuhūr* (2:482-83) and *al-Nujūm* (16:30); it is described in al-Biqā'ī's (d. 1480) *Iẓhār al-'aṣr* as a means of torture (1:364) that involves, perhaps, wrenching or wringing one's body parts, especially fingers and toes, etc., and the result of it could be broken bones or even death (e.g., *rusima bi-'aṣr 'iẓāmihi*, 1:308; *'uṣira ilā an talifat yadāhu*, 1:373; *fa-'uṣira ibhām rijlihi ḥattā takassara 'aẓmuhu wa-'uṣira ka'bāhu ilā an ughmiya 'alayhi wa-ushī'a mawtuhu*, 3:17). In a sense, it was a process that literally "put somebody through the wringer."

[283] Unidentified. Roemer considers this individual to be 'Abd al-Ghanī al-Ḥarīrī, the author of a poem condemning the Muslim collaborators with the Mongols in Damascus; see *Kanz*, 9:index. However, it seems unlikely that the father would attack his sons in this way. The poem is ascribed, by al-Yūnīnī, to 'Abd al-Ghanī al-Jazarī; see the present edition, 112.

[284] Al-Ḥinn, "the lowest, or meanest kind of Ginn" (Lane); for more discussion of al-Ḥinn and al-Binn in Mamluk sources, see Graf, *Die Epitome der Universalchronik Ibn ad-Dawādāris*, 97-99.

[285] I omit the translation of poems here.

started to station themselves from the Post Gate (*bāb al-barīd*) as far as the Citadel and its surrounding districts in order to safeguard their mangonels installed in the Grand Mosque. The siege of the Citadel lasted a few days. Shops around the Post Gate were smashed. They stayed overnight in these places, holding [the reins of their] horses in their hands. The townspeople were afraid to enter the Mosque from this side.[286] The Mongols looted the shops around the Druggists [Market] (*al-'aṭṭārīn*) and the Fāmiya [Market?] as well as other neighborhoods, searching for food and a place to stay. The inhabitants of the Post Gate area as far as the Citadel were increasingly frightened. They moved out of their houses, leaving behind them their belongings and provisions for they were unable to take such things with them. As a rule, people would stay inside their houses, or madrasas and mosques, because they were afraid of being taken [by the Mongols] to fill up ditches and to do other hard labor needed for the siege [of the Citadel] while walking around the city. The gates of the Grand Mosque were closed. Only [a narrow passage was left open] through which people could enter one at a time. And other gates were fully closed. The number of those who participated in sessions (*al-julasā'*) at the Mosque decreased drastically. Merely one or two were seen there. The number of those who attended regular prayer congregations decreased too. All this was due to fears of many things, such as the situation at the Citadel, robbery, being forced to do things like taking care of [the Mongols'] horses or other tasks. [If a person were taken,] he might be forced to stay in their (i.e., the Mongols') place for a day or longer. So people simply stayed home and did not go out unless it was absolute necessary.

The second looting at Mt. Ṣāliḥīya: On the first Friday of this month (January 29, 1300), the Ḥanbalī cloister [at Mt. Ṣāliḥīya] was sacked for the second time. Women and children, including 120 girls, were removed from the cloister. Only a few were spared. The Ḥanbalī qāḍī Taqī al-Dīn[287] was taken prisoner and humiliated in disgrace. He was released [later] this day. Naked, barefoot, and hungry, scores of people fled to Damascus. The scene was horrible.

Damascus burning: As far as Damascus is concerned, the Ashrafīya Dār al-Ḥadīth[288] and its neighborhood up to the Nūrīya [Madrasa][289] were burning.

---

[286] I.e., the side that was facing the Citadel.

[287] Perhaps Taqī al-Dīn Sulaymān Ibn Ḥamza al-Maqdisī; he died in 715/1316 and was the Ḥanbalī chief judge in Damascus during 695/1296-715/1316; see the present edition, 2, 96, 202.

[288] At the eastern gate of the Citadel; see Somogyi, "Adh-Dhahabī's record," 374, note 89.

The [buildings] opposite it also went up in flames. The fire even reached the areas beyond the 'Ādilīya [Madrasa]. The beautiful mansions there were consumed by fire. The fire also reached the area that was next to the [Ashrafīya] Dār al-Ḥadīth on the southern side from the Qaymāzīya [Madrasa][290] and its surroundings up to the Dār al-Sa'āda and the hospital. And on another side from the Dammāghīya Madrasa[291] all the way down to the Faraj Gate. The Mongols surrounded all these districts. As for those places that had not been touched by fire, the Mongols came, plundering and causing damage. Mobs and hooligans also came to loot these burning houses, tearing down wooden [frames] and doors, and taking away everything in the houses: marble, luxury objects, furniture, books, and so forth. They then sold these items at the lowest prices. There is no power and no strength save in God! All these places were laid waste. Nobody dared to pass by or even to get close. Residents of these places and the nearby neighborhoods were leaving. Looting increased in the city from time to time, and in every district and every neighborhood to such an extent that—God knows best!—there was no single shop, block, or street that had not been broken into and looted thoroughly. People were afraid of walking around in the city or shopping. If one had to go out for some reason, he would wear rags and run fast in anxiety and fear. If he managed to get back quickly and safely, he and his family would praise God's mercy.

Damage to the Grand Mosque: As for the Grand Mosque, evening prayers were canceled for several nights and the mosque was closed entirely at night.[292] Only one or two men would show up to perform the prayer at sunset. The same was true for the morning prayer. The mosque was closed early in the evening as well. The Mongols stayed there overnight to watch their mangonels. We were told that they violated the mosque's sanctity by drinking liquor and bringing women [into the mosque] at night. They also soiled the place with urine and other filth. If one happened to stay in the mosque late as it got dark, he would be mugged and his clothes would be taken away. On Friday, Jumādā I 5 (January 29, 1300), most of the populace failed to at-

---

[289] There were three madrasas named al-Nūrīya in Damascus the most famous of which was the Shāfi'ī one; see Pouzet, *Damas*, index. I am not quite sure which one is referred to here. Al-Dhahabī's version does not mention this place.

[290] A Ḥanafī madrasa, to the north of the Ashrafīya Dār al-Ḥadīth; see Pouzet, *Damas*, 49, 52, 59, 63; also Somogyi, "Adh-Dhahabī's record," 374-75, notes 89, 92.

[291] A mixed Shāfi'ī and Ḥanafī madrasa; see Pouzet, *Damas*, 67, 76.

[292] The text has *bayna al-'ishā'ayn*, literally, "between the two evening prayers," that is, between the first evening prayer and the last evening prayer.

tend the Friday prayer lest they should put themselves and their families and properties at home in danger. Only a few showed up.

The situation of confiscation, emergency levying, and taxation (*al-jibāya wa-al-ṭalab*) remained as it had been. Nobody was exempted, regardless of whether he was a prominent scholar, a religious leader, a senior assistant to the ruler (*ṣāḥib malik*), a dignitary holding high-ranking position, or a [commoner] sitting in a shop. The madrasas were charged a tremendous amount, though it was reduced a little bit later. People were in dire straits: nobody was safe from being mugged and having his clothes taken away while walking around at night, even in the Grand Mosque in the daytime. People continued to live with fear, suffering injuries, insults, humiliations, and harassment caused by the confiscators. Some of them were hanged, and others were tortured. Townspeople also suffered from strict rules imposed upon them as well as soaring prices and the shortage of virtually everything.

The [Mongol] vanguard regiment (*al-yazakīya*) continued to block the Citadel from all directions. They were stationed at the Post Gate, the Raṣīf [Gate], and the Ẓāhirīya [Madrasa].[293]

The Mongols' retreat from Jerusalem: It was reported widely that the Mongol troops that had gone to southern regions (*al-bilād al-qiblīya*)[294] were returning, and that they had caused havoc in that area: violence, pillage, and arrest. However, the details have not been brought to us.

Ghāzān's departure for Persia and the Citadel's continuous resistance: On Friday, Jumādā I 12 (February 5, 1300), the news circulated that the ruler [Ghāzān] had decided to return home, and that he would leave his viceroy [Quṭlū-Shāh][295] and troops in Syria.[296] The number of Mongols in Damascus decreased. The vanguard regiment remained as it was on account of the Citadel. We were told that the siege actually helped [deflect the pressure from] the city to the Citadel. The defenders of the Citadel, often invoking God and the Prophet Muḥammad, shot a great many stones by mangonels. A group of

---

[293] A Shāfi'ī madrasa; see Pouzet, *Damas*, index; also Somogyi, "Adh-Dhahabī's record," 375, note 94.

[294] The term usually refers to Jerusalem, Palestine, and the Hejaz on the Red Sea coast; see *QI*, 3:387-89.

[295] He died in 1307. He and Qibjāq were jointly viceroys in Damascus after Ghāzān's departure; see Irwin, *Early Mamluk Sultanate*, 100-1; for his career, see *CHIr*, 5:750 (index).

[296] For the most recent discussion of Ghāzān's sudden withdrawal from Syria in 1300, see Morgan, "The Mongols in Syria," 231-35, in which he argues that in addition to the commonly accepted explanations (the internal political uncertainty, the trouble with the Chagatai khanate on the eastern border, etc.), the lack of sufficient grazing for their horses is a matter worth serious consideration.

them made their way out [of the Citadel] to launch attacks against the [Mongol] vanguard regiment stationed in the city, killing some of them, capturing some, or drawing them out of their strongholds, then they returned safely [to the Citadel].

During the following week, several events took place. One of these was sultan [Ghāzān]'s departure. It was said that on the previous Friday, Jumādā I 12 (February 5, 1300), he left Syria heading home. His viceroy Amīr Bahā' al-Dīn Quṭlū-Shāh, together with a large number of troops, remained [in Syria].

Damascus in the aftermath of Ghāzān's withdrawal: On Sunday, Jumādā I 13 (February 6, 1300), an edict was issued to evacuate the 'Ādilīya Madrasa. The Mongols stood at its gate and forced the people inside to leave. They searched them and seized their belongings as they wished. They also demanded cash. The inhabitants of the madrasa were unable to carry most of their baggage; and they were not allowed to come back to the madrasa. The Mongols then entered [the madrasa]. They smashed the doors of its rooms (*al-buyūt*) and sacked them, taking away as much as they could carry. Late at night, the inhabitants of the madrasa managed to make their way back through terraces to take a look at their rooms. If they found anything left over by the Mongols they would pick it up. People became helpless, with limited means at their disposal; they simply gave up their properties. The 'Uqayba Mosque[297] was burned. The fire continued blazing for several days. Its minaret fell down. Numerous fires engulfed places in the Mt. [Ṣāliḥīya] area, the suburbs, and the orchard and garden areas of Damascus.

Qibjāq's appointment to the office of viceroy: On Friday, Jumādā I 19 (February 12, 1300), after the prayer, two edicts were read on the pulpit in the Grand Mosque. One was the appointment of Qibjāq to the office of viceroy of Syria. The other was the appointment of Amīr Nāṣir al-Dīn Yaḥyā ibn Jalāl al-Dīn to the office of financial agent of Syria. Of Khutan[298] origin, he was the son of Jalāl al-Dīn, the governor of Mosul, Sinjar, and Northwest Iraq (*al-Jazīra*). His grandfather used to be the governor of Khutan in Persia. He was very graceful and gentle. Under his patronage, Sayyid Rukn al-Dīn compiled the *Sharḥ al-Muqaddima*.[299] One of the two edicts also released the money collected from the [Grand] Mosque for arms storage, and returned it [to its original use] for the pilgrimage caravan to the Hejaz. The edict that con-

---

[297] For the 'Uqayba Mosque, which was on the slope of Mt. Qāsiyūn, see Somogyi, "Adh-Dhahabi's record," 376, note 95; also Pouzet, *Damas*, index.

[298] For Khutan, see Le Strange, *Lands*, 487-88.

[299] The author and the work are unidentified.

tained the appointment of Qibjāq mentioned that [by granting him the post] they had fulfilled their promise to him in response to his defection to them and his seeking their help. The text went like this, "On our way to Egypt, we have come [first] to this country (i.e., Syria), . . ." and so forth. The edict also touched upon other matters, such as the commission of religious endowments (*al-awqāf*) and their investment, and the statement that their troops had pursued the Egyptians as far as al-Raml, that they had killed a number of them and arrested others, and that only a few had managed to escape.

Looting after Ghāzān's withdrawal: Saturday morning, Jumādā I 20 (February 13, 1300), the Mongol soldiers climbed on housetops and shot arrows from there. They came to the Shāfi'ī Iqbālīya [Madrasa].[300] Residents of the Ẓāhirīya [Madrasa] neighborhood and those in the nearby areas were frightened. The Mongols looted from the Farādīs Gate, which lay between the two city walls, all the way down to the [Damascus] Citadel, from the Iqbālīya [Madrasa] to the Citadel, from the 'Ādilīya [Madrasa] to the Citadel, and from the Ẓāhirīya [Madrasa] to the Nūrīya [Madrasa], on both sides. That is to say, they looted the Post Gate, the Rab' compound, and the Darb al-Silsila street, from the hospital to the Ḥārat al-Ghurabā' quarter and the Naṣr Gate as well as the entire area surrounding the Citadel; from the Khātūnīya [Madrasa],[301] Ibn Munajjā's madrasa, the Ḥārat al-Balāṭa quarter[302] and all over these districts. Residents of these districts were ordered to evacuate quickly. They thus moved out, leaving behind them their belongings and properties. Then the Mongols came in, plundering and smashing wooden [frames of houses] and doors. They were followed by mobs who did whatever they could, such as tearing down a whole roof to sell its wood for half a *dirham*, . . . and things like that. The civilians' property, provisions, and belongings were all taken away. And their houses were demolished. They escaped with themselves only.

The [chaotic] situation in these areas appeared to be [caused by the resistance of] the Citadel. The Mongols used this as an excuse [for looting], claiming that "these districts are too close to the Citadel, so we want them to evacuate," while their real intention was to loot the area in order to extract sufficient provisions (*al-aqwāt*).

On Sunday, Jumādā I 21 (February 14, 1300), people woke up in the morning only to realize that the 'Ādilīya Madrasa was burning and its dome

---

[300] For this madrasa, see Pouzet, *Damas*, 33, 163.

[301] A Ḥanbalī institution; see Pouzet, *Damas*, 49, 52, 57, 59.

[302] For this district, see Wulzinger, *Damaskus die islamische Stadt*, 70.

had fallen down. The fire was engulfing its wooden frames, doors, storerooms, and books. When the residents of the Ẓāhirīya [Madrasa] area saw this terrible scene, they at once evacuated the women and children [and] moved their clothes and furniture to housetops. They then ran on the housetops, throwing their belongings down from the top to the Asad al-Dīn Public Bath (*ḥammām*) and the 'Uqayq Public Bath, and then they climbed down by ladder or rope. However, there was no way for them to get out of [the city] gate since the [Mongol] vanguard regiments were stationed there. People thereby suffered tremendous difficulties, especially those who carried grain, furniture, and copper vessels; they had no alternative but to hire somebody to carry their [heavy] things at very high prices. This massive exodus happened during the daytime on Sunday. By Monday night, only a few men were seen staying [in the town] to watch their houses.

The withdrawal of other Mongols: On Monday, Jumādā I 22 (February 15, 1300), it was reported that the ruler of Cilicia left [Damascus] early in the morning. It was also reported that the viceroy Quṭlū-Shāh left too. By noon time, a widely circulated rumor had it that a group of soldiers stationed [in the Citadel] launched attacks here and there on the [Mongol] armed escort forces (*al-yazak*) in order to protect the wooden shields covering the wall (*al-satā'ir*) and to safeguard the surrounding areas of the Citadel and its roads. As a result, none of them (i.e., the Mongols) remained in his [posted] place. Before the night fell, people finally managed to go back to their ruined houses near the Citadel and have a chance to inspect the damage to their houses. Some of them found some items (*'udda*) and clothes. Prior to that, they had been unable to do so for the enemies were still there. Then the shields [on the Citadel] began to be taken off and sold as firewood. People realized that there must be some reason behind such an action. Otherwise, how could they afford to abandon something they had taken great pains and a great deal of time to install, and then simply let it be torn to shreds? Having breathed God's blessing and mercy, people spent Tuesday (February 16, 1300) night [in peace].

The Post Gate was [by now as dirty] as a country tavern. Shops [around it] contained nothing but arches (*bawā'ik*), along with a horrible mess of filth and mire. The situation in the Suwayqa [district][303] and the 'Ādilīya [Madrasa] was the same: nothing was left except for windows. The Nūrīya Dār al-Ḥadīth survived, but its doors and storerooms did not. And some of its roofs

[303] Perhaps the Suwayqat Ṣārūjā, a district to the north of Damascus, across the Baradā river; see Brinner, *Damascus*, 1:46, note 282.

were also damaged. As for what were next to it, one could hardly recognize and identify their origins. The [place] and what was facing it were all leveled to the ground. The Dār al-Saʿāda was totally devastated; neither roofs nor a single piece of the wooden [frames] were left intact. Other places were ruined as well.

The situation progressed as Tuesday (February 16, 1300) came. The mangonel installed in the Grand Mosque was shut down. Sayf al-Dīn Qibjāq, accompanied by his entourage, left Damascus on Tuesday night. Some said that his trip had to do with the preservation of the mangonel. The same day, music bands played in the Damascus Citadel, celebrating the triumph.

On Wednesday, Jumādā I 24 (February 17, 1300), the wooden frame of the mangonel was dismantled by the Citadel troopers. Those who had been asking protection from the Mongols were [now] put on a wanted list. Al-Qummī and others were taken to the Citadel. Al-Ḥarīrī's two sons were on the list as well and they went into hiding. On this Wednesday, it was repeatedly called out in the city, "Cheer yourselves up and open your shops! Be prepared to welcome the sultan of Syria Sayf al-Dīn Qibjāq tomorrow with candles!" The town crier's words also included the following, "God has driven away the defeated enemy from you, . . ." and so forth. People were surprised at such an announcement. Opinions varied. As evening came, nobody was able to confirm the news, let alone know what would be the cause behind the Mongols' complete withdrawal from Damascus, giving up the siege [of the Citadel], and abandoning all the equipment they had made a great effort, for nearly a month, to install. Among those high ranking officials to leave Damascus last were Amīr Yaḥyā and his colleague Ṣafī [al-Dīn] al-Sinjārī. His departure from Damascus was in the evening of the above-mentioned Tuesday, Jumādā I 23 (February 16, 1300). On Wednesday (February 17, 1300), none of the Mongols was seen in the city. People thus made their way out to the mountain area and some villages to see what had been burned and what damage had been done to their houses and property.

Ibn Taymīya's account of his negotiations with the Mongols: Shaykh Imām ʿAlam al-Dīn Ibn al-Birzālī told me,[304] "On Thursday, Jumādā I 25 (February 18, 1300), I met with Shaykh Taqī al-Dīn Ibn Taymīya. He told me about his meeting with Amīr Quṭlū-Shāh. He said, 'Quṭlū-Shāh told me that he was a descendant of Jinggiz-Khan. He is a man in his 50s and has a

[304] Again, the first person "me" here is more likely referring to al-Jazarī; see our above source criticism, 41-59. It is also interesting to note that in al-Dhahabī's version, the provenance is given as "Ibn Taymīya related to us"; see Somogyi, "Adh-Dhahabī's record," 377.

yellowish face, without beard.' He also told them (i.e., Ibn Taymīya and his companions) that God sealed the line of Prophets with Muḥammad and that Jinggiz-Khan, his grandfather, was the king of the earth (*malik al-basīṭa*). Therefore, whoever fails to obey him and his descendants is to be regarded as a dissident (*khārijī*). Ibn Taymīya also mentioned his meetings with the ruler Ghāzān, the vizier Sa'd al-Dīn, the vizier Rashīd al-Dīn al-Ṭabīb,[305] the treasurer Sharīf Quṭb al-Dīn and his secretary (*mukātib*) Ṣadr al-Dīn, the Jewish nobleman al-Kaḥḥāl, the shaykh al-mashā'ikh Niẓām al-Dīn Maḥmūd, and the minister of religious endowments (*nāẓir al-awqāf*) Aṣīl (or Uṣayl) al-Dīn, the son of Naṣīr al-Dīn al-Ṭūsī. Ibn Taymīya also mentioned that at Quṭlū-Shāh's place he saw the ruler of Cilicia. He looked pale, having grown a thick beard. Along with him were a small group of men [from Cilicia] who looked humble and guilty. Ibn Taymīya mentioned that Quṭlū-Shāh's departure took place on Tuesday at noon, Jumādā I 23 (February 16, 1300),[306] and that he (i.e., Ibn Taymīya) spoke to him on Sunday, Jumādā I 21 (February 14, 1300) concerning the captives. He then spent Monday night at al-Munaybi',[307] together with the Ḥanbalī qāḍī [Taqī al-Dīn][308] and the Ḥanafī qāḍī because they were on a mission to the Citadel. Ibn Taymīya mentioned that in all of their documents and firmans, the Mongols would write phrases like, 'By the might of God, by the faith of Muḥammad's Religion, . . .' and so forth. Ibn Taymīya also mentioned that he had met one of them (i.e., the Mongols) who appeared to be very pious and quiet. He asked him, 'Why do you come here to fight Muslims?' He replied, 'Our shaykh issued a *fatwā* ordering us to destroy Syria and to seize the Syrians' properties, because they do not worship God without pay, they do not call for prayer without pay, and they do not study or apply Islamic law without pay, and so forth. Our shaykh said, 'If you do all this to them, they will return to God and trust in Him again.'"

An inventory of the Mongols' looting: Wajīh al-Dīn Ibn Munajjā and Ibn al-Quṭayna reported that each one of them had lost 150,000 *dirhams*. Wajīh [al-Dīn] Ibn Munajjā mentioned that the total amount that had been brought

---

[305] His name is, however, given by al-Dhahabī as Rashīd al-Dawla; see Somogyi, "Adh-Dhahabī's record," 377.

[306] The text above states that his departure was on Monday (February 15, 1300) instead.

[307] According to al-Yūnīnī, al-Munaybi' was a suburb of Damascus (*ẓāhir madīnat Dimashq*); see *Dhayl,* M:3. It was around the Khātūnīya Madrasa; see Sauvaire, *Description de Damas*, 435-36.

[308] The name is supplied by al-Dhahabī; however, the Ḥanafī qāḍī is passed over as "another person" instead; see Somogyi, "Adh-Dhahabī's record," 377.

into Ghāzān's private treasury was 3,600,000 *dirhams*, in addition to those official requests (*al-tarāsīm*), bribes (*al-barāṭīl*), and taxes (*al-istikhrāj*) on behalf of other amīrs and viziers. Al-Ṣafī al-Sinjārī alone had managed to collect 80,000 *dirhams* for himself, 200,000 for Amīr Ismā'īl, and 400,000 for the two viziers. As for others in the Mongol army, they all, without exception, quickly got what they wanted.[309] The amount we have mentioned above does not include bribes imposed upon those whose assets had been confiscated. The rest of the Mongols, who were [too numerous] to be named here, also gained an amount at least as much as what has been listed above. Let us ask God for forgiveness!

Qibjāq's return to Damascus: On Thursday, Jumādā I 25 (February 18, 1300), Sayf al-Dīn Qibjāq came back from his farewell trip to Quṭlū-Shāh and the other Mongols.[310] He entered Damascus through the Eastern Gate, while the gate through which he had gone out was the Jābiya Gate. Both gates had been opened for him. Like the rest of the city gates, these two had been closed for some time. He made his way across the city and then arrived at the Ablaq Palace. Amīr Yaḥyā, al-Ṣafī al-Sinjārī, and a group of Mongols accompanying him also returned. They went across the city and arrived at the [Ablaq] Palace as well. Town criers started to announce that Amīr Sayf al-Dīn Qibjāq was now the viceroy of the sultan. The people were surprised at this announcement, wondering how there could be such a coincidence between his homecoming and the coming of Yaḥyā with his companions.

On Friday (February 19, 1300), town criers called out that people ought to go back to their home villages and suburban towns. People were surprised at this announcement, since earlier that morning, it was announced that one should not place himself at risk by going out to the mountain area and the suburban towns, and that whoever did so would be taking his life in his own hands.

The book sale and the soaring prices in Damascus: Islamic books were on sale in Damascus. People did not hesitate about buying those books; on the contrary, they showed increasing enthusiasm for that, although they knew very well that those books belonged either to *waqf* endowments or private collections. If one happened to pass by the book market, he might find books

---

[309] The text has *safā wa-janā;* the verb *safā* means "was quick, or swift" in walking or going and hence "[the wind] raised the dust or carried it away" (Lane). In the present context, it may be used in describing how the Mongol soldiers seized and looted "like whirling wind that carried everything away."

[310] For Quṭlū-Shāh's departure from Syria, see above, 156.

[originally] owned by the ḥadīth scholar 'Abd al-Ghanī,[311] and Ḍiyā' al-Dīn,[312] as well as many *waqf* books that used to belong to his madrasa, the *waqf* books from the Ashrafīya Dār al-Ḥadīth at Mt. [Ṣāliḥīya], the Nūrīya Dār al-Ḥadīth in Damascus, the *waqf* books of Ibn al-Binardī al-Baghdādī,[313] the *waqf* books of the Shiblīya Madrasa,[314] and the books that used to belong to the Ḥanbalīs and inhabitants of the Mt. [Ṣāliḥīya] area. When those from the mountain area saw their books, they were unable to rescue them because they had lost everything and now owned nearly nothing. They did not even have the means to feed themselves, let alone to purchase books.

The prices soared in Damascus. A sack of wheat went for 360 *dirhams*,[315] and a sack of barley 140 *dirhams*. One *raṭl* of bread cost two and a half *dirhams*. Two and a half ounces of oil cost one *dirham*. One ounce of cheese cost one *dirham*. One *raṭl* of meat was sold for seven and eight, or as high as 12 *dirhams*[316] when it was in shortage. One ounce of butter sold for one *dirham* and so did tail fat of sheep (*al-alya*). Ten *raṭl*s of flour were sold for 39 *dirhams*. Five eggs cost one *dirham*. One *raṭl* of syrup cost five *dirhams*. One *raṭl* of honey cost 10 [*dirhams*], sugar 20 [*dirhams*], pomegranate seeds five [*dirhams*], sumac fruit (*al-summāq*) three [*dirhams*], and olives[317] six [*dirhams*]. Other groceries were sold at comparably [high] prices.

Qibjāq's ruling in Damascus: On Jumādā I 29 (February 22),[318] Qibjāq and his retinue entered Damascus. They settled down in the residences of Amīr Sayf al-Dīn Bahādur[319] and al-Maṭrūḥī,[320] both of which were beneath the Fayrūz Minaret. Their presence made the neighborhood overcrowded. Amīr

---

[311] Then the muezzin at the Grand Mosque in Damascus.

[312] Muḥammad ibn 'Abd al-Wāḥid al-Maqdisī; he died in 643/1245 and was the founder of the Ḥanbalī Ḍiyā'īya Madrasa; see Pouzet, *Damas*, 81, 83, 159.

[313] Unidentified. For the *nisba* al-Binardī (or al-Biwardī), see Ibn al-Athīr, *al-Lubāb*, 1:206, 229-30.

[314] A Ḥanafī institution; see Pouzet, *Damas*, 50, 63, 68.

[315] Al-Dhahabī has "300 *dirhams*"; see Somogyi, "Adh-Dhahabī's record," 378. Al-Dhahabī's account, which is much shorter than al-Yūnīnī's, does not mention the book sale.

[316] Al-Dhahabī has "1 *raṭl* of meat 9 *dirhams*"; see Somogyi, "Adh-Dhahabī's record," 378.

[317] The text has *al-zayt* (oil); however, given that oil has already been mentioned above, and the goods listed here are all fruits, I would suggest that the word *al-zayt* is an error for *al-zaytūn* (olives).

[318] The text has Jumādā II, an obvious error for Jumādā I. The text above states that Qibjāq and Yaḥyā entered Damascus on February 18, instead of February 22 as indicated here.

[319] He died in 743/1342. For his biography see Ibn Taghrībirdī, *Manhal*, no. 697; Elham, *Lāǧīn*, passim (index).

[320] I.e., Amīr Jamāl al-Dīn Āqqūsh al-Maṭrūḥī.

Yaḥyā stayed at Ṭūghān's house inside the Tūmā Gate. By the end of the day, town criers called out the following announcement, "The sultan of Syria, the pilgrim to the Two Holy Shrines, Sayf al-Dīn Qibjāq has decreed that people from villages and suburban towns should go home now!"

On the first day of Jumādā II, which fell on a Tuesday (February 23, 1300), and on the following Wednesday (February 24, 1300) as well, they repeatedly urged people to go home, claiming that this edict had been issued by the viceroy and Grand Amīr Sayf al-Dīn Qibjāq. It was reported that Qibjāq promoted some persons to the rank of amīr, among them was his *ustād-dār* 'Alā' al-Dīn, who was given the governorship of the countryside of Damascus, replacing Ibn al-Jākī. Qibjāq promoted a number of his own friends to the rank of amīr as well. Many soldiers thus came to join him. The number of those at his door (*'alā bābihi*) [seeking promotion or benefits] increased too. The city gates were now open, except for those near the Citadel. By the end of this day, the appointment of Qibjāq's *ustād-dār* to the governorship was made public by town criers. It was announced that people with grievances should go directly to him, and that the Riding Animal Market (*sūq al-dawwāb*) was to be located at the Fruit Market (*dār al-biṭṭīkh*).[321]

On Friday [Jumādā II 4] (February 26, 1300), bands with drums played in the Damascus Citadel in celebration. Other [sources] said that the music was played at the gate of Qibjāq's residence instead. Amīr Yaḥyā prayed at the Grand Mosque on this day, and on the following Saturday and Sunday as well. It was mentioned that he had distributed charities to the poor. As for Qibjāq, he attended to state business in Damascus during these days, exercising absolute authority on appointments and removals.

On Monday, Jumādā II 7 (February 29, 1300), Qibjāq(?)[322] and [his] *ustād-dār* 'Alā' al-Dīn rode out, wearing the *sharbosh*-head coverings. Cymbals (*al-kūsāt*) were beaten in Damascus to salute the two. When he rode out, he would be accompanied by the royal band (*al-'iṣāba*) and the honor guard (*al-shāwīshīya*). A host of Damascene soldiers, horsemen and infantry alike, joined him in his service.[323] He issued decrees to appoint senior administrators of Damascus. He organized an army from the [remaining] Mongol

[321] In the district north of the Damascus Citadel; see *Q2*, 194; also Brinner, *Damascus*, 1:61, note 367.

[322] The text has *ṭāshār*, which is not clear to me. From the context, this word must have to do with Qibjāq. My speculation would be that it is an error for *ṭashān*, a Turkish term meaning "one who acts with insolence," hence perhaps a nickname, or title, of Qibjāq.

[323] Literally, "they would ride on horses to serve him and dismount from the horses in his honor."

troops, who were said to be 1,000 horsemen, and sent them to Khirbat al-Luṣūṣ[324] and the Jordan Valley (*al-Ghawr*). They departed on Jumādā II 8 (March 1, 1300). He also appointed the son of al-Ṣafī al-Sinjārī to the office of market inspector at Damascus, and granted him a robe of honor with a *ṭarḥa*-headgear. When he rode out, he would be accompanied by an extravagantly lavish procession made up of a host of dignitaries and soldiers.

What happened during the second 10 days of Jumādā II (the beginning of March, 1300) is as follows:

Qibjāq promoted three [generals] to the rank of amīr and they thus rode on horses, wearing the *sharbosh*-head coverings.

It was proclaimed in the city that bars and brothels around the Dār Ibn Jarrāda district outside of the Tūmā Gate were to be put under state control (*idāra*). The announcement also stipulated that the fees [imposed upon those bars] would be in excess of 1,000 *dirhams*[325] per day.

It was proclaimed also that young mamluks of Egyptian and Syrian [masters] holding belongings of their masters could keep them for preservation.

The Citadel troopers' guerrilla war against the Mongols: A group [of Mamluk soldiers] rode out from the [Damascus] Citadel, swooping down on the Dhabbāb Mosque[326] outside the Jābiya Gate of Damascus. They returned [pursuing] a number of Mongols riding fast in front of them.[327] The masses [in Damascus] thus assumed that the Egyptians had arrived and that the Mongols were running away from them. So they began to attack the Mongols and killed a number of them. However, no report confirming their speculations was forthcoming; and the city was, accordingly, in great confusion. The Ṣaghīr Gate was closed, and it remained closed after this incident. People began to spread rumors that the Mongols were going to seek revenge for their murdered soldiers.

A considerable amount of emergency tax was imposed on the madrasas; none of them, small or poor, was exempted. People were disturbed.

---

[324] This place name appears in Ibn al-Dawādārī's *Kanz* twice (8:241, 273). However, the precise location cannot be found.

[325] Somogyi's translation of al-Dhahabī's version has "(the prohibition) was imposed upon about 1,000 (men) a day," which is perhaps due to the corruption of the original manuscript; see Somogyi, "Adh-Dhahabī's record," 378.

[326] Unidentified. It is listed as "al-Dabbāb" in the index to vol. 8 of Ibn al-Dawādārī's *Kanz*, while the Arabic text in fact has *al-dhabbāb*.

[327] The text has *bayna aydīhim*, which can also be understood as "taking with them" some Mongols [as captives]; however, the text below clearly states that "the Mongols were running away from them . . ." and hence this translation.

It was reported that General Būlāhim[328] and his troops returned from the Jordan Valley. People were scared of them. His arrival on the periphery of Damascus was said to have taken place on Jumādā II 20 (March 13, 1300).

During the last 10 days of the month (the middle and end of March, 1300), troopers of the [Damascus] Citadel came out once more. They seized spoils and weapons from the Mongols and killed a number of them. A large number of Muslims (i.e., the Citadel troopers) were killed as well. A raid occurred outside Damascus. Some persons, who were accused of being the Mongols' accomplices,[329] were arrested [by the Citadel troopers]. Meanwhile, a levy was imposed upon the people on behalf of the Mongol general Būlāhim.

Peacemaking efforts by the local 'ulamā': On Monday, Jumādā II 28 (March 21, 1300), the preacher Badr al-Dīn [Ibn Jamā'a] and Shaykh Taqī al-Dīn [Ibn Taymīya], together with the deputy of Amīr Yaḥyā and a number of his aides, entered the Citadel. People were talking about a peace settlement between the commander of the Citadel [Arjuwāsh] and the deputies of Ghāzān, although what had transpired between them was unknown.

The month of Rajab began with a Wednesday night (March 23, 1300). The preacher Badr al-Dīn [Ibn Jamā'a] and Taqī al-Dīn Ibn Taymīya visited Arjuwāsh and Qibjāq in an effort to make peace between the two and to settle the chaos in the city. No agreement was reached.

On Thursday, Rajab 2 (March 24, 1300) memos signed by Qibjāq were sent to dignitaries: the qāḍīs, 'ulamā', and religious leaders, inviting them to come to his house. Most of them did so. They swore allegiance to Ghāzān's dynasty,[330] promising to provide [loyal] advice and not to be deceitful and the like.

On the same day, Shaykh Taqī al-Dīn [Ibn Taymīya] made his way to the campsite of Būlāhim seeking the prisoners' release. The number of prisoners held by the Mongols was so large that he needed to spend three nights there. He (i.e., Būlāhim) talked to him (i.e., Ibn Taymīya) about Yazīd ibn Mu'āwiya.[331] [He asked,] "Should we admire him or resent him?" Taqī al-Dīn said, "Neither admire nor resent him." Then he (i.e., Būlāhim) said, "He

---

[328] His name is given as Būlāhim and, sometimes, Būlāy in the text. In the following I will retain consistency by citing the name as Būlāhim.

[329] Literally, "having come with the Mongols."

[330] The text has *al-dawla al-Maḥmūdīya*, after Ghāzān's name Maḥmūd.

[331] The second Umayyad caliph, who was responsible for the tragedy of Karbalā' in which Muḥammad's grandson al-Ḥusayn ibn 'Alī was killed. The event is commemorated annually by the Shī'ī's; see "Yazīd b. Mu'āwiya," *EI*², by H. Lammens; also *The History of al-Ṭabarī: The Caliph of Yazīd b. Mu'āwiyah A.D. 680-683/A.H. 60-64*, translated and annotated by I. K. A. Howard (Albany, 1990).

should be damned." At this point, Ibn Taymīya discovered that he had sympathy [towards the 'Alids]. So he kept telling him whatever would please him. He said, "Those Damascenes killed al-Ḥusayn." The shaykh [Ibn Taymīya] said, "No, none of the Syrians was present at the murder of al-Ḥusayn. Al-Ḥusayn was killed at Karbalā' in Iraq." Būlāhim said, "Oh yes, that's true. The Umayyads were the legitimate rulers of this world and they loved the people of Syria. This is the land of prophets and virtuous men." His wrath against Syrians was thereby calmed down. He said that he was of a Muslim background from Khurāsān. He had a wide-ranging discussion with the shaykh [Ibn Taymīya].

On Friday [Rajab 3,] (March 25, 1300), a group of religious leaders went to the campsite of Būlāhim and came back on Saturday [Rajab 4,] (March 26, 1300). They were plundered at the Eastern Gate; their clothes and turbans were taken away and[, as a result,] they came to Damascus bareheaded. On the same day, they were summoned [to the campsite again]. Some of them went into hiding, while others went to [the campsite]. Then they (i.e., the Mongols) set off, taking with them Amīn al-Dīn Ibn Shuqayr al-Ḥarrānī.

The withdrawal of the last Mongols: On the eve of Saturday, Rajab 4 (March 26, 1300), townspeople climbed to the minarets of the [Grand] Mosque and other high places. They reported that they saw a group of Mongols going up the mountain road to 'Aqabat Dummar. Some said that they were leaving [for good]. People remained anxious about them. It appeared that Būlāhim and his troops had gone and that a regiment of [Mongol] troops were scattered in the Mt. [Ṣāliḥīya] area, the village of al-Mizza, and the suburbs of Damascus, causing damage. It was reported that they then headed for al-Biqā' and Ba'labakk.

On Rajab 7 (March 29, 1300), it was widely circulated in Damascus that none of the Mongols was in the suburbs of Damascus. People took this as a good omen. On the same day, Qibjāq's decree was proclaimed [by town criers], urging people to return to their towns and villages, and claiming that the routes were [now] safe. On Thursday [Rajab 9,] (March 31, 1300), a large number of people began to return to the southwest and northward. This home-coming continued on Friday and Saturday (April 1-2, 1300).

On Monday, Rajab 13 (April 4, 1300), while wandering around the quince gardens, people were disturbed by the return of a regiment of Mongols to the outskirts of Damascus. They ran back quickly. Some of them were plundered, and others threw themselves in the river [to escape].

Qibjāq's break with the Mongols: Wednesday afternoon, Rajab 15 (April 6, 1300), there was great confusion among the townspeople. Some said that

Qibjāq was about to break with the Mongols and that the situation of the city and its inhabitants would become dangerous. On Arjuwāsh's behalf, town criers called out from the Grand Mosque the following, "[Fellow Damascenes,] come to protect the city! Stay on the city walls and drive out the enemy!" A flood of people escaped [into the city] from the suburbs. On Thursday eve (April 7, 1300), which happened to be Maundy Thursday (*al-khamīs al-kabīr*),[332] people spent the whole night in anxiety and fear. During the night, Qibjāq left with his companions and followers. And so did 'Izz al-Dīn Ibn al-Qalānisī, the sharīf,[333] and many others. Early Thursday morning, all city gates were closed. So a large number of people, who had fled with some of their belongings and families, were stuck outside the city. When it was late in the morning, the Naṣr Gate was opened because it was in close proximity to the Citadel. Arjuwāsh was in charge of the entire city's welfare. Town criers repeatedly called for the protection of the city walls and proclaimed that whosoever spent the night at home would be hanged and that whosoever, except for bakers, cooks, and druggists, opened his business would also be hanged. The decree was issued in strong terms. Among those who had been collaborating with the Mongols, nobody remained in the city. Then in midday, town criers called out the following, "[Fellow Damascenes,] open your shops and stay on the city walls when night falls!" Arjuwāsh appointed Badr al-Dīn Ibn al-Nakhīlī to run the office of market inspector [in Damascus].

Ibn Taymīya's re-enforcement of Sharī'a *law in Damascus*: On Friday (April 8, 1300), the Friday prayer sermon was resumed at the Grand Mosque in Damascus. The name of the lord of Egypt [al-Malik al-Nāṣir] was mentioned along with the name of the caliph as it had been done before. People rejoiced at that, and their voices of prayer were very cheerful. The names of the two had been eliminated from the Friday prayer sermon since Rabī' II 7 (January 1, 1300) for 100 days.

Early this Friday morning, Shaykh Taqī al-Dīn Ibn Taymīya went around Damascus to inspect the taverns that had opened recently. He and his followers spilt wine, broke jars, and smashed [liquor] containers.[334] They censured

---

[332] See Graf, *Verzeichnis der arabischer kirchlicher Termini*, 43. I like to thank Franz Rosenthal for this reference.

[333] An unidentified member of the Ashrāf (descendants of Muḥammad) in Damascus.

[334] The event is also recorded by al-Dhahabī. However, Somogyi, in his translation ("Adh-Dhahabī's record," 380, and note 113), interpreted this action as out of "general rejoicings [*sic*]," which is obviously missing the point.

wine sellers as well. May God reward him![335] During these nights, people stayed on the city walls. Then they held a military review, displaying their weapons and equipment. Shaykh Taqī al-Dīn [Ibn Taymīya] and his followers made the rounds among them. He recited to them chapters from the Qur'ān on battles (*sūrat al-qitāl*)[336] and Qur'ānic verses on the Muslim holy war (*āyāt al-jihād*), as well as the ḥadīths on the Prophet's raids, campaigns, and garrison. He strove to encourage people and boost their morale.

On Saturday morning, Rajab 18 (April 19, 1300), town criers called people to decorate the city while maintaining guard on the city walls. The people started decorating [the city in celebration].

Al-Malik al-Nāṣir's return from Hims to Cairo: As for sultan al-Malik al-Nāṣir, he retreated from the battlefield in Hims and arrived in the [Cairo] Jabal Citadel on Wednesday, Rabī' II 12 (January 6, 1300).[337] He was followed by Egyptian and Syrian stragglers, most of whom were naked, barefoot, and weak. That is why it took them so long [to get home]. Had there been no blessing and greatness of the Mamluk sultanate of Egypt, an army in such shape would not have managed to survive, not to mention those panicked civilians following them. God bestowed horses and weapons [upon them], but the prices were extremely high;[338] a cuirass originally worth 20 *dirhams* was now sold for 200 *dirhams* or about. All military equipment was expensive. Turbans were in a terrible shortage, and the majority of the soldiers arrived bareheaded. That is because they used to wear helmets in battle, but having been defeated, they had thrown the helmets away in order to ease their burden, and had put kerchiefs (*al-manādil*)[339] or other substitutes on their heads instead. Therefore, they now badly needed to buy turbans. The turbans used to be 50 *dirhams* apiece and [now] cost nearly 200 *dirhams*. Although the sultan spent an enormous amount of money and manpower on equipping the army[, the problem was far from being solved].

A new round of military confrontations with the Mongols: The sultan [al-Malik al-Nāṣir] marched from Cairo to Syria on Rajab 9 (March 31,

---

[335] Ms. Landberg 139 has *atābahu Allāh* (May God make him repent!). The translation here is according to Ms. Ahmet III 2907 which has *athābahu Allāh*.

[336] I.e., the 47th chapter (Sūrat Muḥammad) of the Qur'ān; see Paret, *Der Koran*, 552.

[337] This is a follow-up of the battle of Wādī al-Khazindār in Syria that had taken place in the beginning of this year; for the retreating Mamluk troops, cf. above, 136-37.

[338] According to Peter Thorau, as in European feudalism, the Mamluk individual soldier, not the sultanate, was responsible for his horse, weapons and harness. For a discussion of arms markets during the time, see Thorau, *Baybars*, 151, and note 51.

[339] For the functions of the *manādil* (sing. *mandīl*) in the medieval Islamic world in general, see Rosenthal, "A Note on the Mandīl."

1300) on account of the enemy. He arrived in al-Ṣāliḥīya[340] and encamped there. The viceroy Amīr Sayf al-Dīn Salār and Amīr Rukn al-Dīn Baybars al-Jāshankīr[341] led the troops to Syria. On the way, they encountered Qibjāq, Baktimur, and al-Albakī and brought them to the sultan. They met with the sultan in al-Ṣāliḥīya. On Thursday, Sha'bān 14 (May 5, 1300), the sultan returned to the [Cairo] Jabal Citadel. He was accompanied by the amīrs coming [to join] him: Amīr Sayf al-Dīn Qibjāq, the *silāḥ-dār* Amīr Sayf al-Dīn Baktimur, and al-Albakī.

On Saturday, Sha'bān 10 (May 1, 1300), Damascene troops returned to Damascus.[342] Their general was Amīr Jamāl al-Dīn Āqqūsh al-Afram. People swarmed out to watch them [marching in] and to celebrate their [coming]. They thanked God for His bestowing upon them the favorable turn of events. The remaining Syrian troops arrived on Sunday, Sha'bān 11 (May 2). Among them were the governor of Hama and Aleppo Amīr Shams al-Dīn Qarā-Sunqur,[343] and the governor of Tripoli (*al-Sawāḥil*) Amīr Sayf al-Dīn Quṭlū-Bek.[344] On Monday, Sha'bān 12 (May 3, 1300), the left wing of the Egyptian army, led by the commander, the *amīr-silāḥ* Amīr Badr al-Dīn Baktāsh,[345] arrived. Among those who entered the city in an extravagantly lavish military parade was Sunqur-Shāh. On Tuesday, Sha'bān 13 (May 4,

[340] A town in eastern Egypt, which was on the way to Syria; see Thorau, *Baybars*, 305. This place should not be confused with the Mt. Ṣāliḥīya area on the outskirts of Damascus.

[341] He was also known as Baybars II, a Circassian amīr. For his career, see Irwin, *Early Mamluk Sultanate*, 85-86, 92, 95, 98, 105, 109.

[342] The text has *dakhala jaysh Dimashq al-diyār al-Miṣrīya* (Damascene troops entered Egypt) which is incorrect; it should be *dakhala jaysh Dimashq Dimashq*. This reading is based on the following observations: 1) there is a self-contradiction on the whereabouts of Salār: the previous paragraph says that he had "led the troops to Syria" in Rajab (March, 1300), and this paragraph states that he "entered with [the center]" on Sha'bān 13 (May 4, 1300), while in the next paragraph, we are told that on Ramaḍān 8 (May 28, 1300), "Salār led all the Egyptian troops back to Egypt." There is no way for him to go back and forth several times between Damascus and Cairo in such a short period. It is reasonable that the Mamluk army (both Egyptians and Damascenes) would first return to Damascus after the battle with the Mongols in the upper Euphrates, and then the Egyptians (not Damascenes) would carry on the journey back home; 2) the reference to the Marj in which the troops "encamped" cannot be identified with any locations in Egypt; the term al-Marj usually refers to Marj Rāhiṭ near Damascus; 3) in addition, other sources also state that "Damascene troops entered Damascus"; see Ibn al-Dawādārī, *Kanz*, 9:39; Zetterstéen, 80; al-Dhahabī (Somogyi, "Adh-Dhahabī's record"), 380.

[343] He died in 728/1328. For his biography, see al-'Asqalānī, *Durar*, 3:330.

[344] He died in 729/1328. For his biography and career, see al-'Asqalānī, *Durar*, 3:338; Elham, *Lāǧīn*, 143, 159.

[345] He died in 706/1306. For his biography, see al-'Asqalānī, *Durar*, 3:14.

1300), the right wing, led by the general, *ustād-dār* Ḥusām al-Dīn Lājīn, entered [Damascus]. On Wednesday, Sha'bān 14 (May 5, 1300), the center and the Royal Mamluk regiment entered. The viceroy Amīr Sayf al-Dīn Salār came with them as well. Among those who entered in military parade was Sayf al-Dīn al-Ṭabbākhī[346] and his troops. The same day, Zayn al-Dīn Kitbughā al-'Ādil[347] joined to serve the viceroy [Salār]. All of the troops encamped in al-Marj.[348]

New appointments at Damascus after the Mongols' withdrawal: On Sha'bān 15 (May 6, 1300), Amīn al-Dīn al-Rūmī was appointed to the office of market inspector in Damascus. The preacher Badr al-Dīn Ibn Jamā'a al-Shāfi'ī took over the office of chief judge in Syria.

On Saturday, Sha'bān 17 (May 8, 1300), at the gate of the vizier Amīr Shams al-Dīn Sunqur al-A'sar's [residence], Tāj al-Dīn Aḥmad Ibn al-Shīrāzī assumed the office as head of the administration (*naẓr al-dīwān*) in Syria together with the finance agent Amīr Sayf al-Dīn Aqjubā, replacing Fakhr al-Dīn Ibn al-Shīrajī. The *dawā-dār*[349] 'Izz al-Dīn Aybak al-Najībī assumed the office of governor of Damascus. He was granted the title of amīr at the drum house (*ṭabl-khānah*) during that time. Qāḍī Shams al-Dīn Ibn Ṣafī al-Dīn al-Ḥarīrī was appointed to be the Ḥanafī chief judge on Wednesday, Sha'bān 21 (May 12, 1300). He assumed the office on Thursday [Sha'bān 22,] (May 13, 1300) and people came to congratulate him.

Qāḍī Jalāl al-Dīn, the brother of the chief judge Imām al-Dīn al-Qazwīnī, delivered an inaugural lecture at the Amīnīya Madrasa[350] on Sunday, Sha'bān 11 (May 2, 1300), replacing his late brother. Shaykh Kamāl al-Dīn Ibn al-Zamalkānī[351] took over the teaching position at the Umm al-Ṣāliḥ Madrasa in Damascus on Wednesday, Sha'bān 21 (May 12, 1300), replacing Qāḍī Jalāl al-Dīn al-Qazwīnī, the brother of Qāḍī Imām al-Dīn.

---

[346] Then the governor of Tripoli and Aleppo; he died in 700/1301. For his biography, see Ibn Taghrībirdī, *Manhal*, no. 692.

[347] Al-Malik al-'Ādil Kitbughā II, of Mongol origin, the Mamluk sultan (r. 694/1294-696/1296). His biography is, strangely, not found anywhere. Information of his rule and career can be gathered through the indexes of Irwin, *Early Mamluk Sultanate*; Haarmann, *Quellestudien*; Elham, *Lāǧīn*; Pouzet, *Damas*.

[348] I.e., Marj Rāhiṭ in the vicinity of Damascus.

[349] A word combining Arabic *dawā* (inkwell, pen-box) and Persian *dār* (holder). Under the Baḥrī Mamluks, this was a low ranking position for petty officials; see *Q2*, 139.

[350] A Shāfi'ī institution, it was the oldest madrasa in Damascus; see Pouzet, *Damas*, 25-26, 41, 56, 369; Somogyi, "Adh-Dhahabī's record," 381, note 115.

[351] Muḥammad ibn 'Alī, a Shāfi'ī jurist; he died in 727/1327. His career included the office of qāḍī in Aleppo and Cairo. For his biography, see al-'Asqalānī, *Durar*, 4:192-94; al-Ziriklī, 7:175.

The "clean up" in Damascus: The first day of Ramaḍān fell on a Saturday (May 21, 1300). Early in the day, Arjuwāsh [ordered people to] remove the wooden shields (*al-ṭawāriq wa-al-satā'ir*) from the walls of the Citadel. The army took a break on Ramaḍān 3 (May 23, 1300). On Saturday, the first day of Ramaḍān, Amīr Sayf al-Dīn Salār was seated in the Dār al-'Adl at the Akhḍar Square. Together with him were the qāḍīs and amīrs.

On Saturday, Ramaḍān 8 (May 28, 1300), a royal robe of honor (*khil'a 'aẓīma*) was granted upon the mawlā 'Izz al-Dīn Ibn al-Qalānisī from the vizier Ibn al-Sal'ūs.[352] His son 'Imād al-Dīn 'Abd al-'Azīz was appointed as a public notary (*shāhid*) and officer (*rā'id*) at the state treasury (*dīwān al-khizāna*). The same Saturday, the commander-in-chief and viceroy Amīr Sayf al-Dīn Salār led all the Egyptian troops back to Egypt. These remaining troops had been scattered in Syria in the preceding month [after the battle]. They arrived in Cairo on Tuesday, Shawwāl 3 (June 22, 1300). [On the way,] the viceroy [Salār] and the amīrs celebrated the Fast Breaking festival at Bilbays.[353]

On Ramaḍān 28 (June 18, 1300), the Shāfi'ī chief judge [al-Qazwīnī], and Ḥanafī chief judge [Ḥusām al-Dīn], Tāj al-Dīn Ibn al-Shīrāzī, and the market inspector Amīn al-Dīn were awarded the *ṭayālis*-robes of honor[354] in Damascus. The chief of staff of the administration (*ṣāḥib al-dīwān*) al-Akram Ibn Laqlaq and the senior clerk of the administration (*mustawfī al-dīwān*) Tāj al-Ri'āsa were awarded robes of honor as well.

The month of Shawwāl began on a Sunday (June 20, 1300). The holiday celebration prayer was held in the [Akhḍar] Square. The pulpit [of the Grand Mosque?] was moved to the square [for the occasion].

The punishment of the Mongols' collaborators in Damascus: On Shawwāl 3 (June 22, 1300), Mandūh's eyes were gouged out with hot nails (*akḥalū*). Then some people tried to intercede for him.

On that Wednesday night, Shawwāl 4 (June 23, 1300), three men were fastened with nails (*summirū*) on camels; and other two were hanged. The ones fastened with nails were Sharīf al-Qummī, the *barda-dār*[355] Ibn al-'Awnī, and

---

[352] Muḥammad al-Tanūkhī; died in 693/1294. Information on his career is found in Elham, *Lāǧīn*, 38, 87, 144-47; Pouzet, *Damas*, passim (Index).

[353] A town in al-Sharqīya Province of Egypt, on the way from Damascus to Cairo; see *Q1*, 3:400; 4:27, 66.

[354] Originally a Persian term *ṭaylasān*, "a mantle, scarf or tippet hanging from the shoulder"; see Steingass, *A Comprehensive Persian-English Dictionary*.

[355] From Persian *farda-dār*, "curtain holder," a low ranking officer in the *dīwān* system whose duty, as the title suggests, was to assist and to serve the needs of higher-ranked officers; see *Q2*, 62.

Ibn Ḥaṭlīshā al-Mizzī.[356] The hanged were a clerk of the municipal administration (*masṭabat al-wilāya*) at Damascus and a Jew. They were all accused of having collaborated with the Mongols and causing harm to Muslims. Ibn al-'Awnī was released after three days. He lived until the year of A.H. 702 (1302) and died from colic. The muezzin of Bayt Lihyā[357] Shaykh Ibrāhīm was hanged at the end of Friday, Shawwāl 6 (June 25, 1300). Ibn Ḍā'in's tongue was cut off, and so were al-Daldarmī's one hand and one leg. Al-Shujā' Humām's eyes were gouged out with hot nails. He survived through the night and died afterward. Al-Daldarmī endured for three days and died eventually.

The crackdown on the Druze rebellion: On Friday, Shawwāl 20 (July 9, 1300), the viceroy, His Majesty Jamāl al-Dīn Āqqūsh al-Afram, leading the Damascene troops, was joined by an army of peasants and villagers. They advanced to Mt. Kisrawān and Mt. Druze to launch a [retaliatory] strike on those [mountain people] who had committed crimes of attacking [Mamluk] troops, seizing their weapons, killing [Mamluk] soldiers and harassing them. On Thursday, the second day of Dhū al-Qa'da (July 20, 1300) the first day of which fell on a Wednesday, the mountain people, who were the target of the Syrian expedition, were defeated. They had no choice but to obey. They were charged an enormous amount of levies and were obligated to return all the items they had seized from Muslim soldiers. As a punishment for what they had done to the Muslim lands, their lands and estates were divided [and given] as *iqṭā'* fiefs.

Āqqūsh's preparation for war in Damascus: The viceroy Amīr Jamāl al-Dīn Āqqūsh al-Afram and the remaining army returned from Ba'labakk to Damascus on Sunday, Dhū al-Qa'da 13 (July 31, 1300). People, holding candles, came out in the middle of the day to welcome him and to celebrate. On Wednesday [Dhū al-Qa'da 16,] (August 3, 1300), Damascenes were ordered to hang their weapons in [their] shops. They were also ordered to practice arrow-shooting and to prepare for war. Targets (*āmājāt*) for archers were installed in madrasas and mosques [for practice]. The viceroy's orders were made public by town criers. The chief judge issued a letter to all madrasas on the matter. The [same warning] was sent all over Syria. On Dhū al-Qa'da 21 (August 8, 1300), the armed commoners from different market districts in Damascus were reviewed by the viceroy. Each market had its own commander who was

---

[356] The last two are unidentified. Interestingly, al-Dhahabī's account does not contain any of such information.

[357] Also known as Bayt al-Lihyā, a village east of Damascus; see Brinner, *Damascus*, 1:200, note 1195; also Pouzet, *Damas*, 97, 143, 211.

surrounded by his fellow citizens. The market inspector of Damascus came and brought with him millers and bakers. On Thursday, Dhū al-Qa'da 24 (August 11, 1300), the descendants of al-Ḥasan and al-Ḥusayn, armed with their equipment, were reviewed by the viceroy. They were led by the head of the 'Alids (*naqīb al-ashrāf*) Niẓām al-Mulk.[358]

The revitalization of religious learning in Damascus: On Shawwāl 13 (July 2, 1300), the appointment of Badr al-Dīn Ibn Jamā'a to the office of chief judge was read at the sermon chamber in the Grand Mosque of Damascus shortly after the Friday prayer. The certificate was read by Shaykh Sharaf al-Dīn al-Fazārī[359] in the presence of the viceroy, qāḍīs, and amirs. His duties included the office of chief judge and the management of the religious endowments, in addition to his routine sermon delivery and other responsibilities.

On Sunday, Shawwāl 15 (July 4, 1300), the deputy judge (*nā'ib al-ḥukm*) of Damascus Qāḍī Jamāl al-Dīn Sulaymān al-Adhra'ī assumed the teaching position at the Dawla'īya [Madrasa] in Damascus.[360] He was to replace the late Shaykh Jamāl al-Dīn al-Bājarīqī. On Wednesday, Dhū al-Ḥijja 21 (September 7, 1300), Qāḍī Jalāl al-Dīn, the son of the Ḥanafī chief judge Ḥusām al-Dīn, was appointed by the viceroy to chair the 'Adhrāwīya [Madrasa].[361] On the same day, Raḍī al-Dīn Abū Bakr al-Raqqī delivered an inaugural lecture at the Ma'zīya (Mu'izzīya?) Madrasa on the outskirts of Damascus. He was given the most prestigious [position] and the highest [honor]. His audience was huge. He was to replace Wajīh [al-Dīn] al-Qūnawī who had succeeded al-Majd al-Fakhr Mūsā because of the latter's perpetual residence in the tomb [of his master].[362] Wajīh [al-Dīn] himself did not stay long in that position.

The killing of Muslims in Diyār Bakr: It was widely circulated that at the end of this year, a number of Muslims were killed in Diyār Bakr, which was

---

[358] According to Pouzet, the *naqīb al-ashrāf* in Damascus at the time was Zayn al-Dīn 'Alī ibn Muḥammad of the Banū 'Adnān who died in 708/1308. For his biography, see Ibn Kathīr, *Bidāya*, 14:49; also Pouzet, *Damas*, 200, note 278; 261, note 87. However, the title Niẓām al-Mulk is not found in all these references.

[359] Aḥmad ibn Ibrāhīm; he died in 705/1306. For his biography, see al-'Asqalānī, *Durar*, 1:94; also Pouzet, *Damas*, 112, 133, 421.

[360] A Shāfi'ī madrasa; see Pouzet, *Damas*, 187, 219.

[361] Also as al-'Adhrā'īya, a mixed Ḥanafī and Shāfi'ī institution; see Pouzet, *Damas*, 31, 71, 160-61, 292.

[362] The text has *bi-sabab iqāmatihi*; the term *iqāma* was used in some medieval Arabic texts in speaking of the right of perpetual residence in the tomb of a certain saint or master; see Marmon, *Eunuchs and Sacred Boundaries*, 18. The background of al-Majd Mūsā's *iqāma* here is not explicitly explained by the author.

two horse stations (*marḥala*) away from the fortress of al-Bīra. They were approximately 500 in number. Among them was Shams al-Dīn 'Alī, the son of the shaykh al-Islām Shams al-Dīn ibn al-Shaykh Abī 'Umar al-Ḥanbalī. He had gone there for the sake of [the release of] the captives from the [Mt.] Ṣāliḥīya area. Among those captives, about 70 were the descendants of the shaykh Abū 'Umar and about 4,000 were commoners. Approximately 400 people were killed in the mountain area. As for the looting, nobody was spared.

An inventory of the damage caused by the fires in Mt. Ṣāliḥīya: The Mt. Ṣāliḥīya area and the surrounding region up to the Sukkarīya [Dār al-Ḥadīth],[363] from there to the Māristān Hospital, and then to the Nāṣirīya [Madrasa],[364] was entirely burned. The fire hit one place after another. The Khātūn Mosque[365] burned down as well as the Ashrafīya Dār al-Ḥadīth, the tomb of Ṣāḥib Taqī al-Dīn,[366] and the Asadīya Mosque. God spared the congregational mosque from the fire. In the entire Mt. Ṣāliḥīya area, only five or six metal windows survived the fire. God knows best!

The annual rise of the Nile: In this year, the blessed Nile crested [on the scale of the Nilometer] at 16 cubits and seven fingers [above the old water level].

4. The Year of 700/1300-1

Events of the Maghrib:[367] [Following is a list of] the rulers of the Maghrib: the principality (*mamlaka*) of Tunisia was in the hands of Abū 'Abd Allāh Muḥammad ibn Abī Bakr ibn Zakarīyā Yaḥyā ibn Muḥammad ibn Abī Ḥafṣ.[368] His grandfather Muḥammad has been mentioned in the narrative of the year of A.H. 675,[369] which includes his brief biography as well as the

---

[363] The text has *al-Sharkasīya*, "Circassian," which is unidentified, and a little odd. I doubt it is a scribal error for al-*Sukkarīya*, namely, the Sukkarīya Dār al-Ḥadīth, a Ḥanbalī institution; for the latter, see Somogyi, "Adh-Dhahabī's record," 373, note 87; Pouzet, *Damas*, 333.

[364] Also known as the Nāṣirī Ribāṭ, on the slope of Mt. Qāsiyūn; see Somogyi, "Adh-Dhahabī's record," 376, note 99, with bibliographic references.

[365] Ibn al-Dawādārī has "Ṣābūn Mosque"; see *Kanz*, 9:40.

[366] Ibn al-Dawādārī has "Nūr al-Dīn"; see *Kanz*, 9:40.

[367] The content of this paragraph is originally included in the "list of rulers" that precedes this year's events; see the present edition, 203.

[368] For the Hafsid dynasty in Tunisia, see "Ḥafṣids," *EI*^{2}, by H. R. Idris.

[369] *Dhayl*, 3:209-18.

events during the 15 days after his death. The land of Bijāya (Bougie)[370] was ruled by the cousin of the aforementioned Abū 'Abd Allāh Muḥammad. His name was Abū Zakarīyā Yaḥyā ibn Abī Isḥāq. The ruler of [the land stretching] from the border of Bijāya to Marrākush was Abū Ya'qūb Yūsuf ibn Abī Yūsuf Ya'qūb al-Marīnī. He controlled a vast territory in the coastal area of Alexandria (*barr al-Iskandarīya*).[371] His realm was very large. His army consisted of approximately 200,000 horsemen and infantrymen when he was besieging a city called Sijilmāsa.[372] Some people from the Muslim West recounted that the siege had lasted for a long time—six years up to the end of A.H. 700 (1301)—and he still could not capture it. He swore that he would not leave the place until it was conquered. He had built a [garrison] town near the city. He was in his 40s or 50s. The ruler of Tunisia Muḥammad and his cousin Yaḥyā were all under 40 at the time.

A tax hike in Damascus: On Muḥarram 3 (September 18, 1300), the new administration (*al-dīwān*) held a meeting to [discuss the issue of] collecting emergency revenue (*istikhrāj*)[373] from all the land assets and *waqf* endowments in Damascus and its suburbs. The designated amount (*kirā*) on the city of Damascus was four months' regular dues and on the Ghūṭa suburban area was [as follows]: for each village, if its fixed revenue payment (*ḍamān*) exceeded [the estimated amount according to] its land units (*amdā'*),[374] then one-third of its fixed payment would be collected [this time]; and if *vice versa*, then a seven-*dirham*-per-*mudy* tax would be charged. One *mudy* is 40 square Qāsimī cubits and it is, if counted in fractions, equal to 1,600 [square] Hāshimī cubits.[375] One cubit is three hands (*shibr*) or 24 fingers. The emergency taxes were imposed on villages that grew wheat, barley, cotton, and corn, and were estimated at the rate of the year of A.H. 698 (1298), inasmuch

---

[370] An ancient city on the shore near Algiers. For the principality of Bijāya, see *Ql*, 3:231; 5:109-12; also "Bidjāya," *EI*², by G. Marcais.

[371] Zetterstéen (82) has *barr al-'adwa* (or *al-'udwa*); according to al-Qalqashandī, *barr al-'udwa* lay on the Mediterranean shore, facing Andalusia (Spain) across the sea; *Ql*, 3:229-30.

[372] An ancient town that was 10 day's travel from Fez; see *Ql*, 5:163-73. It is currently being excavated. I thank John Meloy for the information.

[373] For the term *istikhrāj*, see *Ql*, 4:22.

[374] Sing. *mudy*; the word means "measure of corn, bushel" (Hava, Kazimirski); a similar term, though derived from a different root *m-d-d*, is *mudd*, pl. *amdād*, "bushel, a dry measure"; for *mudd*, see Allouche, *Mamluk Economics*, 87. However, the text here shows clearly that the term *mudy* is also used in speaking of "measure of land," in that one *mudy* equals an area of 40 by 40 Egyptian and Syrian cubits.

[375] *Dhirā' Hāshimī* equals .68 m in Syria and .58 m in Egypt (Dozy, *Supplément*). The equivalence of *dhirā' Qāsimī* is not found.

as the year of A.H. 698 saw Syria's good fortune and booming prosperity [although] it was not until the year A.H. 699 (1299) that an agreement on levies on Syria's crops was reached. [However,] Syria suffered a crop failure that year (i.e., 699/1299) due to the Mongols' frequent coming and going; the harvest was poor everywhere. Therefore the current demand for revenues was very difficult for the people. A large number of them escaped and others went into hiding. As for those who were caught, they were [forced] to cut down trees in orchards and sell them as firewood. Each Damascene *qinṭār*[376] [of wood] was sold for three or four *dirhams*. The broker (*al-mukārī*) and the one who cut and chopped [wood] would get two and a half *dirhams*, while the owner would receive only two or one and a half *dirhams*. The destruction to the Ghūṭa area caused by this revenue measure was even worse than that caused by the Mongols. It was indeed the factor that led Damascenes to migrate to Egypt, [fleeing] exorbitant taxes, oppression, and injustice. [As a result,] a large number of Kurds and retired troops (*al-baṭṭāla*) were recruited [for the combat]. Each of them was paid 600 *dirhams*. When the report of the Mongols' advance towards the Euphrates was received, most of those mercenary troops ran away.

The money in the treasury was totally lost. It had either been granted to amīrs or lent to them, while not a single *dirham* was deposited into the treasury. Most of the revenues collected by amīrs were stolen by the Samaritan clerks hired [by the state]. Among those Samaritans, there was one clerk who represented the finance agent and was nicknamed Ibn Iblīs al-Sāmirī al-Muslimānī ("the son of Devil, a Samaritan convert to Islam"). Nobody could do more harm to Muslims than this fellow. He collected bribes so that whosoever wanted to delay the tax payment or get a [tax] break[377] would be granted a permission [if he had paid the bribe]. In his heart, he was even more greedy. People, especially the executive officers of the *waqf* endowments and dignitaries, were humiliated and disgraced by him. They would frequent his place [trying to please him] as he became increasingly tyrannical and brutal. All this was just because he was the deputy of the finance agent and was in charge of collecting revenue. Those [Samaritan] clerks hired by the administration were really lucky and happy given the fact that many people had migrated to Egypt; upon returning to Damascus and Syria [from exile in Egypt], one would find that he was totally unable to keep up[378] with his job

---

[376] One Damascene *qinṭār* equals 256.4 kg.

[377] The text has an obscure *musāḥama* which is perhaps an error for *musāmaḥa* (mercy, grace).

[378] The text has *muta'aṣṣil*, literally, "was pulled out from the root."

and was [therefore forced] to resign and be replaced. The new vizier was not in favor of them any more. Despite all of this, the finance agent 'Alā' al-Dīn[379] was an amīr known for his gentleness towards people, his soft-spoken manner, and his kindness. Some Damascenes complained [to him] that the mother of this Ibn Iblīs used to be a prostitute and that his father had an affair with her; he was therefore put in jail with her during the reign of Amīr Jamāl al-Dīn al-Najībī.[380] When the father was brought to trial in front of the amīr, he converted to Islam for she was a Muslim and he a Samaritan. He married her later and the boy (i.e., Ibn Iblīs) had already been conceived prior to the father's conversion to Islam and his [lawful] marriage. May God let this man and those who initiated this tax hike be far from His heaven and His mercy!

The tax collector [Ibn Iblīs] carried on until Monday, Rabī' II 26 (January 8, 1301) when the town crier announced the repeal of the tax hike after the meeting of the administration. However, the majority of the people, except those mentioned above,[381] had already been taxed by that time.

Ghāzān's new attempt on Egypt and Syria: On Muḥarram 13 of the year A.H. 700 (September 28, 1300), rumors increased in Damascus. Secret agents coming from the East reported that Ghāzān Maḥmūd had gathered a large number of troops and called upon warriors from all over his realm to march to Egypt, and that he himself was advancing towards Syria. Thereupon, from the beginning of Ṣafar to the end of Jumādā I (October 1300-January 1301), all of the Syrians fled from the Euphrates to Gaza; some of them went to fortresses and left their families there [for shelter]; some others made their way to Kerak and the nearby region; and most of them fled to Egypt. As the days went by, reports about their (i.e., the Mongols') arrival kept coming. At this point, sultan al-Malik al-Nāṣir was ready for war. He assembled the Egyptian troops to combat with the enemy.

Al-Malik al-Nāṣir's departure from the Tibn Mosque in Cairo took place on Saturday, Ṣafar 13 (October 28, 1300). They arrived in Budda 'Arsh[382] and stayed on until the end of Rabī' II (December 1300-January 1301). Then they returned to Cairo after having suffered extreme hardship and great difficulties caused by heavy rains, snow, and mud. Since the routes were cut off and the

[379] This is a little confusing: the then finance agent (*shādd al-dawāwīn*) in Syria, as the list of rulers and officials of this year shows (the present edition, 202), was in fact Sayf al-Dīn Aqjubā.

[380] Āqqūsh al-Najībī al-Ṣāliḥī, who was the viceroy of Syria from 600/1290 to 699/1299. For his career, see Ibn al-Dawādārī, *Kanz*, 8:93, 103, 150.

[381] I.e., those who paid bribes.

[382] Also known as Manzilat Budda 'Arsh; the precise location of it is not known to me. It is also mentioned by Ibn al-Dawādārī; see *Kanz*, 8:366.

food supply was thereby jeopardized, the troops and [their] horses had all run out of provisions. Under such circumstances, they could not even make it to Damascus [let alone to battle]. The sultan arrived in the Cairo Jabal Citadel on Monday, Jumādā I 11 (January 22, 1301).

Before leaving Budda 'Arsh, al-Malik al-Nāṣir had allotted 2,000 horsemen to the *silāḥ-dār* Amīr Sayf al-Dīn Baktimur and Bahā' al-Dīn Ya'qūb.[383] They arrived in Damascus on Thursday, Jumādā I 7 (January 18, 1301). The news of the sultan's return to Cairo was circulated at Damascus. The Damascenes who still remained [in the city] began to prepare themselves for war. The governor of Damascus stayed [in the city] to exhort the people personally. He would stop by the markets and say, "What makes you sit there? How dare you still sit there?" On Saturday, Jumādā I 9 (January 20, 1301), town criers called out the following, "Whoever sits down [doing nothing] is risking his own life! Whoever is unable to travel should seek shelter in the Citadel!" Most of the citizens fled [the city] this day. There is no power and no strength save in God!

Ghāzān's troops in Mt. Sumāq and Antioch: As regards Ghāzān, he and his army arrived in Aleppo, while the vanguard regiment approached the edge of Hama and the countryside of Sarmīn.[384] He dispatched his main forces to Mt. Sumāq and the countryside of Antioch, where they snatched an inordinate number of horses, sheep, and cows, and captured a large number of men, women, and children from the region. The reason behind such action was that in the year of A.H. [6]99, a host of refugees had fled to Mt. [Sumāq] to hide; and none of the Mongols had found them. When this year came, contrary to custom, many people climbed up the mountain, in the belief that the Mongols did not know about it and would not attack them since they would be heading for the Syria[n hinterland instead]. Then when Ghāzān's camping in Aleppo became drawn out, and fodder and food were in short supply, some captives caught in Aleppo informed him (i.e., Ghāzān) about the situation in the mountain area. Ghāzān, therefore, sent most of his troops there to plunder and capture civilians. The Muslim men and women captured by them were so numerous that they would sell a female or a male prisoner for 10 *dirhams*. The ruler of Cilicia and some Armenians purchased a lot of them, so did some Georgians and Christians. They dispatched them in many ships and sent them by sea to West Europe under the escort of a group [of soldiers].

---

[383] The text here is probably corrupt. Ms. Ahmet III 2907 has *Ya'qūb* while Ms. Landberg 139 has *Ya'qūbā* which appears to be an error for *Ya'qūb<bi>a<lfay>* . . . (Ya'qūb with 2,000 . . .). The correction is made after Zetterstéen, 84.

[384] To the west of Aleppo; see *Q1*, 4:126.

God summoned rain and snow upon the Mongols. People from that region reported that they had had rain for 41 days, at times rain and at times snow. As a result, a large number of the Mongols died. So they retreated to their homeland in worse shape than defeated troops. Their horses were injured and most of them died. God paralyzed their determination to conquer this land (i.e., Syria) and kill His subjects. *And God sent back those that were unbelievers in their rage, and they attained no good; God spared the believers of fighting.*[385] God made it impossible for the two armies to battle each other. The news of the Mongols' retreat reached [Damascus] in the month of Jumādā II (February 1301). By then Damascus and all the remaining Syrian cities had already been evacuated. The news reached Gaza where the chief judge Badr al-Dīn Ibn Jamā'a, the chief judge Shams al-Dīn al-Ḥarīrī, the chief judge Najm al-Dīn Ibn Ṣaṣrā, Najm al-Dīn Ibn Abī al-Ṭayyib, Ṣāḥib Ibn Sharaf al-Dīn Ibn al-Qalānisī, Niẓām al-Dīn and their sons as well as a large number [of civilians] had been staying [for shelter]. They set off for Cairo on Tuesday, Jumādā II 3, the year of A.H. 700 (February 13, 1301).

Soaring prices in Damascus: Prices soared in Damascus. A *raṭl* of meat cost 10 *dirhams* and billy goat meat six *dirhams*. A sack of wheat cost 300 *dirhams*. Sometimes the price of grain and other kinds of crops went down a little bit.

Persecution of dhimmīs in Cairo and Damascus: In the month of Rajab (March-April 1301), the vizier of the ruler of the Muslim West (*malik al-Gharb*),[386] on his way to the pilgrimage, arrived in Cairo. He met with the sultan as well as the viceroy and Amīr Rukn al-Dīn Baybars al-Jāshankīr. They treated him with hospitality and respect. Then he talked to them about the status of Christians and Jews in their own province where they (i.e., Christians and Jews) were in an extremely humble and contemptible position. They were not allowed to ride, nor to be appointed to state posts and public offices. He expressed his disapproval with the way that Egyptian Christians and Jews had been treated in that they were wearing the most luxurious clothes, riding on mules, horses, and mares, being hired for top-rank offices, and exerting their power and authority over Muslims. He then pointed out that their Pact of Protection (*'ahd al-dhimma*) had expired in the year

[385] *Qur'ān*, 33:25.

[386] I.e., the Hafsid ruler of Tunisia and eastern Algeria; cf. Little, "Coptic Conversion to Islam," 555, note 13; also above, 172-73.

A.H. 600.[387] He then went on and on and said many things like that. His speech had an obvious impact on all the statesmen and won plaudits especially from Amīr Rukn al-Dīn al-Jāshankīr and other amīrs. They all agreed with him on this particular issue and considered such a matter extremely important for carrying forward the rites of Islam.

So when Maundy Thursday, Rajab 20 (March 30, 1301), came, they summoned the Christians and Jews and laid down the rules, proclaiming that none of the Jews and Christians would be appointed to state posts or be hired by amīrs, and that they must change their turbans: the Christians must wear blue turbans and tighten the belts around their waists, while the Jews must wear yellow turbans. The Christians in greater Cairo celebrated a miserable holiday. People of these two communities made their way to visit all the amīrs, Muslim religious leaders, statesmen, and dignitaries. They spread about an enormous amount of money to buy off the imposition of such rules. None of them succeeded. [The measures] were enforced upon them in extraordinarily strict terms. Amīr Rukn al-Dīn Baybars al-Jāshankīr oversaw this action in person. In the greater Cairo area, churches were closed. All doors were nailed up by [wooden or metal] bars and nails. From Rajab 22 (April 1, 1301) on, the Jews started to wear yellow turbans and the Christians blue ones. If anybody [dared] ride on a beast, one of his legs was to be cut off. They were dismissed from state posts as well as amīrs' services and [were forbidden from] riding on horses and mules. A large number of Christians thus converted to Islam.[388] Among them was the assistant to the vizier (*mustawfī al-ṣuḥba*)[389] Amīn al-Mulk, along with others.

The sultan then commanded an edict to be sent to his entire realm, from Dunqula[390] to the Euphrates, in order to carry out such measures. As soon as the edict arrived, residents of Alexandria dashed to demolish two local churches which were said to have been built during the era of Islam (*mustajidda*), along with houses owned by Christians or Jews. If any of these houses were higher than those of their Muslim neighbors, the higher

---

[387] This is referring to the so-called "Covenant of 'Umar"; see "Dhimma," *EI*[2], by Cl. Cahen.

[388] For a general survey of modern scholarship on conversion during the Mamluk period, see Humphreys, *Islamic History*, 256-61, 273-83. Al-Yūnīnī's accounts here have been used as the primary source on the 700/1301 actions against the Dhimmīs in Cairo by Little in his "Coptic Conversion to Islam," 554-58, especially 555 and note 52.

[389] See *Q2*, 311. According to Hassanein Rabie, the official of *mustawfī al-ṣuḥba* "was attached to the person of the sultan, on whose behalf he supervised the work of the *kuttāb* and checked all accounts"; see *The Financial System of Egypt*, 157.

[390] In Nubia.

parts were torn down. If any of them had a shop next to a Muslim shop, the stone doorstep outside the shop was removed so the Muslim shop would [look] higher. They erected signs (*al-shi'ār*) [to indicate non-Muslim shops] as they used to do.

The news of such action was brought to Damascus by the post in the beginning of Sha'bān. On Monday, Sha'bān 7 (April 17, 1301), the regulations upon the Dhimmī's were announced in Damascus in the presence of the viceroy and a large group of amīrs and qāḍīs. They had reached the consensus that those [Dhimmīs] should be laid off from provincial administrations. Certain specific measures were written down, including the ban on riding horses or other animals. On Friday, Sha'bān 25 (May 4, 1301), a measure was called out in Damascus on behalf of the viceroy to force the Dhimmīs to wear the distinguishing garb on their heads: the color of Christians was blue, Jews yellow, and Samaritans red. The measure was vigorously enforced. By Sunday, many Jews appeared wearing the distinguishing garb. They were followed by Christians and Samaritans as well. Praise and blessing be to God!

In the aftermath, people in Cairo started talking about demolishing churches, especially the ones in new Cairo (*al-Qāhira*). Muslim scholars, jurists, and qāḍīs held an assembly to discuss the issue. It was said that the deputy judge of Egypt Qāḍī Najm al-Dīn Ibn al-Raf'a[391] had previously issued a *fatwā* ordering the demolition of churches. So in this later meeting, the qāḍīs and scholars debated the issue for a long time. The chief judge Taqī al-Dīn Ibn Daqīq al-'Īd[392] gave a speech in which he issued a *fatwā* to allow churches to remain, except those proved now to have been built after the Islamic era (*muḥdatha*); if that were the case, then they were to be demolished. The assembly agreed with him unanimously. The final decision was thus made on the guideline drawn by the shaykh Taqī al-Dīn Ibn Daqīq al-'Īd—may God be pleased with him! A clerk named 'Alā' al-Dīn Ibn Waddā'a wrote the following verses [on the event]:

They have forced the infidels to wear sashes of humiliation
Which will add muddle to them,[393] *in addition to God's curse.*
I told them that what they made them wear were not turbans,[394]

---

[391] Aḥmad Ibn al-Raf'a al-Anṣārī; he died in 710/1311. For his biography, see Ibn al-'Imād, *Shadharāt*, 6:22.

[392] Muḥammad ibn 'Alī ibn Wahb al-Qushayrī; he died in 702/1302. For his career and biography, see al-Subkī, *Ṭabaqāt al-Shāfi'īya*, 9:207-49; al-'Asqalānī, *Durar*, 4:91; *GAL*, II:75, and *GALS*, II:66.

[393] This is a pun on the words *shāshāt* (sashes) and *tashwīsh* (confusion, disturbance), both derived from the root of *sh-w-sh*.

But window-sills (barāṭīsh)!

Also:

They have changed their clothing as they have made
The noble God's merciful nature turn [against them].
As you see now they are wearing window-sills,
But they dare to call them "turbans!"

Personal conflicts among the Cairene 'ulamā': In the month of Ramaḍān of this year (May-June, 1301), the Shāfi'ī jurist and court functionary Najm al-Dīn Muḥammad ibn 'Aqīl ibn Abī al-Ḥasan al-Bālisī, a Damascus native, was appointed to the office of deputy judge of Egypt. He was to succeed the chief judge Taqī al-Dīn Ibn Daqīq al-'Īd. As he assumed the position, Qāḍī Najm al-Dīn Ibn al-Raf'a was unhappy and thus left[395] the office of deputy judge and resigned from the post. Ibn Daqīq al-'Īd thus appointed Qāḍī Zayn al-Dīn 'Umar ibn Sharaf al-Dīn ibn Yūnis al-Kinānī to replace Ibn al-Raf'a. He assumed the post in Ramaḍān as well.

In the month of Ramaḍān, Qāḍī Jamāl al-Dīn, known by the name of "the Shāfi'ī ragman" (*al-saqaṭī*) left the office of deputy judge in Cairo and testified on his own behalf for his resignation. All this was due to [the conflicts] between him and some relatives of Shaykh Taqī al-Dīn [Ibn Daqīq al-'Īd]. People in greater Cairo felt sorry for the man. They mentioned that for over 40 years he had been on duty as a judge in Cairo, and that every executive judge knew his integrity. All of them tried to persuade him to stay in the office. He had been in charge of all the civil [legal] affairs and the job was superbly done.

The Mongol envoys in Damascus and Cairo: In this year, on Dhū al-Qa'da 9 (July 16, 1301), an amīr named Sayf al-Dīn Anas came from Aleppo to Cairo to report the enemy's movements. [He said that] the Mongols had sent envoys to them and those envoys were already near the Euphrates. A few days later, postmen brought the news that the Mongols' envoy had arrived in Damascus on Tuesday night, Dhū al-Qa'da 23 (July 29, 1301). They put him up in the [Damascus] Citadel. They (i.e., the envoy and his entourage) were fewer than 20 in number. They stayed in the Citadel for a few days and then,

---

[394] For a discussion of the special concept of turban (*'amā'im*) and those who wear it (*muta'ammimūn*), namely, indigenous aristocracy, see Humphreys, *Ayyūbids*, 23-27, 377-80.

[395] The text has *rafa'a yadahu min*, literally "lifted his hands from. . . ."

on Saturday night, Dhū al-Qa'da 28 (August 3, 1301), three of their representatives were sent to Cairo, leaving their heavy luggage and retinue [in Damascus]. One of those was the Shāfi'ī qāḍī and preacher of Mosul Ḍiyā' al-Dīn [Muḥammad] ibn Bahā' al-Dīn ibn Kamāl al-Dīn ibn Yūnis.[396] The two others were a Persian and a Turkman.[397]

They arrived in the Cairo Jabal Citadel on Monday night, Dhū al-Ḥijja 15, the year of A.H. 700 (August 20, 1301) and received a warm reception. On Tuesday evening [Dhū al-Ḥijja 16] (August 21, 1301), the amīrs and generals gathered in the [Cairo] Citadel with the royal Mamluks, all dressed in their best. When the last evening prayer was over, they lit 1,000 candles and showed off their splendid decorations [of the city]. The envoys were brought in. The qāḍī [Ḍiyā' al-Dīn], wearing a *ṭarḥa*-headgear, was among them. He stood up and delivered a beautiful, eloquent, and brief speech. He cited many Qur'ānic verses on the subjects of peacemaking and consensus building. He was admired [by the audience]. Then he went on to pray for sultan al-Malik al-Nāṣir, and next, for sultan Maḥmūd Ghāzān. He also prayed for the amīrs and the Muslims. [By doing so] he fulfilled the mission with the major theme of their good will for the peace settlement. The envoys then presented a letter signed by the seal of sultan Ghāzān. The letter was accepted but not read that night. The envoys were then led back to the [guest] house. On the eve of Thursday [Dhū al-Ḥijja 18] (August 23, 1301), all the amīrs and generals, as well as most of the troops were summoned and [Ghāzān's] letter was shown and read to them. It was written in a rough hand on half-folio paper (*niṣf qaṭ' al-Baghdādī*).[398]

Ghāzān's letter to al-Malik al-Naṣir: The content of the letter is as follows:

> In the name of God, the Merciful, the Compassionate. After saluting him (i.e., al-Malik al-Nāṣir), we bring the following to his attention: God made us and you people of one community. He honored us with the Faith of Islam. He supported us and assigned us to establish minarets. He showed us the Right Path. Those things [that happened] between you and us were all by God's decree and determination; and they were caused by

---

[396] His biography is not found. His grandfather Kamāl al-Dīn Mūsā (d. 629/1232) was also the Shāfi'ī qāḍī in Mosul; for the latter's biography, see Ibn al-'Imād, *Shadharāt*, 5:206; also Pouzet, *Damas*, 30, note 33 (where the grandfather's name is given as Muḥammad ibn Yūnis).

[397] Ibn al-Dawādārī has "and another was a Mongol and the third a slave soldier"; *Kanz*, 9:52.

[398] For *qaṭ' al-Baghdādī*, see Dozy, *Supplément*.

nothing but by *what your own hands earned*[399] and *for that God is never unjust unto His servants.*[400] The roots [of the confrontation] lie in that a group of your troops attacked Mārdīn and its surrounding areas in the month of Ramaḍān; an attack that has shocked all the people in the region to this day. In it (i.e., Ramaḍān) Satan plunged in and the gates of the Hell were shut off. They *entered the city, at a time when its people were unheeding,*[401] killing and arresting. They committed immoral acts and violated what God declared implacably sacrosanct. They ate forbidden food and committed sins that even idol worshipers dare not do. People of the Mārdīn region thus came to us. Anxious and depressed, they cried and called for help to rescue their children and women. They suffered disasters after having enjoyed happy days. They sought shelter with us and relied on us [for survival]. They came to our door exactly like panic-stricken refugee[s].

Thereupon, we were stirred by noble sentiments and moved by zeal for Islam. We thus immediately maneuvered troops who were at our disposal and, without a stop, came over to the region. We promised God to [intervene in] what had upset Him, fulfilling His resolution. We knew that God was not pleased with the infidelity of His servants, in that they hasten about the earth, creating corruption there.[402] He was angry at [sins of] rape and kidnapping. So, our confrontation with you was out of [our] sincere intent and passionate zeal on behalf of Islam. We have torn you utterly to pieces.[403] The one who drove us to [combat with] you was exactly the One who let us triumph over you. You have struck a similitude: *a city that was secure, at rest, its provision coming to it easefully from every place, then it was unthankful for the blessings of God; so God let it taste the garment of hunger and of fear, for the things that they were working.*[404] And you managed to flee and escaped our swords. We forgave you after [God's] decision and spared you the sentence of the sharp sword. We ordered our troops not to pursue worldly things as you had done and [encouraged them] to spread as much forgiveness and virtue as you had abandoned, for, had you been in a position of power, you would have been neither forgiving nor virtuous.[405] We did not mean to grant you a favor by [following] such [an action]; it was the rule of Islam

---

[399] *Qur'ān*, 42:30.

[400] Cf. *Qur'ān*, 3:182, 8:51, 22:10.

[401] *Qur'ān*, 28:15.

[402] This sentence is slightly adapted, to fit the context, from *Qur'ān*, 2:205.

[403] The sentence is slightly adapted from *Qur'ān*, 34:19.

[404] *Qur'ān*, 16:112.

[405] The term *'affaftum* in the clause *mā 'afawtum wa-lā 'affaftum* reads *'affaytum* in the two manuscripts, which does not make good sense. I thank Dimitri Gutas for suggesting such a reading which perfectly reflects the preceding phrase *al-'afw wa-al-'afāf*.

to fight against oppressors [that motivated us]. All the things that happened in the past and in their pre-existence had already been written down by the pen [of God] on the Divine Tablet.

Then when we saw that people were hurt by our staying in Syria inasmuch as they had to share their drink and food with them (i.e., the troops), and that they were panicking at witnessing our forces accumulating like widespread clouds, we decided to calm their fears by withdrawing from their land with triumph, victory, dignity, and an abundance [of spoils]. We left some troops [in Syria] for the comfort and consultation of the people, as well as for preventing them from assaulting each other *when the earth became strait for* you,[406] until you become self-controlled, able to demonstrate integrity in your behavior, and able to bring forces to Syria in order to protect that land against your enemies as well as those Kurds dispatched [to invade your land]. We instructed two Generals of Ten Thousand from our army that as soon as they have heard about the arrival of any of you into Syria, they ought to retreat to us safely. And they have, in fact, returned home in plain triumph. Praise be to God, the Lord of all beings!

Now, both you and we are still holding the same belief in Islam. The difference between us lies only in what you did to the people of Mārdīn. We have already punished you as the recompense for every rebel. So let us revert now to the matter of restoring people's welfare. Let us, together with you, make an effort to carry out justice in all respects. The situation of the region and its inhabitants has deteriorated since [the confrontation] between you and us. Fear has prevented [people] from resettling in their towns and villages. The trade routes have been closed off and normal life has been interrupted by shortages and travel restrictions. We know that we are asked [to do something] about it and that we are reckoned for that. *From God nothing whatever is hidden in heaven and earth.*[407] And everything, in the past and present, is *with this Book, that it leaves nothing behind, small or great.*[408]

Oh, you honorable ruler! You know that you and I are in charge of [everyone], commoner and noble, and that we are responsible for whatever offense was committed by our most insignificant appointee. Our fate is decided by God. We believe in Islam by word, deed, and intention, performing its duties in all matters. We have charged the chief judge—one of the most learned men of our time, the authority on Islam and a descendant of Muḥammad's family—Ḍiyā' al-Dīn Muḥammad Abū 'Abd Allāh, with

---

[406] *Qur'ān*, 9:118. The original text of the *Qur'ān* has "them" instead of "you."
[407] *Qur'ān*, 3:5, 14:38.
[408] *Qur'ān*, 18:49, 54:53.

an oral message. As a fully authorized delegate (*al-'umda 'alayhā*),[409] he is to deliver that message to al-Malik [al-Nāṣir] in person. If he brings back a [positive] response, he ought to carry with him presents from Egypt to us as a gesture and sign. So it will be known through the sending of presents that your intention to comply with our peace proposal [is sincere]. From our lands, we send our appropriate regards and good wishes to you, God willing!

Al-Malik al-Nāṣir's response to Ghāzān's letter: After [the reading,] sultan [al-Malik al-Nāṣir] consulted with the amīrs. Then they called for a meeting with the above-mentioned qāḍī of Mosul and said to him, "You are one of the greatest scholars and the choicest Muslims. You know what your duty is and what kind of advice [you can offer] in the name of Islam. We will fight for nothing else but in defense of the Faith of Islam. If this [proposal] is made as some sort of deceit and conspiracy on the [Mongols'] part, [tell us, and] we swear to you that we will not leak [our] conversation to any one in this world." They then appealed to him [for his help]. And he, in his turn, swore to them that he believed that Ghāzān and his senior advisors (*al-khawāṣṣ*) meant nothing but to make peace and to avoid bloodshed, as well as to bring about the prosperity of trade and people's welfare. He told them, "It is good for you to consolidate and keep your eyes on your enemies. You used to send patrols once a year to the frontiers of your realm for the sake of its safeguarding and you should continue doing this. If this [proposal] is a trick, then the truth[410] will soon be exposed to you and you will then be on alert; and if it is sincere, your closeness to them will generate peace between the two sides and avoid bloodshed." Upon hearing his advice, they considered it sincere[411] and constructive. Then they began to select [envoys for] the mission [to Ghāzān]. A number of persons were selected, among them were Amīr Shams al-Dīn Ibn al-Taytī,[412] and Shams al-Dīn al-Jazarī.[413] However, the latter, who was then the preacher *(khaṭīb)* at the [Aḥmad] Ibn Ṭūlūn Mosque [in Cairo], was spared [from the mission] after he had solicited many people's pleading on his behalf. They also appointed the preacher of the Ḥākim Mosque and the

---

[409] For the meaning of this phrase, see Kazimirski.

[410] The text has *khilāfuhu*, literally "the opposite of it (i.e., of the deceit). . . ."

[411] The text has *mā fīhi gharḍ*, literally "without ulterior motives."

[412] He was the vizier of the ruler of Mārdīn and died in 704/1304; see Ibn al-Dawādārī, *Kanz*, 9:130.

[413] Muḥammad ibn Yūsuf; he was a Shāfi'ī preacher and died in 711/1312; see al-'Asqalānī, *Durar*, 5:67-68; Ibn al-'Imād, *Shadharāt*, 4:42-43 (gives his death date as A.H. 716). This Shams al-Dīn al-Jazarī should not be confused with the historian Shams al-Dīn Muḥammad al-Jazarī (d. 739/1338), the author of the *Ḥawādith*.

manager of the Dār al-'Adl of Egypt Qāḍī 'Imād al-Dīn Ibn al-Sukkarī,[414] and an *amīr-ākhūr*[415] from the Burjī regiment [to the mission]. This mission was in fact deferred to the coming year[416] and we will report its [journey] below, God willing!

The pilgrim caravan of this year: The month of Sha'bān of this year began on a Monday (April 10, 1301). Greater Cairo was decorated at night for the occasion of the [annual] parade of the *maḥmil* that carried the covering of the Ka'ba [in Mecca] and the Prophet's Shrine [in Medina]. As usual, the qāḍīs, amīrs, generals as well as the entire army, all the preachers, imāms, muezzins, Qur'ān reciters, religious exhortation givers, and all statesmen rode on horses, leading the glorious *maḥmil* and the royal caravan parading in the greater Cairo area. This was a festive day indeed. The leader of this year's pilgrims was the *amīr-jānidār* Grand Amīr Sayf al-Dīn Baktimur al-Jūkandār al-Mālikī al-Manṣūrī.[417] He took this very seriously and spent nearly 85,000 Egyptian *dīnārs* of his own money [for the preparation]. The caravan set off from Cairo and arrived at al-Birka[418] on Monday, Shawwāl 12 (June 19, 1301). It then left al-Birka for Ayla[419] on Sunday morning, Shawwāl 18 (June 25, 1301). The Cairene amīrs who went on this year's pilgrim caravan were: the leader of the caravan Amīr Sayf al-Dīn Baktimur, Amīr of Fifty Horsemen Bahā' al-Dīn Qarā-Qūsh, Amīr of Fifty Horsemen Ḥusām al-Dīn Mughalṭāy, the eunuch (*al-ṭawāshī*) and Amīr of Fifty Horsemen Murshid al-Khādim, Amīr Asad al-Dīn, the son of Amīr 'Izz al-Dīn al-Afram, Ṣāḥib Fakhr al-Dīn Ibn al-Khalīlī, Ṣāḥib Zayn al-Dīn Ibn Ḥinnī, and many others, including Qāḍī Sharaf al-Dīn al-Ḥanbalī as well as a host of Egyptian [civilians], generals, and soldiers. The equipment of the caravan was [loaded on] 100 camels. Among them 80 were of the *zād* and *sawwāqa* ("long-legged") breeds, 10 were of the *muḥāyir* breed, and the rest were of the *hujūn*

---

[414] 'Abd al-Raḥmān ibn 'Abd al-'Alī, the Shāfi'ī chief judge in Cairo; he died in 713/1313. For his biography, see al-Subkī, *Ṭabaqāt al-Shāfi'iya*, 10:138; for his role in this mission, which was deferred to the year 704/1304, cf. Ibn al-Dawādārī, *Kanz*, 9:74-75, 127-28.

[415] Unidentified. The title *amīr-ākhūr* was usually given to the head of the royal stables; see *Q2*, 31-32.

[416] Actually to the year 704/1304.

[417] He was later the commander of the fortress of al-Ṣubayba (706/1306) and then the viceroy of Cairo (709/1309-10); see Ibn al-Dawādārī, *Kanz*, 9:148, 194.

[418] Also known as Birkat al-Ḥājj, an Egyptian town on the Red Sea shore; it was a stop on the Egyptian route to Mecca; see *Q1*, 4:284; 14:381.

[419] Also known as 'Aqaba, 'Aqabat Ayla, or Kūrat Ayla, an ancient village on the Red Sea shore. It used to be a stop on the Egyptian pilgrimage route; see *Q1*, 3:238, 388-89; 7:27-28.

("dromedaries") and *saqqāyīn*. The city of Cairo was decorated on the day the caravan departed. People rode in procession just as they did in the month of Sha'bān as described above.

The celebration of the annual rise of the Nile: In this year, on Saturday night which was the eve of Dhū al-Ḥijja 4 (August 10, 1301), the blessed Nile flooded with an abundant amount of water. People lighted a lantern on the window of the Nilometer (*al-mīqās*)[420] and reported the [news] to the sultan. Marvelous things were happening on the Nile. In the morning, the entire army, led by the viceroy and amīrs, rode forth and marched out. On behalf of the sultan, Amīr Rukn al-Dīn Baybars al-Jāshankīr rode in a light boat (*ḥurrāqa*),[421] and together with him were many amīrs who took different boats. They performed the ceremony of perfuming the Nilometer column (*takhlīq 'āmūd al-sulṭān*).[422] According to the custom, it was the sultan's duty to perform such a ceremony in person. However, on the same day he had some other business to finish, [so he] sent Amīr Rukn al-Dīn to represent him. Having finished the plenitude ceremony, Rukn al-Dīn and the viceroy came back [to the shore] and rode on. They gave orders to open the ancient city canal of Cairo (*kasr al-khalīj*).[423] The canal was opened. The sultan had previously ordered every governor [of Cairo] to declare publicly that whosoever should damage [the canal] would be hanged. So nobody dared even to do things necessary[424] that they used to do. After the opening of the canal, the water increased a great deal. In the year preceding the past year (i.e., A.H. 697), the opening of the Cairo canal had lasted for 17 days and the rise of the Nile in that year was 17 cubits and 19 fingers from the [old water level of] 18 cubits. The plenitude of the Nile, the so-called "water of the sultan," was 16 cubits. Therefore, any amount of [water] above that was considered a great blessing with which people would be very pleased.

The Mongols in Delhi: In this year, at the end of Dhū al-Qa'da (the end of July and beginning of August, 1301), a group of Kārimī merchants[425] came

---

[420] For *al-mīqās*, see Popper, *The Cairo Nilometer*; also *Q2*, 74.

[421] For *ḥurrāqa*, see *Q2*, 104.

[422] For a detailed description of the ceremony, see *Q1*, 3:512-14; *Q2*, 74, 295; also Popper, *The Cairo Nilometer*, 71-73.

[423] Also known as *fatḥ al-khalīj*. According to al-Qalqashandī, whenever the Nile reached the plenitude (*mā' al-sulṭān*), the Cairo canal would be opened; see *Q1*, 3:514-17; *Q2*, 295; also Popper, *The Cairo Nilometer*, 82-85.

[424] I.e., the opening of the Cairo canal when the Nile reached the plenitude, etc.

[425] For the Kārimī merchants, see Lapidus, *Muslim Cities*, 211-13; *Q2*, 73. Some scholars are of the opinion that they were the merchants engaged in the spice trade from India through the Yemeni harbor Kārim. I thank Franz Rosenthal for sharing with me his suspicion of this theory.

from Yemen to Cairo. They said that the ruler of Delhi al-Malik al-Mas'ūd Nāṣir al-Dīn Maḥmūd ibn 'Alā' al-Dīn Muḥammad ibn 'Alam al-Dīn Sanjār, a freed slave (*'atīq*) of Shams al-Dīn Aytāmish who was a freed slave of Shihāb al-Dīn al-Ghūrī, together with his brother sultan Ghiyāth al-Dīn,[426] had dispatched troops in the year A.H. 699 (1299-1300), to the region of Cambay (Kanbāya) of India. As soon as the Mongols, who were stationed nearby and were said to be the so-called Mengü-Temüriya regiment, received the information that Delhi was void of troops at the time, they desired to raid the region. So they assembled troops, deployed forces and then marched towards Delhi. They looted the region, arrested [civilians] and seized half of its capital and assets. Afterwards they advanced towards the city where al-Malik al-Mas'ūd lived. At that time, al-Malik [al-Mas'ūd] had at his disposal no more than 30,000 horsemen while the Mongols were numerous. He thus consulted with his viziers, senior advisors, and statesmen on what to do. They suggested he utilize all the elephants he had and to have warriors ride on them and the main armed forces march behind them. When the Mongols encountered those elephants in the battle they would be troubled with them, and then al-Malik [al-Mas'ūd] and his forces would be able to move into any terrain of their choice between the two armies. As a result, they would not be besieged in the city, killed in captivity, or caught by force. So al-Malik [al-Mas'ūd] rode out for the battle, and approximately 300 elephants were called on. Riding [on horse], al-Malik [al-Mas'ūd] led his army marching behind the elephants. As soon as the Mongols' horses saw the elephants, they [were terrified and] fled the battlefield. As the [Delhi] troops saw the [Mongols'] withdrawal, they pursued them, killing a number of them, capturing others, and tearing the enemy utterly to pieces. Only those [lucky ones] who were destined to live long managed to escape. They (i.e., the Delhi troops) pursued [the Mongols] for 15 days until they expelled them from their land. God let them triumph. And that is their story.

The Delhi army in India: As for the expedition sent by the ruler of Delhi [sultanate] to the land of India, they encountered, and fought with, the Indian troops and defeated them. They captured the king of Cambay. When the Indian king was brought before the general of the expedition, the latter had him shackled in iron fetters. The Indian king said, "Should someone like me be bound with iron fetters? I have prepared golden fetters for you in the hope that if I captured you, I would shackle you in them." The general said, "Bring them here!" The king told them the place. The golden fetters, inlaid with

[426] For more details, see "Dihlī sultanate," *EI*², by P. Hardy.

gems, were brought in. The general said, "I will shackle you in them. And I thank God Who has saved me from this." The king was then shackled in these fetters. The general, who was known for his simple-mindedness, asked the king, "Where is the treasure?" The king said, "Do you want it?" He said, "Yes." The king said, "Go to such and such a place; open it and take whatever is in there. There is plenty of gold." The general then came back and said, "I want [more]." The king said, "What you have gotten isn't enough?" He said, "Not at all!" The king said, "By the Truth I worship, I will tell you another hidden treasure. But if you come back again and ask for more, I will not give any more information to you." The general promised so. Then the king told him about another hidden treasure full of gold. It took them 18 days—others said 28 days—to move all the gold from it. Each day [they carried] 15 loads, in each load 1,500 camels [were utilized]. Having emptied the treasure and moved all the gold to their camp, the general said to the king, "I want more and give me what I want!" The king [had no choice but to] show the Delhi general [other treasures].

Once upon a time, the father of the ruler of Delhi al-Malik [al-Mas'ūd] had seized an enormous amount of captives and booty from India. He found among the captives a young Indian maid whom he liked very much and thus took her as his concubine. She soon became pregnant with al-Malik [al-Mas'ūd]. When the news of the capture of the king of Cambay reached him, he consulted with his mother on what to do with the [captive] king. His mother asked him, "Dear son, don't you know who he is?" He said, "The king of India." She said, "He is your uncle. I am his sister." After learning that, he ordered his general to release the king and treat him gently. He [also] sent him (i.e., the king of India) robes of honor and issued an edict to return his country to him and to appoint him as his deputy there. Upon receiving his nephew's favors, the Indian king was very grateful. He went over to his land and retrieved from hidden treasures an abundance of gems, jewelry, and presents which were decent enough to be presented to any king. Then he sent them to the ruler of Delhi with a letter, saying, "I have many hidden treasures inherited from my forefathers. Whenever you need money and gems, I will send them to you so you can make use of them and triumph over your enemies! I am your deputy and your slave. I own some 40 hidden treasures the smallest of which is as large as what you have taken. Be at ease and don't be afraid of your enemy. Whenever you need money, you will get it from me."

The expedition returned to Delhi with tremendous amounts of booty which were beyond description and were sufficient for them and their offspring forever. As for the treasure taken from the two hidden places, it could be counted only in terms of camel loads. The above story is quoted from Bahā' al-Dīn.[427]

A pseudo-prophet in Ethiopia: It was also reported that at the end of A.H. 698 (1299), a man named Shaykh Muḥammad Abū 'Abd Allāh rose up in Ethiopia (*al-Ḥabash*). He attracted a large number of indigenous followers. He claimed to call for the conversion to Islam and for the establishment of the Faith. He bewitched many people's minds by telling them that angels had come to him and talked to him, and that they had ordered him to conquer Ethiopia. About 200,000 men came to join his cause. At this point, the ruler of Ethiopia al-Amḥarī gathered all of his troops and his followers, approximately 400,000 cavalry and infantry, and led them to battle against Shaykh Abū 'Abd Allāh. [At the same time,] al-Amḥarī secretly sent letters to Shaykh Abū 'Abd Allāh's adherents in an effort to bribe them. So the leading figures of his (i.e., Abū 'Abd Allāh's) followers came to him (i.e., Abū 'Abd Allāh) and said, "We want you to demonstrate some of your miracles (*karāmāt*) so that our hearts would trust [you] and we would go into battle with full confidence." He said to them, "Of course. I will let angels talk to you from a well." After they left, he asked one of his henchmen to go to a designated well and jump in it, and had a secret passage dug out next to the well. [The plan was that] when he came with the others, he would cry, "Oh, Gabriel, am I truthful?" [The man in well would] reply, "Yes." [And he would say,] "Then you should order me and my followers to fight against the ruler of Ethiopia." He coached the man what to say and how to react. Having made sure that the man was ready for the task, and that none could see him, the shaykh and those who had asked him to demonstrate the revelation from angels came, with many other people, to the well. As soon as he approached the well, he shouted, "Oh, angels of my Lord, Oh, Gabriel, am I truthful?" The person in the bottom of the well thus responded, "Yes." And then he went on to order him to do [good] and forbid him [from doing evil], confirming the [above-mentioned] message. [Having seen] all his adherents wholeheartedly convinced, he asked them, "So, what do you people say now?" They said, "Your credibility has been confirmed." Then he said, "So, do whatever I tell you to do!" They said, "Yes." He said, "The first thing I want you to do is to fill this well immediately." They filled the well with earth at once.

The person [buried in the well] happened to have a brother who felt that the man had been absent too long. He came to the shaykh and asked about his

[427] Unidentified.

brother. Prior to that he had [also] made inquiries with some of the shaykh's aides and they told him that the shaykh had sent him on a mission. However, the shaykh denied that. The brother continued the investigation about his brother's whereabouts and eventually discovered that he was the one who had talked to the people from the well. He thus went to the well with a group of people. They dug out the well and found his dead brother. They carried the body out of the well. At that point, the [shaykh's] followers split off. The ruler of Ethiopia al-Amḥarī was very pleased [because by now] the standoff between the two parties on the shores of the Nile had lasted for six months. Al-Amḥarī seized the moment and wrote to him and the two agreed on a truce according to which [al-Amḥarī] promised to cede some lands in the frontiers to Shaykh Abū 'Abd Allāh Muḥammad in which he and his adherents could grow crops without being taxed. [The treaty also stipulated that] the ruler of Ethiopia would give them[428] sufficient provisions to meet their needs as long as the shaykh and his adherents submitted to his sovereignty.

Yemeni 'ulamā's mediation between the Zaydīs and the Rasūlid dynasty: It was also reported that in the year of A.H. 699 (1299-1300), al-Malik al-Mu'ayyad Hizabr al-Dīn Dāwūd, the son of al-Malik al-Muẓaffar Shams al-Dīn Yūsuf ibn al-Malik al-Manṣūr Nūr al-Dīn 'Umar ibn 'Alī ibn Rasūl[429] had reached a covenant with the Zaydīs. The Zaydīs used to ask the ruler of Yemen to pay an annual fee of 20,000 Egyptian *dīnār*s in return for their protection of routes, their assistance to passengers in the transit trade (*al-ajlāb*), [their promise] not to attack the ones who crossed their territory, and their submission to the authority of the ruler of Yemen. Whenever they made the claim they would come [to collect the payment]. In the year of A.H. 699 (1299), the Zaydīs sent their envoys to the ruler of Yemen and told him, "We will not accept anything less than 100,000 *dīnār*s a year." At the same time, they started building up their forces and determined to fight against [the ruler of Yemen]. The latter, in his turn, assembled his troops and deployed them into fortresses. A fierce battle seemed to be inevitable. At this point, religious leaders and scholars in Yemen dashed to interfere. They mediated between the two sides and a peace settlement was brought about. Shaykh Sayf al-Dīn 'Alī al-Āmilī[430] related, "I happened to be with al-Malik al-Mu'ayyad when he was about to wage a war against the Zaydīs; and a settlement was reached afterwards. The root of the problem," said he, "[lies in that]

---

[428] The text has "would *not* give them . . ." the opposite of what seems to be likely.

[429] For the Rasūlids in Yemen at the time, see al-Khazrajī (el-Khazrejiyy), *The Rasuliyy Dynasty,* especially 1:257-64.

[430] Unidentified. This source is also quoted by Ibn al-Dawādārī; see *Kanz*, 9:62.

in the year of A.H. 699 (1299-1300), all kings and rulers in the world were at war."

Bakhtiyah Khān's taking over of al-Qifjāq: In this year, it was mentioned that al-Malik Bakhtiyah,[431] who claimed to be one of the Mongolian khāns, had marched to al-Qifjāq[432] in the year A.H. 699 (1299-1300). He battled there against al-Malik Nughīya (Nogai) and killed him,[433] thus conquering the entire realm of al-Qifjāq. This al-Malik Bakhtiyah was then a young man under 30. He made a peace treaty with sultan Ghāzān, who was his neighbor on the Khurāsān border.

It so happened that all the rulers and kings at that time were young. The kings of Delhi, India, Yemen, al-Amḥarī (i.e., Ethiopia), and the ruler of al-Qifjāq Bakhtiyah and Ghāzān, all of them had not yet reached 30. They began to assume sovereignty in the year A.H. 694 (1294-95). And at that time, the [Mamluk] sultan al-Malik al-Nāṣir was under 20.

Miracles in Syria: In this year, in the first 10 days of Ramaḍān (mid-May, 1301), Amīr Sayf al-Dīn Qibjāq arrived in Cairo. He brought with him a report signed by the deputy judge of Bārīn[434] in the Hama province. The report, which was dated in Rajab of this year (March, 1301), says, "In Bārīn, at the Wādī Rāwīl valley, the district of Ḥiṣn al-Akrād,[435] there was a river that could rotate [water wheels for] mill-stones. Two hills, one to the south and another to the north, stood on its two sides. The length [of the hill] was 110 cubits, its width was half of that, and its height was 26 cubits. The distance between the two[436] was 110 cubits. One hill then moved to the [site of the]

---

[431] He is mentioned also in the text below (the present edition, 240) as "the son of Mengü-Temür and the ruler of al-Khuwārizm, Bulghār (Bolghari), and Sūdāq up to the border of the realm of Constantinople." According to Mongol sources (quoted by Howorth), after Nughīya's defeat, Toktu Khān, the son of Mengü-Temür, was the ruler of al-Qifjāq until his death in 712/1313. We thus have sufficient grounds to assert that the name Bakhtiyah (also as Bukhtay in Ibn al-Dawādārī, *Kanz*) is an error for Toktu (also as Toktogu/Toktubeg in Mongol scripts). It is noted that both Tuqtay (Toktu) and Bukhtay (Bakhtiya?) are found in Ibn al-Dawādārī, *Kanz*, 9:index, but as two different persons, a fact that leads one to believe that Ibn al-Dawādārī might have used different sources of the Mongols. For Toktu's accession and reign, see Howorth, *The Mongols*, II/1:140-48.

[432] Variants Kipchak (Howorth) and Qipchaq (*CHIr*).

[433] Ibn al-Dawādārī states that it was Nughīya that defeated Bakhtiyah and conquered al-Qifjāq (*Kanz*, 9:62). This contradictory account is certainly due to a scribal error. We know for certain that Nughīya had already been the ruler of al-Qifjāq before the battle; see Howorth, *The Mongols*, II/1:123, 135, 139-46, 143-44.

[434] To the west of Hama; see *Ql*, 4:141.

[435] To the west of Hims; see *Ql*, 4:144.

[436] The text has *masāfat al-intiqāl*, literally "the distance of the movement, . . ." which is obscure to me.

other, with all the plants and soil while no dust fell into the water." Only God knows![437]

5. The Year of 701/1301-2

Ghāzān's envoys in Cairo: The year A.H. 701 began on a Wednesday (September 4, 1301). The above-mentioned envoys[438] of the ruler Ghāzān were still staying in the Cairo Jabal Citadel.

The opening of the Cairo canal: On Muḥarram 9 (September 12, 1301), they opened the Cairo canal as well as all the other canals. The annual rise of the blessed Nile increased one finger from [the old water level of] 18 cubits. Because the plenitude of the Nile (*mā' al-sulṭān*) was 16 cubits, so the actual increase was two cubits and one finger. People were very pleased with that.

Aybak al-Baghdādī's appointment to the office of vizier: On Friday, Muḥarram 10 (September 15, 1301), Amīr 'Izz al-Dīn Aybak al-Baghdādī al-Manṣūrī,[439] one of the Burjī amīrs, was appointed to the office of vizier in Egypt, replacing Amīr Shams al-Dīn Sunqur al-A'sar. He was bestowed the robe of the vizierate; the inkwell (*al-dawā*) and inkstone (*ḥajar*)[440] were presented to him after a special royal procession. He was seated in the Cairo Citadel. All the statesmen, dignitaries, amīrs, generals, qāḍīs, and religious leaders came to congratulate him on his appointment to the office. They kissed his hand. It was a memorable day indeed. On the following day, he started passing judgment, issuing orders and proclaiming prohibitions. He requested employees to bring in account records and other documents that were under his jurisdiction. He was the fourth vizier of the victorious [Mamluk] dynasty of Egypt and Syria to be drawn from the so-called "crowned (*al-mukalwatūn*)"[441] Turkish amīrs. Following a custom of Iraq during the 'Abbasid caliphate, the royal military band would play at their gates to honor

---

[437] This paragraph, which is not found in any other sources, appears to describe the change of the course of a river.

[438] Cf. above, 180f.

[439] He died in 706/1306. For his biography, see al-'Asqalānī, *Durar*, 1:452.

[440] According to al-Qalqashandī (*Q2*, 139), *al-dawā* was made from gold and granted to the newly-appointed court functionary (*'ādil*) as a symbol of the office. The inkwell and inkstone here were perhaps the emblems of the vizierate.

[441] Also as *al-mukallatūn*; derived from *kallūta*, of Persian origin *kulota* or Turkish *gyulu-teh*, "a kind of cap." The "crowned" were high-ranking commanders of Turkish origin. According to al-Qalqashandī, the yellow *kallūta* was the official headgear for rulers and amīrs in the Atabek dynasty. The custom had been handed down through the Ayyubids to the Mamluks; see *Q2*, 288.

them. The first of the four was Amīr 'Alam al-Dīn Sanjar al-Shujā'ī who succeeded Ṣāḥib Burhān al-Dīn al-Sinjārī. He was dismissed [and superseded] by Najm al-Dīn Ibn al-Aṣfūnī[442] and then resumed the post after the latter's death. When sultan [Qalāwūn] was at odds with him and, as mentioned above, [issued orders to] torture him (*'aṣarahu*),[443] as mentioned above, he was replaced by Amīr Badr al-Dīn Baydarā.[444] When the martyr al-Malik al-Manṣūr [Qalāwūn] died, Baydarā took over the post of viceroy under al-Malik al-Ashraf, while al-Shujā'ī was put in charge of the office of vizier for a few days until Shams al-Dīn Ibn al-Sal'ūs came from the Hejaz and assumed the office of vizier. By the time al-Malik al-Manṣūr Ḥusām al-Dīn Lājīn became sultan, he appointed Amīr Shams al-Dīn al-A'sar to be his vizier, replacing Fakhr al-Dīn Ibn al-Khalīlī, but only for a short time. He then arrested him (i.e., al-A'sar). After [al-Malik] al-Manṣūr Ḥusām al-Dīn [Lājīn]'s assassination, Amīr Shams al-Dīn [al-A'sar] was released and was appointed to be the vizier of sultan al-Malik al-Nāṣir on the recommendation of the two leading amīrs, Sayf al-Dīn Salār and Rukn al-Dīn al-Jāshankīr. [However,] Amīr Shams al-Dīn [al-A'sar] was then in Syria, and so, following precedent, the post of vizier was passed on to 'Izz al-Dīn al-Baghdādī.

A comet observed in Damascus: In this year, on Sunday night, Muḥarram 11 (September 16, 1301), a bright shining comet appeared in the west after sunset, its tail pointing to the east. It had been invisible and then emerged in a strong light. It kept increasing in brightness one night after another and then it jumped from the site where it was seen [in the first place] towards another direction a lance's throw away. It kept shining for 15 nights and then became faint and eventually disappeared.

Ghāzān's envoys in Damascus: In this year, on Sunday, Muḥarram 19 (September 24, 1301), all the amīrs and generals in the greater Cairo area were ordered to go to al-'Abbāsa[445] on a hunting trip and carry with them fodder for 10 days. They thus had their equipment prepared and set out with most of their troops, all fully armed. The sultan himself marched forward to al-Birka on Monday, Muḥarram 20 (September 25, 1301). He was followed by all the amīrs, generals, and troops. After the sultan's departure, the four chief judges were called upon to join him. They met with the sultan in al-Birka

---

[442] He died in 681/1281. For his biography, see Ibn al-Dawādārī, *Kanz*, 8:260.

[443] For the torture of *'aṣr*, see above, 150, note 282.

[444] His biography is not found. Some information on his career is found in Ibn al-Dawādārī, *Kanz*, 8:338-39, 344-50.

[445] A town in eastern Egypt. It was a meeting place for hunts during the Mamluk period; for details, see Halm, *Ägypten nach den mamlukischen Lehensregistern*, 2:597; "al-'Abbāsa," *EI²*, by G. Wiet.

and then returned to Cairo at night. Then they prepared for a journey and had the Mongol ruler Ghāzān's envoys do the same. The royal pavilion was transported to al-Ṣāliḥīya as the sultan and amīrs came down to the field for the hunt. On the eve of Monday [Muḥarram 27] (October 3, 1301), the sultan and amīrs arrived in al-Ṣāliḥīya. He granted a total of 420 robes of honor upon all the amīrs and generals. The envoys [of Ghāzān] were brought from Cairo and put up in al-Ṣāliḥīya so that they would be able to meet with the sultan upon his return from the hunt. As the well-dressed amīrs, wearing robes of honor, rallied in front of the sultan, [Ghāzān's] envoys were astonished to see the fine clothing on the Muslim [troops which presented] a striking contrast to the Mongols' [ragged] attire. The envoys were led to the royal pavilion at night to meet with the sultan. Numerous candles, torches and lanterns were lit. It was so bright that the place turned all red as if it were aflame with light and fire. The conversation [between the two sides] lasted one hour and then the envoys were given the return letter. They were also given robes for the journey (*khil'at al-safar*). Each envoy received 10,000 *dirhams*, fabric and other gifts. Amīr Sayf al-Dīn Ibn Kurtayh and another amīr were appointed to escort the envoys on their return journey up to the Euphrates. [Nevertheless,] all of them refused to dispatch a single soldier from his regiment [on this mission]. A group of preachers and qāḍīs had thus been appointed to the mission [to Ghāzān].[446]

Al-Malik al-Nāṣir's letter to Ghāzān: The text of the letter was said to be as follows:

> In the name of God, the Merciful, the Compassionate. The ruler [Ghāzān]'s concern and intention have been made clear to us through the statements [in his letter].
>
> Concerning what has been said [in his letter] about our common belief in Islam and that Ghāzān did not lay any claim or have any desire for our land, save insofar as it has been ordained by Divine Decree, this is something nobody ignores and is well known to all of us.
>
> Concerning the raid made by some of our troops on Mārdīn and their killing, arresting, raping, and other blasphemous behaviors, the ruler [Ghāzān] must know that our raids on your territory have been constant ever since your forefathers' days. Those who committed these sins were neither approved by us, nor were they among our amīrs and soldiers;

---

[446] According to Ibn al-Dawādārī, Amīr Ḥusām al-Dīn Aydamur al-Mujīrī and Qāḍī 'Imād al-Dīn Ibn al-Sukkarī were among those who went on to meet with Ghāzān later in 704/1304; see *Kanz*, 9:71ff; also above, 184-85. However, the episode of the Egyptian amīrs' refusal to go on the mission is not recorded in Egyptian sources.

rather, they were a bunch of petty irregulars (*al-aṭrāf*) and greedy bandits whose words and deeds are untrustworthy. Instead, the news we received is that the majority of our troops participating in the raid [on Mārdīn] could not find any food to buy, so they were fasting at the time lest they should eat dubious and forbidden food. Their nights were spent in vigils and their days in fasting.

Concerning the claims made by the ruler [Ghāzān], the grandson of the great Khān, it is very easy to refute. He boasts that all of our movements would reach him within an hour, but he does not know that every time he tossed and turned in his bed from this side to another, or went out riding or walking, we would be informed immediately. He will discover that his most trusted retinue are all our spies. And there are many like them in his court as well. We had the confirmed information that the ruler [Ghāzān] had been building up his strength by winning pledges of allegiance and followers during the past two years. He aggressively recruited in every town and received help from Christians, Georgians, and Armenians. He called on everybody who was able to ride a horse, Arab and non-Arab.[447] He obligated those conquered people (*al-musawwamāt*)[448] to supply horses and riding animals, so his followers increased and his resources multiplied. Then, when he realized that he just could not defeat our troops in the battlefield, he turned to lying, cheating, deceit, and fraud. He pretended to have converted to Islam and publicized his conversion among the elite and commoners. [However,] his innermost [conviction] was just the opposite. [Unfortunately,] our heroic troops believed that, and the majority of the troops thus refused to fight against him. They said, "We should neither fight Muslims, nor kill those who just pretend to be so." That is why they suffered the defeat. And that is why they withdrew from the combat with you in all circumstances. You know that things have turned against you, and you witnessed what it was like: nothing but lamenting, weeping, and mourning for the loss of beloved ones. War has its ups and downs; one day you win and one day you lose. [Our] troops are not to blame, and they shall never be vanquished. That is God's decree and that is what He has preordained.

---

[447] The text has *min faṣīḥ wa-alkan*, literally "who is skillful in using correct literary Arabic and who speaks bad Arabic."

[448] The reading and translation of this term is uncertain. It is read here as a passive participle of the verb *sawwama 'alā*, "to make a raid against" (Hava, Kazimirski); the term, however, might also indicate other things; cf. *al-khayl al-musawwama*, "marked horses," *Qur'ān*, 3:14(12), or *ḥijāra musawwama*, "stone marked with guilt," *Qur'ān*, 11:83, 51:34. It is also curious to note that Ms. Ahmet III 2907 has al-*mushawwamāt* while the parallel text of Zetterstéen (99) has *al-muwashshamāt*, "marked [horses]."

Concerning the ruler [Ghāzān]'s statement that when he fought with our troops he tore them utterly to pieces, it is of course suitable for him to say so in the capacity of a ruler; however, he himself knows very well how our armies fought and how our swords settled on the necks of his forefathers whose blood is still dripping from [our] swords [even] until now. He may not have seen all this, but he may ask the leading statesmen of his dynasty and the amīrs in his army about it! Our swords may be hit once, but they had cut your forefathers to pieces many times! Your troops may trample on our land once, but your land will remain a permanent target for our raids and a lasting abode for our troops! Like you do shall be done to you.

Concerning the ruler [Ghāzān]'s saying that he and his followers had converted to Islam in word, work, deed, and intention, what you have done is in fact everything but the deed of a pilgrim to this House, I mean, the luminous Ka'ba [in Mecca]. What happened to the suburbs of Damascus and Mt. Ṣāliḥīya was with your knowledge [as] the ruler from whom nothing had been concealed. All this is not the behavior of a Muslim, nor that of someone adhering to this Religion. Where, how, and by which excuse [could those things have ever happened]? In Jerusalem, the earthly throne of the Merciful God, wine was drunk, curtains were torn down, virgins were deflowered, religious students residing in the sanctuary were killed, and preachers were arrested. In Hebron, crosses were hung and women were raped. Drunken infidels freely entered into it. If all this [happened] with your knowledge and approval, what a disappointing performance by you in this world and the hereafter! Woe unto you from your birth to your resurrection! Soon there will be declared the collapse of your life and dynasty, and the destruction of your army and troops! If you were not aware of this, we have made it clear to you. So, wake up to redress [your wrongdoing in] the past; nobody needs to do so except you! If you really are, as you have claimed, a believer in Islam, sincere in words and truthful in faith, you should execute those soldiers (*al-ṭawāmīn*)[449] who committed the aforesaid sins, punish them for what they did and let the others learn a lesson! Let it be known that you are on a right path. Your own words and deeds are the most profound proof.

When our troops returned to Cairo, they realized that you had pretended to be sincere and lied about [your] faith and belief, and that you had won the battle by means of an alliance with the Christians. They (i.e., our troops) rallied together and got fully prepared [to fight back]. They marched forward with commendable firm will, pure hearts, and high mo-

[449] The Mongolian word for "ten thousand [soldiers]"; here it is perhaps used as a metaphor for "scores of soldiers."

rale—may God be pleased with those! They marched day and night, shouting the utterance of invocation, "Oh the chosen community of Muḥammad! Hurry! Hurry! Catch your enemies in the country! Quench the thirst of hearts yearning for revenge!" Your army could do nothing but run away. They had neither endurance nor firmness for the battle. Our triumphant troops, with the power of a tidal wave, advanced quickly to Syria. They were determined to conquer your land and reach the utmost goal. Nevertheless, we were concerned about your civilians' lives, the lives of those who could not find any protection while you were running away. Therefore, we ordered them (i.e., our troops) to stay in place and keep alert and watchful, so that *God might determine a matter that was done.*[450]

Concerning [your] message that has been delivered orally by the chief judge, we have listened to and are aware of it. We have also attested to the accuracy of his message. We fully respect [him] as a qāḍī who is well known for his religious knowledge, piety, insight, and belief, as well as his graciousness and asceticism in this world. However, he is not quite familiar with you. Therefore, he has not yet discovered the real nature of your cause and affairs; your hidden motives have not been exposed to him. If you seriously wish to make peace and to repair the situation, if your inner thoughts are as eager for peace as your appearance indicates, and you, the ruler, the seeker of truce and confirmation, if your speech needs no explanation and contains no embellishments so that we should charge you with lies—[as the proverb goes,] "he who pulls out the sword of untruth will eventually be killed by it," and *evil devising encompasses only those who do it*[451]—then you ought to send to us your representative who has the final words, and with your full authorization, on any decision he is to make. He ought to be the most capable and powerful person from your cabinet, a sincere, trustworthy, and fully authorized one. Let us discuss with that person whatever is constructive for [ending] the enmity [between us]. Otherwise, he will return with empty hands.

Concerning the ruler [Ghāzān]'s demand for presents from Egypt, we are not stingy with that at all. Our treasure is endless and the presents given [by us] have been countless. However, [our] response is that he who asks for presents should send *his* first, and we will do the same many times over. In this way, we will be able to confirm his integrity and his sincerity in fulfilling what he announced to us about it, and in doing things that will please God and Muḥammad in this world and the

[450] *Qur'ān*, 8:42.
[451] *Qur'ān*, 35:43.

next. May our business in our life-to-come be profitable, not profligate! May God give us success on the right path!

The return of last year's pigrims: In this year, on Ṣafar 3 (October 8, 1301), the sultan returned from the hunting trip[452] and arrived at al-Birka where he met with the leader of this year's pilgrims, the *amīr-jānidār*, the *jūkandārī*[453] Amīr Sayf al-Dīn Baktimur as well as the pilgrim caravan and the royal *maḥmil* led by him. He (i.e., the sultan) paid a visit to him to congratulate him for the safe [return]. He granted a robe of honor upon him as well. The sultan then went up to the Cairo Citadel in the evening. The *maḥmil* and the pilgrims entered Cairo shortly after him. The pilgrims were very grateful to their leader Sayf al-Dīn. They prayed for him and mentioned that his kindness, integrity, and charity had spread among all. He had given 100,000 *dirhams* to the ruler of Mecca and his sons in charity as well as robes of honor. He had [also] donated an enormous amount of money to religious students residing in the sanctuary and descendants of Muḥammad at Mecca. After coming to Medina he had bestowed robes of honor upon its ruler and his sons aside from numerous presents. He had also given money to religious students residing in the sanctuary and inhabitants of Medina. Shaykh and Qudwa Sayf al-Dīn Abū al-Ḥasan 'Alī al-Āmilī related in Cairo[454] that he had accompanied the leader of the pilgrim caravan all along the journey from Mecca to Cairo, and that upon his arrival at the shrine of Muḥammad [in Medina], the abovementioned Amīr Sayf al-Dīn [ordered him to] vacate the place. Then, taking with him his sons and descendants as well as his money and belongings, he came to the chamber of the Prophet and implored the Prophet to accept all these. He had [also] asked the Prophet's blessing and, in return, promised to do good in the rest of his life. It was mentioned that the sum he had spent [during the pilgrimage] was 85,000 Egyptian *dīnārs*. May God accept it! Shaykh Sayf al-Dīn al-Āmilī [then] went on, "Every time the amīr [Sayf al-Dīn] came to a stop, they would bring scales in front of him to weigh out provisions to pilgrims in the caravan. Everybody, rich or poor, received a sufficient portion for himself and his group. He (i.e., the amīr) did all this in person, [showing] no [sign of] tiredness and boredom. He was committed to doing good with pleasure and joy. May God accept this from him!"

---

[452] Cf. above, 193-94.

[453] Persian, "the *jūkān* holder"; the title of the low-ranking officer who carried the *jūkān* (a kind of polo mallet) for the sultan during the game; see *Q2*, 94.

[454] For this unidentified source, also cf. above, 190, note 430.

Ghāzān's advance towards Syria: In this year, in Ṣafar (October 1301), some secret agents came to Cairo. They reported that Ghāzān had decided to wage a [new] campaign and was advancing towards Syria, and that Būlāhim had already approached the Euphrates. They (i.e., the Mamluks) thus started preparing the troops.

Hailstorms in Syria: The post-master (*al-barīdī*) Amīr 'Alā' al-Dīn al-Fakhrī came [to Damascus] and reported that in the month of Muḥarram (September 1301) a hailstorm had hit the region between Hama, Hims, and Ḥiṣn al-Akrād. Some hailstones took the shapes of mankind, male or female, as well as monkeys and such like. This story was brought to the attention of the sultan in Egypt—may his triumph be strengthened! It was really a strange thing the like of which has never been heard.

Amīr al-Jāshankīr's hunting trip: In this year, on Rabī' I 23 (November 26, 1301), Amīr Rukn al-Dīn al-Jāshankīr went out from Cairo to Alexandria on a pigeon hunt. A large number of amīrs went with him. The sultan proscribed that while he was staying in Alexandria, [the town's] income would be his. There was [also] a decree (*dustūr*) given to all the amīrs who planned to be on leave to take care of their fief lands and to graze their horses [stating that they were permitted to be away] for one month and no more. That was due to the circumstances of the enemy's movements. Therefore, they pastured [their] horses on [nearby] fertile grazing land (*rabaṭū al-khayl 'alā al-rabī'*).[455]

New appointments in the Syrian provinces: At the beginning of this year, Amīr Sayf al-Dīn Quṭlū-Bek left his post as the viceroy in the coastal province [of Tripoli] and came back to Damascus. Amīr Sayf al-Dīn Usun-Damur[456] was appointed to succeed him. Usun-Damur arrived in Damascus on Saturday, Muḥarram 11 (September 16, 1301).

In this year, in the month of Muḥarram (September 1301), a postman came to Damascus to deliver an edict on Amīr Sayf al-Dīn Aqjubā's appointment to the office of finance agent in the province (*niyābat al-salṭana*) of Gaza. He was to replace Rukn al-Dīn al-Muwaffaqī. And his post in the [Damascus] Citadel was taken over by Amīr Sayf al-Dīn Bahādur al-Sinjārī, a Burjī Mamluk. The edict also contained the appointment of Sayf al-Dīn Kāwarkā to the office of viceroy of Bāhasnā. And Sharīf Zayn al-Dīn assumed

---

[455] The meaning of this sentence is not very clear to me. The term *al-rabī'* also refers to "land abounding with the so-called *al-rabī'* herbage" (Lane).

[456] He was the viceroy of Tripoli during 698/1298-699/1230; see Ibn al-Dawādārī, *Kanz*, 9:7, 39, 80.

the office of chief of staff in the administration (*ṣaḥābat al-dīwān*) in Damascus, replacing Fakhr al-Dīn Ibn Muzhir.

A religious trial in Cairo: In this year, on Monday, Rabī' I 24 (November 27, 1301), Fatḥ al-Dīn Aḥmad al-Baqaqī al-Ḥamawī[457] was escorted from the Cairo prison to Bayna al-Qaṣrayn.[458] He was ordered to stand in front of qāḍīs, jurists, and shaykhs, facing the balcony (*al-shubbāk*) of the Kāmilīya Dār al-Ḥadīth. He recited the *shahāda* twice and then appealed to the Shāfi'ī [chief] judge Shaykh Taqī al-Dīn [Ibn Daqīq al-'Īd]. The latter told him, "Your case has been handed over to the Mālikī judge Zayn al-Dīn." The indictment (*al-bayyina*) against him, based on which a death sentence would be inevitable, was prepared by Zayn al-Dīn; it included accusations such as slander on the glorious Qur'ān and the Prophet, declaring forbidden behaviors as lawful, insulting Muslim scholars, and so forth. A court record (*maḥḍar*) had been certified and attested as early as the year A.H. 686 (1286). And since then, more people had come forward [as witnesses]; each of them testified against him as having committed one or another sort of blasphemy (*zandaqa*). It was reported that the witnesses were more than 30 men. At this point, the Mālikī judge Zayn al-Dīn announced that the accused was guilty of infidelity (*kufr*) and was sentenced to death, and that his repentance was not accepted even if he converted to Islam. So on Monday morning, he was brought to Bayna al-Qaṣrayn. He kept appealing to the Muslims [in the audience] by crying out, "I witness there is no God but God! I was an unbeliever but have converted to Islam!" However, the Mālikī judge refused to accept his repentance and ordered his execution. The man was beheaded with a sword. His head was taken away in a reed [mat], and his naked corpse was dragged on the ground and taken to the Zuwayla [Gate] upon which it was suspended. The man had written a *fatwā*[459] in prison and sent it to Shaykh Taqī al-Dīn Ibn Daqīq al-'Īd. The latter thus wrote on it the following, "*Say to the unbelievers, if they repent He will forgive them what is past, but if they return, the wont of the ancients is already gone*!"[460] However, the Mālikīs argued that this Qur'ānic verse had been revealed to address the matter regarding those unbelievers who "returned" [to the previous faith] and then converted [to Islam] and then "returned" again.[461]

---

[457] Unidentified.

[458] A place in downtown Cairo. It was the Royal Way of old Fatimid Cairo.

[459] The use of the term *fatwā*, "appeal(?)," in this context is unusual. The sentence might simply mean that he wrote a *legal opinion* on his own case.

[460] *Qur'ān*, 8:38. The original text of the Qur'ān has *yantahū* instead of *yatūbū*.

[461] I.e., the current case of al-Baqaqī does not fit into this category.

A poem was written about this event. It was ascribed to al-'Azāzī[462] who, in the poem, incited the caliph, the imām al-Ḥākim bi-amr Allāh, to execute the accused. The hostility between the two can be traced back to al-'Azāzī's argument with al-Baqaqī[463] on scholarly matters in the house of Nāṣir al-Dīn al-Shaykhī, the mayor of Cairo. The poem read:

Say to the imām al-Murtaḍā, [with whom God is] pleased,[464]
The detector of dubious men and ambiguous matters,
'Don't let the unbeliever go free! Do whatever has been
Prescribed for Muslims regarding the unbelievers!
Stand up, honoring the true believer of Islam and defend him!
Issue rulings and govern according to what has been set forth by Him.
Let al-Baqaqī, the infamous infidel
And criminal, bleed!'
By God! He (i.e., the caliph) *is truthful. He is [God's] deputy.*
By God! He justified the execution.

New appointments in Damascus: In this year, on Monday, Jumādā I 14 (January 15, 1302), Ṣadr Sharaf al-Dīn Ibn Muzhir assumed the office of inspector of administration (*naẓr al-dīwān*) in Damascus. He was co-appointed with Tāj al-Dīn Ibn al-Shīrāzī.

The moon eclipse: In this year, on Monday night, Jumādā I 14 (January 15, 1302), the moon was fully eclipsed at [the site of the constellation of] *'uqdat al-dhanab*.[465] The eclipse lasted three hours and 20 minutes.

The death of caliph al-Ḥākim bi-amr Allāh: In this year, at the dawn of Friday, Jumādā I 18 (January 19, 1302), the 'Abbasid caliph, the imām al-Ḥākim bi-amr Allāh Abū al-'Abbās Aḥmad died at the Kabsh [Palace],[466]

---

[462] Shihāb al-Dīn Aḥmad ibn 'Abd al-Malik, an Egyptian poet; he died in 710/1310. For his biography, see al-'Asqalānī, *Durar*, 1:205-6; al-Kutubī, *Fawāt al-wafayāt*, 1:48.

[463] The text has *ibn* al-Baqaqī which is perhaps an error for al-Baqaqī.

[464] This a pun between the title of the caliph *al-Murtaḍā* and the noun "the satisfied one (*al-murtaḍā*)."

[465] I thank Franz Rosenthal for suggesting to me that the unidentified words *'aqdat ('uqdat?) al-dhanab* must be the name of a star. However, I have not been able to locate the reference to this star. For *'aqda*, or *'uqda*, see Kunitzsch, *Arabische Sternnamen in Europa*, 153; for various stars named *dhanab* (*dhanab al-asad, dhanab al-dajāja, dhanab al-dulfīn*, etc.) see 239 (Index).

[466] The palace was first built, together with the Aḥmad Ibn Ṭūlūn Mosque, by Aḥmad Ibn Ṭūlūn as his residence. It was renovated by Najm al-Dīn Ayyūb. According to al-Qalqashandī, the palace had been inhabited later by senior amīrs and was destroyed by mobs in 770/1368. For details, see *Ql*, 3:358-59.

which was located outside of Cairo, on the Elephant Lake. As usual, the [Friday] sermons, mentioning his name, were delivered on that day at mosques in greater Cairo. The news of his death was not announced to the public. After the Friday prayer, the viceroy [Salār] summoned the ṣūfis, shaykhs from various zāwiyas and ribāṭs, qāḍīs, jurists, scholars, as well as statesmen and most of the amīrs in the greater Cairo area. Shaykh Karīm al-Dīn, the master of the Sa'īd al-Su'adā' Khānqāh, and 'Umar ibn 'Abd al-'Azīz al-Ṭūkhī, the chief body-washer, undertook the work of washing and shrouding the body of the deceased. It was then moved from the Kabsh [Palace] to the Aḥmad Ibn Ṭūlūn Mosque. The viceroy Amīr Sayf al-Dīn Salār and Amīr Rukn al-Dīn al-Jāshankīr led all amīrs coming down from the [Cairo] Citadel to the Kabsh Palace to attend the body washing ceremony. Then they led the funeral procession marching to the [Ibn Ṭūlūn] Mosque where the shaykh al-shuyūkh Karīm al-Dīn led the prayer for the deceased. His body was then moved to his tomb, which was near the tomb of Lady Nafīsa,[467] and buried there.

The caliph had designated as his successor his son Abū al-Rabī' Sulaymān, who was then 20 years old or so. The event had taken place on Wednesday, Jumādā I 16 (January 17, 1302), as the imām al-Ḥākim bi-amr Allāh asked qāḍīs and a number of court witnesses to come to his palace and called on them to witness his will to secure his son's succession to the throne. Thereupon, after his death, on Friday morning and prior to the Friday prayer, Abū al-Rabī' was summoned to the [Cairo] Citadel. They (i.e., the Mamluk amīrs) testified on his behalf that sultan al-Malik al-Nāṣir—may his triumph be strengthened!—gave to Abū al-Rabī' all the powers that his father, the imām al-Ḥākim bi-amr Allāh, had entrusted to him. Then, after the memorial prayer commemorating the father, they sent the young prince and his nephews, leading the funeral procession, back to the Kabsh [Palace]. Five of the sultan's eunuchs (*khuddām*) came down from the [Cairo] Citadel and sat in front of the gate of the Kabsh Palace watching over them.[468] They remained there for a long time.

[Meanwhile,] the sultan called the Shāfi'ī chief judge Taqī al-Dīn Ibn Daqīq al-'Īd for consultation on the legitimacy of Abū al-Rabī' Sulaymān's succes-

---

[467] A mausoleum situated in the al-Qarāfa area to the south of Cairo, commemorating al-Sayyida Nafīsa bint al-Ḥasan ibn Zayd ibn al-Ḥasan ibn 'Alī (died in 208/824); see "Nafīsa," *EI*², by R. Strothmann.

[468] For discussions of the role of the eunuchs as mediators and guardians of shrines and wealthy households in medieval Cairo, see Marmon, *Eunuchs and Sacred Boundaries*, especially 28, 59, 116 (note 13).

sion. He said, "Yes, it is legitimate." He spoke of Sulaymān highly. [And yet,] the issue remained pending until Thursday, Jumādā I 24 (January 25, 1302). Early in the morning, Abū al-Rabī' Sulaymān, the son of the caliph al-Ḥākim bi-amr Allāh, was summoned, together with his nephews, to the Cairo Jabal Citadel from the Kabsh Palace for [the succession ceremonies]: taking the oath of allegiance, ascending to the throne, and assuming all the authorities devolving from his father upon him. [All this was finally accomplished] after many episodes and twists that would take too long to explain. Everybody was present: the [new] imām al-Mustakfī bi-Allāh Abū al-Rabī' Sulaymān, the son of caliph al-Ḥākim bi-amr Allāh, his brother and nephews. They were led into the [Cairo] Citadel through the gate on the side of the Red Hill (*al-Jabal al-Aḥmar*).[469] Sultan al-Malik al-Nāṣir and all amīrs were seated. The sultan awarded Abū al-Rabī' Sulaymān the robe of the caliphate and granted him the title of al-Mustakfī bi-Allāh ("the Contented with God"). The robe and *ṭarḥa*-headgear were all black. His brother and nephews were awarded four colored robes of the office of grand amīr. After that, the sultan swore allegiance to him. He was followed by amīrs, high-ranking officials, qāḍīs, generals, and dignitaries. As usual, a state banquet was held for the occasion. The sultan then issued his orders to ask him (i.e., the caliph) to stay in the Kabsh Palace and to give them (i.e., the caliph and his brother) the stipend equal to their father's allowance during his last days in addition to some bonus (*ziyādāt*) by which he made them feel at ease and be optimistic.

They stayed in the Kabsh Palace until Thursday, the beginning of Jumādā II (February 1, 1302), when the sultan sent a protocol officer (*mihmandār*) with a team of aides and a flock of camels to move the caliph, his brother, his nephews as well as their wives and all those under their shelter to the [Cairo] Jabal Citadel. They were given accommodations in two halls; one was called the Ṣāliḥīya Hall and the other the Ẓāhirīya Hall. They received their stipends as prescribed.

On Friday, one day after the homage ceremony, namely, Jumādā I 25 (January 26, 1302), sermons were delivered in all mosques in greater Cairo, honoring the [new] caliph, the imām al-Mustakfī bi-Allāh Abū al-Rabī' Sulaymān, and praying for God's mercy upon his deceased father. It was decided [also] to cast the [new] caliph's name on *dīnār* and *dirham* coinage. The caliph was a brown-skinned young man, with thin beard and of medium height.

When still alive, [caliph] al-Ḥākim [bi-amr Allāh] had married off his daughter to Qāḍī Muḥibb al-Dīn, the son of the chief judge Taqī al-Dīn Ibn

[469] On the east side of Cairo; see al-Maqrīzī, *al-Khiṭaṭ*, 33.

Daqīq al-ʻĪd. [That is why] after his death, they (i.e., his descendants) received strong support from Shaykh Taqī al-Dīn.

In Damascus, sermons to honor the imām al-Mustakfī bi-Allāh were delivered on Friday, Jumādā II 9 (February 9, 1302). After the Friday prayer, they prayed for God's mercy upon his father, the [deceased] caliph of Muslims, the imām al-Ḥākim bi-amr Allāh Abū al-ʻAbbās Aḥmad.

The revival of Islamic learning in Damascus: The postman arrived in Damascus from Cairo and delivered an edict to reinstate the Ḥanafī chief judge Shams al-Dīn Ibn al-Ḥarīrī[470] to his former position of deputy judge in Damascus and to dismiss Jalāl al-Dīn[471] from the post. Another edict contained the appointment of Sharaf al-Dīn Ibn Muzhir, replacing Tāj al-Dīn Ibn al-Shīrāzī. Thereupon, Shams al-Dīn resumed his former position. The Khātūnīya [Madrasa] was left in the hand of Jalāl al-Dīn as it used to be. The Nāṣirīya Madrasa was given back to the qāḍī Kamāl al-Dīn Ibn al-Sharīshī. He started teaching on Wednesday, Jumādā II 14 (February 14, 1302), replacing Ibn Jamāʻa.

The Jewish tax rebellion in Damascus: In this year, in the month of Shawwāl (May-June 1302), it was brought to one's attention that the Jews in Damascus claimed to hold a document (*kitāb*) in which the Prophet was said to have canceled their *jizya* tax. They insisted on putting it into effect through a *fatwā* authorized by jurists as well as an edict issued by the viceroy. They produced the document they held. The jurists and imāms recognized its falsity. They pointed out many passages that revealed their forgery. Then, they exhibited another document, one after another, all made by the same hand[472] and full of self-contradictory language. [After the forgery was discovered,] they (i.e., the Jews) became silent (*rajaw*) and wanted to withdraw and to pay the *jizya* tax in full. [The cause of this episode lies in that] they were frightened by the [amount of] taxes imposed upon them in the past. The matter settled down.

A Syrian captive's return from exile: In this year, on Tuesday, Jumādā I 29 (January 30, 1302), Ṣadr ʻAlā' al-Dīn ʻAlī ibn Ṣadr Sharaf al-Dīn Ibn al-Qalānisī returned to Damascus after an exile of several years in the land of the Mongols. [He had been] imprisoned and had been far away from his homeland

---

[470] Muḥammad; died in 728/1328; see Pouzet, *Damas*, 73.

[471] Likely Aḥmad ibn al-Ḥasan al-Rāzī.

[472] Literally "[came] from one valley."

since then. He had stayed in al-Armal [al-Armil?][473] for a while, and then in Ūjān[474] and Tabrīz. God blessed him with rescue after his separation from his companion Sharaf al-Dīn Ibn al-Athīr. He hid in Tabrīz for one month while he spared no effort in finding Ibn al-Athīr's whereabouts. However, God did not allow him to succeed. When the situation became settled, he began to try to get through. He disguised his real identity and kept striving, and finally managed to come back to Muslim lands in two months. His parents, brothers, other relatives, and people of his community had lost [the hope of hearing from] him. Now that he had suddenly come back to them, their joy was overwhelming. This was truly a day of celebration the like of which had never been seen before. People came out to welcome him. Afterwards, he set off on a journey to Cairo with his companion Sharaf al-Dīn Ibn al-Athīr [who had also returned to Damascus]. They arrived in Cairo in Rajab (March 1302) and met with amīrs and the sultan. Ibn al-Athīr then went back to Damascus. He left Cairo on Sha'bān 9 (April 9, 1302). As for 'Alā' al-Dīn, he stayed on [in Cairo] after the Feast [of Fast Breaking?] and then returned to Damascus.[475]

A hailstorm upon Hama: In the middle of Rabī' I (November 1301), a letter was delivered from Hama to Damascus reporting that during these days, a hailstorm had hit the region of Bārīn in the Hama Province. The hailstones took various shapes of animals, some were like lions, snakes, scorpions, birds, goats, and some like men with waist bands. The judge of the region had confirmed the story and reported it to the judge of Hama.

This year's pilgrimage: On Monday, Shawwāl 6 (June 4, 1302), the Syrian pilgrim caravan left Damascus. Its leader was the chamberlain (*al-ḥājib*)[476] Amīr 'Izz al-Dīn Ibn Ṣabra.

The movements of the Mamluk troops: On Thursday, Shawwāl 9 (June 7, 1302), a detachment of Egyptian troops arrived in Damascus. Among them were the *amīr-silāḥ* Amīr Badr al-Dīn Baktāsh al-Fakhrī and the treasurer (*al-khazindār*) Amīr 'Izz al-Dīn Aybak as well as a number of amīrs. On Monday, Shawwāl 13 (June 11, 1302), a large number of Damascene troops

---

[473] Unidentified. I doubt this is an error for Ardabīl, a town near the Caspian shore and not very far from Ūjān and Tabrīz which are to be mentioned below; also cf. Le Strange, *Lands*, 5, 159, 163, 168.

[474] Also known as Uzjān, or Awjān, a town in Persia, to the north of Mayin; see Le Strange, *Lands*, 163, 276, 287.

[475] Lengthy quotations from miscellaneous pieces, on the authority of al-Jazarī, are found inserted between this paragraph and the next and are omitted in the present edition; for details, see above, 55-57.

[476] For the title of *al-ḥājib*, see *Q2*, 102.

marched out. Among them were Amīr Rukn al-Dīn al-Jāliq,[477] Sayf al-Dīn Quṭlū-Bek,[478] and Amīr Sayf al-Dīn Bahādur Āṣ.[479]

The crackdown on the Bedouin rebellion in Upper Egypt: In the year A.H. 701 (1301-2), the Bedouins (*al-'urbān*) rebelled. Two amīrs, Amīr Sayf al-Dīn Salār and Amīr Rukn al-Dīn Baybars al-Jāshankīr, led the major forces of the Egyptian army [to crush the rebellion]. They killed a large number of rebels and confiscated their properties. The sultan's share in booty was 117,200 riding animals and the details are as follows: 22,600 camels and 100,000 sheep, in addition to whatever had been slaughtered and eaten.[480]

The annual rise of the Nile: In this year, the blessed Nile reached [on the scale of the Nilometer] 17 cubits and 15 fingers in the month of Muḥarram (September 1301).

New appointments in Aleppo and Damascus: On Dhū al-Qa'da 11 (July 8, 1302), Qāḍī Zayn al-Dīn, the son of the qāḍī al-Khalīl, went from Damascus to Aleppo to assume the office of judge. The certificate of his appointment, dated from Shawwāl 23, A.H. 701 (June 21, 1302), had previously been delivered from Egypt. He was awarded the robe of the office and *ṭarḥa*-headgear in Damascus and then, wearing the robe and *ṭarḥa*-headgear, rode in the parade in the city.

In the month of Dhū al-Qa'da, the chief of staff of the administration in Damascus, the grand ṣadr 'Izz al-Dīn Abū al-'Abbās Aḥmad Ibn Muyassar al-Miṣrī arrived in Damascus. Wearing an official robe, he assumed the office on Monday, Dhū al-Qa'da 19 (July 16, 1302), replacing Sharaf al-Dīn Ibn Muzhir.

A Jewish judge's conversion to Islam: In this year, on Tuesday, Dhū al-Ḥijja 4 (July 31, 1302), 'Abd al-Sayyid ibn al-Muhaddab, then a Jewish judge (*dayyān*)[481] who inherited the title from his father and grandfather, came over to the Dār al-'Adl. Together with him were his sons. They all converted to Islam. The viceroy granted upon them robes of honor and ordered to have

---

[477] A Syrian amīr; he died in 706/1306. For his biography, see Ibn al-Dawādārī, *Kanz*, 9:151-52.

[478] There were two Syrian amīrs named Sayf al-Dīn Quṭlū-Bek; one was the viceroy of Tripoli (cf. Ibn al-Dawādārī, *Kanz*, 9:41) and the other a chamberlain (*al-ḥājib*) who had been sent by al-Malik al-Nāṣir to Syria in 698/1298 (cf. Ibn al-Dawādārī, *Kanz*, 9:13). It is not certain which one was on this expedition.

[479] A Syrian amīr. For his career, see Ibn al-Dawādārī, *Kanz*, 9:Index.

[480] According to Zetterstéen's version (107), 4,600 horses were brought to the royal stable, 22,000 camels to the royal camel stations, and 100,000 sheep to the royal kitchen. The numbers seem to be exaggerated. It is interesting to note that this story of the Mamluk crackdown is not found in Egyptian sources.

[481] For the word *dayyān*, see Brinner, *Damascus*, 1:168, note 996.

them riding on horses for a parade in the city of Damascus and to have drums be beaten and horns be played after their procession. All this was for the purpose of publicizing their conversion to Islam. They attended the Qur'ān study and religious learning sessions regularly. On holiday, they came to mosque to perform Muslim ritual duties. People treated them with high respect and warm admiration. The viceroy appointed him to head the Nūrī hospital and to be one of its chief physicians. He took up the post in the status of a Muslim. This ʿAbd al-Sayyid influenced a great number of Jews to convert to Islam, either with him or after him.

Ghāzān's new envoys in Damascus: On Monday night, Dhū al-Ḥijja 17 (August 13, 1302), the envoys of the Mongol sultan Ghāzān arrived in Damascus. They stayed in the [Damascus] Citadel. Then on Thursday night, Dhū al-Ḥijja 20 (August 16, 1302), they set off on the journey to Egypt.

The return of the Mamluk expedition from Cilicia: The troops on the expedition to Cilicia[482] returned to Damascus on Thursday, Dhū al-Ḥijja 20 (August 16, 1302). Townspeople came out to welcome them. The Egyptian soldiers who had participated in the expedition then set off for Cairo on Monday morning, Dhū al-Ḥijja 24 (August 20, 1302).

Locusts hit Syria: In this year, God released locusts upon Syria. In some areas, the great number of locusts were devastating; they ruined fruits, trees, grapes, and figs. This occurred in Buṣrā, Zur,ʿ[483] and the suburbs of Damascus. There were many reports of damage in Shawwāl (June 1302). The heat was so intense that the trees lost their leaves. [Then the locusts] came back in Dhū al-Qaʿda (July 1302) to hit the Ghūṭa area in the suburb of Damascus. There is no power and no strength save in God!

---

[482] For this expedition, cf. above, 101-3.

[483] Both are counties in the vicinity of Damascus; see *Q1*, 4:107-8.

APPENDIX I

THE MANUSCRIPTS OF AL-YŪNĪNĪ'S *MUKHTAṢAR MIR'ĀT AL-ZAMĀN*

Hundreds of manuscripts titled *Mir'āt al-zamān* or *Mukhtaṣar Mir'āt al-zamān* have been discovered over the centuries in various Eastern and Western libraries; and most of them have been catalogued. However, what complicates the situation is the widely held belief by scholars—starting from Jewett (1907)[1] and echoed by Cahen (1936),[2] Ritter,[3] and Chase (1954),[4] among others—that many (or maybe most) extant manuscripts under the title of *Mir'āt* contain, in fact, al-Yūnīnī's *mukhtaṣar* version, with or without acknowledgment. That is to say, the actual manuscripts of al-Yūnīnī's *Mukhtaṣar* are far more numerous than those whose title pages or colophons so suggest.

Following is a list of all manuscripts that are known so far for certain as al-Yūnīnī's *Mukhtaṣar*. The list is in a roughly chronological order of the dates on which the manuscripts were copied.

1. *Ahmet III 2907/d. 2* (Istanbul, Topkapı Sarayı), 246 ff.; not dated; covering the pre-Islamic period.[5]
2. *Laleli 2100/1* (Istanbul), 235 ff.; copied in A.H. 71(2?) by Aḥmad ibn al-'Alam al-Ḥakīmī.[6]
3. *Ahmet III 2907/d. 5*, 228 ff.; not dated; covering A.H. 13-36.[7]
4. *Ahmet III 2907/d. 8*, 244 ff.; copied in A.H. 718 by Aḥmad ibn al-'Alam al-Ḥakīmī; covering A.H. 65-92.[8]

---

[1] Introduction to his edition, vii.

[2] Cahen, "Chroniques arabes," 340; and "Ibn al-Djawzī," *EI²*.

[3] Ritter, 672, states that of the 64 manuscripts of the *Mir'āt* in Istanbul, "most of them are from al-Yūnīnī's abbreviated version."

[4] Chase, XIX f.

[5] Karatay, 358; Cahen, "Chroniques arabes," 340. Fu'ād Sayyid, 2:2, 138, states that the manuscript has 248 ff.

[6] Spies, 67. Spies did not indicate whether it is the original or a *mukhtaṣar* version; however, judging from the scribe, date, and the length, I would suggest to link the manuscript to the Ahmet III 2907/d set.

[7] Karatay, 358; Cahen, "Chroniques arabes," 340; Fu'ād Sayyid, 2:2, 138.

[8] Karatay, 358-59 (the scribe's name is given as Aḥmad ibn 'Alam al-Dīn); Cahen, "Chroniques arabes," 340 (but mistakenly given as vol. III); Fu'ād Sayyid, 2:2, 138.

5. *Ahmet III 2907/d. 10*, 248 ff.; copied in A.H. 718 by Aḥmad al-Ḥakīmī; covering A.H. 115-142.[9]
6. *Ahmet III 2907/d. 12*, 249 ff.; copied in A.H. 719 by Aḥmad al-Ḥakīmī; covering A.H. 187-218.[10]
7. *MS arabe 5866* (Paris, Bibliothèque nationale), 243 ff.; copied in A.H. 721 by Aḥmad al-Ḥakīmī; covering A.H. 358-400.[11]
8. *Ahmet III 2907/d. 17*, 250 ff.; copied in A.H. 723 by Aḥmad al-Ḥakīmī; covering A.H. 401-450.[12]
9. *Evkaf 18* (Istanbul, Türk ve Islam Eserleri Müzesi), ? ff.; copied in A.H. 724; covering A.H. 450-489.[13]
10. *Ahmet III 2907/d. 19*, 247 ff.; not dated; covering A.H. 489-561.[14]

11. *British Library 1227* (add. 23,279), 218 ff.; copied in A.H. 762 by Muḥammad ibn Aḥmad al-Anṣārī in Damascus; covering A.H. 577-654.[15]
12. *British Library 1225* (add. 23,275), 145 ff.; copied in A.H. 817 by Muḥammad ibn 'Alī al-Shāfi'ī; covering A.H. 56-74.[16]
13. *British Library 1226* (add. 23,276), 129 ff.; copied in A.H. 817 by Muḥammad ibn 'Alī; covering A.H. 75-96.[17]

---

[9] Karatay, 359; Cahen, "Chroniques arabes," 340; Fu'ād Sayyid, 2:3, 268, states that it was written by one Ibrāhīm ibn 'Alī ibn Maḥmūd. No proof has been given.

[10] Karatay, 359; Cahen, "Chroniques arabes," 340 (states that it covers A.H.188-218); Fu'ād Sayyid, 2:2, 139.

[11] Schefer (Blochet), 2:129; Gabrieli, 1163. The colophon states that the manuscript is "the 16th volume of the *Mukhtaṣar*." It appears to be perfectly fitting in the Ahmet III 2907/d set.

[12] Karatay, 359; Cahen, "Chroniques arabes," 340; the item is not listed in Fu'ād Sayyid's catalogue.

[13] Cahen suggested that the manuscript should be linked to the Ahmet III 2907/d set.

[14] Karatay, 359; Cahen, "Chroniques arabes," 340; Fu'ād Sayyid, 2:2, 139, states, wrongly, that it is of 249 ff.

[15] Cureton, 556-57; Gabrieli, 1163. Jewett suggests that it is, though entitled *Mukhtaṣar*, a revised and enlarged edition of the "original" (the *Mir'āt*?) which is drastically different from the *Mukhtaṣar* version in Ms. Landberg 137; see Introduction to his edition, viii. My spot-check collation of the two manuscripts has yielded the same conclusion. This BL manuscript was used by Chase for his edition (unpublished) which covers the years 1157-1168, 1182-1186; see Chase, XIX-XX.

[16] Cureton, 555; Gabrieli, 1162. According to Cureton's catalogue, the colophon indicates that it is the "seventh volume of the *Mukhtaṣar*"; my examination of the manuscript, however, reveals that the title page says "the fifth volume of the *Mukhtaṣar*." It might well be a collection in which several parts are bound together.

[17] Cureton, 556-57; Gabrieli, 1162. The colophon states that it is the "eighth volume of the *Mukhtaṣar* which has abridged the *Mir'āt* up to the 16th volume."

14. *Yale Landberg 137* (Nemoy 1288), 219 ff.; copied in A.H. 869 by Muḥammad ibn Muḥammad al-Qurashī al-Nastarāwī;[18] the 13th "part" (*juz'*) of the *Mukhtaṣar*, covering A.H. 466-529. This volume is part of the Nastarāwī Set which constitutes a *Mukhtaṣar* and *Dhayl* collection.[19]
15. *Bodleian Marsh 658* (Uri 759), 144 ff.; copied in A.H. 937; covering A.H. 480-553.[20]

16. *Sūhāj 224 ta'rīkh*, 192 ff.; the second "part" (*juz'*), copied in the A.H. 8th century, covering A.H. 58-74.[21]
17. *Yale Landberg 138* (Nemoy 1289), 218 ff.; not dated (1500?); covering A.H. 590-654 (ff. 1a-110b), followed by the *Dhayl*, covering A.H. 654-656 (ff. 111a-219b).[22]
18. *Berlin 9442*, 241 ff.; not dated; a fragment covering, incompletely, A.H. 65-333.[23]
19. *Bankipore Arabic Ms. 967* (Bankipore, Oriental Public Library), 124 ff.; not dated (probably 18th century); the history of the Prophets.[24]

Among the above-mentioned manuscripts, the so-called "Aḥmad al-Ḥakīmī Set"—most of which is preserved in Topkapı Sarayı and the others in Evkaf, Laleli, and Paris—and the Yale Landberg 137 appear to be of special impor-

---

[18]The same scribe of the *Dhayl* (the "Nastarāwī Set"): Yale Landberg 139 and Cairo ta'rīkh 1516/v. 15 and v. 17.

[19]Nemoy, 137; Gabrieli, 1163. The colophon reveals that it is "the 13th volume of the *Mukhtaṣar*." For the Nastarāwī Set, see above, chapter 2, 23-25.

[20]Uri, 1:167-68; Gabrieli, 1163 (mistakenly states that it is of 140 ff.). The manuscript is entitled *Kitāb al-ta'rīkh al-musammā bi-Mir'āt al-zamān fī ma'rifat al-khulafā' wa-al-a'yān*. However, both Jewett and Gabrieli are of the opinion that it is a *mukhtaṣar* version. I have examined a portion of the text and found it very close to an epitome version, from the viewpoints of size (very short) as well as language and style (e.g., A.H. 481, *qultu hādhā mā dhakarahu al-muṣannif raḥimahu Allāh, . . .* "I say: this is what was narrated by the [original] compiler of the work—God's mercy be upon him! . . .").

[21]Fu'ād Sayyid, 2:2, 141; also al-Munajjid, *al-Mu'arrikhūn al-Dimashqīyūn*, 40. The Sūhāj manuscript is listed by both as the *Dhayl*, but is obviously a *Mukhtaṣar*.

[22]Nemoy, 137-38; Gabrieli, 1163. Although the title page claims that this is "the ninth volume of *Mir'āt al-zamān*," it is transparently derived from a *mukhtaṣar* version. It is even shorter than the *mukhtaṣar* mentioned above in that sometimes one single folio contains several years' events and obituary notices.

[23]Ahlwardt, 21:48-49; Gabrieli's catalogue has 9942 for 9442.

[24]Nadwi, XV:12-13.

tance: the former is the most complete and earliest textual evidence known so far, while the latter belongs to a different recension from all the others.[25]

In addition, there are some other anonymous manuscripts bearing the title of *Mukhtaṣar Mir'āt al-zamān*. For example, British Library 279 (add. 9574) is composed of several fragmental texts two of which claim to be the "third and fourth volumes of the *al-Nubadh al-mukhtaṣar*[*a*] *min Kitāb mir'āt al-zamān fī ta'rīkh al-a'yān* (ff. 196a-294b, 295a-326b)." It comprises a very brief narrative, which is approximately one-fifth of the size of al-Yūnīnī's *Mukhtaṣar*, of the events from A.H. 137 to A.H. 645. In my opinion, it is perhaps to be linked to another abbreviated version of the *Mir'āt* by one Muḥammad Ibn al-Sinjāb which is titled *Nubdhat Mukhtaṣar min Kitāb mir'āt al-zamān fī al-tawārīkh al-ḥisān*.[26]

[25] That Ms. Landberg 137 belongs to a different recension from the others (at least those in Europe) was suggested by Jewett who had examined all of the manuscripts in Europe; see Introduction to his edition, vii-ix.

[26] One manuscript of this version is known to me: Bodleian, Marsh 325, ff. 63-92; copied in A.H. 904 by one 'Abd Allāh ibn Abī 'Abd Allāh al-Kināwī(?).

APPENDIX II

THE PUBLICATION RECORD OF SIBṬ IBN AL-JAWZĪ'S *MIR'ĀT AL-ZAMĀN*

Following is a list of the published parts of Sibṭ Ibn al-Jawzī's *Mir'āt al-zamān*:

1. *Recueil des Historiens des Croisades*, Bd. III (Paris, 1884): 517-70. Selected text with French translation, covering the years 490/1096-531/1136, ed. Edouard Dulaurier.
2. *Mir'ât az-Zamân (A.H. 495-654) by Šams ad-Dîn 'l-Muẓaffar Yûsuf Ben Qizughlū Ben 'Abdallāh commonly known by the surname of Sibṭ Ibn al-Jauzī.* A facsimile reproduction of Ms. Landberg 136, ed. with introduction by James Richard Jewett, Chicago, 1907.
3. *Mir'āt uz-Zamān or the Mirror of the Age*, vol. VIII, pts. 1 and 2. Based on the Jewett facsimile, Hyderabad-Deccan, 1952. Some corrections by Ja'far al-Ḥusnī in *MMIA* 29 (1954): 118-22.
4. *The Mir'āt al-zamān of Sibṭ ibn al-Jauzī, years 1157-1168, 1182-1185.* Edward S. Chase, Jr., Ph.D. dissertation, Yale University, 1954.
5. *Mir'âtü'z-zeman fî Tarihi'l-Âyan* [sic]. Years 448/1056-480/1086, ed. Ali Sevim, Ankara, 1968.
6. *Al-Sifr al-awwal min Mir'āt al-zamān fī ta'rīkh al-a'yān*. From the Creation down to the Prophets, ed. Iḥsān 'Abbās, Beirut, 1985,
7. *Mir'āt al-zamān fī ta'rīkh al-a'yān, al-ḥiqba 345-447*. Ed. Janān Jalīl Muḥammad al-Hamūndī, Baghdad, 1990.

APPENDIX III

LIST OF RULERS AND OFFICERS MENTIONED IN THE TEXT EDITED (with special reference to Syria)[1]

1. The Mamluk Sultanate

The sultan
A.H. 697-698 al-Malik al-Manṣūr Ḥusām al-Dīn Lājīn
A.H. 699-701 al-Malik al-Nāṣir Muḥammad ibn Qalāwūn

The viceroy (nā'ib al-salṭana) *in Egypt*
A.H. 697-698 Amīr Sayf al-Dīn Mengü-Temür al-Ḥusāmī (killed in Rabī' II) [1, 57]
A.H. 698 Amīr Sayf al-Dīn Ṭughjī [59]
A.H. 699-701 Amīr Sayf al-Dīn Salār al-Ṣāliḥī al-Manṣūrī [59, 96, 202, 240]

The vizier (Cairo)
A.H. 697 Fakhr al-Dīn Ibn al-Khalīlī [5]
A.H. 698-701 Amīr Shams al-Dīn Sunqur al-A'sar al-Manṣūrī (appointed in Ramaḍān 698) [69, 96, 202, 240]
A.H. 701 Amīr 'Izz al-Dīn Aybak al-Baghdādī (appointed in Muḥarram 701) [241]

The vizier (Damascus)
A.H. 697 Taqī al-Dīn Tawba al-Takrītī [2]

---

[1] This list contains material drawn from "the list of rulers" that precedes each year's events. The data have been adjusted according to the relevant narratives within the text, for most of the appointments were made in the middle of a given year. For the chief judges representing the four Sunnī law schools as well as other religious leaders, also see Pouzet, *Damas*, especially 412-21. The brackets refer to the page numbers in the present edition.

The viceroy in Syria
A.H. 697-698 Amīr Sayf al-Dīn Qibjāq al-Manṣūrī [116]
A.H. 698-701 Amīr Jamāl al-Dīn Āqqūsh al-Afram [62, 96, 202]

2. The Viceroys in the Syrian Provinces[2]

Kerak
A.H. 700 Amīr Jamāl al-Dīn Āqqūsh al-Ashrafī [202]

al-Shawbak (Montreal)
A.H. 700 Amīr Sayf al-Dīn Qibjāq al-Manṣūrī [202]

Hama[3]
A.H. 700-701 al-'Ādil Zayn al-Dīn Kitbughā (the former sultan al-Malik al-'Ādil) [202, 240]

Aleppo
A.H. 698 Amīr Sayf al-Dīn Balabān al-Ṭabbākhī [52]
A.H. 700-701 Amīr Shams al-Dīn Qarā-Sunqur al-Manṣūrī [202, 240]

al-Bīra
A.H. 700 Amīr Sayf al-Dīn Ṭūghān [202]

Tripoli
A.H. 698 (prior to Rabī' II) Amīr 'Izz al-Dīn Aybak al-Mawṣilī [52, 76]
A.H. 698 (after Rabī' II) Amīr Sayf al-Dīn Kurt al-Manṣūrī [76]
A.H. 700 Amīr Sayf al-Dīn Quṭlū-Bek [202]
A.H. 701 Amīr Sayf al-Dīn Usun-Damur [248]

Ṣafad
A.H. 698 Amīr Fāris al-Dīn al-Albakī [52]
A.H. 700 Sayf al-Dīn Balabān al-Manṣūrī [202]

---

[2] The text shows that it was not until A.H. 701 (1301) that the office of viceroy in the Syrian provinces began to be mentioned regularly in "the list of rulers."

[3] Prior to the establishment of the office of viceroy, the ruler (*ṣāḥib*) of Hama was the Ayyubid prince al-Malik al-Muẓaffar Taqī al-Dīn Maḥmūd ibn Muḥammad ibn Maḥmūd ibn Shādhī ibn Ayyūb [1, 48, 90].

3. Municipal Administration in Damascus

The Shāfi'ī chief judge (qāḍī al-quḍāt)
A.H. 697-699 Imām al-Dīn 'Umar ibn 'Abd al-Raḥmān al-Qazwīnī [2, 96]
A.H. 700-701 Badr al-Dīn Muḥammad ibn Ibrāhīm Ibn Jamā'a [202][4]

The Ḥanafī chief judge
A.H. 697-699 Ḥusām al-Dīn Abū al-Faḍā'il al-Ḥasan al-Rāzī (was in Cairo in A.H. 697 and his son Jalāl al-Dīn Aḥmad acted as his deputy) [2, 96]
A.H. 700 Shams al-Dīn Muḥammad ibn al-Ṣafī Ibn al-Ḥarīrī [202]
A.H. 701 Jalāl al-Dīn Aḥmad ibn al-Ḥasan al-Rāzī[5]

The Mālikī chief judge
A.H. 697-701 Jamāl al-Dīn Muḥammad Ibn Sulaymān al-Zawāwī [2, 96, 202][6]

The Ḥanbalī chief judge
A.H. 697-701 Taqī al-Dīn Sulaymān Ibn Ḥamza al-Maqdisī [2, 96, 202][7]

The head preacher at the Grand Mosque of Damascus (khaṭīb al-balad)
A.H. 697-701 Badr al-Dīn Ibn Jamā'a [2, 96][8]

The finance agent (mushidd al-dawāwīn, shādd al-dawāwīn)
A.H. 697-698 Amīr Sayf al-Dīn Jāghān al-Manṣūrī [2]
A.H. 698 Amīr Ḥusām al-Dīn Quṭlū-Bek (appointed in Jumādā I and was removed from the post shortly afterwards) [61, 63]
A.H. 698-701 Amīr Sayf al-Dīn Aqjubā al-Manṣūrī (appointed in Jumādā II) [66, 96, 128, 202, 249]
A.H. 699 (during the Mongol occupation) Amīr Nāṣir al-Dīn Yaḥyā [116]

The governor of the countryside of Damascus (mutawallī barr Dimashq, wālī al-barr)
A.H. 697-698 Amīr 'Alā' al-Dīn Ibn al-Jākī [2, 50]

---

[4] He remained in the position until 702/1303; see Pouzet, *Damas*, 415.
[5] See Pouzet, *Damas*, 416.
[6] His tenure ended in 717/1317; see Pouzet, *Damas*, 418.
[7] His tenure ended in 715/1316; see Pouzet, *Damas*, 417.
[8] He held the position until 702/1303; see Pouzet, *Damas*, 421.

A.H. 698 Amīr Ḥusām al-Dīn Lājīn al-Ḥusāmī al-Manṣūrī (assumed the post in Muḥarram) [50]

A.H. 698-699 'Imād al-Dīn Ibn al-Nashshābī (appointed in Jumādā I 698 to replace Lājīn) [63]

A.H. 699-700 'Izz al-Dīn Aybak al-Najībī (appointed in Sha'bān 699) [123, 202]

The governor of the city of Damascus (mutawallī al-ḥarb bi-Dimashq, wālī al-balad)

A.H. 697-698 'Imād al-Dīn Ibn al-Nashshābī [2, 54, 61]

A.H. 698-700 Amīr Jamāl al-Dīn Ibrāhīm Ibn al-Naḥḥās (appointed to succeed Ibn al-Nashshābī in Jumādā I 698) [63, 202]

The chief of staff in administration (nāẓir al-dawāwīn)

A.H. 697 Amīn al-Dīn Ibn Hilāl [2]

A.H. 699 Fakhr al-Dīn Sulaymān Ibn al-Shīrajī (al-Shīrāzī?) [96]

A.H. 699-700 Tāj al-Dīn Aḥmad Ibn al-Shīrajī (al-Shīrāzī?) (assumed the office in Sha'bān 699) [128, 202]

A.H. 701 Sharaf al-Dīn Ibn Muzhir (appointed in Jumādā I to assist Ibn al-Shīrajī) [250]

A.H. 701 'Izz al-Dīn Aḥmad Ibn Muyassar al-Miṣrī (assumed the office in Dhū al-Qa'da) [255]

The public treasurer (wakīl bayt al-māl)

A.H. 697 Najm al-Dīn Ibn Abī al-Ṭayyib [2]

The supervisor of Mamluk treasury (nāẓir al-khizāna)

A.H. 697 Fakhr al-Dīn Sulaymān Ibn al-Shīrajī [2]

The market inspector (al-muḥtasib)

A.H. 697-699 Amīn al-Dīn Yūsuf al-Rūmī (resumed the office after the Mongols' withdrawal in A.H. 699) [2, 96]

A.H. 699 (during the Mongol occupation) Muḥammad ibn al-Ṣafī al-Sinjār [122]

BIBLIOGRAPHY

ABBREVIATIONS

BEAHIA = *Beiträge zur erschliessung der arabischen Handschriften in Istanbul und Anatolien* (ed. F. Sezgin)
BEO = *Bulletin d'études orientales* (Institut Français de Damas)
BSOAS = *Bulletin of the School of Oriental and African Studies* (University of London)
CHAL = *The Cambridge History of Arabic Literature*
CHIr = *The Cambridge History of Iran*
Dhayl, 1-4 = *Dhayl Mir'āt al-zamān*, Hyderabad edition (vols. 1-4; A.H. 654-686)
Dhayl, M = *Dhayl Mir'āt al-zamān*, Melkonian's edition (A.H. 687-690)
EI = *Encyclopaedia of Islam*, original edition
EI² = *Encyclopaedia of Islam*, second edition
GAL = Brockelmann, Carl. *Geschichte der arabischen Litteratur*
GALS = Brockelmann, Carl. *Geschichte der arabischen Litteratur*, Supplement
HAAS = *al-Ḥawlīyāt al-atharīya al-'Arabīya al-Sūrīya* (*Annales archéologiques arabes Syriennes*, Damas)
IJMES = *International Journal of Middle East Studies*
IOS = *Israel Oriental Studies*
JA = *Journal Asiatique* (Société Asiatique, Paris)
JAOS = *Journal of the American Oriental Society*
JESHO = *Journal of the Economic and Social History of the Orient* (Leiden)
JRAS = *Journal of the Royal Asiatic Society of Great Britain and Ireland* (London)
JSAI = *Jerusalem Studies in Arabic and Islam*
JSS = *Journal of Semitic Studies*
MMIA = *Majallat al-Majma' al-'Ilmī al-'Arabī bi-Dimashq* (Damascus)
Q1 = al-Qalqashandī, *Ṣubḥ al-a'shā*
Q2 = al-Baqlī, *al-Ta'rīf bi-muṣṭalaḥāt Ṣubḥ al-a'shā*
REI = *Revue des études islamiques* (Paris)
SEI = *Shorter Encyclopaedia of Islam*
ZDMG = *Zeitschrift der deutschen Morgenländischen Gesellschaft*

I. MANUSCRIPTS

al-Birzālī, 'Alam al-Dīn al-Qāsim. *al-Muqtafā li-Ta'rīkh al-shaykh Shihāb al-Dīn Abī Shāma*. Istanbul, Topkapı Sarayı, Ahmet III 2951/1, 2.

al-Dhahabī, Shams al-Dīn Muḥammad ibn Aḥmad. *al-Mukhtār min Ta'rīkh al-Jazarī*. Istanbul, Köprülü 1147.

al-Jazarī, Shams al-Dīn Muḥammad. *Jawāhir al-sulūk fī al-khulafā' wa-al-mulūk* (i.e., *Ḥawādith al-zamān*). Paris, Bibliothèque Nationale, arabe 6739.

Landberg, Carlo., et al. *Kurzes Verzeichniss der Sammlung arabischer Handschriften des Dr. C. Grafen v. Landberg in Yale, München, 1900*. Yale University, Beinecke Landberg O., v. 1-5. (v. 6 contains Yale Librarians' processing notes).

Sibṭ Ibn al-Jawzī, Yūsuf ibn Qizughlī. *Mir'āt al-zamān fī ta'rīkh al-a'yān* (vol. VIII). Yale University, Beinecke Landberg 136.

al-Yūnīnī, Quṭb al-Dīn Mūsā. *Dhayl Mir'āt al-zamān* (23 manuscripts; see chapter 2).
—. *Mukhtaṣar Mir'āt al-zamān* (see Appendix I).

II. PRINTED WORKS

Abū Shāma, 'Abd al-Raḥmān. *Tarājim rijāl al-qarnayn al-sādis wa-al-sābi'* (i.e., *Dhayl al-Rawḍatayn*), ed. M. Z. al-Kawtharī. Cairo: al-Sayyid 'Izzat al-'Aṭṭār al-Ḥusaynī, 1947.

Ahlwardt, Wilhelm. *Verzeichniss der arabischen Handschriften der Königlichen Bibliothek zu Berlin*. Berlin: A. Asher & Co., 1897.

Ahmad, H. "Abū Shāma," *EI*[2].

Allouche, Adel. *Mamluk Economics: A study and translation of al-Maqrīzī's* Ighāthah. Salt Lake City: University of Utah Press, 1994.

Amin, Muhammad M. and Laila A. Ibrahim. *Architectural Terms in Mamluk Documents (648-923 H/1250-1517)*. Cairo: The American University of Cairo Press, 1990.

Amitai-Preiss, Reuven. *Mongols and Mamluks: The Mamluk-Īlkhānid War, 1260-1281*. Cambridge University Press, 1995.

Ansari, A. S. Bazmee. "al-Djazarī," *EI*[2].

Arberry, A. J. *The Koran Interpreted*. New York: Collier Books, 1955.

Ashtor, Eliyahu. *A Social and Economic History of the Near East in the Middle Ages*. London: William Collins & Sons, 1976.

'Awwād, Kūrkīs. *Fahāris al-makhṭūṭāt al-'Arabīya fī al-'ālam*. 2 vols. Kuwait: Manshūrāt Ma'had al-Makhṭūṭāt al-'Arabīya, 1984.

Ayalon, David. "Studies on the Structure of the Mamluk Army," *BSOAS* xv/2 (1953): 203-28; xv/3 (1953): 448-76; xvi/1 (1954): 57-90.

—. "Names, Titles, and 'Nisbas' of the Mamluks," *IOS* 5 (1975): 189-232.

—. "The Eunuchs in the Mamluk Sultanate," *Studies in Memory of Gaston Wiet*, pp. 267-95. Jerusalem: The Institute of Asian and African Studies, 1977.

—. "On the Eunuchs in Islam," *JSAI* 1 (1979): 67-124.

al-'Azzāwī, 'Abbās. "Sibṭ Ibn al-Jawzī - al-Quṭb al-Yūnīnī - aw Mir'āt al-zamān wa-dhayluhu: jawāban li-mā ṭalabahu al-ustādh Salīm al-Krankū," *MMIA* 22 (1947): 374-77.

—. "Mu'arrikh al-Shām aw al-Birzālī wa-ta'rīkhuhu," *MMIA* 24 (1949): 519-27.

al-Baghdādī, Ismā'īl Pāshā. *Hadīyat al-'ārifīn: asmā' al-mu'allifīn wa-āthār al-muṣannifīn*. 2 vols. Istanbul: Maarif Basimevi, 1951-55.

—. *Īḍāḥ al-maknūn fī al-dhayl 'alā Kashf al-ẓunūn*. 2 vols. Istanbul: s.n., 1945-47.

Bahnasī, 'Afīf. "al-Miḥrāb al-awwal fī al-masjid al-Umawī," *HAAS* 31 (1981): 9-28.

al-Baqlī, Muḥammad Qindīl. *Fahāris Kitāb ṣubḥ al-a'shā fī ṣinā'at al-inshā' lil-Qalqashandī*. Cairo: 'Ālam al-Kutub, 1964.

—. *al-Ta'rīf bi-muṣṭalaḥāt Ṣubḥ al-a'shā*. Cairo: al-Hay'a al-Miṣrīya al-'Āmma lil-Kitāb, 1984.

Barthold, W. and I. A. Boyle. "Berke," *EI*[2].

Baybars al-Manṣūrī al-Dawādār, Rukn al-Dīn. *Kitāb al-tuḥfa al-mulūkīya fī al-dawla al-Turkīya*, ed. 'Abd al-Ḥamīd Ṣāliḥ Ḥamdān. Cairo: s.n., 1987.

Berkey, Jonathan. *The Transmission of Knowledge in Medieval Cairo: A Social History of Islamic Education*. Princeton, New Jersey: Princeton University Press, 1992.

al-Biqāʿī, Ibrāhīm ibn ʿUmar. *Iẓhār al-ʿaṣr li-asrār ahl al-ʿaṣr: tārikh al-Biqāʿī*, ed. Muḥammad Sālim ibn Shadīd al-ʿAwfī. 3 vols. Jīza (Cairo): Hijr lil-Ṭibāʿa wa-al-Nashr wa-al-Tawzīʿ wa-al-Iʿlān, 1992-93.

al-Birzālī, ʿAlam al-Dīn al-Qāsim. *Mashyakhat qāḍī al-quḍāt shaykh al-Islām Badr al-Dīn Abī ʿAbd Allāh Muḥammad ibn Ibrāhīm Ibn Jamāʿa al-mutawaffā sanat 733 h.*, ed. Muwaffaq ibn ʿAbd Allāh ibn ʿAbd al-Qādir. 2 vols. Beirut: Dār al-Gharb al-Islāmī, 1988.

Blochet, E. *Catalogue des manuscrits arabes des nouvelles acquisitions (1884-1924)*. Paris: Bibliothèque Nationale, 1925.

Boase, T. S. R., ed. *The Cilician Kingdom of Armenia*. Edinburgh: Scottish Academic Press, 1978.

Bonebakker, Seeger Adrianus. "*Adab* and the concept of belles-lettres," *CHAL*, *ʿAbbasid Belles-Lettres*, pp. 16-30. Ed. Julia Ashtiany, et al. Cambridge University Press, 1990.

Braune, W. "ʿAbd al-Ḳādir al-Djilani," *EI²*.

Brinner, William. *A Chronicle of Damascus, 1389-1397, by Muḥammad ibn Ṣaṣrā*. 2 vols. Berkeley/Los Angeles: University of California Press, 1963.

—. "The Significance of the Harafish and their Sultan," *JESHO* 6 (1963): 190-215.

—. "Ibn Ṣaṣrā," *EI²*.

Brockelmann, Carl. *Geschichte der arabischen Litteratur*. Leiden: E. J. Brill, 1937-49.

—. *Geschichte der arabischen Litteratur*. 3 supplementary vols. Leiden: E. J. Brill, 1937-42.

Cahen, Claude. "Les chroniques arabes concernant la Syrie, l'Égypte et la Mésopotamie de la conquête arabe à la conquête ottomane dans les bibliothèques d'Istanbul," *REI* 10 (1936): 335-58.

—. *La Syrie du Nord à l'époque des Croisades et la principauté franque d'Antioche*. Paris: Librairie Orientaliste Paul Geuthner, 1940.

—. "al-Yūnīnī: Dhail Mir'āt al-zamān, Ed. Hydarabad," *Arabica* IV (1957): 193-94.

—. "Editing Arabic Chronicles. A few suggestions," *Islamic Studies* (Karachi) Sept. (1962): 1-25.

—. "Artuḳids," *EI²*.

—. "Dhimma," *EI²*.

—. "Ibn al-Djawzī," *EI²*.

—. "Addenda sur al-Djazarī," *IOS* II (1972): 144-47.

—. "History and historians," *CHAL, Religion, Learning and Science in the ʿAbbasid Period*, pp. 188-232. Ed. M. J. L. Young, et al. Cambridge University Press, 1990.

Chamberlain, Michael. *Knowledge and social practice in medieval Damascus, 1190-1350*. Cambridge University Press, 1994.

Chase, Edward. *The Mir'āt al-zamān of Sibṭ ibn al-Jauzī*. Ph.D. dissertation, Yale University, 1954.

Cureton, W. and C. Rieu. *Catalogus codicum manuscriptorum orientalium qui in Museo Britannico asservantur*. London: s.n., 1846-79.

Dearing, Vinton. *A Manual of Textual Analysis*. Berkeley: University of California Press, 1959.

—. *Principles and Practice of Textual Analysis*. Berkeley: University of California Press, 1974.

Defter-i Kütüphane-yi Ayasofya. Istanbul: Der-i Seʿadet, 1304/1886-87.

Dhahabī, Muḥammad. *al-'Ibar fī khabar man ghabara*. Kuwait: Dā'irat al-Maṭbū'āt wa-al-Nashr, 1960.

—. *Min dhuyūl al-'Ibar fī khabar man ghabara*. 4 vols. Beirut: s.n., 1985.

—. *Mīzān al-i'tidāl fī naqd al-rijāl*, ed. 'A.M. al-Bajāwī. 4 vols. [Cairo]: Maṭba'at 'Īsā al-Bābī al-Ḥalabī wa-Shurakāhu, 1963-64.

—. *al-Mu'jam al-mukhtaṣṣ bi-al-muḥaddithīn*. al-Ṭā'if: Maktabat al-Ṣiddīq, 1988.

—. *Tadhkirat al-ḥuffāẓ*. 5 vols. Hyderabad: Maṭba'at Majlis Dā'irat al-Ma'ārif al-Niẓāmīya al-Kā'ina fī al-Hind, 1333/1915.

Dozy, R. P. A. *Supplément aux dictionnaires arabes*. 2 vols. Leiden: E. J. Brill, 1881 (reprint 1960)

Edwards, Robert W. *The Fortifications of Armenian Cilicia*. Washington, D.C.: Dumbarton Oaks Research Library and Collection, 1987.

Elham, Shah Morad. *Kitbuġā und Lāǧīn: Studien zur Mamluken-Geschichte nach Baibars al-Manṣūrī und an-Nuwairī*. Freiburg: Klaus Schwarz Verlag, 1977.

Elisseéff, N. "Mardj Rāhiṭ," *EI²*.

Farah, Caesar E. *The Dhayl in Medieval Arabic Historiography*. New Haven: The American Oriental Society, 1967.

Fihrist al-kutub al-'arabīya al-maḥfūẓa bi-al-kutubikhāna al-Khidīwīya. 7 vols. Cairo, 1301-06/1884-88.

Fück, J. U. "Ibn Khallikān," *EI²*.

Gabrieli, G. "Appunti descrittivi e critici su alcuni manuscritti arabidi contenuto storico," *Rendiconti dei Lincei (Roma), Serie* V, vol. xxv (1916): 1135-84.

Gaudefroy-Demombynes. *La Syrie au début du quinzième siècle d'après Qalqachandi*. Paris: Librairie Paul Geuthner, 1923.

Glazer, S. "Abū Ḥayyān," *EI²*.

Graf, Georg. *Verzeichnis arabischer kirchlicher Termini*. Corpus Scriptorum Christianorum Orientalium, Subsidia Tome 8. Louvain: Imprimerie Orientaliste, 1954.

Graf, Gunhild. *Die Epitome der Universalchronik Ibn ad-Dawādārīs zur Langfassung: Eine quellenkritische Studie zur Geschichte der ägyptischen Mamlūken*. Berlin: Klaus Schwarz Verlag, 1990.

Haarmann, Ulrich. *Quellenstudien zur frühen Mamlukenzeit*. Freiburg im Breisgau: Klaus Schwarz Verlag, 1970.

—. "Auflösung und Bewahrung der klassischen Formen arabischer Geschichtsschreibung in der Zeit der Mamlūken," *ZDMG* 121 (1971): 46-60.

—. "L'édition de la chronique mamelouke syrienne de Šams ad-Dīn Muḥammad al-Ǧazarī," *BEO* xxvii (1974): 195-203.

—. "Arabic in Speech, Turkish in Lineage: Mamluks and their Sons in the Intellectual Life of Fourteenth-Century Egypt and Syria," *JSS* xxxiii/1 (1988): 81-114.

—. Review of Bernd Radtke, *Weltgeschichte und Weltbeschreibung im mittelalterlichen Islam*, *JAOS* 115/1 (1995): 133-35.

Ḥājjī Khalīfa (Kātib Çelebī). *Kashf al-ẓunūn 'an asāmī al-kutub wa-al-funūn*. Baghdad: al-Muthannā, 1972 (reprint of 1941 Istanbul edition).

Halm, Heinz. *Ägypten nach den mamlukischen Lehensregistern*. 2 vols. Wiesbaden: Ludwig Reichert, 1979-82.

Hamori, A. "Love poetry (*ghazal*)," *CHAL, 'Abbasid Belles-Lettres*, pp. 202-18. Ed. Julia Ashtiany, et al. Cambridge University Press, 1990.

Hardy, P. "Dihli sultanate," *EI²*.

Hava, Joseph G. *al-Faraid: Arabic-English Dictionary*. 5th edition. Beirut: Dar el-Mashreq, 1982.

Hitti, Philip K. *An Arab-Syrian Gentleman and Warrior in the Period of the Crusades: Memoirs of Usāmah Ibn-Munqidh*. Princeton: Princeton University Press, 1987.

Holt, Peter Malcolm. *The Memoirs of a Syrian Prince: Abul-Fida', sultan of Hamah (672-732/1273-1331)*. Wiesbaden: Franz Steiner Verlag, 1983.

Howorth, Henry H. *History of the Mongols: From the 9th to the 19th century*. 4 vols. New York: Burt Franklin, n.d. (reprint London 1876).

Humphreys, Stephen. *From Saladin to the Mongols: the Ayyibids of Damascus, 1193-1260*. Albany, NY: State University of New York Press, 1977.

—. *Islamic History: a framework for inquiry*. Princeton: Princeton University Press, 1991.

al-Ḥusaynī al-Dimashqī, Muḥammad. *Dhayl Tadhkirat al-ḥuffāẓ*. Damascus: al-Qudsī, 1928.

Ibn Abī Uṣaybi'a. Kitāb 'uyūn al-anbā' fī ṭabaqāt al-aṭibbā'. 2 vols. Cairo, 1882 (reprint Beirut, 1965).

Ibn al-'Adīm, 'Umar. *Bughyat al-ṭalab fī ta'rīkh Ḥalab*. 10 vols. Frankfurt am Main: Institute for the History of Arabic-Islamic Science, 1986-89.

Ibn al-Athīr, 'Alī. *al-Lubāb fī tahdhīb al-ansāb*. Vol. 1, ed. M. 'Abd al-Wāḥid. Cairo: Maṭba'at Dār al-Ta'līf, 1971; vols 2 and 3, Beirut: Dār Ṣādir, 1972.

Ibn al-Athīr, 'Izz al-Dīn. *al-Kāmil fī al-ta'rīkh*. 14 vols., ed. C. J. Tornberg. Beirut, 1965-67 (reprint).

Ibn al-Dawādārī, Abū Bakr. *Kanz al-durar wa-jāmi' al-ghurar*. Vol. 8, ed. U. Haarmann, Cairo: Deutsches Archäologisches Institut Kairo (DAIK), 1971; vol. 9, ed. H. R. Roemer, Cairo: DAIK, 1960.

Ibn Ḥajar al-'Asqalānī, Aḥmad. *al-Durar al-kāmina fī a'yān al-mi'a al-thāmina*, ed. M. S. Jād al-Ḥaqq, 5 vols. 2d ed. Cairo: Dār al-Kutub al-Ḥadītha, 1385/1966.

Ibn Hishām, 'Abd al-Malik. *Sīrat al-Nabī*. Vol. 2, ed. Muḥammad Muḥyī al-Dīn 'Abd al-Ḥamīd. Cairo: Maṭba'at Ḥijāzī bi-al-Qāhira, 1937.

Ibn al-'Imād, 'Abd al-Ḥayy. *Shadharāt al-dhahab fī akhbār man dhahaba*. 6 vols. Beirut: al-Maktab al-Tijārī lil-Ṭibā'a wa-al-Nashr wa-al-Tawzī', 1966.

Ibn Iyās, Muḥammad ibn Aḥmad. *Badā'i' al-zuhūr fī waqā'i' al-duhūr*. 5 vols., ed. M. Mustafa, H. Roemer, et al. Cairo and Wiesbaden: Franz Steiner Verlag, 1960-1963.

Ibn al-Jawzī. *al-Muntaẓam fī ta'rīkh al-mulk wa-al-umam*, ed. F. Krenkow. Hyderabad, 1938-40; 18 vols., ed. Muḥammad 'Aṭā' et al. Beirut: s.n., 1992.

Ibn Kathīr, 'Abd Allāh. *al-Bidāya wa-al-nihāya fī al-ta'rīkh*. 14 vols. Cairo: Maṭba'at al-Sa'āda, 1932-34.

Ibn Khallikān, Shams al-Dīn. *Wafayāt al-a'yān wa-anbā' abnā' al-zamān*, ed. Iḥsān 'Abbās. 8 vols. Beirut: Dār Ṣādir, 1977.

Ibn Mufliḥ, Ibrāhīm. *al-Maqṣid al-arshad fī dhikr aṣḥāb al-imām Aḥmad*. 3 vols. Riyadh: Maktabat al-Rushd, 1990.

Ibn Rajab, 'Abd al-Raḥmān. *Kitāb al-dhayl 'alā Ṭabaqāt al-Ḥanābila*. Beirut: Dār al-Ma'rifa, 1982.

Ibn Shaddād, 'Izz al-Dīn Muḥammad. *Ta'rīkh al-Malik al-Ẓāhir*, ed. A. Hutait. Cairo: s.n., 1983.

Ibn Taghrībirdī, Abū al-Maḥāsin Yūsuf. *al-Dalīl al-shāfī 'alā al-Manhal al-ṣāfī*, ed. F. Shaltūt. Mecca: Markaz al-Baḥth al-'Ilmī bi-Jāmi'at Umm al-Qurā, 1399/1978-79.

—. *al-Manhal al-ṣāfī wa-al-mustawfī ba'da al-Wāfī*, ed. Kh. Kh. Amīn. Cairo: al-Hay'a al-Miṣrīya al-'Āmma lil-Kitāb, 1952.

—. *al-Nujūm al-zāhira fī mulūk Miṣr wa-al-Qāhira*. 16 vols. Cairo: al-Mu'assasa al-Miṣrīya al-'Āmma lil-Ta'līf wa-al-Tarjama wa-al-Ṭibā'a wa-al-Nashr, 1963-72.

Ibn Wāṣil, Muḥammad. *Mufarrij al-kurūb fī akhbār banī Ayyūb*, ed. Jamāl al-Dīn al-Shayyāl. Cairo: Maṭba'at Jāmi'at Fu'ād al-Awwal, 1953.

Idris, H. R. "Ḥafṣids," *EI²*.

Irwin, Robert. "The Mamluk Conquest of the County of Tripoli," *Crusade and Settlement*, pp. 246-50. Ed. P. W. Edbury. Cardiff: University College Cardiff Press, 1985.

—. *The Middle East in the Middle Ages: The early Mamluk sultanate, 1250-1382*. London & Sydney: Croom Helm, 1986.

Jewett, J. R. Introduction to the facsimile edition of Part 8 of Sibṭ ibn al-Jawzī's *Mir'āt al-zamān*. Chicago: The University of Chicago Press, 1907.

Jubran, Numan M. *Studien zur Geschichte und Sozialgeographie von Damaskus im Ausgehenden 13. Jahrhundert: mit einer Teiledition der Chronik Šams ad-Dīn Muḥamad* [sic] *al-Ǧazarīs*. Ph.D. dissertation, Albert-Ludwigs-Universität zu Freiburg, 1987.

Kaḥḥāla, 'Umar Riḍā. *Mu'jam al-mu'allifīn*. 15 vols. Damascus: al-Maktab al-'Arabī, 1957-61.

Karatay, Fehmi Edhem. *Topkapı Sarayı Müzesi Kütüphanesi arapca yazmalar katalogu*. 4 vols. Beirut: Cultural Research & Service Center, 1990 (reprint Istanbul 1962-69).

Kazimirski, A. de Biberstein. *Dictionnaire Arabe-Français*. Paris: Editions G.-P. Maisonneuve, n.d.

Khalidi, Tarif. *Arabic historical thought in the classical period*. Cambridge University Press, 1994.

al-Khazrajī (el-Khazrejiyy), 'Alī ibn al-Ḥasan. *The Pearl-strings: a history of the Rasuliyy dynasty of Yemen, by Aliyyu'bnu'l-Hasan 'el-Khazrejiyy: translation and text with annotations and index by the late Sir J. W. Redhouse* (ed. E. G. Browne et al.). 5 vols. Leiden: E. J. Brill/London: Luzac & Co., 1906-18.

Krenkow, Fritz. "Dhayl Mir'āt al-zamān," *MMIA* 21 (1946): 378-80.

Kunitzsch, Paul. *Arabische Sternnamen in Europa*. Wiesbaden: Otto Harrassowitz, 1959.

—. *Untersuchungen zur Sternnomenklatur der Araber*. Wiesbaden: Otto Harrassowitz, 1961.

al-Kutubī, Muḥammad Ibn Shākir. *Fawāt al-wafayāt*, ed. M. M. 'Abd al-Ḥamīd. 2 vols. Cairo: Maktabat al-Nahḍa al-Miṣrīya, 1951-52.

Lammens, H. "Yazīd b. Mu'āwiya," *EI²*.

Lane, Edward W. *An Arabic-English Lexicon*. 8 vols. London and Edinburgh: Williams and Norgate, 1863-93.

Langner, Barbara. *Untersuchungen zur historischen Volkskunde Ägyptens nach mamlukischen Quellen*. Berlin: Klaus Schwarz Verlag, 1983.

Laoust, Henri. "Le hanbalisme sous les Mamlouks Bahrides," *REI* xxviii (1960): 1-72.

—. "al-Bahūt," *EI²*.

Lapidus, Ira Marvin. *Muslim Cities in the Later Middle Ages*. Cambridge, Massachusetts: Harvard University Press, 1967.

Le Strange, Guy. *Palestine under the Moslems: A description of Syria and the Holy Land from A.D. 650 to 1500*. London: Palestine Exploration Fund, 1890.

—. *The Lands of the Eastern Caliphates: Mesopotamia, Persia and Central Asia from the Moslem conquest to the time of Timur*. London: Frank Cass & Co. Ltd., 1966.

Levanoni, Amalia. *A Turning Point in Mamluk History: The Third Reign of al-Nāṣir Muḥammad Ibn Qalāwūn (1310-1341)*. Leiden/New York/Köln: E. J. Brill, 1995.

Lewis, Bernard. "Ibn al-'Adīm," *EI²*.

—. "Kamāl al-Dīn's Biography of Rāšid al-Dīn Sinān," *Arabica* 13 (1966): 225-67.

Little, Donald Presgrave. *An Introduction to Mamluk Historiography*. Montreal: McGill-Queen's University Press, 1970.

—. "The Historical and Historiographical Significance of the Detention of Ibn Taymiyya," *IJMES* 4 (1973): 311-27.

—. "Coptic Conversion to Islam under the Baḥrī Mamluks 692-755/1293-1354," *BSOAS* 39 (1976): 552-69.

—. "al-Ṣafadī as Biographer of His Contemporaries," *Essays on Islamic Civilization: Presented to Niyazi Berkes*, pp. 190-210. Ed. D. P. Little. Leiden: E. J. Brill, 1976.

—. "The Fall of 'Akka in 690/1291: the Muslim version," *Studies in Islamic History and Civilization: in honour of Professor David Ayalon*, pp. 159-82. Ed. M. Sharon. Jerusalem: Cana/Leiden: E. J. Brill, 1986.

Loth, Otto., et al. *Catalogue of the Arabic Manuscripts in the Library of the India Office. London, 1877-1940*; Supplement to Vol. 2, ed. U. Sims-Williams. London, 1991.

Mach, Rodulf. *Catalogue of Arabic Manuscripts (Yahuda Section) in the Garrett Collection, Princeton University Library*. Princeton: Princeton University Press, 1977.

Makdisi, George. *The Rise of Colleges: Institutions of learning in Islam and the West*. Edinburgh: Edinburgh University Press, 1981.

al-Maqrīzī, Aḥmad ibn 'Alī. *Kitāb al-sulūk li-ma'rifat duwal al-mulūk*. 4 vols. Cairo: Dār al-Kutub al-Miṣrīya, 1958-73.

—. *Le Manuscrit autographe d'al-Mawā'iẓ wa-al-I'tibār fī Dhikr al-Khiṭaṭ wa-al-Āthār de Taqī al-Dīn Aḥmad b. 'Alī b. 'Abd al-Qādir al-Maqrīzī*. Texte édité et annoté par Ayman Fu'ād Sayyid. London: Al-Furqān Islamic Heritage Foundation, 1416/1995.

Marcais, G. "Bidjāya," *EI²*.

Marmon, Shaun. *Eunuchs and Sacred Boundaries in Islamic Society*. New York/Oxford: Oxford University Press, 1995.

Martel-Thoumian, Bernadette. *Les civils et l'administration dans l'État militaire mamlūk (IXᵉ/XVᵉ siècle)*. Damascus: Institut Français de Damas, 1991.

Mass, Paul. *Textual Criticism* (a translation of *Textkritik*), tr. Barbara Flower. Oxford: Clarendon Press, 1958.

Melkonian, Antranig. *Die Jahre 1287-1291 in der Chronik al-Yūnīnīs*. Ph.D. dissertation, Freiburg: Universitatsverlag Becksmann, 1975.

Minorsky, V. "Mardin," *EI²*.

Morgan, David O. "The Mongols in Syria, 1260-1300," *Crusade and Settlement*, pp. 231-35. Ed. P. W. Edbury. Cardiff: University College Cardiff Press, 1985.

Morray, David. *An Ayyubid Notable and his World: Ibn al-'Adīm and Aleppo as Portrayed in his Biographical Dictionary of People Associated with the City*. Leiden/New York/Köln: E. J. Brill, 1994.

al-Munajjid, Ṣalāḥ al-Dīn. *al-Mu'arrikhūn al-Dimashqīyūn wa-āthāruhum min al-qarn al-thālith al-hijrī ilā nihāyat al-qarn al-'āshir.* 2d ed. Cairo: Maṭba'at Miṣr, 1956.

—. *Mu'jam al-mu'arrikhīn al-Dimashqīyīn wa-āthāruhum al-makhṭūṭa wa-al-maṭbū'a.* Beirut: Dār al-Kitāb al-Jadīd, 1978.

Nadwi, M. A. *Catalogue of the Arabic and Persian Manuscripts in the Oriental Public Library at Bankipore.* Vol. XV, Calcutta, 1929.; vol. XXIII, 1939.

Nemoy, Leon. *Arabic Manuscripts in the Yale University Library.* New Haven: Connecticut Academy of Arts and Sciences, 1956.

al-Nuwayrī, Shihāb al-Dīn. *Nihāyat al-arab fī funūn al-adab*, ed. M. Elham. *Kitbuġā und Lāǧīn*, Arabic text, pp. 31-88.

—. *Nihāyat al-arab fī funūn al-adab*, vol. 31, ed. al-B. al-'Arīnī. Cairo: al-Hay'a al-Miṣrīya al-'Āmma lil-Kitāb, 1992.

d'Ohsson, Constantin Mouradgea. *Histoire des Mongols, depuis Tchinguiz-Khan jusqu'à Timour-Bey ou Tamerlan.* 4 vols. The Hague-Amsterdam: Les Frères Van Cleef, 1834-35.

Oxford Dictionary of Byzantium. 3 vols. Oxford: Oxford University Press, 1991.

Paret, Rudy. *Der Koran: Kommentar und Konkordanz.* Stuttgart: W. Kohlhammer, 1971.

Pedersen, J. "Ibn 'Abd al-Ẓāhir," *EI²*.

Pertsch, Wilhelm. *Die arabischen Handschriften der Herzoglichen Bibliothek zu Gotha.* 5 vols. Gotha: s.n., 1878-1892.

Petry, Carl F. *Twilight of Majesty: The Reigns of the Mamlūk Sultans al-Ashraf Qāytbāy and Qānṣūh al-Ghawrī in Egypt.* Seattle: University of Washington Press, 1993.

Poliak, A.N. *Feudalism in Egypt, Syria, Palestine, and the Lebanon (1250-1900).* London: Royal Asiatic Society, 1939.

Popper, William. *The Cairo Nilometer: Studies in Ibn Taghrî Birdî's Chronicles of Egypt: I.* Los Angeles/Berkeley: The University of California Press, 1951.

Pouzet, Louis. "Ḫaḍir ibn Abī Bakr al-Mihrānī," *BEO* 30 (1978): 173-83.

—. *Damas au VIIe/XIIIe siècle: Vie et structures religieuses d'une métropole islamique.* Beirut: Dar al-Machreq, 1988.

al-Qāḍī, Wadād, "Biographical Dictionaries: Inner Structure and Cultural Significance," *The Book in the Islamic World*, pp. 93-122. Ed. George N. Atiyeh. Albany: State University of New York Press and The Library of Congress, 1995.

al-Qalqashandī, Aḥmad. *Ṣubḥ al-a'shā fī ṣinā'at al-inshā'.* 14 vols. Cairo: al-Mu'assasa al-Miṣrīya al-'Āmma lil-Ta'līf wa-al-Tarjama wa-al-Ṭibā'a wa-al-Nashr, 1963.

Quatremère, M. *Histoire des sultans Mamlouks de l'Égypte.* 2 vols in 4 parts. Paris: The Oriental Translation Fund of Great Britain and Ireland, 1845.

Rabbat, Nasser O. "The Ideological Significance of the Dār al-'Adl in the Medieval Islamic Orient," *IJMES* 27 (1995): 3-28.

Rabie, Hassanein. *The Financial System of Egypt, A.H. 564-741/A.D. 1169-1341.* London: Oxford University Press, 1972.

Radtke, Bernd. *Weltgeschchte und Weltbeschreibung im mittelalterlichen Islam.* Beirut: im Kommission bei Franz Steiner Verlag Stuttgart, 1992.

Rieu, Charles. *Supplement to the Catalogue of the Arabic Manuscripts in the British Museum.* London, 1894.

Ritter, Helmut. "Mā sāhama bi-hi al-mu'arrikhūn al-'Arab fī al-mi'a al-sana al-akhīra fī dirāsat al-ta'rīkh al-'Arabī wa-ghayrihi: Makhṭūṭāt ta'rīkhiya 'Arabīya fī makātib Istanbūl lam tuṭba' ba'd," *BEAHIA*, pp. 665-78. Ed. F. Sezgin. Frankfurt and Main: Institute for the History of Arabic-Islamic Science, 1986.

Rosenthal, Franz. *The Technique and Approach of Muslim Scholarship*. Rome: Pontificium Institutum Biblicum, 1947.

—. *A History of Muslim Historiography*. 2d rev. ed. Leiden: E. J. Brill, 1968

—. "al-Birzālī," *EI*[2].

—. "Ibn al-Athīr," *EI*[2].

—. "A Note on the Mandīl," *Four Essays on Art and Literature in Islam*, pp. 63-99. Leiden: E. J. Brill, 1971.

al-Ṣabābiṭī, Abū 'Abd al-Raḥmān 'Iṣām al-Dīn. *Ṣaḥīḥ al-aḥādīth al-qudsīya*. [Beirut]: 'Arabīya lil-Ṭibā'a wa-al-Nashr, 1991.

al-Ṣafadī, Khalīl ibn Aḥmad. *al-A'yān al-'aṣr wa-a'wān al-naṣr*, ed. F. Sezgin. Frankfurt am Main: Institute for the History of Arabic-Islamic Science, 1990.

—. *al-Wāfī bi-al-wafayāt*, ed. H. Ritter, et al. 22 vols. Istanbul: Staatsdruckerei, 1931-in progress.

al-Sakhāwī, Shams al-Dīn Muḥammad. *al-I'lān bi-al-tawbīkh li-man dhamma al-ta'rīkh*. Damascus: al-Qudsī, 1930.

Salibi, K. S. "Ibn Djamā'a," *EI*[2].

Sauvaget, Jean. *La Chronique de Damas d'al-Jazarī (Années 689-698 H)*. Paris: Librairie Ancienne Honore Champion, Editeur, 1949.

—. "Noms et Surnoms de Mamelouks," *JA* 238 (1950): 31-58.

—. *Jean Sauvaget's Introduction to the History of the Muslim East*, recast by Cl. Cahen. Berkeley/Los Angeles: University of California Press, 1982.

Sauvaire, Henri. *Description de Damas*. Paris: Imprimerie Nationale, 1895-96.

al-Sawwās, Y. M. *Fihris Majāmī' al-madrasa al-'Umarīya fī Dār al-kutub al-Ẓāhirīya bi-Dimashq*. Kuwait: Manshūrāt Ma'had al-Makhṭūṭāt al-'Arabīya, 1987.

Sayyid, Fu'ād. *Fihrist al-makhṭūṭāt al-muṣawwara*, vol. 2, pts 2 and 3. Cairo: Ma'had al-Makhṭūṭāt al-'Arabīya, 1954-59.

Schoeler, G. "Bashshār b. Burd, Abū 'l-'Atāhiyah and Abū Nuwās," *CHAL, 'Abbasid Belles-Lettres*, pp. 275-99. Ed. Julia Ashtiany, et al. Cambridge University Press, 1990.

Şeşen, Ramazan et al. *Catalogue of Manuscripts in the Köprülü Library*. 3 vols. Istanbul: Research Center for Islamic History, Art and Culture, 1986.

Sezgin, Fuat. *Beiträge zur Erschliessung der arabischen Handschriften in Istanbul und Anatolien*. Frankfurt am Main: Institute for the History of Arabic-Islamic Science, 1986.

el-Shayyal, Gamal el-Din. "Ibn Wāṣil," *EI*[2].

Sibṭ Ibn al-Jawzī, Yūsuf ibn Qizughlī. *Mir'āt al-zamān fī ta'rīkh al-a'yān* (for publication record see Appendix II).

Somogyi, Joseph. "The *Kitāb al-muntaẓam* of Ibn al-Jauzī," *JRAS* (1932): 49-76.

—. "The *Ta'rīkh al-islām* of adh-Dhahabī," *JRAS* (1932): 815-55.

—. "Adh-dhahabī's Record of the Destruction of Damascus by the Mongols in 699-700 /1299-1301," *Ignace Goldziher Memorial Volume*, Part I, pp. 353-86. Ed. S. Löwinger and J. Somogyi. Budapest: s.n., 1948.

Sourdel, Dominique. "Ibn Shaddād," *EI*[2].

Spies, Otto. *Beiträge zur arabischen Literaturgeschichte*. Leipzig: Deutsche Morgenlandische Gesellschaft, 1932.

Spuler, Bertold. *Die Mongolen in Iran: Politik, Verwaltung und Kultur der Ilchanzeit (1220-1350)*. Berlin: Akademie Verlag, 1955.

Strothmann, R. "Nafīsa," *EI*[2].

al-Subkī, 'Abd al-Wahhāb. *Ṭabaqāt al-Shāfi'īya al-kubrā.* 10 vols. Cairo: Maṭba'at 'Īsā al-Bābī al-Ḥalabī wa-Shurakāhu, 1964.

Tauer, Felix. "Dernier volume de la continuation du Mir'āt az-zamān de Sibṭ ibn al-Ǧauzī par Šamsaddīn Muḥammad ibn Maǧdaddin al-Ǧazarī," *Archiv Orientalni* (Praha) II (1930): 89-90.

Thorau, Peter. "The Battle of 'Ayn Jālūt: a Re-examination," *Crusade and Settlement*, pp. 236-41. Ed. P. W. Edbury. Cardiff: University College Press, 1985.

——. *The Lion of Egypt: Sultan Baybars I & the Near East in the Thirteenth Century* (an English translation of *Sultan Baibars I von Ägypten: ein Beiträge zur Geschichte des Vorderen Orients im 13. Jahrhundert.* Wiesbaden, 1987), tr. P. M. Holt. London & New York: Longman, 1992.

al-'Ulaymī, 'Abd al-Raḥmān. *al-Manhaj al-aḥmad fī tarājim aṣḥāb al-imām Aḥmad.* Cairo: Maṭba'at al-Madanī, 1963.

al-'Umarī, Shihāb al-Dīn Aḥmad. *Masālik al-abṣār fī mamālik al-amṣār*, ed. F. Sezgin. Frankfurt am Main: Institute for the History of Arabic-Islamic Science, 1988-89.

Uri, Johannes. *Bibliothecae Bodleianae codicum manuscriptorum orientalium, videlicet hebraicorum, chaldaicorum, syriacorum, aethiopicorum, arabicorum, persicorum, turcicorum, copticorumque catalogus.* Pars prima. Oxford, 1787.

Vajda, Georges. *Le Dictionnaire des Authorités (Mu'jam aš-Šuyūḫ) de 'Abd al-Mu'min ad-Dimyāṭī.* Paris: Centre National de la Recherche Scientifique, 1962.

——. "La mašyaḫa de 'Abd al-Qādir al-Yūnīnī," *JA* 259 (1971): 223-46.

——. "al-Dimyāṭī," *EI²*.

Wensinck, A. J., et al., eds. *Concordance et indices de la tradition musulmane.* 8 vols. Leiden: E. J. Brill, 1933-88.

——. "Ḳunūt," *EI²*.

Wiet, G. "al-'Abbāsa," *EI²*.

Wüstenfeld, Heinrich Ferdinand. *Die Geschichtsschreiber der Araber und ihre Werke.* [Berlin], 1882.

Wulzinger, Karl and Carl Watzinger. *Damaskus: die islamische Stadt.* Berlin and Leipzig: W. de Gruyter, 1924.

al-Yāfi'ī, 'Abd Allāh. *Mir'āt al-janān wa-'ibrat al-yaqẓān fī ma'rifat ḥawādith al-zamān.* Hyderabad: Maṭba'at Dā'irat al-Ma'ārif, 1339/1920-21.

Yāqūt, *Mu'jam al-buldān.* Beirut: Dār Ṣādir, A.H. 1399.

Young, M. J. L. "Arabic biographical writing," *CHAL, Religion, Learning and Science in the 'Abbasid Period*, pp. 168-87. Ed. M. J. L. Young, et al. Cambridge University Press, 1990.

Zambaur, Eduard von. *Manuel de généalogie et de chronologie pour l'histoire de l'Islam.* Hanover: H. Lafaire, 1927.

Zetterstéen, K. V., ed. *Beiträge zur Geschichte der Mamlūkensultane in den Jahren 690-741 der Hiǧra nach arabischen Handschriften.* Leiden: E. J. Brill, 1919.

Ziadeh, Nicola A. *Urban Life in Syria under the Early Mamluks.* Beirut: The American University Press, 1953.

——. *Damascus under the Mamluks.* Norman, Oklahoma: University of Oklahoma Press, 1964.

al-Ziriklī, Khayr al-Dīn. *al-A'lām.* 2d revised ed. 11 vols. Cairo, 1954-59.

INDEX

al-'Abbāsa, 193
'Abbasid, 91, 107, 192, 201
'Abd Allāh, amīr, 116, 123
'Abd Allāh, Zayn al-Dīn, 47
'Abd Allāh al-Anṣārī, Muwaffaq al-Dīn, 69, 87
'Abd Allāh al-Baṭā'iḥī, ṣūfī, 15
'Abd Allāh, Ibn Maḥbūb, Bahā' al-Dīn, 71
'Abd Allāh ibn Marwān al-Fāriqī, Zayn al-Dīn, 135
'Abd Allāh ibn Muḥammad al-Sinjārī, traveler, 44
'Abd Allāh al-Sa'dī, Muḥyī al-Dīn, 89
'Abd Allāh al-Yūnīnī, Ḥanbalī master, 7
'Abd al-'Azīz ibn 'Abd al-Salām, ḥadīth scholar, 11, 72
'Abd al-'Azīz al-Anṣārī, Sharaf al-Dīn, 68
'Abd al-'Azīz ibn Muḥammad ibn 'Abd al-Muḥsin, ḥadīth scholar, 9
'Abd al-'Azīz, 'Imād al-Dīn, 169
'Abd al-'Azīz, Ibn Waddā'a, 'Izz al-Dīn, amīr, 72
'Abd al-Ghanī, muezzin, 130, 144, 145, 160
'Abd al-Ghanī al-Jazarī, poet, 150
'Abd al-Karīm ibn Muḥammad al-Ḥamawī, Sharaf al-Dīn, 50
'Abd al-Majīd, Ibn Abī al-Faraj al-Rūdhrāwī, 91
'Abd al-Qādir ibn 'Alī al-Yūnīnī, al-Yūnīnī's nephew, 16
'Abd al-Qādir al-Jīlānī (al-Kīlānī, al-Jīlī), ṣūfī, 15, 19
'Abd al-Raḥmān, Ṣadr al-Dīn, qāḍī, 69
'Abd al-Raḥmān, Zayn al-Dīn, the brother of Ibn Taymīya, 46, 77
'Abd al-Raḥmān al-Fazārī, Tāj al-Dīn, 67
'Abd al-Raḥmān ibn Muḥammad al-Ba'labakkī al-Yūnīnī, 70
'Abd al-Raḥmān ibn Yaḥyā, Ibn al-Zakī, Kamāl al-Dīn, 99, 100
'Abd al-Raḥmān ibn Yūsuf, Fakhr al-Dīn, 71
'Abd al-Ṣamad, Zayn al-Dīn, known as Ibn 'Asākir al-Dimashqī, 69
'Abd al-Sayyid ibn al-Muhaddab, Jewish judge, 206, 207
Ablaq Palace, Damascus, 118, 159
Abū 'Abd Allāh al-Ḥasan, 27
Abū Bakr Ibn Makārim, ḥadīth scholar, 9
Abū Bakr al-Raqqī, Raḍī al-Dīn, 171
Abū Bakr al-Ṣarṣarī, Taqī al-Dīn, 13
Abū al-Bayān al-Bannā', Shams al-Dīn, *amīr-jānidār,* 75
Abū Ḥayyān, Muḥammad ibn Yūsuf al-Gharnaṭī, Athīr al-Dīn, 48, 58, 74, 75
Abū Muḥammad Ibn Abī Ḥamza, 49
Abū al-Muẓaffar, Shams al-Dīn, 66
Abū Nuwās, poet, 90
Abū al-Qāsim Ibn al-Layth, 27
Abū al-Qāsim Ibn Manṣūr, 13
Abū Shāma, historian, 15, 20, 61, 62, 80, 85, 86
Abū Ṭālib ibn Aḥmad al-Yūnīnī, 70
adab, 31, 35, 67, 82, 87, 89, 90, 91, 92, 96
adab al-kātib, 93
'Adhrāwīya (or 'Adhrā'īya) Madrasa, Damascus, 171
'Ādilīya Madrasa, Damascus, 145, 146, 148, 152, 154, 155, 156
al-Afram, 'Izz al-Dīn, amīr, 75
Aḥmad, Abū al-'Abbās, al-Jazarī's(?) brother, 45
Aḥmad ibn 'Abd al-Dā'im al-Ḥanbalī, 9
Aḥmad ibn 'Abd al-Malik al-A'zāzī, Shihāb al-Dīn, poet, 201
Aḥmad ibn 'Abd al-Raḥmān, Najm al-Dīn, qāḍī al-quḍāt, 71
Aḥmad ibn 'Abd al-Raḥmān al-Maqdisī,

Shihāb al-Dīn, 50
Aḥmad 'Abd al-Wahhāb, scribe, 28
Aḥmad ibn Aḥmad al-Maqdisī al-Shāfi'ī, Sharaf al-Dīn, 47
Aḥmad, Ibn As'ad, 70
Aḥmad, Ibn Athīr, Tāj al-Dīn, 64
Aḥmad, Ibn 'Aṭṭār, Kamāl al-Dīn, 64
Aḥmad al-Baqaqī al-Ḥamawī, Fatḥ al-Dīn, 200, 201
Aḥmad ibn al-Ḥasan al-Rāzī, Jalāl al-Dīn, qāḍī, 49, 97, 128, 136, 145, 171, 204, 215
Aḥmad ibn Ibrāhīm al-Fazārī, Sharaf al-Dīn, 171
Aḥmad ibn Ibrāhīm al-Sarūjī, Shams al-Dīn, qāḍī, 129
Aḥmad ibn al-'Imād al-Qaṣṣāṣ, Shihāb al-Dīn, 120
Aḥmad ibn Isḥāq al-Ḥamdānī al-Abraqūhī, Shihāb al-Dīn, 55
Aḥmad ibn Ma'īn al-Dīn al-Jazarī, Shihāb al-Dīn, 131
Aḥmad ibn Muḥammad, Nāṣir al-Dīn, qāḍī, 92
Aḥmad ibn Muḥammad al-Iṣbahānī, 79
Aḥmad ibn Muḥammad al-'Uqaylī, Shihāb al-Dīn, amīr, 50
Aḥmad, Ibn Muyassar al-Miṣrī, 'Izz al-Dīn, 206, 216
Aḥmad, Ibn al-Raf'a al-Anṣārī, Najm al-Dīn, qāḍī, 179, 180
Aḥmad, Ibn al-Shīrajī(?), see Ibn al-Shīrazī
Aḥmad Ibn Ṭūlūn, see Ibn Ṭūlūn
Aḥmad ibn 'Uthmān, Shihāb al-Dīn, 50
Aḥmad ibn Yaḥyā, Shams al-Dīn, 9
Akhḍar Square, Damascus, 14, 108, 109, 118, 123, 142, 169
Akhū-Ṣārūjā, 104
al-Akram, Ibn Laqlaq, 169
'Alā' al-Dīn, *ustādh-dār*, 150, 161, 175
'Alam al-Dīn Sanjar al-Dawādārī (or al-Duwaydārī), amīr, 48, 64, 69, 101, 102
al-Albakī (Albakī, Bakī, Ilbakī), amīr, 110, 111, 112, 121, 167, 214
Albistān, 62
Aleppo, 2, 13, 46, 62, 65, 101, 103, 104, 110, 112, 118, 121, 122, 123, 129, 130, 131, 144, 167, 168, 176, 180, 206, 214
Alexandria, Egypt, 13, 55, 65, 92, 108, 173, 178, 199
Algeria, 177
Algiers, 173
'Alī, 'Alā' al-Dīn, 13
'Alī ibn 'Abd Allāh al-Shādhilī, Nūr al-Dīn, Abū al-Ḥasan, 67-68
'Alī ibn 'Abd al-Ghanī, Ibn Taymīya al-Ḥarrānī, 'Alā' al-Dīn, 55
'Alī ibn Abī Bakr al-Yūnīnī, 70
'Alī ibn Aḥmad al-Ḥusayn al-'Irāqī, Tāj al-Dīn, 56
'Alī al-'Āmilī, Sayf al-Dīn, 190, 198
'Alī, Ibn Ghānim, 'Alā' al-Dīn, 71
'Alī ibn Muḥammad, head of 'Alids, 171
'Alī ibn Muḥammad al-Dimashqī, Kamāl al-Dīn, 44
'Alī ibn Muḥammad al-Yūnīnī, Sharaf al-Dīn, al-Yūnīnī's brother, 8, 9, 10, 14, 15, 16, 33, 68, 70, 78, 79, 85
'Alī, Ibn Qarqīn, Naṣr al-Dīn, 71
'Alī ibn Shams al-Dīn ibn Abī 'Umar al-Ḥanbalī, 172
'Alī ibn Sharaf al-Dīn, Ibn al-Qalānisī, 'Alā' al-Dīn, 204, 205
'Alī Zayn al-'Ābidīn Mashhad, Damascus, 128, 135
'Alids, 71, 142, 164, 171
Amat al-'Azīz bint 'Alī, al-Yūnīnī's niece, 16
al-Amharī, king of Ethiopia, 189, 190, 191
Āmid, 122
Amīn al-Mulk, *mustawfī al-ṣuḥba*, 178
Amīnīya Madrasa, Damascus, 168
'Āmir ibn Yaḥyā, 72
Anas, Sayf al-Dīn, amīr, 180
Anatolia (*Bilād al-Rūm*), 120, 121, 122
Anatolian(s), 122
Andalusia, 173
Antioch, 10, 176
'Aqaba, 185
'Aqabat Dummar, 164
Aqjubā, Sayf al-Dīn, amīr, 124, 125, 168, 175, 199, 215
Āqqūsh al-Afram, Jamāl al-Dīn al-

Maṭrūḥī, amīr, 53, 103, 107, 112, 115, 119, 122, 160, 167, 170, 214
Āqqūsh al-Ashrafī, Jamāl al Dīn, amīr, viceroy of Kerak, 105, 214
Āqqūsh al-Najībī al-Ṣāliḥī, Jamāl al-Dīn, 175
Aquarius, 123
'Arafāt, Mt., Mecca, 131
Ardabīl (al-Armal, al-Armil?), 205
al-Ardawā', 147
Arjuwāsh, 'Alam al-Dīn, amīr, 108, 117, 124, 136, 142, 143, 144, 148, 149, 163, 165, 169
Armenia, see Cilicia
Armenian(s), 139, 176, 195
Artuqī dynasty, 121
Asad al-Dīn ibn 'Izz al-Dīn al-Afram, amīr, 185
Asad al-Dīn Public Bath, Damascus, 156
Asadīya Mosque, Damascus, 172
al-A'sar, see Sunqur al-A'sar
al-Ashkurī (Laskaris), 102
Ashrafī Mamluks, 98, 103, 104
Ashrafīya Dār al-Ḥadīth, Damascus, 47, 135, 143, 151, 152, 160, 172
Asia Minor, 120
Aṣīl al-Dīn ibn Naṣīr al-Dīn al-Ṭūsī, 158
'Asqalān (Ascalon), 132
'aṣr, a kind of torture, 150, 193
Assassins, 1, 65
Ātish al-'Izzī, Ḥusām al-Dīn, 72
Ayāz, Fakhr al-Dīn, 71
Aybak, 'Izz al-Dīn, *khazindār*, 116, 205
Aybak al-Baghdādī, al-Manṣūrī, 'Izz al-Dīn, vizier, 192, 193, 213
Aybak al-Ḥamawī, 'Izz al-Dīn, amīr, 104
Aybak al-Iskandarī al-Ṣāliḥī, 'Izz al-Dīn, amīr, al-Yūnīnī's son-in-law, 12
Aybak al-Mawṣilī, 'Izz al-Dīn, amīr, veceroy of Tripoli, 214
Aybak al-Mu'aẓẓamī, 'Izz al-Dīn, amīr, the ruler of al-Ṣarkhad, 49, 72
Aybak al-Najībī, 'Izz al-Dīn, 168, 216
Aybak al-Ṭawīl al-Manṣūrī, 'Izz al-Dīn, amīr, 107, 109, 131
Aydak ibn 'Abd Allāh al-Ṣāliḥī, 'Alā' al-Dīn, amīr, 72
Aydakīn al-Ṣāliḥī, see Aydak ibn 'Abd Allāh al-Ṣāliḥī
Aydamur al-Janājī, 'Izz al-Dīn, amīr, 129, 130, 131
Aydamur al-Mujīrī, Ḥusām al-Dīn, amīr, 194
Aydughdī, author of *Mu'jam*, 16
Aydughdī Shuqayr, Jamāl al-Dīn, amīr, 111, 112
Ayla, 185; also see 'Aqaba
'Ayn Jālūt, 22
al-'Aynī, historian, 78, 82
al-'Ayntābī, Shams al-Dīn, amīr, 131
Aytāmish, Shams al-Dīn, 187
Ayyūb, Bahā' al-Dīn, 124, 125
Ayyūb, Najm al-Dīn, 201
Ayyubid(s), 1, 4, 8, 57, 60, 61, 62, 192, 214
al-A'zāzī, Fakhr al-Dīn, amīr, 52, 131
Azdamur, 'Izz al-Dīn, amīr, 49
'Azīzīya Madrasa, Damascus, 144
'Azzāz al-Tatarī, amīr, 111, 112

Bāb al-Barīd (the Post Gate), Damascus, 151, 153, 155, 156
Bāb Saṭḥā, Damascus, 15
Bāb al-Ṣaghīr, see Ṣaghīr Gate
Bāb al-Sirr (the Postern Gate), 52, 99, 119, 124
Bādharā'īya Madrasa, Damascus, 137, 138
Baghdad, 10, 19, 65, 86, 87, 113, 121, 122
al-Baghdādī, Najm al-Dīn, 134
Bahā' al-Dīn, author, 189
Bahā' al-Dīn al-Fā'izī, 11, 12, 13, 72
Bahādur Āṣ, Sayf al-Dīn, amīr, 160, 206
Bahādur al-Sinjārī, Sayf al-Dīn, amīr, 199
Bāhasnā (Behesdin), 122, 199
Baḥrī (Mamluks), 1, 106, 108, 168
Baidu, Hülegü's grandson, 45, 46
al-Bājarīqī, Jamāl al-Dīn, 171
Bakhtiyah Khān, 191
Baktāsh, Badr al-Dīn, amīr, 115, 116, 167, 205
Baktimur, Sayf al-Dīn, amīr, 52, 103,

110, 111, 112, 116, 142, 167, 176, 185, 198
Baktūt ibn 'Abd Allāh, Sayf al-Dīn, amīr, 72
Ba'labakk, 6, 7, 8, 9, 10, 11, 12, 13, 14, 15, 18, 19, 30, 35, 54, 64, 68, 69, 70, 71, 72, 78, 79, 86, 134, 164, 170
Balabān al-Ṭabbākhī, Sayf al-Dīn, amīr, 110, 111, 118, 168, 214
Balqāq, Sayf al-Dīn, 110, 111, 117, 118
Bānyās (Belinas), 125
Baradā river, 105, 109, 156
Bārīn, 55, 191, 205
al-Bārizī, Rukn al-Dīn, 124
Baybars, al-Malik al-Ẓāhir, sultan, 11, 62, 63, 100, 102, 103, 129
Baybars al-Jāshankīr (Baybars II), Rukn al-Dīn, amīr, 116, 167, 177, 178, 186, 193, 199, 202, 206
Baybars al-Manṣūrī, historian, 5, 93, 133
Baydarā, Bahā' al-Dīn, amīr, 193
Bayna al-Qaṣrayn, Cairo, 200
Baysarī, Badr al-Dīn, amīr, 50, 53, 100, 104
Bayt Lihyā, 170
beer, 50, 104, 105
Beirut, 126, 127
Berke (Baraka), 127
Bijāya (Bougie), 173
Bilād al-Shām, see Syria
Bilād al-Rūm, see Anatolia
Bilbays, 115, 169
al-Biqā', 137, 164
al-Biqā'ī, Ibrāhīm, historian, 150
Bi'r Zamzam, 47
al-Bīra, 111, 120, 131, 172, 214
al-Birka, 185, 193, 198
al-Birzālī, al-Qāsim, 'Alam al-Dīn, 8, 9, 14, 18, 22, 41, 44, 45, 46, 47, 55, 75, 76, 77, 78, 79, 80, 81, 82, 84, 85, 86, 94, 100, 157
Bohemond VI, 10
Budda 'Arsh, 175, 176
al-Buhūt (al-Bahūt), Egypt, 25
al-Buhūtī, Muḥammad, scribe, 25, 26
al-Bukhārī, Fakhr al-Dīn, 8, 125
Būlāhim (Būlāy), Mongol general, 112, 113, 121, 122, 163, 164, 199
Bulghār (Bolghari), 191
Burj al-Ḥamām, 117
Burjī regiment, 113, 114, 116, 185, 192, 199
Buṣrā, suburb of Damascus, 207
Buzlār, amīr, 111, 112
Byzantine, 103, 126

Cairo, 2, 11, 12, 13, 45, 46, 47, 48, 50, 52, 53, 55, 56, 58, 59, 63, 72, 74, 75, 86, 87, 92, 93, 94, 95, 97, 98, 100, 101, 103, 108, 109, 110, 115, 117, 118, 119, 123, 126, 128, 129, 166, 169, 175, 176, 177, 178, 179, 180, 181, 184, 185, 186, 187, 191, 192, 193, 194, 196, 198, 199, 200, 201, 202, 203, 205, 207, 213
Cambay (Kanbāya), 187, 188
Caspian, 205
Cave (*al-Kahf*), 145
Christian(s), 87, 141, 176, 177, 178, 179, 195, 196
Cilicia (Armenia), 101, 102, 103, 115, 121, 122, 126, 156, 158, 176, 207
Circassian, 167, 172
Citadel, (Cairo) 113, 114, 115, 116, 119, 166, 167, 176, 181, 192, 198, 202, 203; (Damascus) 8, 43, 69, 75, 97, 99, 101, 102, 103, 108, 117, 119, 120, 124, 132, 136, 142, 143, 144, 145, 147, 148, 149, 150, 151, 153, 154, 155, 156, 157, 161, 162, 153, 155, 169, 176, 180, 199, 207
colloquial language, 82, 94, 95, 96
comet, 14, 53, 123, 193
Constantinople, 44, 102, 126, 191
Coptic, 52, 126, 128
Crusaders, 1, 4, 13, 17, 52, 61

al-Daldarmī, 170
Dam Cavern, 145
Damascus, (city) 6, 7, 8, 9, 11, 12, 13, 14, 15, 18, 22, 29, 30, 31, 36, 38, 41, 44, 45, 47, 49, 50, 52, 53, 54, 55, 59, 61, 63, 64, 68, 70, 71, 72, 73, 75, 77, 78, 81, 82, 84, 86, 87, 88, 92, 97, 98, 99, 100, 101, 102, 103, 104, 105, 107, 108, 109,

110, 111, 112, 117, 118, 119, 120, 121, 122, 123, 124, 125, 126, 127, 128, 129, 130, 131, 132, 133, 134, 135, 136, 137, 138, 139, 141, 142, 144, 145, 146, 147, 148, 151, 152, 153, 154, 156, 157, 158, 159, 160, 161, 162, 163, 164, 165, 167, 168, 169, 170, 171, 173, 174, 175, 176, 177, 179, 180, 193, 196, 199, 201, 204, 205, 206, 207, 213, 215, 216; ("Damascus diary") 38, 54, 132; (the Grand Mosque) 14, 50, 53, 99, 100, 104, 119, 123, 124, 128, 135, 138, 139, 142, 144, 148, 149, 151, 152, 153, 154, 157, 160, 161, 164, 165, 169, 171, 215; (Damascene troops) 101, 107, 111, 112, 167, 170, 205; also see Syrian army
Dammāghīya Madrasa, Damascus, 152
Dāniyāl ibn Mankalī (Menglī?) al-Turkumānī al-Karakī, Ḍiyā' al-Dīn, 49
Daqūqa (Tauk), 121
Dār al-'Adl, 120, 169, 185, 206
Dār al-Biṭṭīkh (the Fruit Market), Damascus, 161
Dār Ibn Jarrāda district, Damascus, 162
Dār al-Sa'āda, 120, 124, 152, 157
Dār al-Ṣāḥib, Damascus, 137
Dārayyā, 147
Darb al-Silsila street, Damascus, 155
Dawla'īya Madrasa, Damascus, 171
Delhi, 87, 186, 187, 188, 191
Dhabbāb (Dabbāb?) Mosque, Damascus, 162
al-Dhahabī, Shams al-Dīn, 6, 7, 8, 10, 14, 15, 16, 17, 18, 19, 20, 22, 36, 38, 42, 55, 59, 62, 78, 82, 86, 96, 132, 133, 135, 137, 138, 139, 142, 144, 145, 146, 147, 149, 151, 152, 153, 154, 157, 158, 160, 162, 165, 167, 170
Dhimmī(s), 177, 178, 179
al-Dimashqī, Yūnus, 'Imād al-Dīn, 43, 44
Dimyāṭ, Egypt, 66
al-Dimyāṭī, 'Abd Allāh al-Mu'min, Ibn Khalaf, Sharaf al-Dīn, 48, 55, 56, 57, 58, 74, 77
dīwān (anthology of poetry) 68, 90
Ḍiyā' al-Dīn (or Ḍiyā'īya) Madrasa, Damascus, 146, 160
Diyār Bakr, 121, 171
Druze, 170
Druze, Mt., 170
Dunqula, 178

earthquake, 52, 58, 75, 87, 126
Eastern Gate (*Bāb Sharqī*), Damascus, 159, 164
eclipse, moon, 201
Egypt, 9, 10, 11, 13, 19, 24, 25, 38, 51, 52, 56, 64, 66, 71, 89, 99, 91, 100, 102, 103, 104, 105, 105, 107, 109, 110, 111, 117, 119, 120, 121, 122, 123, 124, 125, 126, 128, 129, 131, 132, 134, 135, 137, 140, 142, 143, 155, 165, 166, 169, 174, 175, 179, 180, 184, 185, 192, 197, 199, 207, 213; (Egyptian historians, sources) 4, 5, 60, 64, 93, 94, 96, 104, 194, 206; (Egyptian troops) 101, 103, 106, 123, 128, 132, 133, 136, 143, 155, 162, 166, 167, 169, 175, 193, 195, 196, 205, 206, 207
Elephant Lake, Cairo, 202
erotica, 91, 95
Ethiopia (al-Ḥabash), 189, 190, 191
Euphrates, 64, 66, 87, 111, 112, 121, 122, 138, 174, 175, 178, 180, 194, 199
eunuchs (*khuddām*), 128, 185, 202
Europe, 166, 176

faḍā'il literature, 38, 56
al-Fakhrī, 'Alā' al-Dīn, amir, post master, 199
al-fallāḥūn, 106
Farādīs Gate, Damascus, 155
Faraj Allāh al-Muslimānī, Rashīd al-Dīn, nicknamed "Awḥashtanī," 109
Faraj Gate, Damascus, 152
Fāṭima bint 'Alī, al-Yūnīnī's niece, 16
Fatimid, 123, 200
Fayrūz Minaret, Damascus, 160
feudalism, 166
Fez, 173
Franks, Frankish, 66, 105, 126, 127

Gaza, 10, 124, 130, 132, 143, 175,

177, 199
Gemini, 123
Georgian(s), 139, 176, 195
Ghānim, Ibn al-'Ashīra, 71
al-Gharbīya, Egypt, 24, 25
al-Ghawr, see Jordan Valley
ghazal, 88, 89
Ghazān, Maḥmūd, 46, 52, 76, 77, 111, 112, 113, 120, 121, 122, 124, 134, 135, 138, 139, 142, 144, 145, 146, 147, 148, 149, 153, 154, 155, 158, 159, 163, 175, 176, 181, 184, 191, 192, 193, 194, 195, 196, 197, 199, 207
Ghiyāth al-Dīn, sultan of Delhi, 187
ghulāmīyāt, 89
al-Ghurafī ('Uzafī?), Shams al-Dīn ibn Sharaf al-Dīn, 100
al-Ghūṭa, 105, 142, 147, 173, 174, 207
Giza, 56
Golden Horde, 127
Grand Mosque, see Damascus

ḥadīth, 8, 9, 10, 11, 14, 15, 16, 17, 18, 41, 45, 55, 56, 60, 66, 68, 69, 71, 72, 74, 76, 77, 78, 82, 83, 84, 86, 93, 94, 95, 96, 131
Hafsid, 172, 177
Haithon, 133
Ḥākim Mosque, Cairo, 184
al-Ḥākim bi-amr-Allāh, Abū 'Abbās Aḥmad, caliph, 30, 107, 201, 202, 203, 204
al-Ḥakīmī, Aḥmad ibn al-'Alam, scribe, 208, 209, 210
ḥalqa, non-Mamluk troops, 99, 116
Hama, 9, 55, 95, 101, 104, 122, 144, 167, 176, 191, 199, 205, 214
Hamadān (Hamadhān), 113, 124
al-Ḥamawī, Muwaffaq al-Dīn, 104
Ḥamdān, Sayf al-Dīn, amīr, 107, 110, 124
Ḥamza, Ibn al-Miḥaffadār, Najm al-Dīn, amīr, 75
Ḥanafī(s), 49, 97, 100, 124, 125, 128, 128, 136, 138, 144, 145, 152, 168, 169, 171, 204, 215
al-Ḥanafī, Shihāb al-Dīn, 100, 136
Ḥanbalī(s), Hanbalism, 7, 9, 12, 13, 14, 15, 16, 19, 25, 52, 58, 70, 71, 72, 79, 86, 129, 130, 146, 151, 155, 160, 172, 215
al-ḥarāfisha, 98
Ḥārat al-Balāṭa quarter, Damascus, 155
Ḥārat al-Ghurabā', Damascus, 155
al-Ḥarīrī, his *Maqāmāt*, 56
Ḥarīrīya, ṣūfī order, 13
Ḥarrān (Hellenopolis), 56
Ḥasan ibn 'Alī, Ibn al-Ḥarīrī, 50
Ḥasan ibn 'Alī, Fakhr al-Dīn, 71
al-Ḥasan ibn Muḥammad al-Anṣārī, Najm al-Dīn, 72
Ḥasan ibn al-Naqīb al-Kīnānī, Nāṣir al-Dīn, 66
al-Ḥasan al-Rāzī, Ḥusām al-Dīn, qāḍī al-quḍāt, 49, 52, 97, 113, 114, 128, 169, 215
al-Ḥasan, Ibn Sirḥān al-Dimashqī, Najm al-Dīn, 49
Ḥasan Ibn Shāwir, known as al-Nafīsī, poet, 11, 72
al-Ḥasan ibn Yaḥyā, Sanī al-Dawla, 9
Hebron, 196
Hejaz, 153, 154, 193
Het'um II, ruler of Cilicia, 103, 126, 158
Hibat Allāh al-Fā'izī, Sharaf al-Dīn, 12
hijā', 88, 89
Ḥikr al-Sumāq, suburb of Damascus, 142
Hims, 12, 56, 101, 110, 111, 122, 133, 144, 166, 191, 199
Hindu-Ghān, 121
al-Ḥinn and al-Binn, 88, 150
Ḥiṣn al-Akrād, 11, 72, 191, 199
Historiography, 4, 5, 18, 41, 81, 82, 83, 87, 93, 96
homosexuality, homosexual love, 89, 95
Horse Market, (Aleppo) 110; (Cairo) 119; (Damascus) 64
al-Ḥubayshī(?), Sayf al-Dīn, amīr, 123
Hülegü, 10, 45, 46, 62
Ḥumaymiṣ, 102, 103
Ḥusāmī Mamluks, 98
al-Ḥusayn ibn 'Alī, 87, 123, 164, 171
Ḥusayn ibn Dāwūd al-Shahrazūrī al-Kātib, Shams al-Dīn, 46

Ibn 'Abd al-Salām, Nāṣir al-Dīn, 128, 136
Ibn 'Abd al-Ẓāhir, 63
Ibn Abī 'Alī, Ḥusām al-Dīn, amīr, 66
Ibn Abī al-Hayjā', Muḥammad, 'Izz al-Dīn, amīr, 13, 32, 73, 74
Ibn Abī al-Faraj, Zayn al-Dīn, 92
Ibn Abī al-Ṭayyib, Najm al-Dīn, 136, 177, 216
Ibn Abī Uṣaybi'a, 68
Ibn al-'Adīm, 1, 65
Ibn 'Adnān, al-Ḥusayn ibn Muḥammad, Zayn al-Dīn, sharīf, 136
Ibn 'Aqīl Tavern, Damascus, 125
Ibn 'Asākir al-Dimashqī al-Makkī, see 'Abd al-Ṣamad
Ibn al-Aṣfūnī, Najm al-Dīn, vizier, 193
Ibn al-'Assāl, 113
Ibn Athīr, 'Alī, 'Izz al-Dīn, historian, 68, 93
Ibn Athīr, Ḍiyā' al-Dīn, 67-68
Ibn al-Athīr, Sharaf al-Dīn, 205
Ibn al-'Awnī, 169, 170
Ibn Bākhil, Ḥusām al-Dīn, 107
Ibn Bayyā'a, Muḥammad, Shams al-Dīn, historian, 98, 99
Ibn al-Binardī al-Baghdādī, 160
Ibn Ḍā'in, 138, 170
Ibn Daqīq al-'Īd, see Muḥammad ibn 'Alī al Qushayrī
Ibn al-Dawādārī, Abū Bakr ibn 'Abd Allāh ibn Aybak, Sayf al-Dīn, historian, 4, 18, 69, 72, 82, 92, 93, 94, 96, 98, 99, 100, 101, 102, 104, 105, 107, 109, 110, 117, 119, 120, 121, 124, 127, 129, 132, 133, 134, 135, 137, 138, 139, 162, 167, 172, 175, 181, 184, 185, 190, 191, 194, 199, 206
Ibn al-Dhahabī al-Naqīb, 138
Ibn Faḍl Allāh, Badr al-Dīn, 143-44
Ibn Ḥabīb, 14
Ibn Ḥajar al-'Asqalānī, 15, 78
Ibn Ḥamawayh al-Juwaynī, 62
Ibn Ḥaṭlīshā al-Mizzī, 170
Ibn Hilāl, Amīn al-Dīn, 216
Ibn al-Ḥillī, Bahā' al-Dīn, 50, 105
Ibn Ḥinnī, Zayn al-Dīn, 185
Ibn Iblīs al-Sāmirī al-Muslimānī, 174, 175
Ibn Iyās, historian, 94, 96
Ibn al-Jākī, 'Alā' al-Dīn, amīr, 108, 111, 161, 215
Ibn Jamā'a, Abū 'Abd Allāh Muḥammad, Badr al-Dīn, qāḍī al-quḍāt, 71, 79, 100, 135, 139, 163, 168, 171, 177, 204, 215
Ibn Jānidār, 124
Ibn al-Jawzī, 19, 83, 86
Ibn Kalb, 69
Ibn Kathīr, 15, 36, 77, 78, 105
Ibn al-Khalīlī, Fakhr al-Dīn, vizier, 50, 185, 193, 213
Ibn Khallikān, 18, 60, 61, 52, 53, 64, 67
Ibn Laqlaq al-Mustawfī, Karīm al-Dīn al-Ṣaghīr, 129
Ibn al-Miḥaffadār, Sayf al-Dīn, amīr, 43, 45, 48, 58, 75, 85, 126
Ibn Munajjā, Wajīh al-Dīn, 136, 139, 148, 150, 155, 158
Ibn al-Mustawfī, al-Mubārak, Sharaf al-Dīn, vizier, 65
Ibn Muzhir, Fakhr al-Dīn, 200
Ibn Muzhir, Sharaf al-Dīn, 201, 204, 206, 216
Ibn al-Naḥḥās, Muḥyī al-Dīn, 124, 125
Ibn al-Naḥḥās, Shihāb al-Dīn, 104
Ibn al-Najjār al-Baghdādī, Muḥammad, Abū 'Abd Allāh, 65
Ibn al-Nakhīlī, Badr al-Dīn, 165
Ibn al-Nashshābī, 'Imād al-Dīn, amīr, 112, 118, 120, 135, 216
Ibn al-Nashshābī, Nāṣir al-Dīn, 109
Ibn al-Qalānisī, Ḥamza ibn As'ad al-Tamīmī al-Dimashqī, 'Izz al-Dīn, 14, 58, 136, 139, 144, 148, 150, 165, 169, 177
Ibn al-Qalānisī, Jamāl al-Dīn, 47
Ibn al-Quṭayna, 158
Ibn Rāfi' al-Salām, historian, 78
Ibn Rajab, 14
Ibn Rawwāj, ḥadīth teacher, 9, 10
Ibn Ṣabra, 'Izz al-Dīn, amīr, 112, 205
Ibn al-Sal'ūs, see Muḥammad ibn 'Uthmān al-Tanūkhī
Ibn Ṣārim, ḥadīth teacher, 9
Ibn Ṣaṣrā, Amīn al-Dīn, 109
Ibn Ṣaṣrā, Aḥmad, Najm al-Dīn, qāḍī,

14, 58, 67, 135, 139, 150, 177
Ibn Ṣaṣra, Muḥammad ibn Muḥammad, 96
Ibn al-Ṣayqal, see Ma'add ibn Naṣr Allāh
Ibn Shaddād, historian, 62
Ibn Shaddād, Bahā' al-Dīn, 62
Ibn Sham'ūn, Ibrāhīm al-Jazarī al-Kutubī, Shams al-Dīn, 90
Ibn al-Sharīshī, Kamāl al-Dīn, qāḍī, 204
Ibn al-Shīrajī, Sharaf al-Dīn, 136
Ibn al-Shīrajī, Sulaymān, Fakhr al-Dīn, 135, 139, 168, 216
Ibn al-Shīrāzī, Aḥmad, Tāj al-Dīn, 135, 169, 201, 204
Ibn Shuqayr al-Ḥarrānī, Amīn al-Dīn, 136, 150, 164
Ibn al-Sukkarī, 'Abd al-Raḥmān ibn 'Abd al-'Alī, 'Imād al-Dīn, 185, 194
Ibn al-Ṣu'lūk, Asad al-Dīn, 13, 72
Ibn Taghrībirdī, 13, 17, 32, 36, 82, 150
Ibn Taymīya, Taqī al-Dīn, 46, 77, 78, 129, 135, 146, 147, 148, 157, 158, 163, 164, 165, 166
Ibn al-Taytī, Shams al-Dīn, amīr, 184
Ibn Temür-Ṭāsh, Bahā' al-Dīn, amīr, 124
Ibn Ṭūlūn Mosque (Aḥmad Ibn Ṭūlūn Mosque), Cairo, 184, 202
Ibn Waddā'a, 'Alā' al-Dīn, 179
Ibn Wāṣil, Muḥammad, Jamāl al-Dīn, 31, 63, 104
Ibn Yaḥyā, amīr, 14
Ibn al-Ẓāhir, Malik al-Awḥad, 100, 112
Ibn al-Zakī, 'Izz al-Dīn, qāḍī, 104, 136
Ibn al-Zamalkānī, Muḥammad ibn 'Alī, Kamāl al-Dīn, qāḍī, 168
Ibrāhīm, muezzin of Bayt Lihyā, 170
Ibrāhīm ibn 'Abd al-'Azīz, ṣūfī, 13
Ibrāhīm ibn 'Abd al-'Azīz al-Mālikī al-Lūrī, Zakī al-Dīn, 67
Ibrāhīm ibn 'Abd al-Raḥmān al-Fazārī, Burhān al-Dīn, 67
Ibrāhīm ibn 'Alī al-Wāsiṭī al-Ḥanbalī, Taqī al-Dīn, 45
Ibrāhīm, Ibn Luqmān al-Shaybānī al-Miṣrī, Fakhr al-Dīn, 45
Ibrāhīm ibn Muḥammad ibn Ḥamawayh al-Juwaynī, Ṣadr al-Dīn, 46
Ibrāhīm, Ibn al-Naḥḥās, Jamāl al-Dīn, amīr, 120, 135, 216
Ibrāhīm ibn Sa'd Allāh, 71
'Imrān, shaykh, 12, 70
India, 187, 188, 191
Iqbālīya Madrasa, Damascus, 155
iqṭā', 92, 106, 120, 170
Iraq, 154, 164, 192
Irbil, 65
'Īsā ibn Aḥmad al-Yūnīnī, 9, 12, 14, 70
Ismā'īl, Mongol general, 138, 139, 143, 144, 159
Ismā'īlism, 65
al-istikhlāṣ, taxation, 149
al-istikhrāj, taxation, 159, 173

al-Jabal al-Aḥmar (Red Hill), Cairo, 203
Jabal Citadel, see Citadel (Cairo)
Jabal al-Muqaṭṭam, see Muqaṭṭam Mountain
Jābiya Gate, Damascus, 135, 159, 162
Jabrīl (Gabriel) Cave, 145
Jāghān, Sayf al-Dīn, amīr, 50, 52, 102, 111, 112, 117, 118, 120, 130, 131, 215
al-Jāliq, Rukn al-Dīn, amīr, 129, 130, 206
Jamāl al-Dīn al-Raḥbī al-Shāfi'ī, 107, 180
al-Jazarī, Muḥammad ibn Ibrāhīm, Shams al-Dīn, 1, 4, 13, 14, 17, 18, 20, 30, 31, 32, 33, 34, 35, 36, 37, 38, 40, 41, 42, 43, 44, 45, 46, 47, 48, 49, 50, 51, 52, 53, 54, 55, 56, 57, 58, 59, 63, 73, 74, 75, 76, 77, 78, 79, 80, 81, 82, 84, 85, 86, 89, 90, 91, 92, 93, 94, 96, 97, 98, 99, 100, 101, 102, 103, 104, 105, 107, 108, 109, 110, 112, 113, 115, 118, 120, 121, 122, 124, 125, 126, 127, 132, 135, 157, 184, 205
Jazira, Northwest Iraq, 56, 65, 154
Jerusalem, 10, 56, 153, 196

Jew(s), 138, 141, 158, 170, 177, 178, 179, 204, 206
al-jibāya, taxation, 153
Jinggiz-Khan, 157, 158, 195
Jisrayn, village, 105
Jordan Valley (*al-Ghawr*), 162, 163
Jū' Cavern, 145
Jūbān, amīr, 111

Ka'ba, 185, 196
Kabsh Palace, Cairo, 201, 202, 203
al-Kaḥḥāl, Jewish nobleman, 158
Kāmiliya Dār al-Ḥadīth, Cairo, 200
Karbalā', 163, 164
Karīm al-Dīn, head of the Sa'īd al-Su'adā' Khānqāh, 202
Kārimī merchants, 186
Kāwarkā, Sayf al-Dīn, 199
Kerak, 12, 50, 105, 107, 115, 119, 175, 214
al-Khaḍir ibn 'Abd Allāh, Sa'd al-Dīn, see Ibn Ḥamawayh al-Juwaynī
Khaḍir ibn Abī Bakr al-Mihrānī, 11, 71
Khālid ibn Yūsuf, Ibn Nūḥ, scribe, 22, 23
al-Khalīlīya Band, 102
khamrīyāt, 88
Khāṣṣa Square, Damascus, 142
Khātūn Mosque, Damascus, 172
Khātūnīya Madrasa, Damascus, 155, 158, 204
al-Khilāfī, Raḍī al-Dīn, 124
Khirbat al-Luṣūṣ, 162
khuddām, see eunuchs
Khurāsān, 164, 191
Khutan, 154
al-Khuwārizm, 191
Kikaldī, Badr al-Dīn, *ustādh-dār*, 101
Kisrawān, Mt., 170
al-Kiswa, suburb of Damascus, 101, 136, 142
Kitbughā Nūwīn, 10, 11
Kūnjak al-Khuwārizmī, Badr al-Dīn, amīr, 110, 110-111, 112, 124
Kurds, 174, 183
Kurjī, Sayf al-Dīn, amīr, 113, 114, 115, 116, 117
Kurt (or Ibn[?] Kurtayh), Sayf al-Dīn, amīr, 116, 129, 194, 214
Kurtay, Aq-Sunqur, Shams al-Dīn, 101
kutub al-bashā'ir, 61, 63

Lājīn, Ḥusām al-Dīn, sultan, 52, 63, 64, 87, 95, 97, 98, 99, 100, 102, 103, 105, 107, 108 109, 110, 111, 112, 113, 114, 116, 117, 118, 120, 193, 213
Lājīn, Ḥusām al-Dīn, *ustād-dār*, 87, 104, 108, 116, 117, 168, 216
Lead Dome(?), 56
literature, literary work, 34, 38, 66, 67, 76, 83, 84, 87, 96; also see *adab*
Lu'lu' ibn 'Abd Allāh, Ḥusām al-Dīn, 71

Ma'aḍḍ ibn Naṣr Allāh, Shams al-Dīn, known as Ibn al-Ṣayqal al-Jazarī, 56
madīḥ, 87, 88, 94
Maghārat al-Dam, see Dam Cavern
Maghārat al-Jū', see Jū' Cavern
Maghrib, 135, 172
maḥmil, 185, 198
Maḥmūd ibn 'Alī al-Shaybānī, Niẓām al-Dīn, shaykh al-mashā'ikh, 144, 145, 146, 147, 148, 149, 158
Maḥmūd al-Kātib, Shihāb al-Dīn, 63, 64
Maḥmūd ibn Zankī, Nūr al-Dīn, sultan, 146
al-Majd al-Fakhr Mūsā, 171
al-Malik al-'Ādil, Kitbughā, Zayn al-Dīn, sultan, 99, 168, 214
al-Malik al-Ashraf, Ayyubid prince, 8, 15
al-Malik al-Ashraf, Khālid ibn Qalāwūn, 63
al-Malik al-Ashraf, Khalīl ibn Qalāwūn, sultan, 45, 75, 98, 101, 103, 104, 129, 193
Malik Ghiyāth al-Dīn, the sultan of Delhi, 87
al-Malik al-Kāmil, Ayyubid prince, 8
al-Malik al-Manṣūr, see Lājīn
al-Malik al-Manṣūr, see Qalāwūn
al-Malik al-Manṣūr, 'Alī ibn al-Malik al-Mu'izz, 13
al-Malik al-Manṣūr, Ghāzī ibn al-Alpī Qarā-Arslān ibn Ilghāzī, Najm al-

Dīn, ruler of Mārdīn, 121
al-Malik al-Manṣūr, Maḥmūd, 13
al-Malik al-Mas'ūd, Khiḍr ibn Baybars, Najm al-Dīn, 102, 107
al-Malik al-Mas'ūd, Maḥmūd ibn Muḥammad, Ibn Sanjār, Nāṣir al-Dīn, 187, 188
al-Malik al-Mu'ayyad, Dāwūd ibn Yūsuf ibn 'Umar ibn 'Alī ibn Rasūl, Hizabr al-Dīn, 190
al-Malik al-Mu'izz, al-Mu'izz Aybak al-Turkumānī, 13
al-Malik al-Muẓaffar, Quṭuz, 32
al-Malik al-Muẓaffar, Taqī al-Dīn Maḥmūd ibn Maḥmūd ibn Shādhī ibn Ayyūb, 53, 101, 214
al-Malik al-Nāṣir, Muḥammad ibn Qalāwūn, sultan, 50, 87, 105, 115, 116, 117, 118, 119, 121, 126, 128, 132, 133, 134, 143, 165, 166, 167, 175, 176, 177, 178, 181, 184, 186, 191, 193, 194, 198, 199, 202, 203, 305, 213
al-Malik al-Nāṣir, Ṣalāḥ al-Dīn Yūsuf, 87
al-Malik al-Sa'd, Dāwūd Ilghāzī, Shams al-Dīn, 45
al-Malik al-Ṣāliḥ, 'Alī ibn Qalāwūn, 129
al-Malik al-Ṣāliḥ, Ismā'īl Ayyūb, 8, 72, 115
al-Malik al-Ẓāhir, see Baybars
Mālikī(s), 11, 13, 67, 108, 135, 200, 215
Mamluk(s), 1, 4, 11, 12, 34, 58, 60, 61, 69, 72, 73, 88, 89, 94, 102, 106, 113, 116, 117, 119, 120, 121, 122, 123, 127, 133, 134, 136, 137, 162, 168, 170, 181, 199, 202, 216; (military campaigns) 64, 72, 75, 87, 88, 92, 101, 102, 103, 115, 205, 207; (politics) 75, 92; (sultanate) 49, 52, 98, 134, 166, 192, 213
Mandūh, 169
Manṣūr ibn Sālim, 65
Manṣūrī Mamluks, 98, 104, 115, 117
Manzilat Tall al-'Ujūl, 132
maqāmā pl. *maqāmāt*, 38, 56, 91
al-Maqrīzī, 36, 102, 103, 104, 105, 106
Mar'ash (Marash), 102, 103
Mārdīn, 45, 111, 112, 121, 182, 183, 184, 194, 195
Māridānīya Madrasa, Damascus, 145
al-Māristān (hospital), 145, 172
Marj Rāhiṭ, 109, 138, 139, 167, 168
market, 105, 118, 159, 170, 176; also see *sūq*
al-Marqab, 64, 87
Marrākush, 173
al-Mawṣilī, 'Izz al-Dīn, 110
Mayin, 205
Ma'zīya (Mu'izzīya?) Madrasa, Damascus, 171
Mecca, 10, 11, 12, 53, 69, 71, 72, 73, 110, 131, 132, 185, 196, 198
Medina, 12, 61, 69, 77, 87, 110, 185, 198
Mediterranean, 173
Mengü-Temür, ruler of al-Khuwārizm, 191
Mengü-Temür, Sayf al-Dīn, amīr, 98, 102, 104, 106, 114, 115, 117, 213
Mengü-Temürīya regiment, 187
Michael IX Palaiologos, 126
al-Mizza, 51, 147, 164
Mongol(s), 1, 4, 10, 12, 13, 19, 38, 46, 54, 55, 61, 64, 66, 77, 87, 88, 107, 108, 111, 112, 113, 120, 121, 122, 123, 124, 125, 129, 132, 133, 134, 137, 138, 139, 142, 143, 144, 145, 146, 147, 148, 149, 150, 151, 152, 153, 154, 155, 156, 157, 158, 159, 161, 162, 163, 164, 165, 166, 168, 169, 170, 174, 175, 176, 177, 180, 181, 184, 186, 187, 191, 194, 204, 207, 215, 216
Mosul, 111, 113, 154, 181, 184
Mu'aẓẓamīya Madrasa, 50, 100
al-Mubārak ibn Abī Bakr Ibn Ḥamdān, 68
al-Mubārak al-Ghassān al-Ḥimṣī, Mukhliṣ al-Dīn, 69
al-Mubāriz, *amīr-shikār*, 123
Mughalṭāy, Ḥusām al-Dīn, amīr, 185
Mughalṭāy al-Dimashqī, Sayf al-Dīn, amīr, 119
Muḥammad, the Prophet, 7, 8, 17, 87, 88, 94, 95, 123, 134, 140, 153, 158, 163, 166, 183, 185, 197, 198,

200, 204
Muḥammad, Abū ʻAbd Allāh, 189, 190
Muḥammad, Mongol general, 139
Muḥammad, Zakī al-Dīn, qāḍī, 69
Muḥammad ibn ʻAbbās al-Rabīʻ al-Dunayṣarī, 70
Muḥammad ibn ʻAbd Allāh, Fatḥ Allāh, 43
Muḥammad ibn ʻAbd al-Raḥmān, physician, 71
Muḥammad ibn ʻAbd al-Razzāq, 13
Muḥammad ibn ʻAbd al-Wāḥid al-Maqdisī, Ḍiyā' al-Dīn, 71, 160
Muḥammad ibn Abī Bakr al-Fārisī, Shams al-Dīn, 50
Muḥammad ibn Abī Bakr ibn Zakarīyā Yaḥyā ibn Muḥammad ibn Abī Ḥafṣ, Abū ʻAbd Allāh, 172, 173
Muḥammad, Ibn Abī al-Hayjā', see Ibn Abī al-Hayjā'
Muḥammad ibn Abī Saʻd ibn Rājiḥ Ibn Qatāda al-Ḥasanī, Najm al-Dīn Numayya, amīr, 132
Muḥammad ibn Aḥmad, Majd al-Dīn, 12, 71
Muḥammad ibn Aḥmad, Zayn al-Dīn, 53
Muḥammad ibn Aḥmad al-Anṣārī, scribe, 209
Muḥammad ibn Aḥmad, Ibn Manẓūr, ṣūfī, 12
Muḥammad ibn Aḥmad al-Yūnīnī, Taqī al-Dīn, al-Yūnīnī's father, 7, 8, 9, 12, 15, 30, 33, 44, 58, 68, 69, 70, 71, 79
Muḥammad ibn ʻAlī, 71
Muḥammad ibn ʻAlī, Ibn al-Mundhir al-Ḥalabī, ʻImād al-Dīn, 105
Muḥammad ibn ʻAlī al-Qushayrī, Taqī al-Dīn, qāḍī al-quḍāt, known as Ibn Daqīq al-ʻĪd, 55, 179, 180, 200, 202, 203, 204
Muḥammad ibn ʻAlī al-Shāfiʻī, scribe, 209
Muḥammad ibn ʻAlī al-Yūnīnī, al-Yūnīnī's nephew, 16
Muḥammad, Ibn al-ʻĀlima, Shihāb al-Dīn, 70
Muḥammad ibn ʻAqīl Ibn Abī al-Ḥasan al-Bālisī, Najm al-Dīn, 180
Muḥammad ibn Bahā' al-Dīn ibn Muḥammad, Ḍiyā' al-Dīn, qāḍī of Mosul, 181, 183, 197
Muḥammad al-Baʻlabakkī, Shams al-Dīn, 69, 77
Muḥammad al-Ḥanafī, scribe, 25
Muḥammad, Ibn Ḥāzim al-Maqdisī, 49
Muḥammad ibn Ibrāhīm, see Ibn Jamāʻa
Muḥammad ibn ʻImād al-Ḥamawī, Jamāl al-Dīn, 50
Muḥammad ibn Khālid, Shams al-Dīn, 71
Muḥammad al-Maghribī, 127
Muḥammad Muḥammad al-Khawājah, scribe, 28
Muḥammad ibn Muḥammad ʻAlī al-Anṣārī, scribe, 22
Muḥammad ibn Muḥammad, Ibn al-Tibnī, Fakhr al-Dīn, 46
Muḥammad ibn Mūsā al-Maqdisī, 66
Muḥammad ibn Mūsā al-Yūnīnī, al-Yūnīnī's son, 15
Muḥammad, Ibn Qawām al-Nābulusī, 136
Muḥammad ibn Riḍwān, 70
Muḥammad ibn Ṣafī al-Dīn, Ibn al-Ḥarīrī, Shams al-Dīn, qāḍī, 136, 168, 177, 204, 215, 216
Muḥammad al-Shaykhī, Nāṣir al-Dīn, mayor of Cairo, 107, 201
Muḥammad, Ibn Siwār al Shaybānī, Najm al-Dīn, 69
Muḥammad, Ibn Sulaymān al-Zawāwī, Jamāl al-Dīn, qāḍī al-quḍāt, 108, 135, 215
Muḥammad ibn ʻUthmān al-Tanūkhī, known as Ibn al-Salʻūs, vizier, 46, 169, 193
Muḥammad ibn Yūsuf al-Jazarī, Shams al-Dīn, 184
Muhannā ibn ʻĪsā, Ibn Muhannā, Ḥusām al-Dīn, amīr, 107, 109
Muḥibb al-Dīn ibn Taqī al-Dīn Ibn Daqīq al-ʻĪd, 203
al-Mujāhid, muezzin, 139
mukātabāt, 60, 63
al-Munaybiʻ, 158
Muqaṭṭam Mountain, Cairo, 56
Murshid al-Khādim, amīr and eunuch,

185
Mūsā ibn Ibrāhīm al-Sharqāwī, Najm al-Dīn, 70
al-Musallim ibn Muḥammad al-Dimashqī, ḥadīth scholar, 10
al-Muwaffaqī, Rukn al-Dīn, amīr, 199
Muẓaffar ibn Sanī al-Dawla, 'Imād al-Dīn, 70-71

al-Nabk, village, 138
Nafīsa, the tomb of Lady, 202
Najīb Khānqāh, 123
Nakhiya, amīr, 52
al-nās (Mamluks), 119
Nāṣir Ribāṭ, Damascus, 172
Nāṣirīya Madrasa, Damascus, 145, 172, 204
Naṣr Allāh, Jamāl al-Dīn, 71
Nasr Copula, Grand Mosque of Damascus, 123, 139, 144
Naṣr Gate, Damscus, 124, 155, 165
al-Nastarāwa, Egypt, 24
al-Nastarāwī, Muḥammad ibn Muḥammad Maḥlūsī al-Qurashī, scribe, 23-24, 25, 210
Naẓẓāfīn Gate, Damascus, 138
Nile, 50, 107, 128, 172, 186, 190, 192, 206
Niẓām al-Mulk, head of the 'Alids, 171
Nizārī, 65
North Africa, 67
Nubia, 178
Nughiyah (Nogai), the ruler of the Golden Horde, 127, 191
Nughiyah (Nogay, Nogai) al-Karmūnī, 113, 114, 116
Nujayma(?), Cilicia, 103
Nukiyah (Nukay, Nogai), Sayf al-Dīn, 129
Nūr al-Dīn Madrasa, Damascus, 125
Nūrī hospital, Damascus(?), 207
Nūrīya Dār al-Ḥadīth, Damascus, 156, 160
Nūrīya Madrasa, Damascus, 151, 152, 155
al-Nuwayrī, historian, 5, 82, 93, 98, 100, 101, 102, 103

Oriat Mongols, 132

Palestine, 153
Persia, 153, 154, 205
Persian(s), 124, 125, 181
pilgrim, pilgrimage, 11, 12, 47, 52, 71, 72, 73, 103, 107, 109, 131, 132, 161, 177, 185, 196, 198, 205
poet(s), 9, 13, 67, 68, 69, 71, 72, 89, 90, 93, 94
poem, poetry, 7, 9, 30, 31, 34, 35, 38, 43, 44, 45, 47, 48, 49, 51, 57, 58, 61, 64, 66, 68, 69, 71, 73, 74, 76, 77, 82, 84, 85, 87, 88, 89, 90, 91, 92, 93, 94, 96, 98, 99, 150, 201
Post Gate, see Bāb al-Barīd
Postern Gate, see Bāb al-Sirr
price, 12, 50, 105, 133, 136, 137, 160, 166, 177
Pyramid, 56

Qābūn road, suburb of Damascus, 138
Qal'at al-Rūm, 87, 121
Qalāwūn, al-Malik al-Manṣūr, sultan, 12, 52, 61, 63, 64, 72, 98, 103, 105, 109, 117, 129, 193
Qarā-Arslān, Sayf al-Dīn (Bahā' al-Dīn?), amīr, 117, 118
Qarā-Qūsh, Bahā' al-Dīn, amīr, 185
Qarā-Sunqur al-Manṣūrī, Shmas al-Dīn, amīr, 97, 125, 167, 214
al-Qarāfa, Cairo, 202
Qarmanlis, 121
qaṣīda, 68, 88
al-Qāsim ibn Aḥmad al-Andalusī, 'Alam al-Dīn, poet, 80
Qaṣr Ḥajjāj, suburb of Damascus, 142
Qāsiyūn, Mt., 100, 130, 145, 154, 172
Qattāl al-Sab', Mongol general, 123
Qaymarīya (Madrasa?), Damascus, 142
Qaymāzīya Madrasa, Damascus, 152
al-Qazwīnī, Imām al-Dīn, see 'Umar ibn 'Abd al-Raḥmān
al-Qazwīnī, Jalāl al-Dīn, 168
Qibjāq, Sayf al-Dīn, amīr, 52,, 99, 107, 108, 110, 111, 112, 113, 117, 118, 121, 122, 124, 129, 135, 142, 143, 144, 145, 146, 147, 150, 154, 155, 157, 159, 160, 161, 162, 163, 164, 165, 167, 191, 214

al-Qifjāq, 191
Qulayjiya Madrasa, Damascus, 125
al-Qummī, sharīf, 137, 143, 157, 169
al-Qūnawī, Wajīh al-Dīn, 171
Quṭb al-Dīn, sharīf, Ghāzān's treasurer, 158
Quṭlū, Sayf al-Dīn, amīr, 52
Quṭlū-Bek, Sayf al-Dīn, amīr, 118, 120, 129, 167, 199, 206, 214, 215
Quṭlū-Shāh, Bahā' al-Dīn, Mongol general, 77, 133, 153, 154, 156, 157, 158, 159

Rab' compound, Damascus, 155
Rafidites, 17
al-Raḥba, 12, 121, 125
Rāhiṭ Hill, 147
al-Raml, 155
Ra's al-'Ayn, 111, 112, 121
Rashīd al-Dawla, 158
Rashīd al-Dīn al-'Aṭṭār, ḥadīth teacher, 9
Rashīd al-Dīn Faḍl Allāh Hamadānī, 147
Rāshid al-Dīn Sinān, 1, 65
Rashīd al-Dīn al-Ṭabīb, 158
Raṣīf [Gate], Damascus, 153
Rasūlid dynasty in Yemen, 190
Rawāḥiya (Rūḥāniya) Madrasa, Damascus, 138
al-rawk, 50, 106
Red Hill, see al-Jabal al-Aḥmar
Red Sea, 153, 185
rijāl literature, 67, 79, 96
Rita, the sister of Het'um II of Armenia, 126
rithā', 88
Rukn al-Dīn, al-Sayyid, his *Sharḥ al-Muqaddima*, 154

al-Sab'a, suburb of Damascus, 142
Sabian(s), 141
Ṣābūn Mosque, 172
Sa'd al-Dīn Savajī, 147, 158
Ṣafad, 101, 110, 214
al-Ṣafadī, 17, 85
Ṣafī al-Dīn, 105
al-Ṣafī al-Sinjārī, 150, 157, 159, 162, 216
Ṣaghīr Gate, Damascus, 135, 162
Ṣaḥāba Miḥrāb, Grand Mosque of Damascus, 100
Sa'īd al-Su'adā' Khānqāh, Cairo, 202
al-Sakhāwī, 'Alam al-Dīn, 43, 76
Salamīya, 112, 133
Salār, Sayf al-Dīn, amīr, 52, 116, 119, 167, 168, 169, 193, 202, 206, 213
Ṣāliḥī Mamluks, 115
al-Ṣāliḥīya, Egypt, 167, 194
Ṣāliḥīya, Mt., Syria, 130, 145, 146, 147, 148, 151, 154, 160, 164, 167, 172, 196
Ṣāliḥīya Hall, Cairo Citadel, 203
Salīm ibn Muḥammad, Amīn al-Dīn, 53
Samaritan, 174, 175, 179
al-Ṣanawbarī, poet, 75
Sanjar al-Dawādārī, see 'Alam al-Dīn al-Dawādārī
Sanjar al-Shujā'ī, 'Alam al-Dīn, vizier, 109, 193
al-Ṣarkhad, 72
Sarmīn, 176
al-Sāwī, ḥadīth teacher, 9
al-Shādhilī, see 'Alī ibn 'Abd Allāh
Shāfi'ī(s), 11, 51, 55, 62, 67, 69, 72, 100, 128, 135, 137, 142, 144, 145, 152, 153, 155, 168, 169, 171, 180, 181, 184, 185, 200, 215
al-Shāghūr, suburb of Damascus, 142
Shalḥūnah, Shams al-Dīn, 50, 107
Sharb Bazaar, 130
sharī'a, 165
al-Sharkasīya(?) Dār al-Ḥadīth, see Sukkarīya
al-Sharqīya, Egypt, 169
al-Shawbak, 214
Shiblīya Madrasa, Damascus, 160
Shihāb al-Dīn, the imām at the Ḥanafī chamber, the Grand Mosque in Damascus, 124
Shī'ī(s), 17, 70, 87, 163
al-Shujā' Humām, 138, 170
al-Sīb, 113, 121
Sibṭ Ibn al-Jawzī, 1, 2, 16, 17, 18, 19, 25, 29, 35, 62, 82, 83, 86, 212
Sibṭ Ibn 'Abd al-Ẓāhir, 45
Sijilmāsa, 173
Sinjār, 111, 121, 154
al-Sinjārī, Burhān al-Dīn, vizier, 193

Sīs, see Cilicia
Sivas (Sebastea), 122
al-Ṣubayba, 125, 185
Sūdāq, 127, 191
Sülemish ibn Baktū ibn Bājū, 120, 121, 122, 123
ṣūfī(s), 9, 12, 15, 19, 51, 67, 68, 69, 71, 89, 129, 202
Sukkarīya Dār al-Ḥadīth, Damascus, 172
Sulaymān ibn Aḥmad, al-Mustakfī bi-Allāh, Abū al-Rabī', caliph, 202, 203, 204
Sulaymān, Ibn Ḥamza al-Maqdisī, Taqī al-Dīn, qāḍī al-quḍāt, 47, 151, 158, 215
Sulaymān al-Hindī, 'Alam al-Dīn, 147
Sulaymān, Ibn al-Shīrajī, see Ibn al-Shīrajī
Sulaymān ibn 'Umar al-Adhru' (al-Adhra'ī) al-Shāfi'ī, Jamāl al-Dīn, 47, 171
Sultāy (Suntāy), Mongol general, 121
Sumāq, Mt., 176
Sunnī, 70
Sunqur, Shams al-Dīn, amīr, 53, 98
Sunqur al-A'sar, Shams al-Dīn, amīr, 101, 114, 118, 125, 168, 192, 193, 213
Sunqur Shāh al-Ẓāhirī, amīr, 104, 167
Sūq 'Alī, Damascus, 149
Sūq al-'Aṭṭārīn (the Druggists Market), Damascus, 151
Sūq al-Dawwāb (the Riding Animal Market), Damascus, 161
Sūq al-Dhahabīyīn (the Gold-Smiths Market), Damascus, 149
[Sūq] al-Fāmiya, Damascus, 161
Sūq al-Khawāṣṣīn (the Wool-Carders Market), Damascus, 149
Suq al-Khayl, see Horse Market
Sūq al-Rammāḥīn (the Lance-Makers Market), Damascus, 149
Suwayqa district (Suwayqat Ṣarūjā?), Damascus, 156
Syria (*Bilād al-Shām*), 1, 4, 10, 18, 19, 30, 35, 51, 52, 54, 58, 64, 65, 70, 82, 88, 94, 95, 99, 105, 107, 108, 110, 115, 116, 117, 118, 120, 121, 124, 128, 129, 132, 140, 141, 144, 153, 154, 155, 157, 158, 159, 161, 164, 166, 167, 168, 169, 174, 175, 176, 177, 183, 191, 192, 193, 197, 199, 207, 214; (Syrian historians, sources) 5, 17, 18, 32, 33, 60, 64, 78, 81, 82, 83, 86, 91, 92, 93, 94, 96, 132; (Syrian army) 133, 136, 166, 167; also see Damascene troops

al-Ṭabarī, 56, 93, 95
al-Ṭabbākhī, see Balabān
Tabghāz, amīr, 111, 112
Tabrīz (Tawrīz), 121, 205
Tāj al-Ri'āsa, 169
Tajik(s), 139
takhmīs, 87
takhrīj, 79
takhṭīṭ, 79
Tall Ḥamdūn, 101, 102, 103
ta'rīkh, 81, 82, 83, 84, 85, 86, 87, 93, 96; also see historiography
Taurus, 121
Taurus, constellation, 123
Tawba ibn 'Alī al-Takrītī, Taqī al-Dīn, vizier, 53, 213
Thawrā river, 105
Tibn (or Tibr) Mosque, Cairo, 175
Tigris, 113, 122
Toktu Khān, the son of Mengü-Temür, 191
Tripoli, 10, 13, 64, 66, 87, 101, 105, 110, 129, 167, 168, 199, 214
Ṭūghān, Sayf al-Dīn, amīr, 120, 161, 214
Ṭughjī al-Ashrafī, Sayf al-Dīn, amīr, 107, 114, 115, 116, 117, 213
Tūmā (St. Thomas) Gate, Damascus, 138, 161, 162
Tunisia, 29, 68, 172, 173, 177
Ṭuqṣubā al-Nāṣirī, Sanjar, 'Alam al-Dīn, 102
Turk(s), 11, 192
Turkman, 121, 122, 181

Ūjān (Uzjān, Awjān), 205
'Umar ibn 'Abd al-'Azīz al-Ṭūkhī, body-washer, 202
'Umar ibn 'Abd al-Raḥmān ibn 'Umar ibn Aḥmad al-Qazwīnī, Imām al-Dīn,

qāḍī al-quḍāt, 100, 131, 135, 168, 169, 215
'Umar ibn al-Khalīlī, Fakhr al-Dīn, 100
'Umar, Ibn Makkī al-Shāfi'ī, Zayn al-Dīn, 44
'Umar ibn Mūsā, qāḍī, 10
'Umar ibn Sharaf al-Dīn ibn Yūnis al-Kinānī, Zayn al-Dīn, qāḍī, 180
'Umar al-Taflīsī, Kamāl al-Dīn, 67
Umayyad, 89, 164
Umm al-Ṣāliḥ Madrasa, Damascus, 168
Upper Egypt, 108, 206
al-'Uqayba, suburb of Damascus, 142
'Uqayba Mosque, 154
'Uqayq Public Bath, Damascus, 156
Usun-Damur, Sayf al-Dīn, amīr, 199, 214
'Uthmān ibn 'Abd Allāh al-Āmidī, 12, 72
'Uthmān al-A'zāzī, Fakhr al-Dīn, 130
'Uthmān al-Fahrī, Mu'īn al-Dīn, 69
'Uthmān ibn Sa'īd, Mu'īn al-Dīn, 92
'Uthmān Shrine, the Grand Mosque of Damascus, 128

vizier, 12, 50, 64, 65, 100, 109, 126, 147, 158, 159, 168, 169, 175, 177, 178, 184, 187, 192, 193, 213

Wādī al-Khazindār, 133, 166
Wādī Rāwīl, 191
Wādī al-Taym, 137
waṣf, 88
Wāsiṭ, province, 56, 113
wine, liquor, 152, 165, 196
wine sellers, Damascus, 166

Yaḥyā, Ibn Abī Isḥāq, Abū Zakarīyā, 173
Yaḥyā ibn 'Alī al-'Aṭṭār, 11
Yaḥyā ibn Jalāl al-Dīn, Nāṣir al-Dīn, amīr, 154, 157, 159, 160, 161, 163, 215
Yaḥyā ibn Sharaf al-Ḥurrānī al-Shāfi'ī, known as Muḥyī al-Dīn al-Nawāwī, 67
Yaḥyā ibn Yūsuf al-Ṣarṣarī, Jamāl al-Dīn, 68
Ya'qūb, Bahā' al-Dīn, 176
Ya'qūb, Tāj al-Dīn, the uncle of al-Yūnīnī, 9
Yāsīn ibn Yūsuf al-Zarkashī, 67
Yazīd ibn Mu'āwiya, 163
Yemen, 47, 48, 186, 187, 190, 191
Yūnīn, village, 7, 9, 14, 47, 72
Yūsuf ibn Abī Yūsuf Ya'qūb al-Marīnī, Abū Ya'qūb, 173
Yūsuf ibn al-Ḥasan al-Sinjārī, Badr al-Dīn, 64
Yūsuf al-Kurdī, 27
Yūsuf al-Rūmī, Amīn al-Dīn, *muḥtasib*, 168, 169, 216
Yūsuf, Ibn al-Qabāqibī, Majd al-Dīn, 129

Ẓāhirīya group, 129
Ẓāhirīya Hall, Cairo Citadel, 203
Ẓāhirīya Madrasa, (Cairo) 58; (Damascus) 153, 155, 156
al-Zardkāsh, Badr al-Dīn, amīr, 122, 123
al-Zar'ī, Jamāl al-Dīn, qāḍī, 131
Zaydī(s), 190
Zaydīn, village, 149
Zayn al-'Arab bint Naṣr Allāh, al-Yūnīnī's mother, 9
Zayn al-Dīn, Mālikī judge, 200
Zayn al-Dīn, sharīf, 199
Zayn al-Dīn ibn al-Khalīl, qāḍī, 206
Zaynab bint 'Alī, al-Yūnīnī's niece, 16
zuhdīyāt, 88
Zur', suburb of Damascus, 207
Zuwayla Gate, Cairo, 200

ISLAMIC HISTORY AND CIVILIZATION

STUDIES AND TEXTS

1. Lev, Y. *State and Society in Fatimid Egypt*. 1991. ISBN 90 04 09344 3.
2. Crecelius, D. and 'Abd al-Wahhab Bakr, trans. *Al-Damurdashi's Chronicle of Egypt, 1688-1755*. Al-Durra al Musana fi Akhbar al-Kinana. 1991. ISBN 90 04 09408 3
3. Donzel, E. van (ed.). *An Arabian Princess Between Two Worlds*. Memoirs, Letters Home, Sequels to the Memoirs, Syrian Customs and Usages, by Sayyida Salme/Emily Ruete. 1993. ISBN 90 04 09615 9
4. Shatzmiller, M. *Labour in the Medieval Islamic World*. 1994. ISBN 90 04 09896 8
5. Morray, D. *An Ayyubid Notable and His World*. Ibn al-'Adīm and Aleppo as Portrayed in His Biographical Dictionary of People Associated with the City. 1994. ISBN 90 04 09956 5
6. Heidemann, S. *Das Aleppiner Kalifat (A.D. 1261)*. Vom Ende des Kalifates in Bagdad über Aleppo zu den Restaurationen in Kairo. 1994. ISBN 90 04 10031 8
7. Behrens-Abouseif, D. *Egypt's Adjustment to Ottoman Rule*. Institutions, Waqf and Architecture in Cairo (16th and 17th Centuries). 1994. ISBN 90 04 09927 1
8. Elad, A. *Medieval Jerusalem and Islamic Worship*. Holy Places, Ceremonies, Pilgrimage. 1995. ISBN 90 04 10010 5
9. Clayer, N. *Mystiques, État et Société*. Les Halvetis dans l'aire balkanique de la fin du XVe siècle à nos jours. ISBN 90 04 10090 3
10. Levanoni, A. *A Turning Point in Mamluk History*. The Third Reign of al-Nāṣir Muḥammad ibn Qalāwūn (1310-1341). 1995. ISBN 90 04 10182 9
11. Essid, Y. *A Critique of the Origins of Islamic Economic Thought*. 1995. ISBN 90 04 10079 2
12. Holt, P.M. *Early Mamluk Diplomacy (1260-1290)*. Treaties of Baybars and Qalāwūn with Christian Rulers. 1995. ISBN 90 04 10246 9
13. Lecker, M. *Muslims, Jews and Pagans*. Studies on Early Islamic Medina. 1995. ISBN 90 04 10247 7
14. Rabbat, N.O. *The Citadel of Cairo*. A New Interpretation of Royal Mamluk Architecture. 1995. ISBN 90 04 10124 1
15. Lee, J.L. *The 'Ancient Supremacy'*. Bukhara, Afghanistan and the Battle for Balkh, 1731-1901. 1996. ISBN 90 04 10399 6
16. Zaman, M.Q. *Religion and Politics under the Early 'Abbasids*. The Emergence of the Proto-Sunnī Elite. 1997. ISBN 90 04 10678 2
17. Sato, T. *State and Rural Society in Medieval Islam*. Sultans, Muqta's and Fallahun. 1997. ISBN 90 04 10649 9
18. Dadoyan, S.B. *The Fatimid Armenians*. Cultural and Political Interaction in the Near East. 1997. ISBN 90 04 10816 5
19. Malik, J. *Islamische Gelehrtenkultur in Nordindien*. Entwicklungsgeschichte und Tendenzen am Beispiel von Lucknow. 1997. ISBN 90 04 10703 7
20. Mélikoff, I. *Hadji Bektach: un mythe et ses avatars*. Genèse et évolution du soufisme populaire en Turquie. 1998. ISBN 90 04 10954 4
21. Guo, L. *Early Mamluk Syrian Historiography*. Al-Yūnīnī's Dhayl Mir'āt al-zamān. 2 vols. 1998. ISBN *(set)* 90 04 10818 1